CW00538563

# ICONS OF DISSENT

JEREMY PRESTHOLDT

# Icons of Dissent

## The Global Resonance of Che, Marley, Tupac, and Bin Laden

HURST & COMPANY, LONDON

First published in the United Kingdom in 2019 by
C. Hurst & Co. (Publishers) Ltd.,
41 Great Russell Street, London, WC1B 3PL
© Jeremy Prestholdt, 2019
All rights reserved.
Printed in India

A Cataloguing-in-Publication data record for this book
is available from the British Library.

ISBN: 9781849046657 *hardback*

This book is printed using paper from registered sustainable
and managed sources.

www.hurstpublishers.com

Chapter 1 previously appeared as: "Resurrecting Che: Radicalism, the Transnational Imagination and the Politics of Heroes," *Journal of Global History* 7, 3 (2012): 506–526.

Chapter 3 previously appeared as: "The Afterlives of 2Pac: Imagery and Alienation in Sierra Leone and Beyond," *Journal of African Cultural Studies* 21, 2 (2009), 197–218.

Chapter 4 previously appeared as: "Superpower Osama: Thoughts on Symbolic Discourse in the Indian Ocean after the Cold War," in Christopher J. Lee, ed., *Tensions of Postcoloniality: The Bandung Moment and Its Political Afterlives* (Athens, OH: Ohio University Press, 2010), 315–50.

For my parents

# CONTENTS

*List of Images*                                                              ix
*Preface*                                                                      xi

Introduction                                                                   1

1. Until Victory: Che Guevara and the Revolutionary Ideal                     35
2. Rebel Music: Bob Marley and the Cultural Politics
   of Liberation                                                              69
3. Me Against the World: Tupac Shakur and Post-Cold War
   Alienation                                                                 99
4. Superpower Symbolic: Osama bin Laden and Millennial
   Discontent                                                                131
5. One Love: Bob Marley, the Mystic, and the Market                          161
6. Brand Rebel: Che Guevara Between Politics and
   Consumerism                                                               185

Conclusion                                                                   217

*Notes*                                                                      225
*Selected Sources*                                                           285
*Index*                                                                      301

# LIST OF IMAGES

1. Che Guevara banner, Washington, DC, USA, 1967. © Marc Riboud/
   Magnum Photos                                                    36
2. Che Guevara, Ho Chi Minh, and Karl Marx placards, Munich, West
   Germany, 1972. © ullstein bild / Getty Images                   47
3. Jim Fitzpatrick's "Viva Che!", 1968. © Jim Fitzpatrick, 2010    49
4. Che Guevara banner, Mexico City, Mexico, 1968. © A. Abbas / Magnum
   Photos                                                          56
5. Bob Marley performing at the Roskilde Festival, Denmark, 1978.
   © Jorgen Angel / Getty Images                                   76
6. Tupac Shakur mural, Cape Town, South Africa, 2002. © Per-Anders
   Pettersson / Getty Images                                       109
7. Tupac Shakur mural, Freetown, Sierra Leone, 2000. © Teun Voeten  121
8. Tupac Shakur framed picture, Freetown, Sierra Leone, 2004, author's
   own                                                             127
9. Osama bin Laden poster, Rawalpindi, Pakistan, 1999. © B. K. Bangash /
   AP Images                                                       138
10. Osama bin Laden T-shirt, Dhaka, Bangladesh, 2004. © Farjana
    K. Godhuly / Getty Images                                      142
11. Osama bin Laden T-shirt, Pate Island, Kenya, 2005, author's own  145
12. Bob Marley street art, San Cristóbal de las Casas, Mexico, 2007, author's
    own                                                            165
13. Bob Marley flag, Lamu, Kenya, 2008, author's own                176
14. Che Guevara street art, Bergen, Norway, 2006, author's own       189
15. Che Guevara mural, EZLN autonomous zone Oventic, Chiapas, Mexico,
    2007, author's own                                             194

# LIST OF IMAGES

16. Che Guevara flag, New York, USA, 2011. © Ramin Talaie / Corbis via Getty Images     204
17. Che Guevara advertisement, Mombasa, Kenya, 2005, author's own     211
18. Guy Fawkes mask, 2016, author's own     219

# PREFACE

Icons are well-known figures that represent sentiments, ideals, political positions, or something else recognizable to a wide audience. They are powerful symbols that audiences collectively reinterpret over time. This book asks why certain public figures resonate with diverse audiences to become global icons and how perceptions of them change in response to social, cultural, and political currents. To answer these questions I explore popular interpretations of four evocative figures over several decades: Che Guevara, Bob Marley, Tupac Shakur, and Osama bin Laden. These figures differed in ideology, message, and audience, yet each became a highly politicized symbol of dissent that resonated widely and more profoundly than most other global icons. To understand the phenomenon of the icon of dissent, and through it the icon generally, I examine both the commonalities and significant variations in how audiences have interpreted these four figures across differing social environments and historical moments. In this way, *Icons of Dissent* traces a global history of the modern icon.

This book began to take shape after I completed dissertation research in Kenya and Tanzania in 2000. My dissertation and subsequent book, *Domesticating the World: African Consumerism and the Genealogies of Globalization*, shed light on Africa's multifaceted global interface through a survey of nineteenth-century East African demands for imported manufactured goods. I was particularly interested in how East Africans gave locally relevant meanings to imports and how these in turn impacted economic relationships with other world regions and production abroad. This research on consumer demand also piqued my interest in the circulation and reception of less material things such as images, music, and ideas. I was curious, for example, about the extraordinary popularity and strong political resonance of Bob Marley in many African countries, Kenya and Tanzania included. Similarly, I was keen to understand Tupac Shakur's prominence as a symbol for political frustration and hope in East Africa, and indeed around the world.

Events in the wake of the 2001 terrorist attacks in New York and Washington, DC also shaped my research. 9/11 made Osama bin Laden an instantly recognizable figure, both the international face of terrorism and a focus of outrage. At the same time, people around the world began to use posters, banners, and T-shirts bearing bin Laden's image to protest domestic circumstances and international events, including the 2001 invasion of Afghanistan. More surprisingly, bin Laden's face appeared on a great range of mundane consumer goods such as mobile phone cases and cologne bottles. He became a symbol used to represent sentiments, political positions, and even consumer tastes. This astonishing spectrum of bin Laden iconography brought into sharper focus the overlapping spheres of consumer culture and political sentiment that, as I would discover, defined each of the icons in this study. It also highlighted the question of timing: why was Osama bin Laden such an appealing symbol to people in diverse locales at that historical juncture? With this question in mind, I began to focus more intently on the particular historical circumstances of iconic resonance.

After researching Osama bin Laden iconography, it became clear to me that looking at any figure in isolation risked missing dimensions of the larger phenomenon of the icon. To develop a more complete picture of how icons have functioned in global popular culture, I concentrated on several otherwise unrelated figures that gained similar political relevance to international audiences at different moments in time. A sensible place to begin was the most recognizable Cold War-era icon of dissent: Ernesto "Che" Guevara. Guevara became a popular international symbol in the 1960s, a time when the convergence of new modes of communication, patterns of consumption, and shifting political imaginations created new conditions for the creation and circulation of icons. Starting with Guevara and moving forward chronologically to consider the global resonance of Bob Marley since the 1970s, Tupac Shakur since the 1990s, and Osama bin Laden in the early 2000s provided a frame for interpreting global icons over five decades. However, triangulating the histories of these figures, including post-Cold War reinterpretations of Guevara and Marley, proved more challenging than I had initially expected. The research necessarily spanned several continents and took many years to complete. Nevertheless, studying popular perceptions of Guevara, Marley, Shakur, and bin Laden allowed me to consider multiple dimensions of iconic resonance over time and so develop a new perspective on both the global variegation and historical contingencies of the icon.

Researching and writing this book has been an intellectual journey assisted by many scholars, friends, and family members. I owe a great debt to all of those who offered their reflections and suggestions on chapters and manuscript drafts, including Gopalan Balachadran, Timothy Brown, Mona Domosh, Todd Henry, Jeffrey O. Green Ogbar, Ilham Makdisi, Dillon Mahoney, Dilip Menon, Miki Sugiura, and Dixon Wong. Many others have offered their thoughts on the project and thereby assisted in refining the ideas of the book, including Andrew Apter, Jeffrey Babin, Erica Baffelli, Felicitas Becker, Roger Begrich, Ann Biersteker, Dimitri Bogazianos, James R. Brennan, Martin Bunzl, Jeffrey Burds, Thomas Burgess, Rainer Buschmann, Judith A. Byfield, Shane Carter, Conerly Casey, Sohail Daulatzai, Rachel Dwyer, Andrew Eisenberg, Ivan Evans, Laura Fair, Duana Fullwiley, Karl Gerth, Adam Green, Joseph D. Hankins, Patrick Harries, Ariana Hernández-Reguant, Deborah Hertz, William Hitchcock, Shamil Jeppie, Bennetta Jules-Rosette, Hassan Kassim, Hasan Kayali, Nancy Kwak, Peter Limb, Ghislaine Lydon, Zethu Matebeni, Everard Meade, Bettina Ng'weno, Farish A. Noor, Patrick Patterson, David Pedersen, Kristin Peterson, Deborah Posel, Doug Pray, Michael Provence, Zeke Rabkin, Allen F. Roberts, Susan Rosenfeld, Nayan Shah, Eric Tagliacozzo, Julie Weed, Edward Watts, Daniel Widener, and Peter Zinoman.

I greatly appreciate the reflections of many other colleagues at the University of California, San Diego as well as graduate and undergraduate students at UCSD and Northeastern University, notably Naomi Greckol-Herlich, Greg Kosc, Mychal Odom, Reuben Silverman, and Caine Jordan, who acted as research assistant and always approached the work with great enthusiasm. Sarah Bly, Sam Hitz, Robert Strand, Charles Weed, and my sister, Jennifer Prestholdt, offered valuable

PREFACE

observations and encouraged this project for more than a decade. I am
likewise very grateful to mentors Edward A. Alpers, Mary Jo Arnoldi,
Robert Edelman, Jonathon Glassman, and David Schoenbrun, who have
given so generously of their time and advice over many years. My
department chair, Pamela Radcliff, offered both guidance and support,
which I greatly appreciate. Sincere thanks go to Matthew S. Hopper, for
his friendship and valuable feedback on many aspects of this project
since its inception. Similarly, I cannot thank Jacob S. Dorman enough
for his friendship, enduring enthusiasm for this project, and his ideas for
improving the manuscript. Jake has always been a primary sounding
board for the book and the final product is much stronger as a result of
his insights, keen eye, and suggestions.

This book has benefited immensely from comments received at
workshops, conferences, and lectures, including events at Cornell
University, Dartmouth College, Northeastern University, Stanford
University, the University of California, Berkeley, the University of
California, San Diego, the University of Kansas, Centro Incontri
Umani, the Centre for Indian Studies in Africa at the University of
Witwatersrand, Copenhagen Business School, the Graduate Institute
of International and Development Studies-Geneva, the Institute for
Humanities in Africa at the University of Cape Town, and the
University of Hong Kong. I owe an additional debt to Anne K. Bang for
inviting me to the University of Bergen, facilitating an ideal environ-
ment in which to work, and for her valuable reflections on this and
other research. Similarly, Madeleine Herren-Oesch and the Institute
for European Global Studies (Europainstitut) generously hosted me at
the University of Basel, and I benefited immensely from this experi-
ence. Research for this book was facilitated by grants from the Harry
Frank Guggenheim Foundation and the University of California, San
Diego Division of Arts and Humanities as well as the Academic Senate.
I greatly appreciate all of the efforts of Karen Colvard at the Harry
Frank Guggenheim Foundation. Additionally, I appreciate the impor-
tant work and assistance of archivists at the National Archives of the
United Kingdom, the National Archives of South Africa, Cape Town
Archives Repository, and Dag Hendrichsen and Anna Vögeli at Basler
Afrika Bibliographien.

My sincere thanks go to the anonymous reviewers of this manuscript
whose comments and suggestions made for a more cogent final itera-

tion. I am similarly grateful to editors William Gervase Clarence-Smith, Christopher J. Lee, and Lutz Marten as well as anonymous reviewers for earlier versions of chapters that appeared in the *Journal of Global History*, *Making a World After Empire: The Bandung Moment and its Political Afterlives*, and the *Journal of African Cultural Studies*. I am especially appreciative of the teams at Hurst Publishers, including Daisy Leitch, Kathleen May, and Jon de Peyer, and Oxford University Press. Lara Weisweiller-Wu at Hurst was an expert editor and worked tirelessly to guide this book to publication. A heartfelt thanks to Michael Dwyer for seeing the potential of this project while it was still in its infancy. I have always valued his commitment to the book, his input, and his friendship.

My deepest thanks go to my wife, Nicole, who has enriched both my life and this book in countless ways. She encouraged and supported me over many years of research and writing, and I am extremely grateful for her reflections on this project as well as her myriad other contributions to the realization of this book. I cannot imagine a more ideal partner with whom to have shared this intellectual journey or with whom to share my life. I am also incredibly thankful for our daughter, Sofia Liv, who came into our lives as this book reached completion and who has given her parents so much joy. Finally, I thank my parents, Cynthia and Perry, who, as with all I have undertaken, enthusiastically encouraged this project from its earliest stages. They have given me everything in life and made me who I am. As a small token of my gratitude, I dedicate this book to them.

# INTRODUCTION

Since the 1960s the world has seen a significant increase in the number and diversity of globally recognizable figures, including those who personify dissent. The images, music, and ideas of iconic figures such as Che Guevara, Bob Marley, Tupac Shakur, and Osama bin Laden have circulated with ever-greater rapidity and found a wide audience. In an epoch defined by connectivity and audiovisual technologies, these and other icons have condensed the anxieties, frustrations, and dreams of people across the planet. As a means to articulate individual and collective sentiment, global icons of dissent have affected political culture, social movements, national conflicts, consumerism, and other modes of interface.

For example, in 1967 the Argentine hero of the Cuban Revolution, Ernesto "Che" Guevara, became a martyr for socialist internationalism. Over the following decade his dramatic visage was so frequently reproduced that it became one of the most widely circulated images in world history. More remarkably, after the end of the Cold War Guevara regained political allure but his image was largely emptied of its socialist content, and in this guise it was transformed into a brand-like logo for the fashion industry. Despite this unbridled commercialization, in the twenty first century Guevara's iconic image once again became a ubiquitous symbol of dissent. Similarly, Robert Nesta "Bob" Marley, a Jamaican convert to Rastafari who was born into extreme poverty, emerged as an international symbol for emancipatory social justice in the 1970s. By the end of the 1990s, long after his death from cancer in 1981, Marley was one of the most recognizable artists in the world.

1

Yet, this meteoric rise was facilitated to a great degree by the reconceptualization of him as a spiritual figure and popular emphasis on his refrain "One Love". Tupac Amaru Shakur, an American hip-hop artist murdered in 1996, released only a handful of albums during his short life, yet he became an omnipresent voice of post-Cold War disillusionment. As his renown grew, young people in many parts of the world embraced him as an icon of both antiestablishment defiance and masculinity. More surprisingly, in the wake of the 9/11 attacks, the world's most notorious terrorist, the Saudi-born Osama bin Laden, became a transnational icon of anti-imperial sentiment and his face became a popular T-shirt logo in many parts of the world. Though most people saw bin Laden as little more than a mass murderer, some interpreted him differently. Across the global South, in Africa, Latin America, the Middle East, South Asia, and Southeast Asia, many imagined bin Laden to represent diverse social and political grievances, even though few shared his worldview.

How do we explain the remarkable trajectories of such iconic figures? More precisely, why do certain individuals become martyrs, heroes, villains, and commercialized symbols at specific historical junctures? What meanings do transnational icons have for diverse audiences? And what can the popular attraction to these figures tell us about both the global past and contemporary cultural politics? This book seeks to answer these questions by studying the history of popular attraction to iconic figures over the past fifty years, a period of significant global integration. It explores the transformation of individuals into idealized symbols and the circulation of those larger-than-life icons in mass culture. In the first instance this is a story of symbolic communication in a media age. I explore how flesh and blood has become a foundation for modern mythology and an object of consumer culture. In the second instance this is a book about the larger contexts of iconic resonance and the people that embrace icons, young people in particular. It is an inquiry into why so many people are drawn to iconic figures, how such figures condense larger ideals and desires, mirror and affect popular sentiments, and gain or lose meaning. By considering the resonances of four very different figures across the globe over several decades, *Icons of Dissent* seeks to shed new light on the transnational factors and historical contingencies that define icons.

2

# INTRODUCTION

In the process it reveals both their dynamism and volatility, and it offers a perspective on global cultural politics that highlights the convergence of consumer culture and political sentiment since the 1960s. Che Guevara, Bob Marley, Tupac Shakur, and Osama bin Laden are more than recognizable personas. They have each become emblems of popular dissent, social identity, and political community. However, they are very different historical figures and it is not my intention to equate them. Beyond the fact that they are men (a point to which I will return), they are an unusual set because they had little in common. They ascribed to different worldviews, represented different subject positions, advocated divergent political strategies, and attracted different audiences. This raises the question: why study these four icons together? The comparative study of four contrasting figures offers insight into the phenomenon of the icon across social and ideological divides. It reveals dimensions of iconic resonance that considering either a single figure or closely related figures would not. For instance, while Guevara, Marley, Shakur, and bin Laden have appealed to different audiences, they have done so in remarkably similar ways. Each acted as a focal point for the popular imagination and so came to represent collective sentiments, even though such sentiments did not necessarily align with their personal philosophies. By giving form to collective sentiment, their images focused communal energies, shaped actions, and provided symbols of transnational solidarity. Guevara, Marley, Shakur, and bin Laden were each heavily commoditized as well. As a result, each personified the intersection of politics, consumerism, and transnational connectivity. Additionally, while many politically oriented icons have gained global popularity, few have resonated as widely or to the same degree as these four. Indeed, Guevara, Marley, Shakur, and bin Laden are among the most galvanizing and omnipresent icons to emerge in the past fifty years.

Guevara, Marley, Shakur, and bin Laden are also worthy of study together, despite their ideological differences and contrasting audiences, because they belong to a poorly understood category of figures: the global icon of dissent, or figures that challenge the socioeconomic norms of their times and so attract audiences beyond their nations of origin. They are not only antiestablishment but also "antisystemic".[1] They represent the rejection of, or resistance to, global structures of power and

3

hegemonic systems such as colonialism, imperialism, and capitalist exploitation. Their stance against systemic forms of domination and inequality has encouraged audiences to invest them with inherently political meaning. This in turn distinguishes icons of dissent from other popular personalities. Icons of dissent are not new, but a great many have risen to global prominence since the end of the Second World War. Political figures such as Mao Zedong, Mahatma Gandhi, Gamal Abdel Nasser, Angela Davis, and Nelson Mandela have appealed to wide audiences, as have prominent artists including Miriam Makeba, John Lennon, and Peter Tosh. Other celebrities have also transcended their particular fields to become icons of dissent. Notably, Olympic gold medal winner and heavyweight champion of the world Muhammad Ali used this platform to speak out against racism and the US war in Vietnam. As a result of his political stance, he was both celebrated and vilified. [2]

Icons of dissent are dynamic products of the communal imagination whose meanings are constantly changing. In image form they relay more than words, while their actual words are at times superseded by popular projections. Icons of dissent also represent less conscious phenomena. As symbolic figures of resistance they act as proxies for traumas and unspoken desires. [3] They become mediums through which individuals and groups simultaneous broadcast and claim shared sentiments and emotions. In this sense, they function as communal reservoirs from which diverse audiences draw and contest meaning. They also function as romanticized folk heroes, reflecting particular virtues, transcendent values, and revolutionary sentiment, which in turn makes them inherently controversial. In appealing across conscious and unconscious planes, icons of dissent fortify social identity and focus communal energies. They can also demonstrate solidarity, spark the imagination, reflect dreams of possibility, and offer a sense of empowerment. As a result, studying icons of dissent allows for a greater appreciation of agency and imagination, of marginalized and young people in particular, in the overlapping spheres of political thought and popular culture. Just as important, icons of dissent offer a lens through which to view linkages among seemingly disconnected social actors, events, and historical moments. In sum, icons of dissent grant us a valuable window on collective interests and the popular imagination. In this way, they help us to understand how diverse audiences make sense of the world and attempt to shape it.

4

# INTRODUCTION

*Icons and Iconic History*

Iconic figures are often studied in biographical form and within relatively narrow time frames.[4] This approach has yielded great insight into the lives and motivations of figures such as Che Guevara, Bob Marley, Tupac Shakur, and Osama bin Laden. But this tack often reveals little about their iconic histories, or how and why they attracted international audiences. As a result, the critical questions of iconology, including the global context of their appeal, the social impact of their images, and how these resonated differently across time and space, have received insufficient attention.[5] Tracing the iconic histories of Guevara, Marley, Shakur, and bin Laden can address these questions and significantly augment biographical approaches to well-known figures.

Emphasis on the historical and transnational dimensions of iconography reveals several critical points. First and foremost, icons are to a significant degree composite products of the popular imagination. Audiences and marketers collectively transform famous individuals into powerful, myth-like figures who represent ideals, emotions, and aspirations. More precisely, the iconic imagery of each of the four figures surveyed in this book reflects individual and collective interpretations of them.[6] This imagery recalls elements of the four figures' lives, but it also reduces their actions to abstract concepts, amplifies limited elements of their messages, and obfuscates their individual complexities. Iconic representations of historical figures are thus more than images of well-known individuals. They are the building blocks of popular myths based on the lives of individuals, but which substantially reduce, reimagine, or otherwise distort those lives.

For example, the most common image associated with Che Guevara, a two-dimensional rendering of him with long hair, beard, and beret, is not simply a photograph of Che. As we will see in Chapters One and Six, it is an image that has been interpreted and strategically modified by graphic artists, manufacturers, and diverse audiences to serve numerous social, cultural, political, and economic ends. It has acted as an attractive symbol for rebelliousness, antiestablishment sentiment, and revolutionary action. The image became iconic in part because it so neatly represented the kind of heroic figure that artists and audiences longed for. It has remained iconic because multiple generations have found it similarly evocative. This transformation of the human into a meaningful symbol defines the phenomenon of the icon in global culture. To understand this transformation, my focus in this book will not be Guevara, Marley, Shakur, or bin Laden per se. Rather, the overarching emphasis will be on their resonance—how they have been interpreted and reimagined by artists and audiences to address particular sociocultural concerns.

The iconic histories of Guevara, Marley, Shakur, and bin Laden highlight several additional points. As products of the popular imagination, their meanings have exhibited significant dynamism across space and time. Such variegated interpretations, or the malleability of iconic figures, has often increased their appeal. At the same time, the iconic histories I sketch in this book suggest that shifting collective interpretations determine whether an icon's significance will be resilient or fleeting. Thus, understanding how icons work in mass culture necessitates an emphasis on revisionist interpretations. In other words, to appreciate the appeal of iconic figures, we must understand not only the variegated local meanings of global icons but also the temporal dimensions of iconic resonance, or how and why perceptions of icons change over time.

The historical and transnational analysis of icons also reveals that while transcultural iconography has seen a historical shift from a field dominated by the sacred to one dominated by the secular, the modern secular icon has retained core elements of the sacred. Much like religious relics, secular icons act as screens—audiences not only draw meaning from them but also project meaning onto them. Individuals develop emotional, even quasi-spiritual relationships with iconic figures, including icons of dissent, and thus they often function as totemic identity markers. Audiences even blur the distinction between sacred and secular by representing modern iconic figures as saint-like or superhuman, as we will see throughout this book.[7] Finally, the history of global icons offers a window on a broad phenomenon that deserves greater attention: the desire for transnational connection. I will return to this point in the next section.

This survey of Guevara, Marley, Shakur, and bin Laden as iconic figures relies on evidence from both the West and the global South, Africa in particular. I look beyond the national spaces of each icon's genesis to highlight the ways in which they circulate across national boundaries, how like rhizomes they appear, disappear, appeal to, and connect social actors beyond the control of the state.[8] In short, this book is interested in how icons have been created in transnational dialog and domesticated by diverse audiences. Accordingly, it highlights the social actors who raised these figures to global iconic status and why they did so. It also pays close attention to cultural products, such as murals, graffiti, T-shirts, posters, and other renderings, as these provide important evidence of how audiences transform popular figures into symbols. However, I do not trace the resonance of Guevara, Marley, Shakur, and bin Laden everywhere in the world. Rather, I focus on those social and national environs where strong empirical evidence of each figure's popularity is available.

Icons gain popularity because they resonate with contemporaneous sociopolitical contexts, ways of thinking, and emergent trends. Therefore, the meanings of icons are linked to a number of social and historical circumstances. Drawing on insights from theories of the image and cultural translation, I suggest that icons have two degrees of connotation: general and particular.[9] The general connotations of icons are often consistent across social space and only change gradually. Particular connotations, on the other hand, vary significantly across space and can change rapidly over time. For example, since the Cuban Revolution, the image of Che Guevara has connoted rebellion and rebelliousness.[10] In the 1960s and 1970s, however, the particular meaning of rebellion associated with him varied, from general anti-Vietnam War sentiment to revolutionary internationalism. We can see greater variance in popular interpretations of Che in the post-Cold War era. Guevara remained a metonym for rebelliousness, and he was once again associated with anti-war sentiment. But he was less frequently associated with militancy or socialism. Instead, antipolitical and even apolitical connotations influenced popular perceptions of Che, both of which were affected by the commercialization of his image.

Che Guevara's iconic history highlights the malleability of icons on the one hand, and their ability to maintain general symbolic value on the other. This combination of malleability and endurance, or the capacity to act as vessels of both shared and divergent meaning, gives iconic figures their broad appeal. It can also contribute to their remarkable longevity. One of the most important conclusions we can draw from the study of icons of dissent is that while their ideological positions may contribute to their initial popularity, most obtain their greatest notoriety once they are abstracted from those particular positions. Reduction to a finite number of attributes, stereotypical gender roles, and even a single mantra, as I will address below, invariably does violence to the complexity of the individual.[11] Detractors frequently engage in this form of reduction as a means to critique iconic figures, as we will see. On the other hand, the selective interpretation of historical figures ensures their appeal to audiences well beyond those who share their convictions. Guevara, Marley, Shakur, and bin Laden resonated most widely when their messages were stripped of nuance and their images assigned less complicated, broader connotations. In sum, iconic figures tend to gain larger audiences as they are distilled into essences of general sentiment or common values.

Icons have also been made and remade by consumer culture and marketing. Since their attractiveness is contingent on how they are popularly perceived, they function much like, and are often made into consumer goods.[12] For example, the images of icons of dissent have been reproduced as popular commodities that reflect political or social identity. But even though iconic resonance is affected by marketing, it is by no means determined by it. Just as consumers reinterpret and transform cultural products to serve their interests, diverse audiences reimagine icons.[13] And while the marketing of icons of dissent has certainly led to recuperation, or cooptation and banalization by the cultural forces of global capital, this banalization is not the inevitable outcome of marketing icons of dissent.[14] The presumption that consumer culture necessarily militates against the subversive uses of symbols assigns too narrow a role to the commodity. For example, the resurgence of Malcolm X as a global icon of dissent in the 1990s (see Chapter Four) was in part a consequence of director Spike Lee's 1992 biopic *Malcolm X*.[15] The transnational political import of Bob Marley provides another case in point. As we will see in Chapter Two, Marley's mainstream record label marketed his group as a "black rock band", but his music was bootlegged around the world and many embraced him as an indefatigable advocate for national liberation, racial equality, freedom, and social justice. As a result, Marley's tracks were radically decommercialized as a soundtrack for political struggle and human rights. Thus, the popularity of icons of dissent can develop in spite of or in tandem with significant commercialization.

*Icons and Iconic Resonance*

The term "icon" is used to refer to such a great range of people, things, and phenomena that it has been rendered almost meaningless. It is now frequently used as a synonym for little more than being well-known. Common references to iconic figures rarely note what, precisely, such figures represent in the popular imagination. However, the etymology of the word evidences two overarching senses, both of which are useful for our purposes. The first sense is archaic: that of an image or totem. This usage is close to its Greek derivation, *eikōn* (likeness, image), and has been applied to representations of sacred figures since the Byzantine era.[16] The second sense of the term is more contemporary and broad, exhibiting only traces of its ancient origins. Since the nineteenth century, the term "icon" has referenced a personality, thing, or phenomenon that occupies a prominent place in the popular imagination and is often, as W.J.T. Mitchell noted, "provocative of powerful emotions."[17] This book unites these two senses, the image and the celebrity. Thus, I use the term icon in a precise sense: a person who becomes a totem or brand-like symbol and occupies an important place in the public imagination because he or she represents something acclaimed, loathed, or otherwise recognizable.[18] The iconic figure is thus a synthesis of person, image, and mythos, with evocative connotation and recognizable form.

A great range of historical figures, from athletes to actors, musicians, intellectuals, political figures, and many other people of note fall within this definition of icons. Some only attained this status within national or other circumscribed spaces, while others gained transnational prominence.[19] Regardless of their reach, popular icons connote specific traits such as courage or strength. More precisely, audiences transform them into Jungian archetypes: seemingly superhuman figures of the collective unconscious that condense virtues and values into human form.[20] These recall a range of mythic figures and speak to a transhistorical yearning for "exemplars". Specifically, icons such as those in this study are often perceived as "moral agents".[21] As with religious figures, audiences rework and embellish the life stories of icons of dissent until they

9

become virtual hagiographies, punctuated by the figure overcoming seemingly insurmountable odds.[22] Another leitmotif for the icon of dissent is that she or he occupies a position of relative weakness, but makes significant self-sacrifices in service of a greater struggle. Like the mythological warrior-hero, he or she personifies the idea that one person can challenge powerful forces and change the world.

As an inherently social phenomenon, the icon is a mode of interface. In this, the icon's form is essential. As a vessel in human form, the icon appeals in ways more seductive than popular logos or insignias. Indeed, representations of iconic figures tend to focus narrowly on the face, the most recognizable and emotive of human aspects. In its material form as artwork or consumer good, the icon fixes sentiment to visual cues in a process Jeffrey C. Alexander aptly referred to as reification. Thus, as Alexander has outlined in his groundbreaking work on iconicity, the icon features both "surface" and "depth": it conjoins aesthetics with social meaning in compelling ways.[23] What Dominik Bartmański and Jeffrey C. Alexander have termed "iconic power" derives from this graphic connection between "discursive meanings" and "sensual force."[24] Like "iconic brands" that, in Douglas B. Holt's words, allow consumers to "express who they want to be," icons of dissent appeal to particular social yearnings.[25] For instance, disenfranchised members of the post-Cold War generation searched for a figure such as Tupac Shakur, a symbol of self-determination who could speak truth to power with charisma and courage. Much as the social import of religious icons derives from a desire for salvation, Shakur fed a hunger for inspirational figures, particularly among the young and marginalized. It is therefore no coincidence that few secular icons have been as sacralized as Shakur and other figures in this study (see Chapter Three).[26]

Icons condense history and history affects the interpretation of icons. In this way iconic figures often become fictions, serialized visages abstracted from the collectives or movements of which they were a part. Additionally, biography and conjuncture are often conflated in popular memory, such that world events are consumed like melodrama. More precisely, popular memory tends to compress complex historical dynamics into essentialized stories of victors and victims, heroes and villains.[27] And historical changes are made more comprehensible when movements, conjunctures, and epochs are reduced to evocative images, as with the photographs of "Raising the Flag on Iwo Jima" and Tiananmen Square's "Tank Man".[28] Nationalist sentiment and state propaganda have encouraged this conflation and deftly employed iconic visages to relay patriotic messages. Authoritarian leaders such as Benito Mussolini and Joseph Stalin created cults of personality, presenting themselves as the embodiment of their respective nations' history and future.

This association of person with conjuncture has also transcended state directives. For example, after the 1961 assassination of Patrice Lumumba, Prime Minister of then Republic of the Congo (Léopoldville), he became a widely evoked symbol of resistance to neocolonialism.[29] Similarly, at the end of the decade, international anti-Vietnam War sentiment coalesced in the image of Ho Chi Minh. While it is clear that individuals and groups project meaning onto iconic figures, what is perhaps less evident is the fact that these projections reshape interpretations of such figures over time.[30] In fact, the totemic nature of icons makes them subject to significant historical revisionism. For example, over the course of several centuries Jesus Christ was transformed in the popular imagination from a "revolutionary Jewish nationalist," as Reza Aslan put it, into a "peaceful spiritual leader."[31] In the age of electronic mediation, a similar transformation of Bob Marley from revolutionary to mystic took just over a decade.

Like people and commodities, iconic representations have remarkable social lives.[32] As expressions of human relationships they stir emotion and trigger debate. Most importantly, icons act as catalysts for building relationships: they offer a bridge between the individual and the collective. As Bishnupriya Ghosh demonstrated in her pioneering analysis of contemporary global icons, they are apertures that "open us" to others. In articulating shared experience or struggle they offer a sense of connection with others.[33] Icons, and particularly icons of dissent, become something akin to Durkheimian "collective representations", which, by representing shared values and ideas, define and bind otherwise disjointed international communities.[34] Referencing an icon of dissent can be an empowering act of solidarity and thus a means to build community. As focal points for solidarity, the icons in this study have facilitated what Stephen Howe termed "imaginative solidarities". The neologism evokes Benedict Anderson's insights into the fashioning of nations from imagined communities. Yet, Howe directs our attention to relationships that are more fluid and incoherent than national citizenship. As collective representations, iconic figures facilitate imaginative solidarities by linking individuals across national, social, and cultural lines—and they do so in virtual as well as material form.[35]

Icons of dissent frequently act as references for individuals and movements with common interests. They have also facilitated joint endeavors. However, icons more commonly act as references for disparate groups with shared outlooks but who rarely engage in concerted action. In either case, the celebration of icons reflects a desire to be part of a translocal collective.[36] It is a means of affecting worldliness, from collective action to simply feeling connected to others. Wearing or reproducing an iconic image can be a means of projecting a particular relationship with the wider world.[37] Graphic artists, for example, have frequently represented this cosmopolitan desire by interpolating global icons into domestic symbolic sets. In the 1980s Nicaraguan artists depicted Che Guevara alongside Augusto Sandino, leader of the resistance to US occupation, and Carlos Fonseca, founder of the Sandinista National Liberation Front. In the 1990s Mexican mural artists juxtaposed Guevara with revolutionary hero Emiliano Zapata and Zapatista spokesperson Subcomandante Marcos (see Chapter Six). Such associations represent an aspirational fusion of national and international signs and struggles. In these and other examples, the domestication of icons reflects a desire to engage a great collective or wider struggle, to be part of history.

Thus far I have focused on the general social functions of global icons, but a number of other characteristsics also deserve attention. For instance, icons of dissent are highly gendered. The world has seen a great many female icons of dissent at the national level, including, for example, Harriet Tubman, Celia Sanchez, and Phoolan Devi. Many other women, such as Angela Davis, Gloria Steinem, Winnie Mandela, Arundhati Roy, Wangari Maathai, Aung San Suu Kyi, and the Russian dissidents Pussy Riot, have gained substantial global audiences. Though icons of dissent are by no means exclusively male, in the twentieth and twenty-first centuries global audiences have frequently gravitated towards male antisystemic icons, particularly those perceived to represent archetypal male attributes. This is a critical point. If indeed male icons of dissent are more prevalent on the global stage, this may in part be a consequence of the fact that dissent is so closely associated with traits widely perceived to be masculine. A great many icons of dissent have emerged from social fields dominated by men, and these figures have been vaunted for their performance of roles commonly seen as masculine. More precisely, they have proven attractive because they perform, confirm, and amplify conventional male traits, including aggression. While men such as Mahatma Gandhi and Martin Luther King, Jr. gained iconic status in part as a result of their emphasis on non-violence, it is nevertheless a recurring trait among global icons of dissent that their resistance to structures of power entails redemptive violence. As we will see, diverse audiences have celebrated the hyper-masculine traits of icons such as Guevara and bin Laden, so-called "men of action" willing to translate their ideas into extreme acts.

The gendering of icons of dissent evidences a wider sociocultural phenomenon. The concept of the "hero" offers an instructive parallel. As Joan Fayer has shown, the preponderance of male "heroes" in the popular imagination stems from their association with leadership and violence, both of which are often stereotyped as masculine or dominated by men. This conspicuous masculine bias in the definition of heroes has contributed to the greater invisibility of women as heroes.[38] The historical preponderance of male heroes thus reflects the highly gendered profile of the hero as an iconic category. The same could be said for icons of dissent. And the tendency for audiences to gender iconic categories and reduce complex historical figures to gender stereotypes extends well beyond the categories of hero and icon of dissent. Global icons of religion, the entertainment industry, and many other fields evidence various forms of gender reduction.[39] For instance, some of the most vaunted female icons are those such as the Virgin Mary, Florence Nightingale, Mother Teresa, and Princess Diana whom audiences perceive to encapsulate values associated with motherhood, including love, compassion, and care.[40] The iconic histories of figures such as Mother Teresa and Che Guevara thus reveal a recurring phenomenon: the reduction of individuals to gender archetypes in the production of iconography. Moreover, extreme forms of gendering are perhaps most common among figures that gain substantial international audiences. Reduction to an archetypal "mother", "rebel", or other

13

social ideal that defines a specific iconic category has in many cases broadened an icon's appeal. As the case studies in this book demonstrate, the allure of many iconic figures is linked to the distillation of their personas and actions into transnational common denominators of gender performance.

The core messages, modes of delivery, and aesthetic dimensions of icons are also critical to their transnational appeal. Dogmatism can attract admirers, but gravity of message, passion, sincerity, and perhaps most importantly charisma have proven more critical to the appeal of icons of dissent. Rather than detailed plans for social change, the antisystemic messages that attract the widest audiences are those that address everyday injustices and suffering.[41] For instance, the figures in this study denounced the contemporaneous socioeconomic order, and their critiques were calculated to engage a large audience. Even Osama bin Laden, whose ideology appealed to very few, developed an antiimperial message aimed at a broad cross-section of listeners.[42] Moreover, the appeal of icons of dissent has generally increased as their core messages were reduced to key concepts. Rousing mantras such as Guevara's *"Hasta la victoria siempre"* (Always Onward Until Victory) and Shakur's "Me Against the World" have captured the imagination of diverse audiences, acting as hooks for those who ascribed to no common ideology. In short, icons can be both seductive and liberating because they appear attuned to the plight of their audiences and offer charismatic voices for diverse listeners.

Other affective dimensions of these four icons have also proved attractive. They have each appealed to their audiences' senses. For example, popular attraction to Bob Marley and Tupac Shakur's music was essential to their global resonance. Popular culture, and music in particular, is an important arena in which social identities are developed and transformed, and Marley and Shakur's music offered an enveloping style and soundtrack for self-definition. Similarly, icons' physical attributes have contributed to their resonance.[43] Not only are icons often physically attractive but their appearance also conveys symbolic messages. Specifically, the images of iconic figures that capture the widest audiences are those that offer visual evidence of their exceptional nature. As we will see in Chapters One and Six, the image of Che Guevara with a beret, long hair, and beard was so imbued with social, political, and affective meaning that by the 1970s it superseded nearly every other image of him. Similarly, Osama bin Laden's beard, white *dishdasha* (long shirt), and camouflage jacket relayed the message of combined piety and militancy, which many found appealing. Global audiences have read Bob Marley's signature dreadlocks and beard as a public refutation of conservative social conventions. Marley's hairstyle also demonstrates how popular attraction to affective dimensions of iconic figures can translate into aesthetic emulation. Influenced by Marley, many around the world embraced dreadlocks and red, gold, and green apparel—symbols of Rastafari culture (see Chapter Two)— as fashion and a political statement.[44]

Death can also widen the appeal of icons. Violent death can even confer martyr status, as it did for Che Guevara. Untimely death frequently bestows a seductive mystique on popular figures, as in the cases of John F. Kennedy and Janis Joplin. Moreover, as the afterlives of both Kennedy and Joplin demonstrate, the particular salience of a figure's death is often a consequence of historical timing. As we will see in Chapter One, Che Guevara's death sent a shockwave through the global left, in part because he died at a moment in which his ideals were resonating widely. Similarly, death can lead to significant iconic resonance when a historical figure regains a wide audience before their demise, as in the case of David Bowie. On the other hand, death can ensure greater irrelevance. For instance, Osama bin Laden died at a moment when popular interest in him had waned substantially. Therefore, unlike Che Guevara, bin Laden's death did not enhance his mystique. In virtually every case, however, death makes iconic figures all the more malleable. Their silence makes them readily idealized and allows admirers to burnish desired traits. Moreover, the dead cannot engage in activities that contradict their stated moral positions. Most importantly, as we will see throughout this book, when iconic figures die young they preserve the dream of what they could have been. They become totems for potential unfulfilled.

The postmortem transfiguration of people into nearly superhuman figures highlights another critical point we can draw from the study of popular icons: for iconic figures to remain relevant, they must be reimagined for new historical junctures. Icons tend to remain in, or return to, the popular imagination because audiences see them differently in new historical moments and ascribe alternative meanings to them. Those icons that do not take on new meaning fade more readily from the collective memory.

## Icons and the Transnational Imagination

Accounting for the popularity of global icons of dissent requires an appreciation of the proximate circumstances of attraction to them as well as the cultural currents and technologies that deliver them to the world. Shared sentiments, diverse communication technologies, and a desire to create community beyond the boundaries of the nation have increased popular demand for iconic figures in the last half-century. Yet, the majority of antisystemic figures have emerged from just two realms: politics and the arts. In the chapters that follow I will sketch how myriad forces aligned across the spheres of subversive politics and artistic expression to produce Marley, Shakur, Guevara, and bin Laden as icons of dissent. First, however, we should appreciate the shifting intersections of cultural politics and communication technology that have shaped the broader spectrum of modern global icons.

The intensification of human connectivity over the past several centuries has become a primary focus of historical analysis. Literature in the burgeoning fields of world, global, and transnational history emphasizes the mobility of people, goods, and capital as fundamental to understanding historical change.[45] Yet, the cognitive dimensions of global interrelation have received less attention.[46] How humanity has become interfaced, how we have come to see the same images and hear the same cues deserves much more reflection in current debates about the history and consequences of globalization. Exposure to print, film, television, popular music, and the Internet have opened new windows on distant societies.[47] As humanity has become more networked, diverse symbols, ideas, artworks, and personages have attracted wider audiences. As a result, in the epoch of electronic media humanity has shared more cultural references than ever before, from pop songs to lingua francas (notably the English language) and celebrities. We might think of this historical development as a "great symbolic convergence", or common familiarity with cultural signs and references facilitated by access to diverse media.[48] This convergence has augmented earlier forms of human interface and engendered new imaginations of community.

16

INTRODUCTION

Symbolic convergence has entailed myriad permutations of what I will refer to as the "transnational imagination", a mode of perception that frames local circumstances within a global historical trajectory and shapes collective desires and actions as a result.[49] This cognitive sensibility is transnational in two ways: it is attentive to inter-societal linkages and embraced by people in very different cultural and social milieus. As a collective social phenomenon, the transnational imagination is the product of global exchanges, but it has also contributed to the acceleration of global integration, particularly in the twentieth and twenty-first centuries.[50] In short, the transnational imagination is an engine and consequence of historical forces, including the desire to be part of history. Since at least the early twentieth century, the sense of the world becoming more interdependent has been a social force shaping geopolitical strategy, economic policy, and religious community.[51] Public and foreign policy as well as trade and investment decisions are now frequently predicated on the notion that distant places are immediately relevant to our everyday lives.

The transnational imagination has taken form in international bodies such as the Communist International and United Nations as well as in refrains such as Marx and Engels' "Workers of the world unite!" and Bob Marley's anthem "One Love". In the digital age, economic integration, symbolic convergence, and the transnational imagination have further encouraged people to think and act collectively beyond the nation-state. These have created unprecedented "communities of sentiment", which Arjun Appadurai defined as groups that feel and act together.[52] Online communities, for instance, occupy no single territory, yet they open spaces for international consensus. In some cases, communication technologies can facilitate disembodied debates that engender mass action. For instance, social media and other modes of electronic communication created a virtual space for public discourse in Egypt. This, in turn, emboldened a community of sentiment that mobilized for collective action in 2011. Events in Egypt and elsewhere in the Middle East then inspired similar reform movements beyond the region, including the global Occupy movement.[53] At the same time, transnational communities of sentiment rarely share more than anxieties, fears, passions, or moral sensibilities. Nevertheless, martyrs and other iconic figures can channel the aspirations of these communities, giving physical form to the transnational imagination and acting as badges to fortify the boundaries of group membership. Therefore, as products of the transnational imagination, icons offer a unique window on how people see the larger world and their relationship to others in an epoch of global interface.

## Icons and the Symbolic Idiom

The modern icon recalls a range of recurrent figures in human history, from the rebel to the bandit, hero, and prophet.[54] Considering this range of figures, as well as the political circumstances and communication technologies that facilitated their resonance, sheds important light on the rise of the global icon of dissent. Venerated symbols of power, including religious figures and divine rulers, are ancient phenomena. Before the modern era, the iconic plane was dominated by figures that blurred the line between the human and divine. At the same time, a great many icons such as Salah-ad-Din and Joan of Arc, as well as fictional figures such as Robin Hood, became plebeian heroes. However, while luminaries of the arts such as William Shakespeare altered the English lexicon and popular understandings of the past, few non-religious icons shaped the daily imaginations of people beyond their immediate regional or linguistic environs.[55]

With the expansion of early modern empires and the creation of postcolonial nations, a host of new secular, anticolonial, and transnational icons emerged. Heroes of revolution such as George Washington, Toussaint Louverture, the Peruvian Túpac Amaru II (José Gabriel Condorcanqui), and Simón Bolívar captured the imagination of political thinkers beyond their respective political spheres. Political leaders also became symbolic tools for national identity construction, and patriotic icons became cornerstones of modern nationalism. Much like earlier figureheads and folk heroes, state icons such as Napoleon Bonaparte became the object of romantic tableaus that extolled their exploits and heralded them as nearly superhuman.[56] As a result of the nineteenth-century explosion in print media and the advent of photography, the number of globally recognized icons increased exponentially, including secular figures such as Queen Victoria.

Just as importantly, awareness of one's position in the world and one's connection to distant regions affected ideology, consumer desire, and economic policy. Specifically, disparate groups developed a strong sense of affecting and being affected by global socioeconomic changes. This variegated transnational imagination intensified as steam navigation and imperial expansion drew disparate world regions into unequal, yet ever more interdependent, relationships.[57] Moreover, the ease of textual reproduction in the latter nineteenth century gave the world flexible media that reflected and affected this consciousness. As John Lonsdale explained in the case of colonial Kenya, increased literacy "deepened political imaginations by enabling people to place themselves in a larger framework of space and time."[58] Newspapers, the telegraph, and later the telephone facilitated rapid, nuanced communication in an age of empires.[59]

Imperial consolidation, international organizations, and interstate alliances evidenced new forms of thinking about space and relation—as did anarchism, collectivism, and struggles against colonial rule.[60] The popularization of recorded visual and audio material, and ultimately radio, accelerated this process. Telephone, film, and recorded sound created a new sense of simultaneity, a new sense of "now". The experience of the present, as Stephen Kern argued, "became an extended interval of time that could, indeed must, include events around the world." In the fateful days leading up to the outbreak of the First World War, this simultaneity created excitement, anxiety, confusion, and ultimately pressure to go to war.[61] The electronic media of the twentieth century ushered in an era in which circulating audiovisual artifacts significantly shaped perceptions and social relations.[62] Images, songs, works of art, and other cultural products constituted a planetary "symbolic idiom", or a shared audiovisual vocabulary.

In the early twentieth century, the world entered an age in which audiovisual technologies, the transnational imagination, and the symbolic idiom would markedly shape social relations. Messages, music, ideas, and commercial slogans crackled through the airwaves. Capturing the wonder of those heady times, *The New York Times* proclaimed, "in the very air one breathes are words written by electricity."[63] Mass production of images ensured greater "visual reciprocity", to use W.J.T. Mitchell's evocative phrase, and so dramatically increased the number of globally recognizable secular figures, from political leaders and athletes to actors, musicians, and radical thinkers.[64] Figures

19

such as Charlie Chaplin's The Tramp appealed to audiences around the world. Well-known personalities such as Paul Robeson popularized political causes while revolutionary leaders including China's Sun Yat-sen and Mexico's Pancho Villa gained international acclaim. In the aftermath of the First World War, antisystemic figures such as Russian revolutionaries Vladimir Lenin and Leon Trotsky, the Polish-German Marxist theorist Rosa Luxemburg, and the Jamaican activist Marcus Garvey developed global audiences for their messages and inspired significant international solidarity linked to class, race, and other forms of transnational identity.

Moreover, artistic movements such as Constructivism and agitprop developed compelling iconography for mass consumption. Though these visual messages served specific political agendas, they both borrowed from and influenced emerging marketing paradigms. The rise of fascist states and the outbreak of the Second World War saw the further application of print, visual media, and the tropes of the advertising industry for mass mobilization. To this inherently political end, states produced representations of vaunted heroes and shameful villains.[65] But in this media-charged milieu, antifascist and anticolonial figures such as Ethiopian emperor Haile Selassie I and Mahatma Gandhi also gained international recognition, even sacred auras.[66] For example, from the early 1930s the fledgling Rastafari community of Jamaica hailed Selassie as a messianic figure (see Chapter Two).

The spectrum of common references, from revolutionaries to pop stars, expanded exponentially after the Second World War, facilitated by popular media including film, radio, the LP, and television. The Cold War era saw the planet defined by political spheres: a capitalist First World, communist Second World, and a non-aligned Third World. Political iconography remained a valuable tool for states, totalitarian regimes in particular. Moscow, Beijing, and Pyongyang created cults of personality by representing leaders and former leaders as demigods.[67] At the same time, performers of transnational musical forms, including jazz, Afro-Cuban, soul, and rock found enthusiastic audiences across political fault lines.[68] In the West, diverse media in the late 1940s and 1950s encouraged an iconography of popular figures and consumer brands. In the entertainment and political milieus, figures such as Marilyn Monroe, James Dean, Elvis Presley, and Fidel Castro found adoring audiences beyond their nations of origin. North America also saw the increasing popularization of fictional iconic figures. Super-heroes such as Superman, Wonder Woman, and Captain America articulated clear sociopolitical values, vanquished formidable villains, and so captured the imagination of young people.[69]

More important, challenges to European imperialism contributed to the rise of a great number of iconic anticolonial figures. India's Jawaharlal Nehru and Egypt's Gamal Abdel Nasser, for example, were inspirational models, icons of decolonization celebrated far beyond their respective nations.[70] As nationalist movements across the colonial world gained ground, audiences gravitated towards charismatic anti-systemic figures. These figures embodied overlapping visions of trans-national unity (albeit without compromising state sovereignty) that hinged on diverse forms of identity, including class, race, ethnicity, and geography. Vietnam's Ho Chi Minh, Ghana's Kwame Nkrumah, Algeria's Ahmed Ben Bella, and Tanzania's Julius Nyerere became sym-bols of anticolonialism, postcolonial possibility, and an emergent Third Worldism (see Chapter One).[71]

In the early 1960s, ideas, images, and music pulsed through the circuits of an electronically mediated world. Film, television, popular music, and other forms of entertainment animated an international image-making industry. National and international celebrities—those known for their "well-knownness" as Daniel J. Boorstin famously put it—multiplied, and marketing focused ever more intently on the cre-ation of signs that could deliver complex, layered, and convincing mes-sages. Much like marketers, states and political movements attempted to harness the power of evocative images.[72] Advertising and political art evidenced a convergence that would deepen over the following decades. For instance, the global left developed a sophisticated graphic art of dissent that drew on the grammars of advertising to promote symbolic yet meaningful solidarity in struggles for equality and free-dom. Artists and thinkers of the left produced posters, leaflets, news-letters, magazines, and many other works as a means to circulate and affirm demands for systemic change.[73] Famously, from the mid-1960s, the Organization of Solidarity of the People of Asia, Africa, and Latin America produced images of Che Guevara, Nelson Mandela, Guinea-Bissau's Amílcar Cabral, Chile's Salvador Allende, and other celebrated socialist figures. Stylistically, these images departed from conventional state propaganda and promoted an idealization of solidarity that appealed to young radicals.[74]

The luminaries of diverse movements for freedom, self-determination, and social change, such as Martin Luther King, Jr., the Martinican anticolonial theorist Frantz Fanon, and Chinese Communist revolutionary Mao Zedong, became key elements of the global symbolic idiom. As antisystemic icons, such figures gained depth of meaning and sometimes even breadth of popularity that surpassed that of celebrities and other well-known political icons. As we will see in Chapter One, posters of Che Guevara circulated from Havana to Milan, New York, Paris, Mexico City, Dar es Salaam, and Tokyo through routes of transmission that included mail order businesses, radical collectives, and personal connections. Mao Zedong's *Little Red Book* became one of the most reproduced texts in history and Mao's image, in the form of pins and posters, traveled from Beijing to Berkeley, West Berlin, Ayacucho, and Kathmandu, distributed by sympathetic governments or sold by leftist organizations. Icons of dissent, then, offered inspiration for new social movements and political struggles well beyond their national origins and ideological confines.[75]

Revolutionary icons also merged with the counterculture and popular fashion. For example, in 1967 poster vendors in Paris sold Che Guevara's image alongside those of Lenin, Trotsky, the Beatles, and Peter Fonda.[76] In the countercultural mode, style too functioned as a form of dissent. As I suggested above, the personal styles of antisystemic figures spurred imitation, and the material culture of iconic figures became closely associated with political stances. Mao Zedong caps had radical affect, and Che Guevara's beret, long hair, and beard resonated with the antiestablishment style of many young radicals. Thus, not only did Guevara's ideas inspire political organizations such as the New York-based Young Lords and radicals such as Ilich Ramírez Sánchez (see Chapter One), but his iconic aesthetic also influenced their self-presentation.[77] In the sixties and seventies, Guevara's signature combination of starred beret, long hair, and beard became synonymous with antiestablishment sentiment and struggles for freedom.

Media events such as the 1968 Olympic Games and the 1969 Apollo 11 moon landing also augmented the transnational imagination by enhancing the sense of being part of a global collective. Benjamin Lazier has dubbed this interfaced historical conjuncture the "Earthrise era", in reference to the collective view of the earth as an integrated whole.[78] The widely circulated Earthrise image, which was sold as a poster alongside those of political and pop icons, was an example of the shared lenses through which audiences viewed world events. Just as important, the Earthrise-era perception of the world as a deeply integrated sociopolitical space led a greater number of people than ever to conclude that resistance to Western capitalism and imperialism required both a systemic understanding of injustice and concerted, transnational action.[79]

While the global left put a premium on solidarity, coordinated action across borders tended to be more symbolic than material. Additionally, in the late 1960s and 1970s, left movements in both the global South and the West encountered coordinated national and international resistance. The ongoing imprisonment of Nelson Mandela and the murder of outspoken critics such as Salvadoran archbishop Óscar Romero offered additional transnational focal points of solidarity. Yet, as reactionary leaders gained greater power and exerted overwhelming force in Argentina, Italy, and elsewhere, the allure of militancy faded. Many antisystemic icons also began to lose their appeal. In much of the postcolonial world, the late 1970s and 1980s were marked by political repression. One-party states, in some cases with the aid of the United States or the Soviet Union, frequently embraced authoritarianism (see Chapter Two), which compounded popular disillusionment. In such environments, where the media acted as the mouthpiece of the state and social movements were fatigued, music and the arts continued to provide an avenue for political critique.

In the West, visions of systemic change eroded further with the rise of the New Right and free trade orthodoxy. Among a new generation of left activists, the postcolonial world was no longer seen as the vanguard of world historical change. This represented a conceptual departure from left movements of the sixties. Nevertheless, the desire for solidarity remained critical for issue-oriented activism, such as the women's rights, anti-Apartheid, antinuclear, and environmental movements. In the final decade of the Cold War music circulated through the plastic medium of the cassette tape to give voice to angst and aspiration across the global North and South. Indeed, the late 1970s and the 1980s saw an effervescence of populist and underground music, including reggae, punk, and hip-hop, which provided new idioms of transnational dissent and solidarity.[80] Bob Marley, for example, would develop a popular aesthetic platform for articulating disenchantment with contemporary politics.

*Icons and Post-Cold War Convergence*

As the Cold War neared an end, a world of familiar divisions and ideological binaries began to fall away. Alongside Bob Marley, figures such as the Philippines' Corazon Aquino, Poland's Lech Wałęsa, South Africa's Bishop Desmond Tutu, and Pope John Paul II came to symbolize demands for political reform. With the demise of state socialism, new possibilities percolated into popular consciousness. Policy-makers, commentators, and academics searched for ways to understand the emergent world order. Many Western analysts framed this watershed as the triumph of a benign capitalism. Francis Fukuyama, for example, proposed that the universalization of Western liberal democracy represented the final vista in human ideological evolution, or the "end of history". Exactly what this meant for liberal democracy was not clear, particularly as many political actors turned to increasingly exclusive notions of citizenship and belonging.[81]

Capitalism was triumphant in the post-1989 world, but it quickly became evident how important socialism had been as an ideology against which Western capitalism defined itself. Without what Ernesto Laclau termed a "constitutive outside", capitalism's inadequacies became increasingly evident. Despite economic growth, unfettered capitalism appeared unable to deliver prosperity to the global majority, much less greater equality.[82] Nevertheless, capitalism's ideological dimensions receded from view. It became a masked ideology, so normalized that it appeared an inescapable fact of life. Western nations and a great many political thinkers in the postcolonial and formerly Communist worlds promoted liberal democracy and technocratic forms of free market thinking. Yet, dissatisfaction encouraged a range of counterhegemonic movements, including extreme forms of nationalism and social movements that emphasized the correlation of religion and the state. In nations such as Afghanistan and Sudan, the rejection of socialist and liberal democratic templates fueled alternative models of religion-oriented governance. The most radical figures in this vein, such as Ayman al-Zawahiri and Osama bin Laden, went much further. Drawing on the political thought of Sayyid Qutb and others, they sought theoretical and divine justification for new forms of international militancy.[83]

World leaders trumpeted the post-Cold War era as one of a liberating social and economic integration, or "globalization". Yet, it was an era of economic integration governed by an extreme form of free market dogma often termed neoliberalism. This new orthodoxy encouraged economic growth through the deregulation of the financial sector, the privatization of resources, lower taxes, and consumerism, while discouraging certain barriers to trade.[84] These priorities, and the uneven application of trade regulations, negatively impacted poorer nations and stifled alternative forms of socioeconomic organization. At the same time, new technologies and falling barriers to the circulation of information continued to expand the global symbolic idiom.[85] In the Information Age, satellite news media and the Internet deepened a sense of proximity and mutual familiarity. These technologies made it possible for a great many figures to be so ubiquitous as to feel familiar to people across the globe.[86]

Film, television, music, and the Internet acted in concert to make the world what Marshall McLuhan termed a global theater: a condensed visual space through which people received images and translated experience.[87] In this theater pop icons such as Madonna and fictional characters such as Rambo resonated with global audiences to become meaningful symbols of youth culture, femininity, or masculinity. As I suggested above, political icons were totems that could be recast in light of local and transnational circumstances. For instance, during the 1990 American military mobilization in the Persian Gulf, many around the world celebrated Saddam Hussein as a heroic underdog challenging American global hegemony.

Barriers to the circulation of media continued to fall in the post-Cold War world. Cassette tapes and videocassettes gave way to CDs, DVDs, and Internet downloads. The films *Jesus* (1979) and director James Cameron's *Titanic* (1997) reached wider audiences than any other films in history. Their ubiquity evidenced the new possibilities for circulation in the context of analog and digital replication. The global theater also evidenced the possibilities of the spectacle. In September 1997, as many as two and a half billion people—a third of humanity—watched Princess Diana's funeral live on television, catapulting Elton John's ballad "Candle in the Wind" to the second best selling single of all time.[88] Four years later, the visual dramaturgy of the 9/11 attacks ensured that they too constituted a simultaneous, planetary media spectacle.[89] The global outpouring of sympathy for the victims of the attacks, including a rolling global candlelight vigil, was remarkable. 9/11 also evidenced the conflation of a media event with an iconic figure. Media outlets cast Osama bin Laden as the singular face of global jihad and thus many interpreted him as a symbol of antisystemic sentiment (see Chapter Four).

In the new millennium, information and images tore through the ether of a networked world, creating a more diverse and in some cases more democratized mediascape. As alternative information sources, the Internet, citizen media, and social media proved galvanizing forces for communities of sentiment and social movements. Communication technologies offered a more accessible, albeit siloed, media universe, but neoliberal capitalism delivered little else to the majority. While globalization generated great wealth for a small few, among those who fared worse this new world order catalyzed discontent. Unemployment, restrictions on migration to wealthy countries, and the devastating consequences of structural adjustment policies created multiple socioeconomic strains that directly affected the lives and aspirations of young people in the global South.[90] Neither Marxism-Leninism nor any other formal school of thought provided broadly attractive theoretical grounding for criticism of what some referred to as global apartheid. Yet, economic inequality and a host of other social concerns encouraged various forms of radicalism and dissent.[91]

In the 1990s and 2000s, multiple issue-oriented social movements coalesced in a new internationalism, or a transnational imagination manifest in highly charged cyber environments and demonstrations against the World Trade Organization, authoritarian governments, and US military interventions.[92] Governments, social movements, and militants each exploited new media to promote specific images and

INTRODUCTION

ideas. Political disillusionment linked both to local and global injustices renewed the appeal of antisystemic figures, including those of earlier eras. Popular nostalgia nourished this interest. Specifically, nostalgia for a radical past that could have been helped to kindle the desire for retro styles, music, and symbols.[93] The technologies of the turn of the century likewise supercharged a public culture of celebrity, and exposure to the intimate details of celebrities' lives made such iconic personalities feel more familiar than ever before.[94] Similarly, through the online medium individuals could more easily identify and engage with others who held similar ideas, interests, and tastes. In short, digital audiovisual technology encouraged a sense of common experience. Hip-hop offers a case in point.

Much as with rock and reggae, hip-hop was a medium of critique propelled by the global corporate entertainment industry but not always diluted by it. This was particularly evident in the success of socially conscious groups such as Public Enemy and Boogie Down Productions. Tupac Shakur, one of the most celebrated MCs of his generation, also developed a sociopolitical message, which helped to propel his global popularity. His was a non-dogmatic grammar that remixed multiple ideological strands to denounce intersecting forms of racial, class, and gender inequality. Despite Shakur's antisystemic stance, the celebrity-obsessed multimedia milieu catapulted him to stardom, and audiences around the world interpreted his messages as profound articulations of their own experiences. Through a combination of digital media and piracy, audiences in every corner of the globe—often where no label promoted his music—embraced Shakur and other hip-hop artists. In this way, their music gave voice to angst and aspiration.[95] By the late 1990s, hip-hop was an ever-present expressive form, or what Paul Gilroy termed the preeminent "communicative idiom" of youth culture.[96]

Despite its potent critiques, hip-hop and other elements of the global symbolic idiom communicated no clear alternative vision for the world. At the dawn of the millennium, most new forms of social criticism often fell short of imagining an alternative future. Even jihadist movements, led by ideologues abhorred by both the global left and right, often refrained from articulating clear visions of a world transformed.[97] The most recognizable antisystemic figure to capture the world stage in the twenty-first century, Osama bin Laden, offered only a vague and qualified definition of what his ideal future entailed. At the same time, Che Guevara, Bob Marley, and other historical icons continued to gain relevance in the new millennium as symbols of rebellion and unity on the one hand and consumerism and fashion on the other. As I will demonstrate in the chapters that follow, these seemingly divergent trajectories were a consequence of collective reimagination. Guevara and Marley were emptied of much of their personal philosophies and encoded with alternative, though not unrelated, meanings in the post-Cold War era. Largely shorn of their ideological positions, Guevara and Marley became more malleable as symbols, flags for revolution as well as icons of dispassionate consumerism.

The dreams of millennials have found overlapping outlets in political, media, and consumer cultures. Internet radicalism, the decline of the social welfare state, and a sense of political opening have animated dissent in the twenty-first century, spurring movements of resistance to authoritarianism, austerity, sexism, racism, and the excesses of capitalism. Much as in earlier moments, antiestablishment sentiment has placed emphasis on symbols of solidarity, from Tunisia's Mohamed Bouazizi to Che Guevara and the Guy Fawkes mask featured in the cult film *V for Vendetta* (2005). The visions of alter-globalization thinkers, Arab Spring demonstrators, and Occupy activists have shown an acute awareness of the transnational dimensions of local concerns. Yet, they have been grounded more in national than international demands. While external support for protesters in Egypt in 2011, for example, demonstrated the possibilities of international solidarity, coordinated action across borders continues to prove difficult.[98] Millennial political thinkers have keenly diagnosed contemporary global ills, and movements such as Occupy have reinvigorated critiques of capitalism.[99] But they less frequently speak of a utopian future and their path towards the realization of another world is often opaque. The zeitgeist is both antidogmatic and, in many cases, antipolitical.

Yearnings for change in the new millennium and a desire to connect with planetary communities of sentiment transformed Che Guevara, Bob Marley, Tupac Shakur, and Osama bin Laden into galvanizing figures. These and other antisystemic icons have occupied positions of prominence in the global symbolic idiom, yet they reflect a world in which history has no direction. In this world, politics, popular culture, and consumerism are so intertwined as to be indistinguishable. At the same time, the ubiquity of icons and other symbols of dissent evidences a popular imagination reignited by the structural economic forces, political frustrations, and social inequalities of our time.

## Structure and Chapters

In the chapters that follow, I track the popularity of Che Guevara, Bob Marley, Tupac Shakur, and Osama bin Laden across multiple spatial scales in a roughly chronological fashion. By working across space—from the neighborhood to the nation, region, and globe—I consider the local and the transnational stereoscopically. Specifically, the book consists of semi-autonomous chapters that explore the popularity of one iconic figure at a particular historical juncture. Each chapter can be read on its own and in any order, though all engage and build upon the wider themes of the volume. Since each period in an icon's popularity coincides with a historical conjuncture, each chapter offers a different perspective on the transnational imagination, desires for community, and the global symbolic idiom. To provide both chronology and balance, I begin by addressing Guevara and Marley, figures who rose to prominence in the Cold War era. Then I consider Shakur and bin Laden, figures whose global notoriety post-dated the Cold War. The final two chapters return to Guevara and Marley in the 1990s and move forward to the present to highlight contrasts between their earlier popularity and their post-Cold War mythos.

The first chapter, "Until Victory: Che Guevara and the Revolutionary Ideal," takes a wide-angle approach to Guevara as a symbol of antisystemic and antiestablishment sentiment in the late 1960s and 1970s. Guevara's popularity offers a critical point of entry into two principle dispositions of the global left: commitment to antiestablishment struggle and a desire for transnational solidarity. This spirit of emancipatory internationalism, which bridged multiple doctrinal positions, was born of egalitarian aspirations, a transnational imagination, and the belief that global socialist revolution was possible, even imminent. As a renowned proponent of radical-emancipatory politics, Guevara neatly embodied this internationalist ideal. In an era when coordinated action across national boundaries was difficult and radical politics was marred by factionalism, Guevara became a medium for claiming and broadcasting shared sentiments. As a link among movements in North America, Western Europe, Latin America, Africa, and the Middle East, Guevara iconography helped to create and sustain communities of sentiment and dissent.

The second chapter, "Rebel Music: Bob Marley and the Cultural Politics of Liberation," also applies a wide lens to appreciate the multifaceted popularity of Marley in the late Cold War era. More precisely, the chapter explains how a commercial musician became a potent symbol for social justice and so bridged the worlds of politics and popular culture. In the mid-1970s, Island Records marketed Bob Marley to Western listeners as an exotic rock star. Yet, fans around the world soon embraced his critiques of inequality and state repression as well as his liberation anthems, notably "Get Up, Stand Up". By rejecting ideological binaries and emphasizing morality, Marley became an important reference for transnational left youth culture, activism, and militancy. Young West Indians, Africans, Europeans, North Americans, Pacific Islanders, and many others celebrated Marley as an authentic antiestablishment voice both articulating common experiences of oppression and offering a new countercultural aesthetic. In dispensing with conventional politics and articulating the dreams of the freedom fighter, Marley invigorated liberation discourse.

Chapter Three, "Me Against the World: Tupac Shakur and Post-Cold War Alienation," narrows the analytical scope to examine a transnational icon's audience in one nation. More precisely, I explore the convergence of mass media and social discontent in the early post-Cold War era by focusing on the popularity of American hip-hop artist Tupac Shakur in Sierra Leone. Shakur's worldview was more nihilistic than that of either Guevara or Marley, and his iconic resonance has not reached the level of these figures. Nonetheless, Shakur offered poignant critiques of contemporary inequalities and so came to embody post-Cold War disillusionment and social alienation, particularly for young male audiences. To demonstrate this point I take a close look at rebel combatants' attraction to Shakur during the Sierra Leone civil war, one of the most harrowing conflicts of the late twentieth century. Militant factions embraced Tupac as an inspirational figure representing those attributes combatants wished for: empowerment and the ability to overcome great odds. They used Shakur T-shirts as uniforms and incorporated his lyrics into their everyday rhetoric. As a result, Tupac references in Sierra Leone offer a window on how young people sought broader relevance for their experiences and searched for meaning through the iconography of global popular culture.

The fourth chapter, "Superpower Symbolic: Osama bin Laden and Millennial Discontent," charts the popularity of bin Laden's image in the first decade of the twenty-first century, a period marked by the 9/11 attacks, US military interventions, and growing resistance to global inequalities. More than any other icon to emerge in the new millennium, Osama bin Laden provided a symbol for popular frustrations with the neoliberal world order in the global South. His popularity was also more fleeting than that of the other figures in this study. Nevertheless, the 9/11 attacks and subsequent media focus on Osama bin Laden led many across the non-Western world to conclude that he embodied a range of desirable qualities. Bin Laden T-shirts, graffiti, and other iconography became a means to articulate a sense of marginalization and demands for systemic change. At the same time, few of those who wore bin Laden T-shirts subscribed to his beliefs or endorsed his tactics. Rather, many simply perceived bin Laden as a figure of extraordinary ability, a figurative "superpower" that symbolically approximated the United States. To account for this interpretation I narrow the analytical focus further to concentrate on the urban environments of coastal Kenya, where some young people represented a range of grievances through bin Laden iconography. In an effort to explain why they did so, I highlight acute feelings of alienation within religious and ethnic minority communities along Kenya's Indian Ocean coast. I show how some Kenyans perceived their experiences of marginality as part of a larger system of repression that bin Laden's actions appeared to address.

Chapter Five, "One Love: Bob Marley, the Mystic, and the Market," widens the analytical aperture once again to explore how antisystemic figures of the Cold War era were reimagined in the post-Cold War world. I begin by considering the exponential growth of Bob Marley's popularity after his death as well as the amplification of discrete elements of his message. Specifically, I concentrate on the alternative meanings listeners have projected onto Marley since the 1980s, notably the view of him as a spiritual lodestar. From the mid-1980s Marley's record label and many fans began to champion him as a suprareligious figure and a symbol for politically neutral concepts such as "One Love". This reinterpretation of Marley flattened his message but substantially widened his appeal. In the 1990s a new generation of Bob Marley fans looked to him as a voice of imprecise yearnings for spiritual fulfillment as well as social change. But Marley's skyrocketing popularity also contributed to increasingly vapid forms of commodification, which reduced Marley's message to cultural style. By the early 2000s, Marley's image appeared on a dizzying array of products, from underwear to soft drinks. As a result, an intense debate ensued over the meaning of Bob Marley's music and legacy, one in which Marley's heirs, seeking to redeem his name as an ethical brand, have played an increasingly important part.

The final chapter, "Brand Rebel: Che Guevara Between Politics and Consumerism," traces Guevara's unlikely resurgence in the post-Cold War era. As with Bob Marley, Guevara was reimagined for the new millennium in ways that isolated and extended particular dimensions of his complex profile. Guevara reemerged in nearly singular form: with long hair and beard, wearing a beret and looking into the distance, an image dubbed "Heroic Guerrilla" (*Guerrillero Heroico*). Through this image Guevara once again became a ubiquitous antiestablishment symbol. For many political thinkers critical of contemporary globalization and domestic repression, Guevara became a symbol of defiance that recalled the radicalism of the 1960s and early 1970s. Even though Guevara's rebellious aura proved alluring, admirers frequently deemphasized his socialist beliefs. Moreover, as Guevara regained political relevance, he also began to appeal as a brand-like logo. The commercialization of Guevara's image quickly surpassed that of earlier historical moments as myriad adaptations of the Heroic Guerrilla appeared on everything from baby clothes to candles and mud flaps. This commoditization introduced Che to yet wider audiences, including many who ultimately embraced him as an antisystemic icon. Guevara's political and consumerist dimensions were thus mutually reinforcing. And while Guevara's ideology was to a great degree excised, an often implicit politicality continued to underwrite his potency as a symbol

INTRODUCTION

for diverse movements. Che Guevara therefore came to function
simultaneously as an apolitical object of consumption, an inspirational
symbol for alternative social possibilities, and the most prominent icon
of dissent in the world.

1

# UNTIL VICTORY

## CHE GUEVARA AND THE REVOLUTIONARY IDEAL

On 7 October 1967 Ernesto "Che" Guevara surrendered to US-trained counterinsurgency forces in Bolivia. Two days later the Bolivian military executed him. Though Guevara failed to gain support in South America for the socialist revolution he envisioned, his death had global reverberations. In Italy, after hearing of Che's execution, demonstrators in Turin descended on the US Consulate while protesters in Milan took to the streets with cries of "Che Lives!" Arab, African, Asian, and Latin American students at Moscow's Lumumba University defied their Soviet hosts by staging a demonstration at the US Embassy. Labor organizations in Panama City held a memorial service in Guevara's honor, as did the government of Congo-Brazzaville. Che admirers gathered at London's Mahatma Gandhi Hall to remember the fallen revolutionary, and in the United States demonstrators marching on the army's Oakland induction center scrawled "Viva Che" and "Che Lives" on streets, sidewalks, and walls. Soon thereafter, at America's first national protest against the Vietnam War, tens of thousands paused for a moment of silence on the National Mall in Washington, DC in homage to Guevara.[1]

Che Guevara's Bolivian venture coincided with the adoption of increasingly confrontational strategies by many left movements around the world. The timing of Che's death, and the fact that he died while

35

1. Demonstrators with Che Guevara banner in front of the Lincoln Memorial during the first national protest against of the Vietnam War. The banner is captioned "¡Venceremos!" (We Will Win!) and "Che vive donde los pueblos lucha" (Che lives where the people struggle). Washington, DC, 21 October 1967. © Marc Riboud/ Magnum.

attempting to foment revolution, made him an ideal martyr for this new ethos of direct action. Thus, in the late 1960s and 1970s Che was one of the most celebrated icons of the global left. Leaders of protest and guerrilla movements claimed him as a personal hero. The poets Pablo Neruda, Derek Walcott, Peter Weiss, and Allen Ginsberg exalted him in verse. A 1968 poll revealed that a greater percentage of US university students identified with Che than with the current presidential candidates.[2] Demand for books by and about Che grew exponentially after his death, and in 1968 demonstrators from Tokyo to West Berlin to Mexico City carried placards bearing his image.

In Latin America Che became a common signifier for resistance to domestic oligarchs and US imperialism. Moreover, Che's example provided inspiration for diverse proponents of "revolutionary violence", from the Southern Cone to Palestine. The North Vietnamese government, for example, vaunted Guevara as a "shining example of revolutionary heroism." For many around the world Che represented a romanticized concept of radical action and socioeconomic change: an ideal revolutionary and a revolutionary ideal. Indeed, the time, place, and fashion in which Guevara died cemented him in the imagination of young people around the world. As a result, Guevara's ideas and iconography shaped the politics and culture of left militancy well into the 1970s.[3]

Che Guevara's execution was a momentous event for a transnational community of antiestablishment sentiment. As such, the celebration of Che in the years after his death offers a critical point of entry into iconic resonance in the Cold War era as well as the spirit of emancipatory internationalism espoused by left-wing radicals in the late 1960s and 1970s. This spirit was born of transnational egalitarian aspirations and the belief that global socialist revolution was possible, perhaps imminent. As one of the most ardent proponents of revolution, Che Guevara neatly embodied this zeitgeist. For many radicals, he also encapsulated the desire for international solidarity. In an era when coordinated action among militants was difficult and many left movements occupied the political margins, the materialization of common ideals in symbols such as Che Guevara provided graphic confirmation that each movement was part of a larger struggle. In the late 1960s and 1970s Guevara and other icons of dissent were easily readable and replicable signs of two principle dispositions of the youthful left: belief in a global struggle for self-determination and a yearning for meaningful solidarity.[4] Che Guevara embodied a transcendent idea of revolution, the binding ideal of not simply national revolts but "the revolution", or radical world historical change.

The rise of radical youth movements in the 1960s, their influence on each other, and the simultaneity of uprisings in 1968 have been the subject of much important research.[5] Less analytical attention has been given to the common symbols of these movements, their shared meanings, and their varied interpretations across contrasting sociopolitical landscapes. Recent research on Che Guevara as an icon has yielded many valuable insights into his global popularity. However, this body of work focuses less on Che's doctrinal allure than on the aesthetics of his iconography and its currency in popular culture.[6] Studies considering Guevara's influence on the political imagination of radicals have deepened our understanding of his appeal in this period, but these fall short of a holistic assessment of his utility as a symbol across the sociopolitical spectrum, from the counterculture to insurgent movements.[7] This chapter seeks to bridge these complementary literatures and so widen the analytical lens through which we view both the global left in the 1960s and Guervara's afterlife. More precisely, it explores the politics of claiming Che as an icon of dissent and how his example gave direction and confidence to social movements and guerrilla organizations on multiple continents.

*Revolution in the Long Sixties*

Che Guevara's death coincided with a series of seismic global historical phenomena, including decolonization, a rights revolution, the war in Vietnam, and the rise of student protest movements. These both were affected by and helped shape a shift in consciousness.[8] In the early 1960s radicals on every continent perceived a meaningful link between their individual circumstances and a system of domination that transcended national boundaries. At the same time, many young leftists rejected the gradualist policies of the Soviet Union and the orthodox communist parties of the Old Left. Instead, young radicals embraced Maoist and Castroite visions of global revolution. Thus, "internationalism", to use the idiom of the era, became central to the identity of radical movements and part of a wider "structure of feeling", to borrow Raymond Williams' term, which transcended many ideological differences. Grounded in what Alain Touraine called a "unity of attitudes", including a commitment to the global antiestablishment struggle, internationalism entailed new radical networks, coordinated actions, and symbolic demonstrations of solidarity.[9]

At the core of this emerging consciousness was the transnational imagination: a cognitive sensibility that frames local circumstances within a global historical trajectory and so shapes collective action. In radical circles of the long 1960s, the imagination of the global arena was integral to political theory, strategies for action, and group identity. Leftist movements in different socioeconomic environments held varying perspectives on the world, but many shared common egalitarian ideals, including self-determination, "universal liberation", Marxism-Leninism, and so forth. Just as important, the individual and collective project of "making connections", or recognizing the relationships between circumstances of oppression at home and abroad, shaped a new generation of radicals.[10] Western radical movements, for instance, came to see oppression and exploitation in the decolonizing world as manifestations of the same reactionary forces in their own societies. From this perspective, the struggles of the metropole and postcolony were indivisible, part of one anti-imperialist community.[11]

The collective imagination of radical movements held that because local circumstances and actions were inextricable from distant struggles, each movement contributed to a substantial world historical shift. The fact that 1960s radicals imagined a deeply integrated world and mutual struggle was not without precedent. For instance, many in the West saw themselves as inheritors of the spirit, though not the praxis, of the nineteenth- and early twentieth-century Communist Internationals. Nonetheless, for many young radicals the adoption of an explicitly internationalist lens through which to view local events was electrifying. The anti-imperialist imagined community of the 1960s also found a common language through what Benedict Anderson has termed a "transnational library".[12] Influential thinkers such as Guevara, Frantz Fanon, Antonio Gramsci, Vladimir Lenin, Herbert Marcuse, Karl Marx, Jean-Paul Sartre, Leon Trotsky, and Mao Zedong offered concepts for apprehending current circumstances and a grammar to articulate radical perspectives.[13] This *communitas* of shared ideals bound by a transnational imagination helps to account for the timing of antiestablishment uprisings (particularly 1968), commonalities among urban guerrilla movements (notably in Latin America), and the celebration of shared heroes, including Che Guevara.[14]

Many radical movements operated from a position of relative weakness. As a result, by the late 1960s the concept of solidarity was critical to the morale and identity of a great many leftist social movements and guerrilla factions. In the global South, like-minded groups drew inspiration from each other's successes, and movements or states with shared interests acted in concert. Networks and conventions such as the Non-Aligned Movement, the Organization for Solidarity for the People of Africa and Asia (OSPAA), and the Organization of Latin American Solidarity (OLAS) attempted to build connections across national and ideological divides. Perhaps the most noteworthy effort in this respect, albeit one dominated by the Cuban model of "immediate revolution", was OSPAA's reincarnation in 1966 as the Organization for Solidarity with the Peoples of Africa, Asia, and Latin America.

Liberation movements in the global South also embraced Western radicals, though solidarity with Western movements was not always of strategic importance.[15] For Western radicals, on the other hand, the affirmation of Third World grievances and solidarity with liberation movements in the South, a posture termed "Third Worldism", was vital. Western European and North American radical movements had local roots and differing ideological moorings, but the Third World proved a catalyst for action and a key frame of reference.[16] Western radicals saw Third World liberation movements—Marxist-Leninist, Maoist, or similar ideological orientations—as the vanguard of anti-capitalist struggle, and their successes seemed to signal that the overthrow of the capitalist system was within reach. Militant organizations such as the Vietnamese National Liberation Front (NLF), Fidel Castro's 26th of July Movement, and the Algerian National Liberation Front (FLN) offered inspiration— examples of victory in the face of overwhelming odds and proof that anything was possible. Additionally, for organizations such as the Black Panther Party (BPP), the Che-Lumumba Club of the Communist Party, the Brown Berets, and the Young Lords, narratives of exploitation and oppression articulated by liberation movements in the global South offered analogies to their own experiences.[17] By the late 1960s Western radicals had come to see the global South as an "ersatz proletariat", or the great masses implementing a new world order, and believed that they too had an important role to play in this effort.[18]

Though radical movements shared a commitment to the anti-capitalist struggle and sometimes even acted in unison, solidarity was more often symbolic than material. Common attitudes crystallized in a number of visible ways, but perhaps their most evocative forms were flags, ideograms, and images, including the NLF standard, the red flag of socialism, and Che Guevara's visage. This symbolic discourse provided a de-territorialized means of expressing transnational alliances, invoking global consensus, and creating spectacles of resistance. For example, as a statement of "universal and international principles of social justice," the Chicago 8 (radicals indicted for organizing protests during the 1968 Democratic Convention in Chicago, including BPP co-founder Bobby Seale) placed an NLF flag and Che Guevara's portrait on the defense table during their trial.[19] As mediums for simultaneously claiming and broadcasting consensus, ideograms, flags, and icons of dissent became essential components of the radical collective identity. By offering the trappings of a common identity, they contributed to the production of affinity among diverse movements. Thus, symbols, symbolic acts, and revolutionary discourse were not simply evidence of solidary. They were critical acts of solidarity.

Iconic figures were profound symbols of shared ideals and transnational solidarity because they condensed multiple virtues in a single, extraordinary human life. As suggested in the Introduction, icons frequently act as symbols of individual vision and courage, putting flesh on the bones of political rhetoric. They stand at the center of an inspirational horizon as practically superhuman backdrops onto which people project their hopes and dreams. In the late 1960s national heroes remained relevant to radical movements, but young people also embraced a small number of shared transnational icons that reinforced a sense of affinity. Alongside evocative national figures such as Emiliano Zapata, Augustino Sandino, Rosa Luxemburg, or José Martí, radicals around the world celebrated Che, Mao, Marx, Lenin, Castro, and Ho Chi Minh. The central role of radical icons in fostering solidarity helps explain why the protest chant "Che, Che, Che Guevara," first raised by

West German students, was echoed by radicals in Nanterre, Mexico City, and East Los Angeles.[20] Protest placards of Che and the slogans attributed to him, including "*Hasta la victoria siempre*" (Always Onward to Victory) and "*Venceremos*" (We Will Win), sounded a global chorus of revolution with each voice emboldening the others and confirming the idea of a common struggle.

In the late 1960s analysts of Guevara's meteoric rise to celebrity described him as a "folk hero", "icon", "revolutionary archetype", "idol", "cult figure" and "revolutionary pin-up". The fact that Che was a theorist of revolution and romantic hero who confronted seemingly unassailable forces made him a common denominator of radical ideals and ensured that his legend was multidimensional. Indeed, he became a popular rebel well beyond radical circles. Che personified utopian dreams of revolution better than almost any other figure because, as Andrew Sinclair explained in 1968, he "made the impossible appear to be possible." Guevara was, in Frantz Fanon's words, the "world symbol of the possibilities of one man." For young people who enjoined each other to "demand the impossible," Che neatly encapsulated the "antirealist" political imaginary of the late 1960s.[21] Because Che's heroic life and untimely death accorded well with antirealist youth rebellion, his popularity seeped into the counterculture and beyond.

By the spring of 1968 Guevara's image, as Richard Holmes recorded, hung "like an icon in a million bedsits, *apparts*, pads and communal kitchens, in London, New York, Hamburg, Paris and Rome."[22] Posters, flags, and T-shirts bearing the most popular image of Che, dubbed the Heroic Guerrilla (see below), first gained popularity in radical circles and then found an eager audience in the wider counterculture. In 1968 Guevara entered a contemporary pantheon of iconic figures that included film stars and pop musicians. As the market for pop art, music, and celebrity posters mushroomed, Che was sold on posters in Paris alongside the Beatles and Shirley Temple.[23] By May 1968, his image was subject to even greater commercialization. It was emblazoned not only on posters and T-shirts but also on blouses, sweatshirts, and handkerchiefs.[24] The British designer Antony Price tapped this developing trend and opened a shop in London's Kensington High Street named Che Guevara.[25] Additionally, after an international row over the rights to Che's final work, *Bolivian Diary*, the volume was translated into several languages and sold over a million copies. Books by and about Che were bestsellers at the bookstores of universities such as Columbia.[26] Recognizing this allure, the Italian typewriter manufacturer Olivetti even used his image in an advertising campaign. And less than three years after his death, Che was the subject of a major Hollywood motion picture, a Dutch opera, and several other films and plays.[27]

Though Che became a pop icon whose appeal transcended his political views, he remained a highly subversive and controversial figure. For instance, Brazilian police seized a cache of women's blouses that featured Che's image. Similarly, when a Barcelona publisher released a volume of Guevara's writings without the approval of the Spanish Ministry of Information, the Francisco Franco government ensured that copies of the offending material were destroyed. More gravely, the Turkish government banned Bolivian Diary and arrested poets Metin Demirtas and Arif Damar for praising Guevara in verse.[28] Chilean authorities likewise arrested an Italian priest in 1974 for possessing two Che Guevara posters, which they deemed "subversive propaganda." Even Hollywood's depiction of Guevara fueled a backlash. When the 1969 motion picture Che! opened, right-wing groups attacked the studios of Twentieth Century Fox, which produced the film, as well as cinemas that screened the movie in New York, Los Angeles, and West Palm Beach, Florida.[29] While many critics saw Guevara admirers as dangerously subversive, others perceived them as simply naïve. The British sitcom Citizen Smith reflected and popularized this perception whilst lampooning left radicals. The focus of the series was a young Marxist South Londoner named "Wolfie" Smith who had long hair, wore a black beret, sported a Che Guevara T-shirt, and claimed to represent the "Tooting Popular Front". Smith idolized Che, but his actions showed him to be both gullible and incompetent.[30]

In 1970, Time Magazine lamented that it had become "difficult to determine whether Che is actually a moving force or merely a symbol of a mood."[31] In fact, Guevara was both. He was a symbol of transnational sentiment but also a source of great inspiration for radicals. By the end of 1968, Heroic Guerrilla, the evocative image of Che with long hair and beard wearing a starred beret and looking intently into the distance, occupied a central place in radical iconography. Onto this image and its multiple permutations radicals inscribed a confident socialist future, a vision that motivated protesters and insurgents alike.

The following sections will plot the circulation of this image and the ideals associated with Che across these two broad, overlapping aspects of his appeal: as a symbol of the possible and as a revolutionary role model. I begin by exploring the logics of attraction to Guevara and the itineraries of the Heroic Guerrilla image—circuitous routes that link Cuba with radical movements around the world. I argue that while Guevara's image and ideas were blended into various discursive cocktails, Che proved alluring for several reasons: he was one of the most high-profile proponents of revolutionary internationalism; his words and actions aligned; he projected an ideal image of youthful rebellion; and he seemed a kindred spirit to many young radicals. In the second section I examine the crosscurrents and synchrony of New Left activism in 1968 through a reflection on the ways in which radicals in the US, UK, West Germany, France, and Mexico used Che's image and drew inspiration from his example. In the final section, I address more extremist interpretations of Guevara's ideas—how militants in the US, Latin America, and the Middle East applied his theory of revolutionary violence and employed his image as a symbol of transnational alliance.

## Ascent of the Heroic Guerrilla

Even decades after Che Guevara's death, Tariq Ali vividly recalled the day he learned of his hero's execution. Ali was a prominent member of Britain's Vietnam Solidarity Campaign, and when he heard of Che's fate in October 1967 he was preparing for the first large-scale Vietnam War demonstration in London. After receiving the news Ali was overpowered by a sense of loss. "I sat at my desk and wept," he remembered. Ali would later record that his grief was only eased by the fact that "[o]n every continent there were many others who felt and reacted in a similar fashion."[32] Like others in this broad *communitas*, Tariq Ali was a self-described revolutionary socialist who greatly admired Mao Zedong, Ho Chi Minh, and Che. Just as important, Ali embraced Guevara as a new beacon of idealism. Disillusioned with the Labour Party, Ali believed that egalitarian ideals had died in British parliamentary politics. For him and many others, revolution in the global South offered the inspiration and direction that Western democratic institutions lacked.[33]

Che's popularity among radicals like Tariq Ali was inextricably linked to the Cuban Revolution and its privileged position in the imagination of the New Left. In the late 1950s and early 1960s, Fidel Castro and Che Guevara became anti-imperialist luminaries. Many radicals hailed the Cuban success as a significant repulse of US influence in Latin America and lionized its two most recognizable personalities. As George Mariscal has suggested, post-revolutionary Cuba became a popular screen onto which a range of leftist dreams for a more egalitarian society were projected.[34] Che's association with Castro and the Cuban victory thrust him into the international spotlight, but his celebrity also stemmed from the fact that he was not Cuban. As one of the few outsiders and the sole Argentine in Castro's army, Che emerged from the revolution an unparalleled internationalist figure, a man willing to fight injustice in a foreign land.

In the years after the Cuban Revolution, Guevara embraced Marxism and revolutionary internationalism with greater zeal. In the early 1960s he became an emissary for the Cuban doctrine of "immediate and uncompromising armed struggle."[35] The writings and speeches of Che's final years reflect his ardent internationalism and commitment to guerrilla war. Perhaps his most famous work in this respect was "Message to the Tricontinental," published just before his death. Widely circulated in radical circles, Che's "Message" called for a dedication to international revolution. "[L]et us develop a true proletarian internationalism," Che proclaimed, in which "each nation liberated is a phase won in the battle for the liberation of one's own country." In his "Message" Guevara dreamed of a world in which "two, three, many Vietnams [could] flourish," resulting in conflicts too taxing for the American Goliath and its allies to sustain.[36] Moreover, Che was a paragon of unconditional solidarity with the wider Third World. Guevara was concerned with the suffering of the weak, and he believed that contributing to the alleviation of suffering was his obligation. "It is not a matter of wishing success to the victim of aggression but of sharing his fate," Guevara wrote in 1967. "[O]ne must accompany him to his death," he concluded, "or to victory."[37] In Cuba, Congo, and Bolivia, Che put this ideal of self-sacrificial internationalism into practice.

Tariq Ali also admired Che because he was more than an idealist; Guevara was a "man of action" who gave his life for his beliefs. Though Che occupied ministerial positions in Cuba's post-revolutionary government, he forfeited his comfortable new life to fulfill what he deemed the "most sacred of duties," that of fighting imperialism.[38] In 1965, Che traveled to Central Africa to assist insurgents in the Republic of the Congo (Léopoldville). When the Congo venture failed he turned to South America. Che calculated that Bolivia could become the epicenter of a continental uprising, and in late 1966 he traveled there to lay the groundwork for this revolution. Less than a year later he was captured by the Bolivian military and executed, his body put on display for the international media. Soon thereafter, his hands were removed and his remains were burned and buried in a secret location. Bolivian policy-makers believed these efforts would prove that they had killed Guevara and this would diminish his mystique. On the contrary, Che's death in Bolivia at only thirty-nine years old froze him in time as the perpetual revolutionary: young and idealistic, uncompromising and courageous. Both Che Guevara's life and death seemed to epitomize the spirit of the New Left, anti-colonial movements, and emancipatory projects generally.

Che Guevara's commitment to action also proved appealing because of the hyper-masculine culture that characterized left movements of the late 1960s and 1970s. As Sara Evans explained, Che was a "brash, gun-toting, self-confident image of the masculine rebel."[39] This revolutionary archetype, imbued with machismo, appealed to young men such as Mark Rudd of the American Students for a Democratic Society. In 1968 the twenty-year-old Rudd dreamed of being like Che, a "daring commander of rebels, willing to risk his life to free the people of the world." Like Che, Rudd hoped that his own death would inspire others to "greater sacrifice and victory."[40] Moreover, Guevara felt like a kindred spirit to many young radicals because his background mirrored their own.

Che was a precursor to 1960s radicalism typified in Europe, Latin America, and to a lesser extent the US by young, educated and empowered people who questioned the social and economic basis of their power. Born into a middle-class Argentine family in 1928, Che earned a medical degree before embarking on journeys that would introduce him to the plight of the Latin American underclass. The educated young people who constituted the core of protest movements and guerrilla organizations in Mexico, Uruguay, West Germany, and elsewhere saw elements of their own trajectories of political awakening in Guevara's

2. Student demonstrators carrying placards of Che Guevara, Ho Chi Minh, and Karl Marx. The placard in the foreground is a reprint of Alberto "Korda" Díaz Gutiérrez's photograph "Heroic Guerrilla", which was initially distributed in Europe by Italian publisher Giangiacomo Feltrinelli. Munich, West Germany, January 1, 1972. © ullstein bild / Getty Images.

story.[41] Che's heady allegory of self-sacrifice and passionate internationalism led many to see him as the ultimate icon of political, social,
even cultural revolution. Thus, from late 1967, Che imagery appeared
on placards, banners, and posters across the globe. Chief among these
images of Guevara was Heroic Guerrilla.

The popularity of this single image highlights channels of radical
connectivity as well as simultaneity within radical circles. While simultaneity across radical communities was not unprecedented, rarely had
a single image captured the imagination of so many young people at the
same time. Cuban fashion photographer-turned-journalist Alberto
"Korda" Diaz Gutiérrez snapped Heroic Guerrilla in 1960 and gave the
image its evocative name. It gained little attention until 1967, when
Korda offered a print to the Italian publisher Giangiacomo Feltrinelli.
In the months before and after Che's death, Feltrinelli made thousands
of posters from the image in Italy. As a result, many of the demonstrators who took to the streets of Milan after learning of Che's death
carried these prints of Korda's photo. Around the same time, Cuban
artists also began producing images based on Korda's photograph,
some of which appeared at the 1967 OLAS conference in Havana just
before Che's death. Another version, produced soon after Che's death
by Antonio Pérez Gonzalez (Ñiko), featured a two-tone, high-contrast
close-up of Guevara's face.[42]

Heroic Guerrilla circulated widely within Western radical circles,
but it was a stencilized version created in Ireland (and somewhat similar to Gonzalez's image) that would have the greatest impact on subsequent iterations of the image. It would also highlight converging interests in Che's visage. Irish artist Jim Fitzpatrick, like many young
radicals, was a great admirer of Che. In 1967 he received a print of
Heroic Guerrilla from members of the Dutch anarchist Provo movement. After creating multiple stylized adaptations, Fitzpatrick stripped
the original photograph of its grey tones and cast Che as a two-dimensional black stencil. He then erased the background and replaced it
with 'socialist' red. Fitzpatrick's version of Heroic Guerrilla, which he
dubbed "Viva Che!", transformed Guevara into an easily reproducible
work of pop art that signified courage, militancy, and socialism.[43]

Accordingly, Fitzpatrick set about printing thousands of copies of his
stenciled Heroic Guerrilla. He gave many away, posted a number abroad,

3. A two-dimensional rendering of Alberto "Korda" Diaz Gutiérrez's photograph "Heroic Guerrilla" by Jim Fitzpatrick, titled "Viva Che!", 1968. © Jim Fitzpatrick, 2010.

and sold others at low prices to shops in Ireland and England. Within a few months of its creation, demand for Fitzpatrick's image skyrocketed. For example, in early May 1968, one of France's most prominent activists, Daniel Cohn-Bendit (see below), acquired one of the posters, copied it, and distributed it among Parisian demonstrators.[44]

Che Guevara gained admirers around the world in the late 1960s, but nowhere was his example and image as important as in Cuba. In the months before Che's death the Cuban government began to cast Guevara as a national symbol of individual and collective aspiration. The Castro government believed that Che's selfless example could become a valuable moral apparatus that would give direction to the post-revolution generation. Soon after learning of Che's fate, the government commissioned a photomural of Korda's Heroic Guerrilla to span six stories of the Ministry of the Interior building on Havana's Plaza de la Revolución.

In a speech memorializing his fallen comrade, Castro predicted that Che would live on as a lodestar for revolution. "If we wish to express what we expect our revolutionary combatants, our militants, our men to be," Castro bellowed, "let them be like Che!"[45] Castro's predictions would come to pass, in part as a result of his own efforts. Several weeks later, on 2 January 1968—the ninth anniversary of the 26th of July Movement's victory—Castro gave another speech in which he decreed that the entire year was to be dedicated to Che and the Vietnamese freedom fighters. Castro declared 1968 to be the Year of the Heroic Guerrilla. The Cuban government funded more Guevara murals and promoted aspirational phrases such as "*Hasta la Victoria Siempre*" and "Be Like Che". Even Cuban school children were taught a daily pledge to emulate the national hero's behavior.[46] The Castro government thus projected Che Guevara as the crystallization of the revolution's founding ideal—that revolutionaries should act as servants of the masses.

The promotion of Che to the status of patriotic symbol also created an enduring point of connection between the Castro government and leftist movements around the world.[47] Fidel Castro's charge to "be like Che" struck a chord with people who had no connection to the Cuban Revolution. As I will outline in the next section, Guevara's revolutionary example became a model for the new generation of radicals. When Columbia University's Students for a Democratic Society (SDS) organizer Mark Rudd visited Cuba in March 1968, Che's image already adorned the nation, from the international arrival terminal at Havana Airport to provincial towns. The image made a great impression on the young radical. Rudd would later recall the transformative moment when, while traveling in the Cuban countryside, he looked down from a high ridge to see an enormous image of Guevara's face painstakingly plotted in stones. It was then that Rudd became a devotee of what he would later call the "cult of Che."[48]

*Che Guevara and Social Movements*

For Mark Rudd, Che's ideas and selfless example were exemplary. Before visiting Cuba, Rudd was inspired by, among other works, *The Autobiography of Malcolm X* and Frantz Fanon's *The Wretched of the Earth*. Yet, it was a book that expounded on Che's ideas written by the French intellectual Régis Debray, *Revolution in the Revolution?*, that gave Rudd's life clear direction. Debray's 1967 treatise outlined the foco theory—the concept that radical paramilitary cells can spark revolution through exemplary action. With insights drawn from Guevara's *Guerrilla Warfare* and the assistance of Fidel Castro, Debray outlined the Cuban model of revolution, one that rejected orthodox Marxism's emphasis on the mobilization of the proletariat as a precondition of insurrection. Debray argued that insurgents can become the nucleus, or "focal point", that creates the conditions for a broader antiestablishment insurrection. Echoing Guevara and Castro's conclusion, and feeding the New Left's hunger for alternative strategies, Debray suggested that the lesson of the Cuban Revolution was that a small revolutionary vanguard can mobilize the masses.[49]

For Mark Rudd and other radicals disillusioned with the political process and desirous of rapid social change, the notion that a fringe group could light the spark of revolution was intoxicating. In 1967 radicals in Latin America and the West had already begun to embrace direct action tactics. Thus, the foco theory, in Todd Gitlin's words, "heightened the feeling that with sheer audacity we must—and therefore could—bull our way past the apparent obstacles."[50] The wide circulation of *Revolution in the Revolution?* and the increased interest in Che after his death converted the foco theory into what Edward Said termed a "traveling theory", or an idea reinterpreted and transformed by its application beyond its original context.[51] In the case of the foco theory, it was neither the minutiae of the Cuban model nor the nuances of Debray's thesis that would fire radical imaginations. Instead, many radicals embraced a simplified traveling theory, which held that spontaneous action could create change, even revolution, virtually anywhere. In this form, the concept offered a theoretical basis for diverse strategies of direct confrontation, from protest tactics to urban guerrilla campaigns.

In the spring of 1968 Mark Rudd's experiences in Cuba and the foco theory stirred a new zeal in the student leader. He was now guided by a dictum commonly repeated in Cuba: "the duty of the revolutionary is to make revolution."[52] Once back at Columbia, Rudd helped organize a number of SDS members into a cell called the Action Faction that tried to put the foco theory into practice. Instead of using violence, the Action Faction staged militant political acts such as protests and walkouts. These events attracted greater attention and support for the SDS, and so they appeared to confirm the foco theory. Events came to a head in April 1968 when a coalition of Columbia students led by the SDS and the Student Afro-American Society (SAS) occupied a clutch of university administration buildings. The uprising was born of multiple concerns, but students focused on two main issues: the administration's decision to build a gym in Harlem's Morningside Park and Columbia University's institutional support for the war in Vietnam by way of its affiliation with the Institute for Defense Analysis.

Student demands for reform may have been local in scope, but both the SDS and the SAS viewed the occupations as acts of international solidarity. In the aftermath of the occupations Mark Rudd explained that "[e]very militant in the buildings knew that he was there because of his opposition to racism and imperialism and the capitalist system that needs to exploit and oppress human beings from Vietnam to Harlem to Columbia." SAS representative Bill Sales was equally explicit: "You strike a blow at the gym, you strike a blow for the Vietnamese people," he told an audience in student-occupied Hamilton Hall. "You strike a blow at Low Library [another occupied building] and you strike a blow for the freedom fighters in Angola, Mozambique, South Africa."[53] Students in Hamilton Hall celebrated shared heroes by hanging posters of Stokely Carmichael, Malcolm X, and Karl Marx on the walls. They afforded Che Guevara's image pride of place over the door of the Acting Dean's office. The Columbia revolt was short-lived, but in its wake even more students joined the radical cause, thus further validating the foco strategy. Militant actions, in Mark Rudd's estimation, had changed the consciousness of Columbia students, just as Régis Debray posited.[54] Moreover, efforts of the SDS and SAS emboldened direct action campaigns on campuses across the US and Europe. Their acts of resistance encouraged other radical organizations, in Tom Hayden's adaptation of Che's call, to "create two, three, many Columbias."[55]

Like Columbia's SDS and SAS, West German students at universities in Munich, Frankfurt, West Berlin, and Hamburg saw themselves as catalysts for revolutionary change. For Rudi Dutschke, the most prominent representative of the Socialist German Student Union (Sozialistischer Deutscher Studentenbund, or SDS), the struggle of

West German students was for "international emancipation." The West German SDS saw its political agitation as an act of solidarity with Third World liberation movements and reform movements in Eastern Europe. For many in the SDS, Che Guevara struck a powerful cord as a daring and selfless rebel fighting for a just international order.[56]

As Timothy S. Brown has demonstrated, for West German radicals Heroic Guerrilla and other iconic images acted as "ritual objects" that conferred authenticity to political struggle and conveyed "the appearance of a mass revolutionary base" that transcended West Germany.[57] The revolutionary example of Che Guevara would also provide a common reference, or "point of contact", between East and West German radical movements.[58] Rudi Dutschke even named his son after Che and claimed that the West German SDS aimed to create "two, three Prague Springs." Dutschke and other SDS radicals also believed that opposition to the American war in Vietnam was a critical first step towards challenging imperialism and liberating humanity from capitalist and bureaucratic oppression. Thus, much like their American counterparts, West German radicals embraced Che as a revolutionary icon and drew inspiration from the foco theory.[59]

At a student convention in 1967, Dutschke and fellow organizer Hans-Jürgen Krahl spearheaded an effort to push the SDS in a more confrontational direction. The guiding spirit of student agitation would be, in Ingrid Gilcher-Holtey's words, "organization by action, and not action by organization."[60] During a February 1968 Vietnam War teach-in in Frankfurt, Dutschke attempted to implement this more confrontational strategy by calling on the crowd to occupy the American consulate. Dutschke and the protestors descended on the US Consulate in Frankfurt but failed to penetrate the complex. Instead, in a heavily symbolic gesture, they stripped the West German flag from the nearby US Trade Center and replaced it with the NLF standard and a picture of Che.[61]

The same month, at West Berlin's Technical University, the SDS convened its first International Vietnam Conference, which was attended by representatives from the West German SDS, French and American student organizations, and the Italian Socialist Party of Proletarian Unity (Partito Socialista Italiano di Unità Proletaria). The West German SDS hosts decorated the conference hall with symbols that represented the causes uniting the groups present at this landmark event. Above the podium was an NLF flag, a sign of solidarity with Vietnam. As a symbol of global revolution, the organizers hung a banner bearing Che's image and a maxim commonly associated with him, "the duty of every revolutionary is to make revolution." French students who attended the conference were inspired by the militancy and devotion of the West Germans. It would be the first time they would hear the chants "Ho, Ho, Ho Chi Minh" and "Che, Che, Che Guevara." Three months later they repeated these chants on the streets of Paris.[62]

One of the French student groups that attended the West Berlin conference and later played a role in the French May uprising was the Revolutionary Communist Youth (Jeunesse communiste révolutionnaire, or JCR). The JCR adopted elements of Trotskyism, voiced solidarity with Vietnam and Cuba, and celebrated Che as a revolutionary hero. Inspired in part by the foco theory, JCR members believed that they could ignite a revolution that would lead the metropolitan working classes to socialism. In February 1968, one of the JCR's founders, Janette Habel, argued that western European youth should draw inspiration from Guevara as a true internationalist. "We must defend Che like a flag," Habel argued, "defend his concept of the new human being, who is involved in the anti-imperialist fight ... who is sensitive to the fate of all the exploited." Che's "many Vietnams" call to arms, and other axioms such as "the duty of a revolutionary is to make revolution," peppered JCR discourse.[63]

In May 1968 French radicals staged a series of protests that began as demonstrations against the war in Vietnam and the structure of French universities but quickly gained such force as to threaten the Charles de Gaulle government. One organizer of the uprising was Daniel Cohn-Bendit. Like the JCR, Cohn-Bendit's Movement of 22 March drew inspiration from Che and the foco theory. The movement reckoned that vanguard actions by students could create the conditions for revolution. Cohn-Bendit became a seasoned agitator in Nanterre, where the Movement of 22 March gained a number of concessions. Emboldened by victories that seemed to confirm the foco theory, Cohn-Bendit turned to central Paris and helped students there to organize demonstrations. In May, Parisian students occupied the Sorbonne and plastered it with posters of Che, Marx, Lenin, Trotsky, and Mao. They also renamed its main auditorium Che Guevara Hall.[64]

The relevance of the foco strategy seemed to grow exponentially when workers joined the striking students. What had begun as student demonstrations quickly became the largest strike in French history, a spontaneous wildcat strike that counted roughly nine million laborers, about half of all French workers. A loose confederation of labor, anti-Gaullists, and students paralyzed Paris, brought the economy to a standstill, and applied significant pressure to the de Gaulle government.[65] Yet, the coalition dissipated as quickly as it coalesced. Concessions to workers and severe police reprisals against student demonstrators effectively ended the uprising. Yet, the failure of the students to usher in a new order in France did not dampen the zeal with which young people embraced Che and the foco theory. In the eyes of many radicals in and beyond France, the general strike that followed from student agitation validated the idea that exemplary action can rouse the masses.

In the summer of 1968, students in Mexico City resurrected Che's spirit in a more explicit fashion. Activist and later Guevara biographer Paco Ignacio Taibo II recalled that within Mexican radical circles of the late 1960s Che was the ideal revolutionary hero, or "the man to follow."[66] More than any other figure, Guevara represented the anti-authoritarian and internationalist sensibilities of the Mexican student movement. By August 1968 Che was a primary symbol of Mexican radicalism as well as a point of connection with other movements. As one student explained, Che was "our link with student movements all over the world."[67]

Less than two months after the end of the French strike, students in Mexico City initiated a series of protests. Student demands included the release of political prisoners and an end to police aggression. Launched just ahead of the 1968 Mexico City Olympics—the first Olympic Games to be held in Latin America—protest leaders placed significant pressure on the Gustavo Díaz Ordaz government at the very moment when Mexico was poised to capture the world's attention. On 26 July students led a mass demonstration in solidarity with Cuba's 26th of July Movement. On 13 August, two months before the games were scheduled to begin, university and secondary school students marched to the center of Mexico City. Che's inspirational role was manifest. Protesting students chanted, "Create two, three, many

4. Student demonstrators carrying an image of Che Guevara similar to Jim Fitzpatrick's rendering, captioned "Hasta la Victoria Siempre" (Always Onward Until Victory). Mexico City, Mexico, 1968. © A. Abbas / Magnum Photos.

Vietnams!" and "Che, Che, Che Guevara." "Che is not dead," a banner read, "he lives in our ranks." As more protesters swelled the student ranks, events seemed to validate the foco theory. One demonstrator declared that "Che's thesis is proven in Mexico."[68]

Che's symbolic presence grew with the size of the demonstrations. Those at the front of a 17 August march carried a giant banner reminiscent of Fitzpatrick's stylized Heroic Guerrilla, inscribed with the slogan "*Hasta la Victoria Siempre*". "We had all linked arms and were chanting in unison, 'Che, Che,Che Guevara,'" one student recalled. "Just as we passed into the Zócalo [Mexico City's central plaza] ... the bells [of the National Cathedral] started ringing. All of them at once. Many of us turned and looked at the picture of Che and began cheering and screaming. I looked over at the person marching next to me and there were tears in his eyes."[69] As in the US, West Germany, and France, Guevara was a lodestar for the dreams of Mexicans radicals, a spirit that guided and emboldened their acts of resistance. Ten days later, on 27 August, an even larger group of students, numbering roughly 400,000, entered the Zócalo carrying portraits of Che alongside those of Mexican national heroes, including José María Morelos, Benito Juárez, Emiliano Zapata, and Francisco "Pancho"Villa.[70]

Che was the most important transnational hero of the Mexican student movement, but from late August 1968 he became a significant political liability for the protesters. The Mexican government and the popular press pointed to Che Guevara references as evidence that the student movement was being controlled by external, communist powers, notably Cuba.[71] To deflect this charge, on the eve of the Great Silent March, a solemn demonstration set for 13 September, organizers asked demonstrators to carry only placards of Mexican national heroes. Despite such efforts, the government responded to the student demonstrations with violence, culminating in a massacre of protesters at Tlatelolco the following month.[72] Che symbolism had become a liability, but Guevara's example and ideas continued to influence Mexican radicals.

Many other political organizations also embraced Guevara as both a revolutionary archetype and point of linkage with a wider *communitas*. The Black Panther Party (BPP) offers a case in point. Founded in Oakland, California in 1966, the BPP was an anti-racist, Marxist-Leninist-Maoist group that developed a broad political program.

Though initially focused on community protection from police brutality, later BPP activities emphasized housing, education, healthcare, and other means to bring dignity and greater autonomy to marginalized urban communities. Maoism greatly influenced BPP thinking, but its leaders also embraced Che and the Cuban Revolution as examples of the revolutionary potential of a small, determined group. Che's *Guerrilla Warfare* was mandatory reading in BPP political education classes, and Panther leaders regularly referenced Che in speeches and party literature. Guevara's image was also posted in many BPP offices and appeared on the masthead for the *Black Panther* newspaper's international news section.[73]

BPP co-founder Huey P. Newton, much like Tariq Ali and Mark Rudd, saw Che as a kindred spirit. Newton explained that the Panthers, as disenfranchised African Americans, read Guevara's work alongside Mao's because they saw both "as kinsmen" who suffered at the hands of the same oppressor. "We believed it was necessary to know how they gained their freedom," Newton concluded, "in order to go about getting ours."[74] The BPP was also internationalist, and it gained the recognition of a number of liberation movements abroad. BPP solidarity chapters were established in France, Sweden, Denmark, West Germany, the Netherlands, Italy, and Japan.[75] In an attempt to build bridges connecting disparate radical movements around the world, in 1970 the BPP organized a plenary session in Philadelphia called the Revolutionary People's Constitutional Convention. Delegates representing many different political organizations from across the US as well as from Africa, Europe, the Middle East, and South America attended the event. As a sign of solidarity, at the venue the BPP flag flew alongside the internationalist standards of the NLF, Black Nationalism, Yippie (Youth International Party), and a flag bearing Che Guevara's visage.[76] In the US as elsewhere, Guevara's image reflected the transnational imagination and articulated a desire for global solidarity in the struggle against imperialism and oppression.

## Che Guevara and Guerrillas

A few days after Guevara's death in 1967, US National Security Advisor Walt Whitman Rostow explained to President Lyndon B. Johnson that Che's execution would have "a strong impact in discouraging would-be guerrillas."[77] Rostow had it wrong. In the late 1960s and early 1970s, many radicals emphasized the emancipatory power of violence and emulated Che Guevara by taking up arms, often against greatly superior forces. Che was a principal role model for many guerrillas, and the application of the foco strategy of armed struggle came to be known as Guevarism, or *foquismo*. Guevarists in Peru, Venezuela, Sri Lanka, Nicaragua, and many other countries drew heavily on the Cuban experience and Che's writings, though most guerrillas who aspired to follow in Che's footsteps borrowed selectively from his canon.[78]

Much as with protest movements, the foco theory was attractive to those willing to adopt violent tactics because it held that the revolutionary could bypass the proletariat, political parties, and other precursors to revolution prescribed by orthodox communism. "It is not necessary to wait until all conditions for making revolution exist," Che explained in his 1961 treatise *Guerrilla Warfare*, "the insurrection can create them."[79] Revolution by sheer audacity appealed to radicals who were frustrated by the reformist approaches of the Soviet Union and the Old Left, alienated from the working class, and driven by a profound optimism that the dominant socioeconomic system could be toppled. For instance, in 1968 an overzealous admirer of Guevara at the University of Colorado-Boulder explained to his fellow students that, contra orthodox Marxism, the revolution did not need the masses behind it. Just one man, he wrote, "can bring a city to its knees."[80]

The foco theory was popular in leftist circles, but Guevara and Debray's prescription for revolution was, in fact, quite narrow: a rural insurrection led by a revolutionary vanguard and supported by the peasantry. The foco theory may have provided a theoretical frame for interpreting the Cuban Revolution, but this formula for insurrection was not easily transposed. Che's own death demonstrated the limited applicability of the theory. After only a few months of fighting in Bolivia, Guevara's forces had alienated the Bolivian Communist Party, failed to gain the support of local peasants, and encountered stiff resistance from US-trained counterinsurgency forces. By the time the Bolivian military finally captured Che his band had dwindled to just a handful. As resourceful and determined as he was, Che Guevara could not recreate the Cuban Revolution by sheer force of will.

The foco theory also obscured many dimensions of the Cuban Revolution. For instance, Guevara and Debray's model rejected any role for urban agitation in the revolution, arguing that the city has a corrupting effect on the guerrilla. This doctrinal position was at least in part a product of Cuban politics. Both Castro and Guevara minimized the contributions of other players in the Cuban Revolution so as to emphasize the centrality of their rural guerrilla movement. It is no small irony, therefore, that in the 1960s and 1970s the foco theory inspired a great number of urban guerrilla movements. Much as protest movements adapted a traveling foco theory, Che's exhortations on the necessity of revolution inspired urban guerrillas to launch campaigns that diverged substantially from the Cuban model.[81]

For instance, *foquista* guerrilla movements based in the city tended to focus on spectacular martial acts, which they believed could deliver the masses to the revolutionary cause. As a result, urban guerrillas who embraced Che's spirit often engaged in actions more akin to nineteenth-century anarchists than Cuban revolutionaries. Additionally, *foquismo*'s emphasis on immediate revolt widened ideological divides within the left. In many instances frictions between *foquistas*, Maoists, and those committed to less violent forms of agitation led to the Guevarists' detachment from mass movements. Unlike Castro and Guevara's 26th of July Movement, most of the urban guerrillas of the 1960s and 1970s found themselves isolated from potential bases of support, including the urban and rural working classes and student movements.

Perhaps the most famous militant to emulate Guevara's commitment to emancipatory violence—and replicate his image—was the Venezuelan internationalist Ilich Ramírez Sánchez, aka Carlos the Jackal. Sánchez joined the Venezuelan Communist Party at a young age, but he was expelled for his support of Douglas Bravo's Guevarist movement, the Armed Forces of National Liberation (Fuerzas Armadas de Liberación Nacional). In his late teens or early twenties, Sánchez became enamored of Che and soon began to fashion himself as an international revolutionary.[82] Sánchez began studies at the London School of Economics but soon transferred to Moscow's Lumumba University. There he became known for wearing a black beret in tribute to Guevara. However, Lumumba University expelled Sánchez in 1969 after he participated in a demonstration in solidarity with Arab students.[83] Sánchez did not return to Venezuela. Moved by Che's example of revolutionary internationalism, in 1970 he joined the Popular Front for the Liberation of

Palestine (PFLP). He fought in Jordan during Black September, and in 1975 he was appointed to lead a PFLP operation to disrupt the 1975 OPEC summit and take the attendees hostage. In homage to Guevara, Sánchez grew his hair long for the operation, donned a leather jacket, and sported a black beret. For Sánchez, the Heroic Guerrilla image constituted the revolutionary ideal.

In Western Europe, the US, and Latin America, many proponents of revolutionary violence emerged from the student movements. One group that transitioned from protest to armed struggle was a faction of the American SDS known as the Weathermen, formed in 1969 by militant wings of the SDS, including the Action Faction in New York (see above) and the Jesse James Gang in Ann Arbor, Michigan. Under the leadership of Bernardine Dohrn, Mark Rudd, Cathy Wilkerson, Bill Ayers, and others, the group produced a position paper, "You Don't Need a Weatherman to Know Which Way the Wind Blows," which borrowed a popular Bob Dylan lyric to argue for the necessity of revolutionary violence. It explained that the world was locked in a battle between American imperialists and those who resisted them. They saw Vietnam as a primary theater in this war, but held that a new front should be opened on American soil. This, the group suggested, would add internal conflict to the "many Vietnams" that would "dismember and dispose of US imperialism." To rally militants around this idea, the Weathermen adopted the slogan "Bring the War Home."[84]

The Weathermen initiated the war at home by setting off a bomb in Haymarket Square, Chicago on the second anniversary of Che Guevara's capture: 7 October 1969. Two days later the Weathermen staged an anti-Vietnam War demonstration in Chicago's Lincoln Park, timed to coincide with the anniversary of Che's death and the trial of the Chicago 8. The Weathermen hoped that the demonstration would propel the protest movement towards armed clashes with the police. The event only drew a modest crowd, but those who attended were committed to active resistance. The radicals assembled in the park carried NLF flags and a banner bearing Fitzpatrick's rendering of Heroic Guerrilla, captioned "Avenge Che Guevara." Bernardine Dohrn announced to the crowd that Che's death had "not killed the revolution." The chants "Che Lives", "Venceremos", and "Ho, Ho, Ho Chi Minh" filled the night air. From Lincoln Park the demonstrators took to the streets, smashing symbols of conspicuous consumption and fighting running battles with the police.[85]

The Chicago police bludgeoned the Weathermen, but many members remained convinced of the necessity of revolutionary violence. Soon after the confrontations in Chicago, national leaders of the SDS met in Flint, Michigan to discuss the future of the student organization. Dohrn and the Weathermen called for armed struggle and argued that the non-violent tactics of the student movement were an impediment to true revolution.[86] The exodus of Maoist Progressive Labor Party members from the SDS had already split the organization, and Dohrn's call to arms alienated many of its remaining members. As the Weathermen hastened the SDS' collapse, the faction reconstituted itself as a clandestine network of urban cells known collectively as the Weather Underground Organization (WUO).

WUO guerrillas fashioned themselves a fifth column of the worldwide revolution and initiated a carefully orchestrated bombing campaign to demonstrate solidarity with the Vietnamese NLF, the Uruguayan Tupamaros, and the Black Panther Party. Founding WUO member Cathy Wilkerson explained that the organization sought to create links with revolutionaries in Vietnam, Cuba, Algeria, and elsewhere while positioning themselves "to bring down the critically weakened center [of the capitalist system] from the inside." They would accomplish this through bombings that would rouse the masses and encourage similar acts of revolutionary violence. To honor Che Guevara's inspirational example cell members hung photos of him in their safe houses.[87]

The murder of BPP spokesman Fred Hampton by the Chicago police in December 1969 prompted the WUO to expand its bombing campaign. The cells focused on targets of political and symbolic significance, though they were careful not to injure anyone. In August 1970 the WUO bombed the Army Math Research Lab in Madison, Wisconsin, which had developed an infrared device used to locate Guevara and his fellow insurgents in Bolivia. In 1972 the WUO even planted a bomb inside the Pentagon. WUO actions continued into the mid-1970s, but after the end of the Vietnam War and the disintegration of the Black Power movement the WUO dissolved.[88] The application of the foco theory to urban America had not inspired the proletariat to revolt. Instead, revolutionary violence had effectively isolated the WUO from nearly all support bases.

*Foquismo* reached its zenith in Latin America, where Che's doctrine of immediate revolution captured the imagination of a great number of radicals. By the middle of the 1960s radicals across the region saw few prospects in non-violent agitation and therefore embraced the Cuban model of uncompromising armed struggle. In this milieu, Che became the central moral and political reference for revolutionary leftist movements from Chile to Nicaragua, a generational symbol for the regional struggle against US imperialism. In 1968, journalist Norman Gall argued that Che's *Guerrilla Warfare* was likely the most influential book published in Latin America since the Second World War. *Guerrilla Warfare* was hardly a bestseller, but in Gall's estimation it profoundly altered the tone and focus of Latin American revolutionary struggles.[89]

Che's internationalism and personal sacrifice resonated with the revolutionary fervor of Latin America's urban middle-class radicals, who constituted a sizable proportion of the militant community. Since these revolutionaries lacked substantive links with rural communities, they often adapted Guevara's ideas to the city. For instance, Brazilian tactician Carlos Marighella reworked many of *Guerrilla Warfare*'s themes for an urban context in his 1969 manual on insurgent tactics.[90] Che also influenced Latin America's clergy. The Brazilian Bishop of Santo Andre, Jose Marcos de Oliveira, referred to Guevara as a "heroic" man "who sought justice."[91] Uruguayan clergyman Juan Zaffaroni called Guevara "the revolutionary I idolize." But the most celebrated cleric to integrate Che's ideas with Christian precepts was the Colombian Roman Catholic priest Camilo Torres. For Torres, the lives of Jesus and Che were analogous since both men were devoted to the liberation of the oppressed and fearlessly challenged social inequalities. Adapting the famous phrase associated with Guevara, Camilo Torres declared that "the duty of every Christian is to be a revolutionary, and the duty of every revolutionary is to make the revolution."[92]

At the end of the 1960s Guevarist guerrillas were more numerous in Latin America than any in other part of the world. Among the most notable were the Chilean Movement of the Revolutionary Left (Movimiento de Izquierda Revolucionaria, MIR), the Bolivian National Liberation Army (Ejército de Liberación Nacional, ELN), Uruguay's Tupamaros, Venezuela's Armed Forces of National Liberation (Fuerzas Armadas de Liberación Nacional), the Peruvian Revolutionary Left

Movement (Movimiento de Izquierda Revolucionaria), the Nicaraguan Sandinista National Liberation Front (Frente Sandinista de Liberación Nacional), the People's Revolutionary Army of Argentina (Ejército Revolucionario del Pueblo, or ERP), and Brazil's Revolutionary Movement of October 8 (Movimento Revolucionário 8 de Outubro). Each group looked to Che as a revolutionary role model, even though each interpreted Guevarist doctrine somewhat differently.

Guevara's influence was perhaps most symbolically evident in the Brazilian Revolutionary Movement of October 8, or MR-8. MR-8 grew out of a popular student campaign to oppose the 1964 military seizure of power. In 1966 a core group of student radicals took up arms against the military dictatorship. The following year, members chose what they believed to be the date of Che's execution as the name of their organization. This choice both memorialized the fallen revolutionary and symbolically linked Brazilian efforts with the global liberation struggle. Under the leadership of a former military officer, Captain Carlos Lamarca, MR-8 commandos organized a series of bank robberies in an effort to lay the groundwork for a larger, rural insurrection. The most fantastic of their exploits, the 1969 kidnapping of the US Ambassador to Brazil, succeeded in bringing international attention to the group. However, MR-8's revolutionary actions, as well as those of other militant factions in Brazil, failed to foment a broad uprising.[93]

In neighboring Uruguay the Tupamaros launched a similar urban insurgency. Tupamaros members were mainly students, academics, and other middle-class intellectuals who believed that they could create a revolution in Uruguay. The Tupamaros argued that "the revolution cannot wait" and that they were its vanguard. Echoing Guevara, they outlined their overall strategy as an attempt to create "many Vietnams" in order to challenge US imperialism and its regional agents.[94] The Tupamaros emerged in the early 1960s but only began to execute notable operations on the second anniversary of Che's death. In October 1969 the Che Guevara Commando Unit, which consisted of at least fifty guerrillas, led an assault on the town of Pando, about 30 kilometers outside of Montevideo. The raid aimed to demonstrate the ability of the people to rise up against the forces of oppression, and the targets included a police station as well as three banks. Though the Tupamaros would continue their efforts for several years and win the sympathy of many Uruguayans, no popular revolt materialized.[95]

64

The People's Revolutionary Army (ERP) of Argentina held Che in similarly high regard. Che Guevara was Argentina's most famous revolutionary, and he was the ERP's primary inspiration because of what they referred to as his "exemplary practice of proletarian internationalism." The ERP's goal, like Che's, was to pave the way for socialism in Argentina and "be in whatever place people are fighting imperialism arms in hand."[96] ERP guerrillas vowed to take up Guevara's banner of internationalism, and so in 1973 they joined forces with the Tupamaros, the Chilean MIR, and Bolivia's ELN to create a popular front against their respective governments and US influence in the region. The four insurgent groups established the first international coordinating committee of Guevarist guerrillas, the Junta for Revolutionary Coordination (Junta de Coordinación Revolucionaria), or JCR.

The foco theory, Che's spirit of defiance, and his vision of global socialist revolution united the JCR. In an April 1974 communiqué the consortium argued that their collaboration was a necessary first step towards concretizing "one of the principal strategic ideas of comandante Che Guevara": the internationalization of revolution. The JCR claimed that, as a transnational league of guerrilla fighters, they were sowing the seeds of "the second [Latin American] independence," which would eliminate the "unjust capitalist system" and establish "revolutionary socialism." For their flag the alliance adopted a red banner emblazoned with a seal in the shape of the globe. Superimposed on this seal were Fitzpatrick's rendering of Heroic Guerrilla and the words "Che Guevara".[97] The image of Che the revolutionary, filtered through Korda, Fitzpatrick, and the radical circuits of the era, thus became the standard for a collective insurgency that saw each national movement as a component of a global revolution. The transnational imagination, by way of Guevara's example, had helped to inspire a regional guerrilla war.

The JCR was the most advanced attempt to realize Guevara's dream of regional insurrection, but its constituent movements had few successes. For instance, the ERP was subdued after initiating a *foco* in Argentina's remote Tucumán Province. The Isabel Perón government responded to the ERP threat with overwhelming force, granting the military and police extraordinary powers to neutralize the insurgents. By 1977 security forces had broken the back of the guerrilla movement through a counterinsurgency program that included targeted assassinations, "disappearances", and torture. Other regional governments likewise used heavy-handed tactics to crush members of the JCR. This overwhelming state response to Guevarist insurrection shifted the political landscape of Latin America in ways that the radicals could not have foreseen. Instead of installing revolutionary socialism, Guevarism emboldened regional governments to act with impunity, encouraged greater coordination among them, and led to a significant increase in US counterinsurgency assistance. *Foquismo* thus became a justification for greater repression.[98]

South American guerrilla organizations embraced Che's ideas with the greatest verve, but Guevara's example inspired many other militants around the world, including prominent members of the Irish Republican Army (IRA), the People's Mojahedin Organization of Iran, the Palestinian National Liberation Movement (Fatah), and the Popular Front for the Liberation of Palestine (PFLP). Guevara played a central role in inspiring one of the PFLP's best-known commandos, Leila Khaled, to join the armed struggle. The combination of the Six-Day War and Che's death convinced Khaled to become part of the resistance. She pledged to fight Israel and its American ally and believed Guevara to be the ideal role model for Palestinian revolutionaries. Sounding notes similar to radicals in the US and Latin America, Khaled admired Che because, she explained, "his commitment was total." "[M]y people needed revolutionaries and heroes of Che's calibre," Khaled argued, and so she vowed to follow Guevara's example by committing herself to the liberation of Palestine.[99]

As with the WUO in the US and the JCR in South America, PFLP militants saw Che as a lodestar for anti-imperialism and a crucial link with the global emancipatory struggle. Guevara was so important to PFLP operatives that they referenced him during a hijacking designed to bring international attention to the Palestinian cause. In 1969 the PFLP leadership selected Leila Khaled to head a cell called the Che Guevara Commando Unit on a high profile mission to commandeer a Transworld Airlines flight. The choice of an American airliner was significant. After taking control of the airplane Khaled explained to the passengers that the PFLP had hijacked the flight because of the US government's support of Israel. "We are against America because she is an imperialist country," Khaled told the hostages, "[a]nd our unit is called the Che Guevara Commando Unit because we abhor America's assassination of Che and … we are a part of the Third World and the world revolution."[100]

In 1970 the Che Guevara Commando Unit attempted another hijacking operation in coordination with three other PFLP cells, a series of events that would be widely known as the Dawson's Field hijackings. To demonstrate their solidarity and affinity with guerrilla movements elsewhere, during hostage negotiations representatives of the PFLP gave interviews to the international press under posters of Che Guevara, Mao Zedong, and Ho Chi Minh. In the wake of the hijackings the Israeli intelligence agency, Mossad, exploited the PFLP's interest in Che to launch a counterattack. PFLP leader Bassam Abu Sharif claimed Guevara as one of his "special heroes"; and so Mossad agents tried to assassinate him by sending him a copy of *The Memoirs of Che Guevara* packed with explosives. The PFLP leader was nearly killed when he opened the book.[101]

Che was a common symbol for revolution because he offered leftist guerrillas like Leila Khalid both inspiration and theoretical grounding for the practice of revolutionary violence. However, with few exceptions, the dream of liberation that fostered armed struggles soured in the inability of violence to mobilize the masses, particularly in the West and Latin America. Moreover, *foquismo* exacerbated doctrinal divisions within the left and isolated many guerrilla movements from larger bases of support. In most cases, attempts to realize Guevara's dream of "many Vietnams" led militants to political suicide, while the concept of immediate revolution lost its rhetorical strength under the weight of state repression. Che's spirit continued to inspire militants in Guatemala, Nicaragua, Colombia, Palestine, South Africa, and elsewhere, but by the late 1970s few still believed that violence alone could awaken the masses and germinate a revolutionary consciousness.[102]

### Conclusion

In the late 1960s and 1970s, left-wing radicals on every continent struggled against what they saw as a world system of imperialist oppression with myriad local manifestations. Galvanized by the transnational imagination, radicals sought to internationalize movements that were, in practice, national and to domesticate ideas borrowed from very different sociopolitical milieus. In this internationalist context, the death of Che Guevara, one of the greatest proponents of global socialist revolution, was momentous. Soon after his death, Guevara became a martyr for revolutionary internationalism and a symbolic link among a great many radical movements. Since most leftist movements were circumscribed by national boundaries, the celebration of Che and other aspirational figures offered graphic affirmation of a transnational unity of attitude and vision. In this way, the resurrected Che provided psychological solace that any movement, no matter how marginal, could be part of a global fight for liberation and social justice.

Radicals projected onto and drew from Che Guevara a politics of morality, solidarity, and possibility that transcended the particularities of the era and ensured Che's long-term relevance. While the symbolic legacies of 1960s radicalism have been more ambiguous than the successes of national liberation and civil rights movements, the emphasis that radicals placed on symbols as a means of building solidarity continued to imprint the left. Long after the protest movements that Che inspired dissolved and Guevarism withered, Che remained an important reference. Perhaps there is no better example of the power that 1960s radicals vested in the revolutionary ideal of Che than the fact that, as we will see in Chapter Six, subsequent generations resurrected Guevara as both a symbol of rebellion and a means of critiquing the inequities of the post-Cold War world.

Nevertheless, Che Guevara was among the last figures of the twentieth century to represent the ideal of a revolutionary utopia. The anti-systemic figures that would follow came to symbolize social change, but often in a different fashion. Perhaps no iconic figure of the late Cold War era demonstrates this better than reggae musician Bob Marley. Marley's worldview and prescriptions for change represented a radical departure from Guevara's, but in the decade after Che's death Marley took up the mantle of militant critique through what he dubbed "rebel music". During Che's life, few could have imagined that a progenitor of an art form almost unknown beyond the Caribbean would become one of the world's most celebrated voices for liberation and social justice. Yet, by the time of Marley's death in 1981, he had captured the imagination of audiences around the world and offered them a new lexicon for emancipatory politics.

2

# REBEL MUSIC

## BOB MARLEY AND THE CULTURAL POLITICS
## OF LIBERATION

On the morning of 13 March 1979, rebels stormed the national radio
station of Grenada, a small island in the eastern Caribbean. After taking
control of the station the insurrectionists renamed it Radio Free
Grenada and announced that a revolution, led by the Marxist-Leninist
New Jewel (Joint Endeavour Welfare, Education and Liberation)
Movement, had unseated the island's prime minister, Eric Gairy.
Maurice Bishop, the New Jewel Movement's leader, then delivered a
speech outlining the aims of the revolution. However, most Grenadians
were wary. Many thought the announcement a ruse by the Gairy government to lure dissenters onto the streets where they could be appre-
hended. New Jewel Movement members were surprised by this tepid
response to revolution and so looked for ways to assure Grenadians
that the uprising was authentic. Soon Radio Free Grenada began to
broadcast music banned by the Gairy regime, including subversive
tracks by the Jamaican singer Bob Marley. Broadcasts of Marley and
other antiestablishment reggae artists proved more convincing than
Maurice Bishop's speech. When Grenadians heard songs of liberation
on the radio they recognized that the announcement was genuine and
that a revolution was indeed underway.[1]

In the years after the Grenadian revolution Bob Marley would become the most recognizable popular icon of the postcolonial world. He would also become one of the first truly global pop stars.[2] But as the use of Marley's music during the Grenadian revolution suggests, the reggae artist was much more than a pop star. "To the 'downpressed' of the third world," the *New York Times Magazine* recognized in 1977, "Bob Marley is a hero."[3] As a consequence of his charisma, musical acumen, and antiestablishment message, Marley was synonymous not only with reggae as an emerging art form but also with liberation as an overarching concept of self-determination—Third World liberation in particular. For instance, in the late 1970s Nicaraguan Marxist-Leninist insurgents, the Sandinista National Liberation Front (Frente Sandinista de Liberación Nacional), listened to Marley's music before going into combat.[4] During the final months of the Zimbabwe War of Liberation, Marley's 1979 track "Zimbabwe", which praised Marxist-Leninist and Maoist guerrillas fighting to end white minority rule in Rhodesia, lifted militants' morale. Marley's label, Island Records, even released a 7-inch record with a sleeve featuring a clenched fist Robert Mugabe, leader of the Zimbabwe African National Union liberation movement, and the slogan "Majority Rules OK." Marley's tribute to the southern African freedom fighters brought attention to the Zimbabwean conflict and made Marley one of the most recognizable international voices in the struggle against white minority rule in Africa.[5]

More than any other artist of his generation, Marley bridged the political space between the global South and the West. In cultural theorist Paul Gilroy's words, Marley was "a rebel voice of the poor and the underdeveloped world that made itself audible in the core of the overdeveloped social and economic life he called Babylon."[6] As a voice of the Third World, Marley also raised sensitivity to global inequalities among a new generation of Westerners. US president Barack Obama recalled that in the early 1980s Marley raised his awareness of "how people outside [of the United States] were thinking about the struggles for jobs and dignity and freedom."[7] In Western Europe, Marley's emancipatory message echoed and fortified critiques of racial and class-based discrimination, particularly among people of West Indian and African descent. Social critique was not new to popular music, but Marley's articulation of the grievances of the global South would contribute to the redefinition of subversion in popular music and politically motivated art generally.

During the 1980s Bob Marley's songs became transnational anthems for social justice, equality, and political reform. For instance, in 1988 Amnesty International selected Marley's song "Get Up, Stand Up" (co-written with Peter Tosh) as its anthem to promote the tenets of the Universal Declaration of Human Rights. In the context of an Amnesty concert tour, some of the most popular Western musical artists of the era performed the song to hundreds of thousands of concertgoers on five continents. As a powerful symbol of the "social idealism" of rock music, Bob Marley's words were an international anthem of human rights.[8] In 1989, when young East and West Berliners rose up to dismantle the wall that had come to symbolize the divisions of Cold War Europe, those who congregated on both sides sang Bob Marley's songs.[9] On the other side of the globe in Beijing's Tiananmen Square, Marley's music was a symbol of the reformist, student-led protest movement. At the height of the demonstrations in 1989, protesters chanted "Get Up Stand Up, Stand Up for Your Rights!" and carried posters bearing Marley's image.[10]

Bob Marley was not only emblematic of a wider structure of feeling in the late Cold War era. He also gave form and voice to the transnational cultural politics of the left. As a symbol of Third World liberation, Bob Marley was an artistic and spiritual parallel to Che Guevara.[11] For many fans, Marley's long hair, beard, and clothes, like Che's, signified rebelliousness. More importantly, Marley, like Guevara, gained popularity as a critic of imperialism and inequality while also acting as a general symbol of a youthful, defiant spirit. Both Guevara and Marley harbored utopian visions for the world, but Marley gravitated away from the radical left's vision of global socialist revolution. Indeed, Marley articulated ambivalence towards socialism and violence, with notable exceptions such as the Zimbabwe War of Liberation. Rather, he embraced the idea of self-reform and introspection. As we saw in the previous chapter, the appeal of Guevara and other militant heroes, notably Mao Zedong and Ho Chi Minh, waned in the late 1970s. At the same time, Marley's critical yet hopeful message of social equality rooted in communal soul-searching struck a chord with many young people. Thus, Marley's fatigue with the political strategies of the long

1960s reflected and amplified a wider shift in the political sensibilities of the late Cold War left.

This chapter aims to understand how Bob Marley, a musician and avowedly antipolitical figure, became a potent symbol for social equality and resistance to the status quo. More precisely, it addresses why Marley's songs, which articulated the experiences and struggles of the Jamaican underclass, became clarion calls for political, social, and cultural liberation among those who had little knowledge of Jamaica or Marley's Rastafari beliefs.[12] In short, this chapter asks why Marley's lyrics and image resonated well beyond the immediate political and cultural environs of Jamaica, and it explains how Bob Marley became a vessel for the articulation of dissent, a prominent voice of the postcolonial world, and a global symbol for a spirit of liberation. To these ends I focus on attraction to, and the marketing of, Marley's music alongside interpretations of his lyrics and image between the mid-1970s and the end of the Cold War. I place special geographical emphasis on Sub-Saharan Africa, the Pacific Rim, North America, and Europe.

Chapter One explored why Che Guevara's call for global revolution and his image of romantic determination appealed to diverse audiences. This chapter similarly asks how one popular performer became so globally influential in the late 1970s and 1980s. Marley's popularity derived from the fact that he was a charismatic performer and gifted songwriter who packaged his message in a powerful new art form. Just as important, Marley emphasized ethics over political ideology and so eschewed conventional politics and the factional debates that divided the left. This, when conjoined with an emergent popular music, made his intertwined messages of revolution, spirituality, and love feel universal.

Marley's medium was the essential element of his global popularity. In the late Cold War era, popular music was an important factor in the creation of collective identities and common references (a theme to which we will return in Chapter Three). For Marley, the music industry, whose global influence was growing in the early 1970s, was a platform for the dissemination of his message. Radio, 78s, LPs, and, perhaps most importantly, cassette tapes allowed for the dissemination of his music and ideas. Moreover, his tracks would be amongst the most pirated in history, and a substantial number—perhaps a majority—of listeners were exposed to his music in this way.[13] In sum, the aesthetics, ease of replication, and intrinsic politicality of Bob Marley's music allowed him to bridge the worlds of art, consumer culture, and politics in remarkable ways.

## Cultural Politics in the Late Cold War Era

In the late 1970s and early 1980s calls for revolutionary violence appealed to an increasingly small audience. On the other hand, Third Worldism, or the concept of shared experiences and desires for solidarity across the global South, retained its value. Bob Marley's iconic ascent reflected Third Worldism, and the concept of liberation in particular.[14] In this period, the term "liberation" entailed a holistic demand for social justice, equality, and self-determination. As with the various understandings of revolution, it functioned as a multi-faceted reference that included clearly defined concepts of change as well as more amorphous notions of national, global, or personal reform. However, liberation did not necessarily entail the militant sentiments often implicit in contemporary notions of revolution. In contexts of national liberation, as in Zimbabwe, Namibia, or East Timor, the term was indeed synonymous with political revolution. Yet, liberation also referenced a more general desire for equality and greater economic, social, cultural, or political freedoms. Thus, in the latter Cold War era the term "liberation", in its most catholic sense, referred to gender, racial, and sexual transcendence of contemporary social or political constraints—an ideal that did not necessarily imply revolutionary violence.

In much of the global South the concept of liberation spoke to concerns over repressive postcolonial regimes and neocolonialism, or the lingering influence of the former colonial powers. Bob Marley became a prominent voice of this broader demand for equality and social justice. His music, Henderson Dalrymple wrote in 1976, was "the spiritual food of a hungry, frustrated and oppressed people."[15] Refining this point, cultural critic Kwame Dawes has argued that Marley used music "to speak to those who oppressed the poor and to let them know that the poor had a sophisticated understanding of what oppression was about."[16] His music thus became a soundtrack and inspiration for myriad political, social, and spiritual movements.

Bob Marley explored general themes of marginalization and oppression. While he did not write all of the songs he performed, he used his medium to bolster a sense of shared interests in justice, equality, and freedom. The British-South African singer Johnny Clegg noted that in the 1980s many young people seemed to be yearning for a "moral force" apart from conventional political dogma.[17] Marley's message aligned neatly with this antipolitics, and he delivered it with conviction. By developing an alternative language—with strong spiritual overtones—to articulate dissent, rebelliousness, and ethics, Bob Marley spoke to the popular emphasis on morality. He sang about weighty issues such as slavery, poverty, and political repression, making these into what Paul Gilroy deemed an interpretive tool "turned towards innumerable varieties of injustice and unfreedom."[18] Indeed, Marley's narrations of pain and possibility carried an unusual "moral authority."[19] Though not the leader of any movement, Bob Marley articulated liberation discourse and the plight of the world's marginalized more memorably than most icons since the Second World War.

Marley's political philosophy was rooted in a refusal of the dominant culture of politics.[20] Though his message was antipolitical, it evidenced elements of Rastafari, revolutionary socialism, Black Power, and the New Left.[21] He repeated North American themes of black resistance and empowerment, and he appropriated more general phrases of the left, including the refrain "make love, not war" ("No More Trouble", 1973). Just as important, he revitalized the symbolic linkage between the West and the global South. Writing for *The New York Times* in 1978, John Rockwell emphasized Marley's unique capacity to reach across this socioeconomic divide. Reflecting on Marley's performance of the song "War" during his US tour—a song that set Haile Selassie I's words to music—Rockwell asked, "Who would have believed that Madison Square Garden would have swayed en masse to a speech by Haile Selassie...?"[22] The caliber of Marley's music and musicianship would gain him audiences on every continent, even amongst listeners who had difficulty deciphering his lyrics. Moreover, Marley was widely perceived as an authentic, antiestablishment voice of the Third World, one who also offered a new rebellious aesthetic. In attracting fans across the global South as well as the West, Marley represented a profound culmination of Third Worldism.

Bob Marley echoed many of the antiestablishment sentiments of the contemporary left. But unlike other political icons of the 1970s, he spoke truth to power in a language free of the ideological baggage of Marxism-Leninism, Maoism, or any other another socialist paradigm.[23] Drawing from the self-corrective tenets of Rastafari, Marley eschewed over-determined definitions of social change. As Keisha and Louis Lindsay have suggested, Marley's sense of revolution was plural and complex, a "process" as opposed to an event, a "fundamental reformation" of the heart and mind over time.[24] Marley's revolution was one of self-reform and a shift in consciousness.[25] Thus, Marley spoke directly to the spiritualist turn among many on the left in the 1970s and 1980s, or an increasing concern with self-transformation and redemption. One of the most repeated lines from Marley's 1980 track "Redemption Song" articulated this internal and transcendent form of liberation by borrowing from a 1937 speech by Marcus Garvey in which he emphasized the necessity of self-emancipation from "mental slavery" as "none but ourselves can free the mind."[26] The track "Burnin' and Lootin'" offers another example. As Marley explained to a reporter in 1977, "[w]e're not talkin' bout burnin' and lootin' for material goods … [w]e want to burn capitalistic illusions."[27] The revolution necessary for "a solution", Marley concluded in the track "Revolution" (1974), was not on the Cuban or Chinese models but rather the destruction of inherited ways of thinking.[28] Thus, Bob Marley saw his music as enacting a kind of resistance by spreading seditious messages and raising popular consciousness. He was a self-styled soul rebel: a sharp-tongued musician on a spiritual, and often introspective, campaign with great social implications.

Bob Marley's music explored, celebrated, and translated the experiences of the marginalized, giving a resolute and spirited voice to the global underclass. Marley's primary point of reference was his home country of Jamaica. Yet, his lyrics referenced many transnational themes, including political repression and extreme poverty. His uncanny ability to articulate shared experiences of suffering was to many listeners around the world both empowering and liberating.[29] For instance, Samuel Haile Maskal, who lived through the Ethiopian political upheavals of the late 1970s, remembered that on hearing Marley's music he felt that "someone did care about what happened to us." "It's hard to explain how liberating that is," Maskal recalled. "The feeling that you are not alone allows you to hope again…"[30] Marley's clarity of

5. Bob Marley performing at the Roskilde Festival, Roskilde, Denmark, 1 July 1978. © Jorgen Angel / Getty Images.

observation encouraged young people around the world to repeat his lyrics as broadly applicable messages of hope as well as a means to articulate their own anxieties and aspirations. In short, Bob Marley gave listeners not only a frame for understanding the world but also a lexicon to articulate suffering, morality, and dreams of liberation.

Bob Marley saw himself as a messenger. Whereas Guevarists, Maoists, and political thinkers of other stripes sought to raise popular consciousness through acts of defiance, Marley believed music to be a powerful tool that could contribute to a shift in consciousness. As Marley explained in a 1979 interview, he imagined himself a revolutionary without weapons or political influence, fighting "single-handed, with music."[31] Music is indeed a direct and efficient means of communication, since it can convey complex ideas in an enjoyable form. More precisely, popular music communicates across two powerful registers: melody and words. George Lipsitz has suggested that music also holds out a political transcendence that other forms of communication do not. Though political parties and social movements often remain bound to relatively parochial identities, music can easily connect diverse individuals and communities of interest. For instance, in the absence of a shared political or social institution, Bob Marley's music became a shared reference among members of the Black Power movement in Australia, liberation movements in southern Africa, and the British punk scene.[32] Music thus bridges the intimate and the universal in ways more profound than most other art forms, and it does so as a quintessentially "disembodied" form of global mobility.[33]

Music has the ability to catalyze identity in a more general sense as well. In his analysis of the popularization of reggae, Neil J. Savishinsky suggested that in the second half of the twentieth century pop music became increasingly important as a reference for cultural and social identity. It transcended ethnic, linguistic, and social boundaries and so lent itself to aesthetic and discursive fashions that were intrinsically cosmopolitan.[34] Popular music also offered a shared rhetorical structure, or a framework for interpreting the world. As a result, in the second half of the twentieth century, music played an integral role in social movements and liberation movements, both domestic and global.[35] The freedom songs of the US Civil Rights Movement, notably "We Shall Overcome", were performative acts of defiance and solidarity both within the movement and for many abroad. Similarly, in postwar Eastern Europe, rock came to stand for both democracy and freedom.[36] As we will see in the next chapter, hip-hop became a platform for sociopolitical grievances in the 1980s and 1990s. Even in circumstances where the lyrical content has been apolitical, music has had important political resonances. For instance, in mid-1980s Brazil, heavy metal came to be associated with popular anti-authoritarian sentiment even though the lyrics of most popular songs did not address political circumstances, per se.[37]

Other twentieth-century artists such as Paul Robeson, Mahalia Jackson, and Bob Dylan had become synonymous with political movements or sentiments.[38] Bob Marley aimed to follow in this tradition and was inspired by what Gilroy termed the "moral energy and political acumen" of many contemporary African American artists. As Marley's global popularity grew in the 1970s, critics began to refer to Marley as "the Third World's own Bob Dylan."[39] Like Dylan, Marley appealed to a wide audience while maintaining a distinctly political edge. This signaled a departure from contemporary mainstream Western popular music, which in the mid-1970s pivoted away from the social critiques of the late 1960s (a point to which I will return). Meanwhile, Marley's music, and reggae generally, continued to broadcast overtly antiestablishment messages.

In the late 1960s reggae emerged as a distinct art form that spoke of and to the experience of the postcolonial Jamaican underclass. As we will see, its lexicon and aesthetic was rooted in the rejection of elite social norms in and beyond Jamaica. For both fans and critics, reggae was inherently subversive. It offered an alternative political and cultural discourse for young West Indians, and by the mid-1970s it also began attracting large audiences well beyond the region. Bob Marley's brand of roots reggae shared many elements with other popular Jamaican groups of the era, yet the finely wrought lyrics of his "message songs" had a distinct air of universality.[40]

As Kwame Dawes succinctly explained in his masterful analysis of the Marley canon, Marley's lyrics were "rich with metaphor, thick with allusions, elevated by biblical references and fired by passion and energy."[41] Marley's allusions effortlessly oscillated between the language of the Old Testament, revolutionary socialism, and Rastafari neologisms.[42] Moreover, Marley often delivered his message in parables so richly layered that diverse audiences drew multiple meanings from them. While his songs frequently referenced circumstances in Jamaica and Marley's personal life, in crafting lyrics rooted in allegory and allusion, Marley ensured sufficient ambiguity for other meanings to be grafted onto his songs.[43] The popular track "Get Up, Stand Up" (1973) exemplifies this point.

"Get Up, Stand Up" was Bob Marley's best-known refrain in the final years of his life, and often the final song he would perform in concert, largely because audiences embraced it as a clarion call for social justice and political reform. No other Marley track, or perhaps any other popular refrain of the 1970s and 1980s, resonated as widely within contemporaneous, transnational youth culture. However, "Get Up, Stand Up" was conceived around a relatively narrow theme. The lyrics, co-written with Peter Tosh, were not a general charge to rise up against oppressive forces. Rather, they were a critique of Jamaica's dominant Christian culture. Every lyric emphasizes the folly of mainstream Christianity, its denigration of the Rastafari community, and the need for Rastas to take a stand against their oppression. Yet, Marley's listeners largely ignored

Marley and Tosh's emphasis on Rastafari beliefs. Instead, most listeners interpreted the song as a general affirmation of both individual and common rights.[44] Indeed, the fact that few of Marley's non-Rasta listeners were versed in Rastafari belief made the charge to "Get Up, Stand Up" all the more transposable. More precisely, American rock critic Robert Hilburn noticed that a poor understanding of Rastafari allowed Marley's audiences "to sidestep the specifics" of Marley's lyrics and identify more broadly with his "sincerity" and "freedom-oriented stance."[45]

As the lyrics of "Get Up, Stand Up" suggest, Marley's spirituality provided a primary anchor for his political thought. Unlike most mainstream religions, Rastafari is not dogmatic. It emphasizes tenets such as self-empowerment, Afrocentrism, and a rejection of imperialism, the Western capitalist system, and "Babylon" generally. In Rastafari thought, Babylon refers to the modern world and its attendant destructive social forces: greed, envy, desires for power and control as well as the general promotion of sociocultural mores that denigrate people of African descent.[46] As Ennis B. Edmonds has noted, the Rasta critique of the "Babylon system" echoed neo-Marxist analyses of capitalism as a drive to maximize profits without regard for the consequences. Yet, Rastas also saw the Soviet Union and the Catholic Church as components of the Babylon system, a "vampire" figuratively sucking the life from ordinary people ("Babylon System", 1979).[47] By joining liberation discourse with Judeo-Christian thought, Rastafari echoed many threads of contemporary liberation theology, particularly that in Latin America and southern Africa.[48]

Rastafari beliefs also drew on the history of Pan-Africanism and Garveyism, adding to this intellectual package elements of contemporary black liberation rhetoric of the 1960s and '70s. The Rastafari faithful emphasized African and African diaspora solidarity, and they placed great emphasis on Africa as a spiritual and metaphysical homeland to all people of African descent. Rastas overlaid this intellectual superstructure with the revelation that Haile Selassie I (1892–1975), Emperor of Ethiopia, was the Messiah. Therefore they championed the red, gold, and green of the Ethiopian flag and idealized Ethiopia as a place of resettlement, a spiritual Zion.

Rastas developed a distinctive cultural style as well. They grew beards, dreadlocks, and embraced cannabis, or "ganja", as religious sacrament. Ganja, they asserted, had the capacity to heighten individual and communal consciousness. As a defiant, politically conscious countercultural movement of the underclass, in the 1960s Caribbean Rastas were widely perceived as dangerous and often treated as criminals.[49] Reggae was strongly influenced by the Rastafari subculture, to the extent that the two often seemed synonymous. As a result, they gained popularity in tandem, particularly from the end of the 1960s. Yet, negative stereotypes of Rastafari and reggae influenced the way that many beyond the Caribbean viewed Rastas, and Bob Marley specifically. For example, after several concerts in the United Kingdom in 1976, *The Sunday Times* wondered if Bob Marley represented a passing fad "or an extremist cult that could incite violence."[50]

Bob Marley became a practicing Rasta as early as 1966. Like other Jamaican musicians of the 1960s, he adapted Rasta critiques and philosophy to reggae music, building on a rhetorical edifice steeped in Garveyism, the Black Power movement, and contemporary left debates as well as biblical references and Rastafari neologisms. By the 1970s Marley saw himself as a vessel for the faith, a messenger proselytizing through music. In fact, from the mid-1970s Marley would be a primary force in Rastafari's internationalization, doing more to popularize the belief system than any other figure.[51] The earliest audiences for Marley's messages beyond the Caribbean were in Western Europe. Both Rastafari and reggae appealed to working-class people of West Indian descent as an alternative set of cultural, political, and moral values.[52] In 1970s London, Amsterdam, and Paris, the popularity of Marley's music contributed to a surge of interest in Rastafari, particularly among people of African descent.

## Rebel Rising

Bob Marley was born in 1945 in Jamaica's Saint Ann Parish. His childhood was defined by extreme poverty and the social alienation he suffered in consequence of his biracial background: Marley's mother was black and his father was white. Bob Marley's father was also absent from his life. As a result, Marley strongly identified with his mother and the rural black community of his birth. Yet, because of his biracial background, Marley was often ridiculed. When he was twelve years old, he and his mother relocated to the bustling capital of Kingston. As poor migrants from the countryside, the family settled in Trench Town, one of the city's most notorious slums. During his teen years, Marley focused intently on singing and songwriting because he believed music offered the only path out of the deprivation of Trench Town. Marley's voice was high and raspy, but it was also memorable and sincere. While still in his teens, Marley collaborated with fellow Trench Town resident Peter Tosh and childhood friend Bunny Wailer to form a musical ensemble dubbed The Wailers.

The Wailers released their first single, "Judge Not", in 1962, the same year that Jamaica gained independence from Britain. "Judge Not" had strong moral overtones and unmistakable biblical references, both of which foreshadowed the group's later music. The Wailers' first number one hit came two years later with the up-tempo ska tune "Simmer Down". It too had a sociopolitical message. It called for an end to the violence that was engulfing Trench Town and Kingston's other slums. The Wailers recorded several other hits, but their success came with no financial reward and the trio gained little recognition beyond Jamaica. In the meantime, Marley's mother relocated to Wilmington, Delaware and urged her son to join her. Arriving in the US in 1966, Marley witnessed racial violence, the nationwide campaign for civil rights, and the growth of the Black Power movement. Less than a year after his arrival in Delaware, Marley returned to Jamaica and reunited with the Wailers. On his return he also became a devotee of Rastafari.

The Wailers' prospects for international success rose after signing with the British label Island Records. With an advance from the record company, the band recorded many tracks for their first full-length album, *Catch a Fire* (1973). It proved a watershed. Producer Chris Blackwell hoped to build on the rebellious spirit of the popular Jamaican film *The Harder They Come* (1972) and therefore selected many tracks from the Wailers' recordings that were militant and defiant. The album addressed slavery and racial oppression, and it cited common refrains of Pan-Africanism and contemporary black internationalism. The record was so politically charged that Henderson Dalrymple, writing in the mid-1970s, believed it had the power to "kindle the consciousness of thousands upon thousands of black brothers all over the world."[53] However, Blackwell wished to market the

Wailers as a "black rock band". To this end he attempted to blur the lines between reggae, soul, and rock by augmenting the Wailers' tracks with rock riffs as well as other elements unusual for reggae. In a further effort to develop an overtly rebellious image, the *Catch A Fire* record sleeve featured a close-up image of Marley shirtless and smoking a large spliff. Island Records calculated that this and other images of Marley with long hair, beard, and in denim would cement his rebellious image and draw Western audiences. The message of the album was clear: Bob Marley was a rebel.[54]

*Catch A Fire* was the Wailers' first step towards recognition beyond the Caribbean, and Bob Marley became the undisputed frontman of the group. The group's second album with Island Records, *Burnin'* (1973), addressed equally explosive themes. For instance, "I Shot the Sheriff" contended that rebellion was the price of oppression and abuse. The album also included the enduringly popular "Get Up, Stand Up". Neither *Catch a Fire* nor *Burnin'* were great successes in the European charts, but they captured the imagination of black audiences in Western Europe. As Simon Jones and Paul Gilroy have argued, the politically conscious themes of both albums resonated strongly among young UK Afro-Caribbean listeners. Young people of West Indian descent were searching for a voice that could speak to a shared sense of marginality and alienation. Marley's music offered this.[55] For instance, the track "Concrete Jungle" reflects on contemporary urban poverty and the elusiveness of true freedom for people of African descent. "Slave Driver" makes similar reference to the shackles of poverty, linking contemporary circumstances to a long history of oppression and exploitation. For people of Caribbean descent in Western Europe, Marley's music spoke to broader concerns of social justice as well as the more particular historical experiences of slavery and racial oppression. Thus, Bob Marley and reggae generally offered a voice for black Britons and other people of African descent as well as a defiant new cultural style.[56]

Black reggae enthusiasts in Western Europe constituted Marley's earliest fan base outside of the West Indies, but Island Records continued to pursue wider audiences. Marley's next album, *Natty Dread* (1974), reached a larger audience, including the coveted North American market. Rock guitarist and singer Eric Clapton's 1974 cover of "I Shot the Sheriff", which reached number one on the Billboard charts in the US, also delivered Marley's music to a mass audience. Yet, Marley had not altered his antiestablishment message to gain new listeners. Tracks such as "Rebel Music (Three O'Clock Road Block)", "Them Belly Full (But We Hungry)", and "Talkin' Blues" spoke to the repressive practices of the postcolonial state, resultant inequality, and a spirit of resistance. With *Natty Dread*, Marley developed a multiracial fan base in the US and drew rock and punk devotees as well as reggae enthusiasts. Within two years of *Natty Dread*'s release, *Rolling Stone* magazine elected Bob Marley and the Wailers Band of the Year.[57]

By 1976 Bob Marley had become a folk hero in Jamaica. *Time Magazine* concluded that his popularity was so great that it made him a force "to rival the [Jamaican] government."[58] This may have been hyperbole, but, fearing Marley's influence, the Jamaican government banned four potentially subversive tracks from Marley's release of the same year, *Rastaman Vibration*. Moreover, Jamaican political factions also vied to coopt the rising star.[59] Kingston was divided between rival political groups affected by larger Cold War geopolitics. In 1976 confrontations turned violent between supporters of the socialist Michael Manley government (People's National Party, or PNP) and Edward Seaga's pro-US Jamaica Labour Party.[60] Disgusted by the brutal tactics of both parties, and disillusioned with the political process in Jamaica, Bob Marley rejected the parties and distanced himself from their leaders.[61] But in an effort to stem the political violence engulfing Kingston's slums, Marley arranged to play a free concert promoting national unity. The Smile Jamaica concert nearly cost Marley his life, and it forced him into temporary exile.

Smile Jamaica was organized through the Ministry of Culture, and thus many Jamaica Labour supporters presumed that Marley's sympathies lay with the ruling People's National Party. Additionally, the Manley government attempted to capitalize on the event by setting the date for national elections immediately after the concert's announcement. Two nights before Smile Jamaica, gunmen entered Bob Marley's Kingston home and fired on Marley and several others. One of the bullets grazed Marley's chest and struck him in the arm. His wife Rita and his manager were also wounded. Marley survived, but the attackers were never formally charged. Their motives therefore became the subject of great conjecture. For their part, Marley and many around him interpreted the assailants' motives as political. This emboldened the reggae star. On the night of the Smile Jamaica concert, Marley arrived at the event with bandaged wounds and virtually no security. In a direct challenge to his erstwhile assassins, Marley sang for ninety minutes. He called for unity in a bold effort to diffuse the explosive political rivalries that were wracking Jamaica.[62] Early the following morning he left Jamaica, and for more than a year he would live in self-imposed exile in London.

While in exile Marley released yet another studio album: *Exodus* (1977). The record enjoyed considerable commercial success. The title track, which developed a liberation message through its overtly biblical trope, reached the top spot in the Jamaican, British, and German charts. Marley followed this success with *Kaya* (1978), an album that took a different tack from his previous releases. It featured much lighter subject matter, including songs about spiritual introspection, romantic love, and the virtues of ganja. Unlike his earlier, defiant album art, the record sleeve for *Kaya* featured Marley smiling broadly. While the album's praise of ganja had political overtones, the subdued nature of *Kaya*'s tracks led to charges that Bob Marley had gone soft.[63]

Despite this fleeting criticism, Marley remained a towering figure in Jamaica. In the spring of 1978 he agreed to play a second free concert in Kingston. The One Love Peace Concert was billed as a plea for an end to politically charged violence once again threatening to destabilize Jamaica. During his performance, Marley called Prime Minister Manley and opposition leader Edward Seaga to the stage and held the rival politicians' hands together above his head. It was a Gandhian moment that punctuated Marley's calls for a truce in the deadly political wars. It also gained him greater international attention. In recognition of his role as a mediating voice in the Jamaican political crisis, the UN awarded Marley its Medal of Peace.[64]

Marley's final releases aimed to refute charges that he had lost his militant edge. Between early 1979 and the spring of 1980, Marley recorded what would be the last records to be released during his short life: *Survival* (1979) and *Uprising* (1980). Both albums featured anthems of the meek standing against dominant powers, "quixotic figure[s]," Kwame Dawes keenly described them, "facing all the machinations of

Babylon."[65] *Uprising*'s sleeve placed Marley squarely within the emancipatory matrix of revolutionary self-transformation and liberation politics. It featured Marley rising out of the ground with fists reaching towards the sky and dreadlocks cascading down to form a mountain. This image of Marley, which drew heavily from contemporary Third World liberation iconography, provided the backdrop for his final live performances during the Uprising Tour of 1980. The *Uprising* record sleeve would be an apt visual metaphor for Marley's transfiguration into a seemingly supernatural force promoting emancipatory ideals.

## Bob Marley and Global Liberation

In the West, Bob Marley's music filled a void in the popular music scene. Rock gained a strong critical edge in the 1960s, but by the middle of the 1970s it had became largely apolitical and the famous excesses of contemporary rock outfits typified an increasingly nihilistic pop culture. Thus, it would be through Bob Marley's music that "a generation of white rock-fans," according to Simon Jones, "rediscovered the oppositional values which so much contemporary rock music appeared to have lost."[66] In 1976, for example, teenage Dubliner and future U2 frontman Bono discovered Bob Marley. When he first heard Marley's music he "not only felt it," he recalled, "I felt I understood it."[67] Like many other listeners, Bono connected with Marley in intuitive ways. In the 1970s and 1980s, Marley's popularity among the UK's white working-class youth grew out of abiding interests in ska and punk rock. Within the late 1970s antiestablishment punk movement, reggae was both influential and inspirational.[68] The synergy between the antiestablishment sentiments of young, working-class whites and blacks led to an effervescence of artistic cross-fertilization. As early as 1978, promoters in the UK began pairing reggae and punk acts in a series of concerts dubbed Rock Against Racism.

In early 1980s Britain, many young whites began to see Bob Marley as a political thinker of "heroic proportions."[69] This was in part because young white Britons read Marley's critiques as not only rooted in anti-racism. They interpreted Marley as also speaking to British systems of class.[70] Simon Jones conducted extensive interviews with UK listeners in the 1980s and discovered that white fans celebrated Bob Marley as an artist who communicated universal messages, offered a grammar of social critique, and "spoke for everybody." Indeed, young white UK listeners perceived songs such as "Get Up, Stand Up" through the lens of class. One of Jones' informants explained his interpretation of Marley's lyrics in this way: "I could relate very strongly to 'sufferation' and 'sufferers' music even though I wasn't black … you know, 'stop pushing me Mr. Boss Man' … And the ones about freedom too. 'Cos I hated school, I felt *I* was captive by school, and by people in authority."[71] Such liberal interpretations of Marley's social critique cemented his songs as a cornerstone of white working-class counterculture in 1970s and 1980s Britain.[72]

In neighboring France, Bob Marley's popularity followed a trajectory similar to that in the UK. French Caribbean immigrants and others from former colonies—Pacific nations, in particular—constituted Marley's earliest fan base. Yet, Marley soon also appealed to the antisystemic zeal of members of the largely white middle-class student movement, particularly those who identified with liberation movements in the global South. By the late 1970s, Marley's fan base included a cross-section of white rock listeners attracted both to reggae and Marley's rebellious image. Bruno Blum argued that in France, as in the UK, Bob Marley filled a "long-overdue gap" among left-wing youth, those who in the past gravitated to avant-garde and politically oriented artists such as Miles Davis and Bob Dylan. Yet, Marley did more than fill a political void. According to Blum, he "felt wider in ambition and scope" than other musical figures and so became a "universal hero."[73]

In North America, Bob Marley's popularity increased dramatically in the early 1980s.[74] Unlike in Europe, Marley's earliest audiences in the United States were predominantly white. Much as in the UK, the intersections of punk, ska, and reggae heightened Marley's heroic appeal among young white audiences.[75] Yet, Marley's popularity was in no way limited to whites. For instance, members of the pioneering African American punk-reggae outfit Bad Brains attended a Marley concert in 1980, which inspired them both to embrace Rastafari and modify their message.[76] Marley had long worked to gain an African American fan base. After touring with top R&B acts and marketing directly to African American listeners, at the end of the 1970s he began to draw a substantial African American audience.

In the early 1980s, Marley would be an important political reference, particularly within the anti-Apartheid and anti-nuclear movements as well as among young leftists, radical political thinkers, and artists. Future president Barack Obama's interest in Bob Marley is a case in point. According to biographer David Maraniss, in the early 1980s Obama and his friends were particularly interested in Marley's music. They pored over the song lyrics of the album *Survival*, debating their meaning and Marley's intention. According to a college friend, Obama's consciousness "was influenced by music, influenced by a recognition, an understanding of the world through music." Bob Marley, he recalled, "stirred something deeper inside" the young Obama.[77] Marley's music struck a similar chord with civil rights and Black Power leader Kwame Ture (formerly Stokely Carmichael). During a 1985 tribute to Bob Marley, Ture praised the singer for taking "the music of the people to inspire the people."[78] Acclaimed author Alice Walker refined this point. She saw in Marley "the radical peasant-class, working-class consciousness that fearlessly denounced the *wasichu* (the greedy and destructive)."[79]

In the southwestern United States, many young people of the Native American Hopi tribe similarly found inspiration and solace in Marley's messages.[80] He likewise gained a fan base in the Havasupai community of the Grand Canyon, Arizona. In the late 1970s, many young Havasupai embraced Marley as a lodestar figure who spoke directly to their circumstances.[81] Marley's lyrics reflected Native experiences of oppression and marginality, while Marley's demands for social justice amplified Native aspirations. For instance, songs about systemic oppression and liberation such as "Get Up, Stand Up", "400 Years", and "Crazy Baldhead", resonated with Havasupai listeners.[82]

In Hawaii and across the South Pacific, Bob Marley and reggae gained large audiences. Marley's rise to iconic status coincided with the emergence of indigenous movements inspired by notions of a global black experience. More precisely, Marley's core message of liberation attracted many cultural and sovereignty activists in the Pacific Region.[83] In Australia and New Zealand, for example, Marley became a key international reference and inspiration within emergent social movements addressing the rights of indigenous peoples. In the 1970s, identification as black had become an evocative political claim in Australia that linked the struggle of Aboriginal peoples with Third World liberation discourse.[84] Bob Marley's message of black empowerment, self-direction, and self-realization therefore found a sizable audience among Australia's indigenous minority.

Early Aboriginal reggae bands such as No Fixed Address and Mixed Relations domesticated Bob Marley's emancipatory politics (and reggae generally) by framing the plight of Aboriginal Australians within the context of global black liberation.[85] For example, Bart Willoughby, drummer and guitarist for the pioneering group No Fixed Address, credited Bob Marley as an important role model, both because of the power of his music and emphasis on black pride.[86] According to Willoughby, Bob Marley's revolutionary fusion of Black Power politics and music "changed everything" for him.[87] As in the UK and US, Marley's influence on Australian Aboriginal musicians transcended reggae. For instance, Mandawuy Yunupingu, lead singer of the Aboriginal rock band Yothu Yindi, explained that Marley's "freedom themes" greatly influenced his songwriting.[88] As a global icon, Marley proved a critical bridge connecting the cultural politics of a new generation of Aboriginal artists and activists with liberation struggles around the world.

Bob Marley's message, and that of reggae generally, accorded with New Zealand's Black Power movement as well. As in Western Europe and North America, most New Zealanders were introduced to reggae through Marley. Marley's visits to Australia and New Zealand in 1979 while promoting *Survival* drew substantial crowds that included a broad cross-section of young people. Reggae's message of liberation resonated strongly with indigenous rights activists. For instance, among Maori seeking to reclaim an indigenous cultural heritage, Bob Marley's criticisms of colonialism and white domination struck a powerful chord.[89] Marley's vision of redemption through a return to a more authentic cultural heritage—a more "natural" way of life than that offered by Western civilization or the Christian Church—also appealed to many young Maori.[90] In Wellington, a city that would become the largest reggae market in the southern hemisphere, multiple reggae bands emerged in the wake of Marley's visit. Politically oriented ensembles, such as the group Herbs, employed reggae to articulate Maori and wider Polynesian experiences alongside concerns about nuclear weapons testing and proliferation. Reggae's popularity contributed to and reflected new forms of individual and communal identity that explicitly linked the experiences of black people in New Zealand to others around the world.[91] Marley and reggae also offered a new countercultural style for young Maori and other Polynesians. Many grew dreadlocks and wore clothing that referenced the imperial Ethiopian red, gold, and green.[92]

Bob Marley's music had equally profound resonance in many African nations. Marley visited several African countries in his final years and concluded that his largest audience was in Africa, not, as many of his contemporaries assumed, in the Caribbean, Europe, or the US.[93] In previous decades, Caribbean music, including calypso, rumba, and cha-cha, had found receptive audiences in urban Africa. However, the ease of replication facilitated by the cassette tape ensured that reggae would be more accessible and ubiquitous than earlier forms of imported music. Moreover, reggae's political dimensions, which frequently referenced contemporary African concerns, added an alluring element that would attract young audiences right across the continent.[94] So strong was the affinity for Marley's music on the African continent that many fans claimed him as one of their own. For example, a 1981 graffito in Abidjan, Ivory Coast declared, "Bob is not Jamaican, he is African."[95]

Bob Marley's popularity was perhaps most palpable in southern Africa, a region that he addressed directly through songs about decolonization and national liberation. Marley's most powerful commentary on contemporary African circumstances was the track "Zimbabwe" from the album *Survival* (1979). Released in the final year of the Zimbabwe War of Liberation, the track portrays what Marley biographer Timothy White called an "apocalyptic battle" against Babylon in southern Africa.[96] More precisely, the lyrics condemned one of the last vestiges of white rule on the continent and praised the Marxist-Leninist-Maoist guerrillas working to unseat Ian Smith's minority government. The track's first line was a firm declaration of the right to self-determination, while the chorus voiced solidarity with Zimbabweans and affirmed the necessity of their struggle. In the final months of the war, Marley's song gave Zimbabwean combatants a moral lift while simultaneously raising their global profile. By the time the war ended in 1980, Marley's homage to the liberation struggle had become so popular that *Survival* was Zimbabwe's top-selling record.[97]

"Zimbabwe" became so closely associated with the struggle for majority rule that in 1980 Robert Mugabe's newly elected Zimbabwe African National Union-Popular Front government invited the reggae star to perform at the nation's independence ceremony.[98] At great personal expense, Marley delivered his full band, crew, sound system, and a stage to Harare in April 1980. Marley's performance would be the crowning moment of the independence ceremony, which was attended by dignitaries such as Zambian president Kenneth Kaunda, Indian prime minister Indira Gandhi, and Charles, Prince of Wales. Just after the new Zimbabwean standard was raised at Rufaro Stadium, the MC introduced Bob Marley and the Wailers.[99] Soon thereafter, fans clamoring to hear Marley began to force their way into the stadium. Security forces launched tear gas into the crowd, but Marley was able to perform several of his most politically charged songs, including "Dem Belly Full" and "I Shot the Sheriff", before being driven from the stage by wafting tear gas. Once the gas cleared, Marley again took the stage. After playing "Zimbabwe" to an enraptured audience, Marley saluted the crowd and proclaimed, "A Luta Continua! Viva Zimbabwe! Pamberi Zimbabwe! (The struggle continues! Long live Zimbabwe! Forward Zimbabwe!)"[100]

Bob Marley found keen audiences in neighboring South Africa as well. Because his music was so closely associated with the politics of liberation and resistance, much of his music was banned during the Apartheid era. Songs of romantic love such as "Is This Love?" and "She's Gone" passed the censors, but potentially subversive tracks such as "Real Situation" and "Zimbabwe" (indeed the entire album *Survival*, on which it featured) were deemed officially "undesirable" under the South African Publications Act of 1974. To restrict access to subversive tracks, the Apartheid government blacked out lyrics on Marley's record sleeves and censored specific tracks by scoring them. Nevertheless, Marley's political messages circulated widely in South Africa as uncensored records were smuggled in from neighboring nations, including Zimbabwe.[101]

South African musicians played an important role in the dissemination of Marley's music, often at great personal risk. For example, bandleader Colbert Mukwevho recalled a concert in Musina, northern Limpopo Province, in which his group covered the proscribed song "Real Situation" from *Uprising*. Though "Real Situation" was more of a pensive statement than a call to resistance, the track included the explosive refrain, "[it] seems like total destruction is the only solution." When Mukwevho's band played their cover version in Musina, the local police arrived before the band had even finished the song.[102] Only in 1992, as the Apartheid system collapsed, did the South African government officially reclassify Marley's album *Survival* as "not undesirable."[103]

## Bob Marley's Legacy and the Politics of Dissent

In late 1980 Bob Marley was diagnosed with cancer. The melanoma quickly spread from his toe to his lungs and ultimately to his brain. Yet, he continued to tour relentlessly. In Marley's last two years he traveled to Japan, Australia, New Zealand, and Zimbabwe as well as to Western Europe and North America. Hardly a month after Zimbabwe's independence celebration, Marley kicked off what would be his final world tour, dubbed Uprising. Across Europe Marley drew capacity crowds, breaking many venue records. When he played San Siro stadium in Milan, which had hosted Pope John Paul II only a week earlier, his concert drew over 100,000 people—more than had come to see the Pope and more than any previous music event in Italian history. Much as during Zimbabwe's independence ceremony, fans in Milan forced their way into the stadium, pushing it beyond capacity.[104]

The first European date on the Uprising tour, however, was Zurich, a concert that would be linked in memory to a youth uprising popularly known as the Opera House riots (*Opernhauskrawalle*). Marley had never played Zurich, but the capacity crowd in May 1980 was indicative of what the band would see throughout the tour. Marley and the Wailers gave an impassioned performance. The last song the band played was "Get Up, Stand Up", a tune the concertgoers knew well. Marley exited the stage with a resounding "Don't give up the fight. Cuz I never give up!" Meanwhile, on the street, a demonstration at the city's historic Opera House was beginning to spiral out of control. Leftist students and young workers, invigorated in part by an increasingly defiant punk rock scene, had been pushing for greater public funding for alternative cultural expression.[105] Specifically, activists demanded autonomous centers for alternative arts, a "sovereign space

91

of difference" in Francesa Polletta's words. They also eschewed any clear political agenda: "No power to nobody," some would chant.[106]

The city of Zurich had other priorities. Just before Marley's concert, Zurich's city council announced a multi-million-franc loan for the renovation of the historic Opera House. At the same time, it voted down a measure to fund a youth arts space. As Marley's concert ended, fans enraged by the city's decision joined the demonstrators at the Opera House. When the police responded with force, the demonstration became a riot. In the following months, police and youth battled in Zurich's streets and the protests spread to other Swiss cities. "Get Up, Stand Up" would become part of the soundtrack of this period of recurring clashes, known as "Zurich Burns".[107]

Some young people interpreted the uprising as actively bridging youth angst in Switzerland and global antiestablishment sentiment. One Zürcher recalled that he was able to "link what happened in Zurich with the Third World and Bob Marley." In the riots he "saw that there were people [in Switzerland] ... [who were] unhappy with some things and wanted to change them." He concluded that through the protests Zurich "became part of the rest of the world."[108] Once again, Marley functioned as a critical bridge across global space. While his performance was not the cause of the Zurich Burns uprising, its uncanny timing and his emotive message helped to propel simmering youth discontent into outright rebellion.

Bob Marley was a national symbol in Jamaica, but he spent less time in his home country during his final years. Nevertheless, leaders of both national political parties embraced him as a means to attract voters. During Prime Minister Michael Manley's 1980 reelection campaign, supporters used songs from *Uprising* (1980), including "Coming in from the Cold" and "Bad Card", to draw crowds to PNP rallies. Challenger Edward Seaga campaigned using the same songs.[109] Seaga would win the election and continue to seek association with Marley while in office. Just before Marley's death, Seaga's government conferred on him Jamaica's Order of Merit, one of the nation's highest honors. The move recognized the high regard in which Jamaicans held the reggae star, but it was likely also a means to coopt Marley's legacy as his life was nearing its end.

Bob Marley died of cancer in 1981. Rastafari culture prohibited him from undergoing chemotherapy for the advanced melanoma. After an unsuccessful effort to find holistic means to fight the disease, Marley succumbed. He was only thirty-six years old. Marley's funeral would be the largest in Jamaica's history and an official government event. During the funeral Prime Minister Seaga, borrowing a phrase from sociologist Émile Durkheim, proclaimed that Marley had become "part of the collective consciousness" of Jamaica. His music, the prime minister continued, was "an omnipresent cry in our electronic world."[110] In death Marley became an even more alluring instrument for the Jamaican government. Much as Cuban leaders used Che Guevara as a propaganda tool, the Jamaican government searched for ways to appropriate Bob Marley's memory for political purposes. For instance, soon after Marley's passing, the Seaga government issued postage stamps bearing the late singer's visage.[111]

Bob Marley's symbolic power was similarly harnessed by the US military during its 1983 invasion of Grenada. In an effort to unseat leaders of the New Jewel Movement government that had come to power in 1979, American forces decimated Grenada's infrastructure. Among US targets during the invasion, dubbed Operation Urgent Fury, was Radio Free Grenada: the station that broadcasted Bob Marley's music during the rebel takeover in 1979 as a means of authenticating the revolution. The American military appreciated the importance of radio in Grenada. Thus, while US forces destroyed Radio Free Grenada, an American psychological operations (PSYOP) team began broadcasting on the same frequency. In an effort to legitimate the pro-US messages now filling the airwaves, the PSYOP team played Bob Marley and music by other reggae artists.[112]

Over the following decade, Bob Marley's international popularity soared. For many admirers, his "omnipresent cry" was a soundtrack for demands for social justice. In 1985 the *Washington Post* asserted that Marley's music had become a "hi-fi doctrine of peace and liberation, heard from Nicaragua to South Africa."[113] Among the remarkable examples of Bob Marley's global resonance was the use of "Get Up, Stand Up" as Amnesty International's anthem for its human rights awareness campaign, which culminated in the 1988 Amnesty-sponsored concert tour Human Rights Now! The tour visited over twenty countries and featured some of the most popular musical figures of the 1980s, including Bruce Springsteen, Youssou N'Dour, Sting, Tracy Chapman, and Peter Gabriel.

Human Rights Now! coincided with the fortieth anniversary of the Universal Declaration of Human Rights and aimed to raise awareness about human rights violations around the world. Its organizers hoped that it would focus international attention on rampant abuses in places such as Chile and South Africa. In an effort to engage wider audiences, the tour visited not only conventional host countries such as the US, Japan, and Italy but also less common destinations such as Zimbabwe, India, and Argentina. Additionally, it offered a shared platform for rights activists and popular performers. Throughout the landmark tour, the full ensemble of performers, joined by tens of thousands of concertgoers, sang "Get Up, Stand Up" at both the beginning and the end of each concert, often under a banner that read "Universal Declaration of Human Rights 1948–1988".[114] Bob Marley's words thereby linked human rights discourse with popular music in an unprecedented way.

As the Cold War drew to a close, Bob Marley remained a primary vehicle for sociopolitical critique. He also continued to be a lodestar for armed movements from Southeast Asia to the Pacific and West Africa. For example, among those resisting the 1975 Indonesian military occupation of East Timor, Marley became an inspirational icon of "just rebellion", alongside Che Guevara and Nelson Mandela.[115] Specifically, Marley's image became associated with support for the Timorese rebels, Armed Forces for the National Liberation of East Timor (Forças Armadas da Libertação Nacional de Timor-Leste, or Falintil). Marley's calls for neocolonial liberation were attractive to Falintil supporters, but affinities also went beyond his message. Since many saw parallels between Bob Marley's hairstyle and that of Falintil guerrillas, Marley's personal style also acted as a bridge.[116] Marley became so synonymous with hyper-masculine concepts of rebelliousness in East Timor that even street gangs in Dili began using his image as an emblem.[117]

Many other militant movements embraced Marley in the 1990s. In 1991, a rebel group called the Revolutionary United Front (RUF) initiated a civil war in Sierra Leone (see Chapter Three). In the years immediately preceding the rebellion, reggae, and Bob Marley in particular, had been a popular means of articulating antiestablishment sentiment. Dissenters frequently repeated Marley's lyrics in their critique of the oppressive political and economic conditions under the ruling All

People's Party. As in Switzerland, Marley and reggae represented a sub-versive youth culture in Sierra Leone and a link to transnational cur-rents of dissent. In early 1995 RUF combatants began to use Bob Marley T-shirts as impromptu uniforms. This led to the government's effective outlawing of Marley apparel. Since Marley was now associated with the rebels, anyone wearing his image was often perceived as either an RUF member or sympathizer. As a result, young Sierra Leonean men were detained and sometimes killed for wearing Bob Marley shirts. Nevertheless, the singer continued to feature in the RUF constellation of icons throughout the war. In 2000, for instance, RUF combatants in Kono celebrated 10 May as Bob Marley Night, presumably to com-memorate the date of Marley's passing.[118]

Throughout the 1990s, Marley was a youth culture hero par excel-lence in many African countries. His popularity often evidenced both frustration with conventional politics and resistance to authoritarian governments as his music accorded with a cosmopolitan, pro-democ-racy stance. For instance, in early April 1994 demonstrations ahead of the first democratic South African elections saw activists in Soweto rallying under images of Bob Marley, Che Guevara, and Chris Hani, the slain general secretary of the South African Communist Party. In Tanzania, Bob Marley held a singular position in the youth imagination of the early 1990s. When I studied at the University of Dar es Salaam from 1992 to 1993, no international popular culture figure approached Marley's popularity among young people. His music served as a set of common references for Tanzanians of diverse backgrounds. While many students at the university voiced disdain for former president Julius Nyerere and his socialist-inspired programs, most perceived Marley as a true voice of freedom and social justice. In 1992 a fellow student confided in me that while Nyerere, the nation's first president, was considered the "Father of the Nation" (Swahili: *baba wa taifa*), Marley's omnipresence suggested that he deserved the title. "Bob's face, not Nyerere's, should be on the [national] currency," he suggested.

A few years later, anthropologist Eileen Moyer conducted a formal analysis of Bob Marley's appeal among young men in Dar es Salaam. Moyer found that young urbanites were familiar with Marley's biogra-phy and highlighted elements of his personal story that they saw as analogous to their own experiences. For instance, many young men argued that the realities of Jamaican poverty, so eloquently expressed by Marley, had direct parallels in Tanzania. Many also saw similarities between Marley's condemnation of Jamaica's postcolonial government and their own critiques of the Tanzanian state. Young people often echoed Marley's lyrics as articulations of their frustration with postcolonial social and economic injustices, which they perceived as the result of bad governance. Tanzanian youth revered Marley as a true revolutionary because of his clear-eyed criticism of postcolonial power structures, both domestic and global.[119]

Bob Marley continued to be a symbol for liberation and armed resistance as the new millennium approached. For example, in 1999 an Aboriginal insurgent group in the Solomon Islands called the Guadalcanal Revolutionary Army (GRA)—later incorporated into the the Isatabu Freedom Movement—embraced Bob Marley as a symbol of indigenous rights in their war against the government of the Solomon Islands and settlers from neighboring Malaita Island. Much like the RUF in Sierra Leone, the GRA donned Marley T-shirts as uniforms.[120]

## Conclusion

Bob Marley was an entertainer, but he also became a symbol for justice, equality, resistance to the status quo, and liberation writ large. Indeed, Marley had an uncanny ability to join melody and the voice of suffering in such a way as to capture the global imagination. Since his concept of liberation was antidogmatic, his message remained malleable and his music attracted a diverse transnational audience. Marley's popular ascent was also a consequence of timing. His star rose as emotional and political investments in revolutionary socialism—and its icons—began to wane. Marley's words reflected the political sensibilities of the mainstream global left, but his unconventional aesthetic and language of social critique also offered new antisystemic imagery that appealed to a generation seeking an introspective vision of social change and an authentic Third World voice.[121]

Bob Marley's brand of roots reggae captivated international audiences, while his reflections on poverty, depravation, injustice, love, and spiritual joy ensured a depth of appeal beyond musical style. Through an emphasis on ethics rather than conventional politics, Marley both

embodied and invigorated Rastafari praxis and simultaneously catalyzed a wider global community of sentiment. His perceived moral
authority and critique of structures of power appealed to alternative
youth cultures searching for new heroes. Regardless of the specifics of
Marley's Rastafari message, his antiestablishment image proved attractive to a range of young people, from Marxist-Leninist insurgents in
Nicaragua to an avowedly antipolitical youth movement in Switzerland,
young men at the margins of Tanzanian society, and combatants in
Sierra Leone. As the Cold War drew to a close and a new epoch of
global interface emerged, Bob Marley was the unparalleled voice of
popular sentiments ranging from frustration to aspiration and the
desire for revolution.

Today, Marley remains socially relevant, but interpretations of his
image have changed significantly. As we will see in Chapter Five,
Marley underwent an overhaul as an icon in the 1990s. Specifically,
Marley fans and marketers gravitated towards a more conciliatory
image. The king of reggae was yet a symbol of youthful rebellion, but
the militant edges of his message would be progressively blunted as
many emphasized the spiritual, romantic, and lighthearted elements of
his canon. By the turn of the millennium Bob Marley would be more
commonly perceived as a transcendent mystic than a revolutionary.

In 2009, on the twentieth anniversary of the fall of the Berlin Wall,
the rock band U2 and hip-hop luminary Jay-Z evoked Bob Marley's
nearly four-decades-old words in a concert at the Brandenburg Gate.
Jay-Z and Bono, the U2 frontman who had first heard Bob Marley as a
teenager in Dublin, intoned, "Get up, stand up; stand up for your
rights!" Yet, it was not at all clear what "Get Up, Stand Up" meant for
German audiences celebrating the end of the Cold War. The world had
changed dramatically in the previous two decades. Global capitalism
stood without significant challenge and Marley was now far more than
a rebel. Nevertheless, it was telling that U2 performed Marley's signature refrain with one of the brightest stars of hip-hop, not reggae.
From the second half of the 1980s, the emergent musical genre of
hip-hop was rapidly eclipsing reggae as a vessel for articulating the
suffering and grievances of marginalized young people. Hip-hop's
stripped-down aesthetic and direct, uncompromising lyrical style captivated audiences across the globe. Moreover, digital media and reced-

ing limitations on the reproduction of audiovisual material facilitated the rapid global popularization of hip-hop performers.

In addition to the artistry and aesthetics of hip-hop, its keen social criticism would be key to the genre's transformation into a mouthpiece for a new generation. In the late 1990s and 2000s, one of the most widely celebrated voices of hip-hop was the prolific and controversial American MC Tupac Shakur. In the wake of his murder at the age of twenty-five, Tupac Shakur's tracks would become anthems of post-Cold War alienation, defiance, and aspiration, heard and repeated across the globe. It is to these resonances of Shakur's music that we now turn.

3

# ME AGAINST THE WORLD

## TUPAC SHAKUR AND POST-COLD WAR ALIENATION

Gunfire woke the residents of Kukuna, a small town in northwest Sierra Leone. At least 100 young men and women soon appeared, all wearing T-shirts bearing the image of American rapper Tupac Shakur. There were so many young people wearing Tupac shirts that some townspeople assumed that Kukuna was hosting a hip-hop concert. However, as screams filled the night air and buildings were set ablaze, residents recognized those wearing the T-shirts as the Revolutionary United Front (RUF), a rebel group seeking to overthrow the government of Sierra Leone. Defenseless, Kukunans watched their town burn, their food carried away, and twenty-eight of their neighbors and relatives killed.[1]

It was late September 1998, and Kukuna was one of many towns in northern Sierra Leone decimated by the RUF in their advance towards the capital, Freetown. The rebels had come to depend on local communities for sustenance. They had also come to believe that civilians could be terrorized into complacency. In the early years of the war, RUF commanders had calculated that they did not need to win the support of civilians, only their acquiescence. Thus, the RUF preyed on rural populations. The rebels conscripted juveniles to replenish their ranks, looted and raped civilians, and humiliated or killed figures of authority. These were graphic illustrations of the extreme power young combatants wielded over civilians and the ways in which combatants externalized their own psychological traumas. By 1998 Tupac references had become another, albeit more subtle dimension of the war's psychodynamics. The RUF's symbolic appropriation of Shakur in its advance towards Freetown was an example of how young people sought broader meaning for their experiences, psychological solace from the chaos of war, and a transnational figure onto whom they could project their aspirations for power.

Two years earlier, in September 1996, Tupac Shakur was killed by an unidentified gunman in Las Vegas. Shakur was only twenty-five when he died, but his remarkable life and shocking death elevated him to the position of an almost mythic figure in mass culture. For example, I was in East Africa several months after Tupac's murder and he was on the minds of many young people. Was Tupac really dead?, many asked. If so, who killed him? In Nairobi, Mombasa, Arusha, and Dar es Salaam Tupac's music and visage were ubiquitous: on walls and buses, in barbershops and video cafes, in cassette stalls and on car sound-systems.[2] In the years that followed, murals in Los Angeles, New York, Tijuana, Tokyo, Saint Petersburg, Lomé, Cape Town, and Freetown honored Shakur. His image adorned shops and homes from Johannesburg to Lima and Port-au-Prince. Graffiti in Norway, Germany, Slovenia, Cyprus, Guinea, the United Arab Emirates, and New Zealand praised him. His image was even featured on the national stamps of Tajikistan and Moldova. In 2014 Tupac's music was the subject of a Broadway musical, and in 2017 Shakur was the focus of the feature length Hollywood film, *All Eyez on Me*.

Tupac Shakur's music and iconography has become a point of reference for audiences around the world. Yet, appreciating his transnational popularity requires considering, simultaneously, the commonalities and particularities of references to him. For some, Tupac may be little more than an empty signifier. But his global resonance suggests that the act of evoking him is, in degrees, a symbolic engagement with the two core sentiments that have been projected onto other icons of dissent: alienation and aspiration. Like Che Guevara and Bob Marley, Tupac appealed to diverse self-images in ways that constituted and reflected a disjointed community of sentiment across differing social and political landscapes. The RUF's references to Shakur were but one manifestation of the transnational imagination and a larger fascination with the hip-hop star. At the same time, the use of Tupac's image in Sierra Leone is of exceptional import since it was often of greater gravity, under circumstances more extreme, than almost anywhere else.

In this chapter we narrow the analytical focus to consider the meaning of a global icon of dissent in one national context. By taking this tack, we can probe deeper into local circumstances to understand precisely how and why an antisystemic figure became important to the identities and worldviews of young people in the post-Cold War era. During Sierra Leone's civil war (1991–2002), one of the most harrowing of the late twentieth century, it was Tupac's global popularity as well as the severity of life and proximity of death—circumstances that mirrored Shakur's lyrical imagery—that attracted young people to the rap icon. This stereoscopic view of Tupac's popularity in the post-Cold War era brings into sharp focus both a common sense of Shakur's significance as well as the convergence and divergence of individual interpretations of him. More precisely, in this chapter I argue that the global circulation of Tupac's music, Sierra Leone's decade-long civil war, and the ways these intersected provide evidence of the domestic repercussions of post-Cold War geopolitical shifts and the expansion of the global symbolic idiom. Tupac Shakur's popularity in Sierra Leone thus offers a window on a devastating war and its relation to broader patterns of alienation in the post-Cold War world.

## Tupac Shakur and the Post-Cold War World

The end of the Cold War and the collapse of global socialism as a doctrinal alternative to liberal democratic capitalism altered both the geopolitical order and the transnational imagination. In the absence of an overarching contest of ideological influence and strategic positioning, the priorities of powerful nations shifted. The United States, for instance, now often showed less concern for political instability in the postcolonial world. This new geopolitical calculus did not signal an end to interventionism, as the invasions of Afghanistan and Iraq would evidence. Rather, it demonstrated a general shift in powerful states' attitudes to the circumstances of the global South. For nations such as Sierra Leone, what came at the "end of history" (to use Francis Fukuyama's phrase) was neither benign capitalism nor peace, but rather the realization that much of the world viewed its disintegration as inconsequential.[3]

As we saw in Chapter One, during the Cold War, socialism, concepts of revolution, and liberation discourse offered social movements and guerrillas the "providential self-assurance" that they were part of a worldwide battle.[4] This self-assurance largely waned in the 1980s, but this did not diminish dissent. As we saw in the last chapter, Bob Marley became a global icon of dissent in the late 1970s in part because he addressed this shift and articulated alternative concepts of transnational solidarity. The end of the Cold War posed vexing challenges to transnational networks of action and support. With some exceptions, in the early 1990s popular political imagination gravitated towards domestic concerns. Those transnational alliances that did persist or emerge tended to focus on relatively narrow concerns, not worldwide social change. At the same time, the seismic historical shifts of the 1990s enhanced popular attraction to symbols that could link the individual to global currents. This intensifying symbolic convergence was to a great degree a consequence of a more diverse and accessible mediascape.[5]

Media proliferation—television, music, and the Internet—was crucial to the accelerated symbolic convergence of the 1990s. The increasing availability of video and commercially produced music offered a means to interpret the world that was open to diverse translations. Music was also easily replicated. In Sierra Leone and across the global South pirated music (usually in cassette tape form) was accessible to almost everyone. It required neither literacy nor access to more costly technologies such as video or the Internet. This transnational aural popular culture and the surging international interest in hip-hop would be key to Tupac Shakur's rise to global iconic status. As the introduction to this book outlined, hip-hop was not only an attractive new art form. It also offered a compelling medium for the conveyance of social and political messages. In many African nations, hip-hop made limited inroads in the 1980s, but by the mid-1990s it was supplanting reggae as the most popular musical genre of critique, rebellion, and global connection. Hip-hop's establishment as a popular art form across Africa and much of the postcolonial world roughly coincided with Shakur's rise to celebrity status in the United States.[6]

Like Che Guevara and Bob Marley, Tupac's attractiveness and charisma, as well as the specifics of his message, contributed to his popularity. He developed many antisystemic messages consonant with those of Bob Marley. Shakur, like Marley, used stories of the marginalized to critique racism and systemic oppression. He also favored complex narratives of pain and liberation that emphasized internal conflict and the necessity of self-knowledge. Tupac's trajectory also exhibited a number of similarities with Marley's. Both experienced the depravities of urban poverty and racial injustice. Both gravitated to and then popularized an emerging musical genre that in turn gave them platforms for their messages. Both were the targets of assassination attempts, in the wake of which both artists produced their most memorable material: Marley's *Exodus* (1977) and Shakur's *All Eyez on Me* (1996). It is thus no surprise that Shakur identified with Marley's music, or that he tattooed the word "Exodus" across his back in the style of Marley's album cover.

Yet, Tupac's lyrics departed from Marley's often utopian message. Tupac was defiant, but he offered no idealized vision for the world. He sought no salvation, nor did he call for an internal revolution. Though he became a sign of rebellion endlessly resignified, the world he inhabited was different from Marley's. By the end of the 1980s, for instance, the notion of Third World solidarity found an increasingly small audience. Marley and Shakur shared experiences of suffering and used an emerging art form to critique injustice, but they also developed messages shaped by and attuned to contrasting circumstances, both personal and world historical.

Born in East Harlem, New York City in 1971, Tupac Shakur was given the name Lesane Parish Crooks. Soon thereafter, his mother, Afeni Shakur, renamed the infant in honor of the eighteenth-century indigenous Peruvian revolutionary leader, Túpac Amaru II (José Gabriel Condorcanqui). It would be a name in which Tupac took great pride.[7] He grew up in a radical household and this would shape his worldview. His stepfather, Mutulu Shakur, was a member of the Black Liberation Army (BLA). His step-aunt, Assata Shakur, was perhaps the best known member of the BLA as she was imprisoned in the US and received asylum in Cuba. Tupac's godfather, Geronimo Pratt, was a prominent Black Panther Party (BPP) member and one of the postwar era's best-known political prisoners. Tupac's mother was also a Black Panther and the target of significant political persecution. She gained international notoriety in 1969 when she was accused, along with other BPP members (often referred to as the Panther 21), of planning a bombing campaign in New York City. Many charged that the case was an elaborate attempt by local and national authorities to neutralize the BPP. The resulting trial was the among the longest in New York's history. Just one month before Tupac's birth, Afeni Shakur and her co-defendants were acquitted of all charges.[8]

Tupac Shakur embraced his family's radical politics. In his late teens he was the national chairman of the New Afrikan Panthers, a youth organization affiliated with the New Afrikan People's Organization. A peripatetic childhood also exposed him to the arts, notably theater and hip-hop. After attending a school for the arts in Baltimore, Tupac toured with the Oakland-based hip-hop outfit Digital Underground. In 1991, at age twenty, he released his first solo album, *2Pacalypse Now*, which addressed social issues such as poverty and racism. Between 1991 and his death in 1996, Tupac released six albums; the last three, *Me Against the World* (1995), *All Eyez on Me* (1996), and the posthumous *The Don Killuminati: The 7 Day Theory* (1996) reached number one in the American charts. Just as impressive, Shakur pursued a successful film career, starring in six Hollywood films, including box office hits such as *Juice* (1992) and *Poetic Justice* (1993).

Tupac's death at the height of his career undoubtedly accelerated his rise to superstardom. His music was widely known beyond the United States before his death, and the drama of his murder during a highly publicized feud between his Los Angeles label Death Row and New York-based Bad Boy Records added significant mystique to his image. The war of words between acclaimed MCs of both camps—a war that had only just subsided when Tupac was shot—captivated hip-hop fans around the world.[9]

Tupac Shakur was spectacularly productive during his short career, and he received great acclaim. His intellect, passion, and musical acumen seeded a meteoric rise in the hip-hop world, while his charisma and Janus-like personality propelled his acting career. Though Tupac's recordings spanned just five years, they showcased his great versatility. He was equally comfortable with themes such as gender inequality and police brutality as he was with vacuous materialism. Tupac indulged in the conspicuous consumption and braggadocio that had become common to mainstream hip-hop, yet his lyrics were often as eloquent and incisive as they were audacious and raw. His messages also seemed to come directly from the heart. His sincerity of expression, regardless of the topic, added great weight to his words. In the facile milieu of the early 1990s music industry, Tupac spoke about myriad aspects of life in ways both vulnerable and relatable. Just as important to Tupac's popularity was the fact that he embodied many ideals of black masculinity recurrent in hip-hop: personal strength, fearlessness, and defiance of social restraints.[10]

However, Tupac's career was marked by controversy. The popular media often derisively referred to his music as "gangsta" rap.[11] High-profile political figures, including US Vice President Dan Quayle and Senator Bob Dole, charged that Tupac's music incited violence and called for its censorship. Detractors painted Shakur as an archetypal hoodlum. Quayle even asserted that his music had "no place in our society."[12] It was in this context that Shakur embraced the term "thug", which critics used to describe him. For Tupac, the term was a means to valorize those dismissed by the wider society. He titled his 1994 release *Thug Life: Volume 1*, and defined "Thug Life" as an acronym that encapsulated his systemic critique of inequality: "The Hate U Gave Little Infants Fucks Everybody".[13] As a result, the motto "Thug Life" became shorthand for resistance to the dominant social order and an increasingly popular reference in the years after Shakur's death.

Tupac also embraced the image of the outlaw during his tumultuous final years. Not only did he name his group the Outlaw Immortalz but he also gave his supporting rappers aliases such as Kastro, Kadafi, and Hussein Fatal. Additionally, the final years of Tupac's life were marked by a series of legal battles. These cases, and several months spent in prison after being convicted of sexual abuse, inspired one of his most referenced refrains, "Me Against the World". Yet, more than any other development in Shakur's life, his public feud with acclaimed New York-based rapper Biggie Smalls, aka The Notorious B.I.G., gained the world's attention. It began in November 1994, when Tupac was attacked by unknown assailants outside of a New York recording studio. The attackers shot the young rapper five times, including twice in the head, and stole US$40,000 in jewelry. Miraculously, Tupac made a full recovery, which earned him an air of invincibility. He soon went on the offensive. He believed that individuals associated with Bad Boy Records, including the label's famous MC Biggie Smalls, were behind the attack. As a result, he launched a verbal assault on both Smalls and his label.

This feud, interpreted narrowly by the popular media as a rivalry between the East and West Coast hip-hop scenes, colored the final year of Tupac's life with overtones of violence and retribution. His earlier concern with broader issues of social justice and racial equality seemed to fade into aggressive and nihilistic imagery that culminated in the stage persona Makaveli. Through this alter ego, assumed for Tupac's final studio release, *The Don Killuminati* (1996), Shakur narrated a world of dangers and redemptive violence. The angst he expressed in his remarkably prolific last year, which included the albums *All Eyez on Me* (1996), *The Don Killuminati*, and posthumously produced records such as *Still I Rise* (1999) and *Better Dayz* (2002), responded directly to Tupac's sense of being under attack. They emphasized resiliance, as Tupac proclaimed, "Against All Odds" (*The Don Killuminati*).

Many lyrics featured on these albums conveyed a sense of righteous violence. One of *All Eyez on Me*'s greatest chart successes, "Hit 'em Up", encapsulates this discursive shift. Instead of a critique of racism or police brutality, common themes in Tupac's earlier recordings, "Hit 'em Up" is an attack on Biggie Smalls and Bad Boy Records. Many of his last tracks were also tinged with paranoia, regret, and references to violent death. "Troublesome '96", which likewise appeared on *All Eyez on Me*, outlines the necessity of fighting violence with violence, as well as the psychological repercussions of this response for the victim-turned-aggressor.[14] The dual aggression and despair that marked many of Tupac's later songs offered a resonant soundtrack to the lives of many young people in the late 1990s. Moreover, the vulnerability displayed on tracks such as "Troublesome '96" cemented Tupac's place as a larger-than-life hero with empathy, someone who understood the experiences of those suffering from injustice and trapped in poverty.

Tupac Shakur's reflection on multiple dimensions of violence in urban America—from the perspective of victims as well as perpetrators—struck a chord with young people living in circumstances analogous to those he described. Carlos D. Morrison referred to Tupac's "death narratives," or regular reflection on violent death, as powerful articulations of the realities experienced by many of his American listeners. The other side of Tupac's message was equally resonant. Specifically, his lyrics are steeped in the rhetoric of resilience, of overcoming unjust conditions. As Tupac often pointed out, he had succeeded despite America's social constraints of racism, classism, and poverty. He was, to borrow a reference from his poetry, a "rose that grew from concrete."[15] What Tupac offered, according to Morrison, was an example of how to survive the "killing fields" of America.[16] His perceived invincibility offered psychological solace for young people, and men in particular, who experienced violence as part of their everyday lives. More precisely, in Tupac's voice young people found a presence that was equally fearless and encouraging.[17]

Tupac's ability to narrate the experiences of diverse listeners and his resistance to hollow, reassuring metanarratives created a discourse that Eithne Quinn summed up as embracing the "confusions of overlapping, conflictual, and commodified narrative."[18] Yet, to many American critics, such contradictory and usually third-person narration seemed incoherent. During Tupac's life this narrative multipositionality, or his convincing articulation of the subject positions of those whose experiences were different from his own, left many wondering what Tupac's values really were. Nevertheless, his multidimensionality, combined with his general criticism of systemic injustice and empathy for both perpetrators and victims of violence, made Tupac a potent mirror of diverse desires. He became an archetype of courage and power, even among those who shared few experiences. As a result, in the years after his death Tupac Shakur became, in Michael Eric Dyson's words, "his generation's defining voice."[19]

In death, Shakur became an omnipresent planetary hook for shared alienation and aspiration. Much as with the other figures addressed in this book, those who identified with him and looked for inspiration and comfort in his words occupied different, even opposed subject positions. This, more than anything, suggests the plasticity of Tupac's image, a quality central to his emergence as a global icon. As with Bob Marley, young people in many parts of the world grafted their experiences onto Tupac's iconography and words. The hyper-masculinity and glamour that Tupac Shakur exuded led many young men to embrace him as a model of manhood akin to Che Guevara, while interpretations of Tupac's lyrics as reflections of universal pain, frustration, and grievance ensured a wide popularity. This breadth of appeal also helps to explain why, like Che Guevara and Bob Marley, audiences have embraced Tupac as alternatively fashionable, inspirational, and prophetic.

As hip-hop transcended the United States, Tupac Shakur's music resonated around the world.[20] South Africa offers a microcosm of the perceived relevance of Tupac's rhetoric for young people of diverse backgrounds. In 1999 (about the same time that the Sierra Leonean RUF gravitated towards Tupac) a Johannesburg barbershop was covered with Tupac posters and stickers. The owner, teenager Shaku Biserat, asked his family and friends to call him Tupac. "All the things [Tupac] sings about are the things that happen in real life to me and my friends," Biserat explained in an interview. "The way we grew up, the poor life," he continued, "is the life Tupac lived. And he made it out ... That's what we want, too."[21]

Gangs in Johannesburg and Cape Town also embraced Tupac as an inspirational figure.[22] For instance, in Boksburg, an eastern suburb of Johannesburg, Jermaine "Turbo" Van Wyk, the slain head of a gang named the Thugs in reference to *Thug Life: Volume 1*, gained the world's attention in 2002 when he masterminded an airport cash and diamond heist. Van Wyk was so moved by Shakur's music that he adopted the personal motto "To Live and Die in SA", an unambiguous reference to Tupac's 1996 hit "To Live and Die in LA".[23] In Cape Town's poverty-stricken Manenberg district, gang members in the Beatrix Court housing block commissioned towering murals of Tupac in 1997, captioned with Tupac's famous phrases, "Thug Life" and "West Side".[24] Another Cape Town gang even boasted the name Thug Life, and graffiti referencing Shakur, including "W[est] S[ide] 2PAC" and "Fuck The World", has long dotted the urban terrain.[25] Similarly, in 2000 fans in a small town near the rural Eastern Cape's Magusheni tribal authority covered local signs with Tupac references. Fans wrote his name on almost every official road sign, and they even erected new signs along the main road reading "PAC", "West Coast", and "Live by the Gun".[26] Research on the popularity of Shakur among Cape Town gang members in the 2000s suggested that many young men imagined Tupac to represent a masculine "outlaw" ideal.[27] Across South Africa this image and

6. Mural depicting Tupac Shakur, captioned "West Side" in reference to Shakur's refrain. Manenberg, Cape Town, South Africa, 2002. © Per-Anders Pettersson / Getty Images.

Tupac's spirit of defiance has drawn wide audiences since the late 1990s. The notion that Shakur's words derive from a fount of experience that mirrors and gives broader relevance to shared depravities, combined with his "outlaw" status, made him a compelling icon.

Tupac's narration of violence has gained particular relevance in contexts of conflict. For instance, in the late 1990s indigenous rebels on Guadalcanal in the Solomon Islands referenced Tupac in ways reminiscent of the RUF in Sierra Leone. When, in 1997, Guadalcanal authorities began to raid cannabis farms managed by armed groups, one such organization, the Outlaws, planted rows to spell out "West Side". As a member of the group explained in 1999, the popularity of Tupac was in consequence of the perception of Shakur as "a man of action" who "wasn't afraid of dying."[28] Soon thereafter, in the Haitian capital, Port-au-Prince, Shakur appealed to gangs-turned-militias in support of the Jean-Bertrand Aristide government. Like combatants in Sierra Leone, a prominent militia leader in the impoverished Cité Soleil neighborhood chose 2Pac as his nom de guerre.

In Bunia, Democratic Republic of the Congo, both ethnic Hema militias and members of the Congolese armed forces used Tupac T-shirts as uniforms in the early 2000s.[29] In 2002, multiple rebel groups in northern Ivory Coast similarly began wearing Tupac T-shirts.[30] The Young Patriots, a group that supported the Ivoirian government, similarly recognized hip-hop as a mobilizing force. Their leader, Charles Blé Goudé, explained young people's attraction to American hip-hop stars such as Tupac: "When [American rappers] sing, you listen, and the message comes straight to you."[31] Indeed, it was the power of hip-hop as a medium, its rawness and the metaphorical proximity of its lyrics to many young people's experiences that Shakur came to represent. Sgt Delmus McGill, a US Marine serving in Iraq in 2004, framed this sentiment concisely. As he explained to the television network VH1, "When your soul is hurting, you can listen to Tupac." "When you're hurting," he added, "you can feel everything he's saying."[32]

Tupac likewise proved attractive to Libyan combatants during the rebellion against the Muammar Gaddafi regime in 2011. Many young Libyan admirers of Tupac turned to his music for solace and courage. "I only listen to 2Pac before going to shoot Gaddafi boys," one young militant explained.[33] Rapper and activist Yousef Ramadan offered greater insight. According to Ramadan, during the Libyan uprising many saw Tupac as a kind of "sacred man" and drew inspiration from his words.[34] Shakur's music proved inspirational to a great range of other listeners. For instance, Omar Hammami, the young American who traveled to Somalia to fight alongside al-Shabaab insurgents, used Tupac's "Hail Mary" (1996) as the score for his 2011 recruitment rap, "Make Jihad With Me".[35] A larger reevaluation of Tupac was also underway in the new millennium. There is perhaps no better example of this than the fact that Tupac's single "Changes" (1998), which addresses police brutality and racial violence, appeared on the Vatican's MySpace page in 2009 as one of its twelve favorite songs. In 2012, conservative US senator Marco Rubio similarly revealed his fondness for Tupac Shakur's music.[36]

By the beginning of the 2010s, Tupac's global resonance was multifaceted. From the US to South Africa and the Solomon Islands, he appealed as an authentic and transcendent voice for social justice as well as a hyper-masculine hero and rebel archetype. To fully understand the complexity of Shakur's resonance, let us turn to Sierra Leone's civil war.

## Tupac Shakur and the Psychodynamics of War

Baimba Bompa-Turay was a child soldier in Sierra Leone. In 1999, he was abducted by the RUF during their invasion of Freetown. His father was brutalized by the rebels and his sister was killed. Though spared death, Bompa-Turay had little choice but to fight alongside his captors. Like many other boys, he was forcibly addicted to crack cocaine and trained to kill. The drugs and his camaraderie with fellow juvenile combatants initiated Bompa-Turay into extreme violence. "We were invincible," he recalled, and he did "vicious things."[37]

During his years with the RUF, Bompa-Turay's best friend had chosen Tupac as his nom de guerre. In September 2000 the boys' unit was ordered across the border into Guinea. Outgunned and malnourished, they suffered a terrible defeat. Bompa-Turay was shot twice. Tupac was fatally wounded and died in his arms; most of Bompa-Turay's friends were killed that day. Though Bompa-Turay recovered from his physical injuries, the psychological trauma was far deeper, and thus at the end of the war he was committed to a mental hospital in Freetown. Baimba

Bompa-Turay and his friend Tupac's experiences reflect those of many young Sierra Leonean conscripts who both suffered and inflicted great suffering on others while using global popular culture references to give meaning to these experiences.

In Sierra Leone, young combatants were neither steeped in the theories of Marxist-Leninist ideologues nor offered providential self-assurance in their killing. Nevertheless, war intensified the need for a broader significance to their actions. It also deepened young people's desires for myth-like heroes. Throughout the war, iconic figures both fictitious and real, including Rambo, Chuck Norris, Bob Marley, and Tupac Shakur, were critical frames of reference for young people, both because they already constituted a broader symbolic idiom in and beyond Sierra Leone and because they represented qualities to which young combatants aspired. Tupac was particularly important in the late 1990s because his rhetoric of alienation seemed so resonant with the experiences of young Sierra Leoneans. He offered allegories of invincibility, a voice for feelings of frustration and angst, and reassurance that those caught in cycles of violence, including perpetrators, were not alone.

During the civil war, more pressing matters made reflection on the interface of iconography and violence tangential. When the RUF's use of Tupac did gain attention, reflections often had a dismissive tone that demonstrated a lack of consideration for the circumstances of his popularity and interpretations of Shakur's life and death. Many analysts presumed combatants' embrace of Tupac was little more than a disturbing evocation of the worst of American culture: misogyny, violence, and drug abuse. Sierra Leonean government officials even blamed Tupac himself, and aspects of American popular culture generally, for inciting violence—a refrain reminiscent of critiques of Tupac's music in the United States. In the desperation of the war, analysts overlooked the reality of Tupac's relevance and appeal to young people, particularly combatants. In hindsight, the fact that young combatants who carried out terrible acts evoked Tupac suggests that there is value in considering the meanings attributed to him during the war. Moreover, incorporations of Tupac into the symbolic idioms of other places and other wars since the end of the conflict in 2002 indicate that his appropriation in Sierra Leone represents an early manifestation of an evolving transnational phenomenon.

The uses of Tupac by combatants in Sierra Leone require concentration on the psychology of violence, the strategic logic of the war, and the global nature of a conflict that seemed to have little international relevance. More precisely, Tupac iconography offers a unique way to understand both conflict and the global symbolic idiom, because it necessarily moves analysis beyond politics to the life-worlds of combatants, a shift in focus that many analysts of the war deemed necessary.[38] To understand the actions of young combatants and the relevance of Tupac to them, we must appreciate both how the war was fought and the specific logics of its violence. During the war, Yusuf Bangura suggested that combatants were developing their own ideologies, ones that he suspected "may have reinforced their views about their own marginality and provided rationales for the looting and outrageous violence they committed against society."[39] For Bangura, Sierra Leone could not be fit into preconceived frames for understanding the perpetuation of conflict, since rebels neither advocated a clear ideology nor articulated specific social goals. Bangura, Ibrahim Abdullah, Lansana Gberie, Danny Hoffman, David Keen, Kieran Mitton, and other analysts have convincingly argued that the particular kinds of violence manifest in Sierra Leone are only explicable through the self-perceptions of those who formed the majority of the RUF, the Sierra Leone Army (SLA), and other factions.[40]

The RUF's foot soldiers, as well as a sizable proportion of the SLA, were the most marginalized of the rural and urban poor, often with little education or social mobility. Many were volunteers, but by the end of the conflict most were conscripts. In a war without guiding ideologies, fought by many forced into combat, young combatants sought ways to express what Ibrahim Abdullah and Ishmail Rashid typified as the conflicting "zeal" and "pain" with which they carried out their orders.[41] Bridging these two positions, or understanding the psychodynamics of violence as a community of spirit, requires a conceptual leap that Tupac iconography can help to propel. Like young people in other parts of the world, Tupac resonated with Sierra Leonean combatants because his was a voice of simultaneous criticism, alienation, empathy, and aspiration. He outlined a way of understanding the world that both accorded with and helped to articulate the psychological trauma of wartime violence. As Brad Weiss has shown in the case of urban Tanzania, Tupac's themes and imagery offered a means to assert a communal identity fixed in pain. By identifying with the "positive value of pain" in Tupac's voice, young people aligned themselves, as Weiss noted, with a "worldwide community of affliction."[42] For young Sierra Leoneans coopted to fight and goaded to externalize their pain, Tupac offered motivation and solace in the layered experience of alienation and brutality.

Between 1991 and 2002, civil war ripped apart the daily life of Sierra Leoneans. It was a war that knew no boundaries. All sides targeted and preyed on civilians, though the most notorious faction was the RUF. In the early years of the war, the RUF relied on a vague populism that it later articulated in its manifesto, *Footpaths to Democracy*.[43] The RUF's populist message, however, never extended beyond grievances against the federal government generally, and figures of authority whom it claimed were responsible for the poverty and marginalization of Sierra Leoneans in particular. What weight this populist rhetoric carried was lost after its ideologue proponents were expunged from the group during the early years of the war. In order to consolidate his power, the anti-ideologue RUF commander Foday Sankoh embarked on a campaign of executing rival leaders and so gained full control over the faction. Ultimately, Sankoh's faith that violence alone was sufficient to unseat the "corrupt system" of Sierra Leone's political elite overrode any interest in gaining popular support. Because of Sankoh's indifference to violence against civilians and the RUF's habitual looting, most Sierra Leoneans rejected the movement.[44] This rebuff angered the rebels, who responded by inflicting greater violence on local populations. If the RUF developed any overarching strategy, it was that of terrorizing civilians into acquiescence while financing the insurgency through control over rutile, diamond, and gold mining areas.

Violence against civilians aimed to intimidate both ordinary citizens and opposing factions. But the actions of young combatants also hinged on less conscious drives. For the rank-and-file conscripts, the war became a theatre for exerting power over the lives of others. Acts of violence were often displaced responses to feelings of alienation on the part of young combatants, a response intensified by the experience of military indoctrination (a point to which I will return). For most combatants, destroying the conventions of the "corrupt system", looting civilians' possessions, and forcing their will on those in positions of power was a psychological salve. The war opened up possibilities for addressing the frustrations and humiliations of life, and the gun offered unprecedented opportunities. As one SLA corporal explained to Ishmael Beah, a teenage recruit who would later write an account of his years fighting with government forces, "[the] gun is your source of power in these times."[45]

The gun not only offered unusual power, but also forced the performance of respect. Those young people who had been powerless before the war, and who were then systematically degraded as child soldiers, used the gun to demand respect from those over whom they wielded their newfound power. Theirs was a desire to be in control of their own lives for the first time, albeit through the proxy of others' suffering. Longings for respect and recognition would prove powerful psychical drives among conscripts and volunteers alike throughout the war.[46] Killing became an indulgence of the desire to be someone of import; it demonstrated that the killer, though in many cases quite young, wielded the power of life and death over others. This unambiguous demonstration of domination, which Achille Mbembe termed "necro-power", revealed itself in the worst of the war's atrocities: forcing young people to kill their parents; asking victims if they wanted just their hand cut off or their whole arm; forcing victims to dance after the murder of their family members; systematic rape. These were calculated attempts to humiliate civilians, overturn a gerontocratic system, and demonstrate the power of those committing such atrocities.[47]

Since the RUF could not depend on popular support for recruits, and its leaders believed that soldiers did not need to be ideologically motivated, it turned to abducting and conscripting juveniles—the most malleable of all potential soldiers. Recognizing that children as young as five, but more commonly between the ages of ten and fourteen, could be coerced into doing virtually anything their commanders wished, the RUF created a core of teen and preteen combatants. While the SLA attracted many young men seeking to avenge the death of a family member or loved one, by the mid-1990s the RUF was to a great degree dependent on forcibly conscripted juveniles. A post-war survey revealed that as many as 72 per cent of ex-combatants claimed to have been forcibly conscripted, while 70 per cent were either small children or adolescents at the start of the war.[48]

Recruitment was a process of psychologically distancing the conscript from his or her family. Children captured by the RUF were often compelled under the threat of death to kill, maim, or rape members of their communities, even family members. This served to alienate young people from their families and make them believe that returning home would be difficult. To ensure that they did not try to escape, conscripts were often branded or cut with the faction's initials. They were then alienated from whatever moral precepts they maintained by being forced to repeatedly kill, maim, and rape. To alleviate some of the psychological trauma of such violence, juveniles were given cannabis, ephedrine, crack cocaine, heroin, and diazepam. When this drugging resulted in addiction, many conscripts became easier to manipulate.[49] Finally, older combatants convinced conscripts that they should accept their new comrades as their family. Orphaned, or at least estranged from their families, young people usually came to trust and build relations of reciprocity with their captors. In the chaos of war, the structure of combat units offered a kind of patriarchal, familiar order.[50] Though initially traumatized and disoriented, initiates became accustomed to the values and beliefs of their captors-cum-comrades as well as the extreme violence of everyday life during the war.

Young conscripts were socially dead and then reborn into killing.[51] Through this social engineering factions developed juvenile fighting forces fiercely loyal to their commanders and that exhibited little sympathy for their victims. Indeed, initiates were encouraged to show no mercy for perceived enemies, military or civilian, and instead focus their anger and feelings of humiliation on them. For many combatants violence became a comfort that they could not easily forgo even once out of combat.[52] This cycle of violence—abduction, violent indoctrination, and the externalization of pain—contributed to the perpetuation of the war. As a result, civilians as much as opposing forces suffered the displaced angst and psychological pain of those juveniles whom the Sierra Leone Truth and Reconciliation Commission (TRC) described as "victim[s] turned perpetrator[s]."[53]

Though perhaps the majority of RUF combatants were conscripted at a young age, others joined willingly. Immediately after the war, the Sierra Leone TRC heard testimony from young, mostly male combatants who had joined the RUF voluntarily. Their stories were remarkably similar. They were lower-class young men whose parents had worked in the agricultural sector and who had received no benefit from the long reign of the pre-war ruling party, the All People's Congress (APC). Many gained a limited education before the war, but higher education was not available for the majority and university scholarships were controlled by the ruling party.[54] Clientelism, corruption, and nepotism were rife under the APC, and so opportunities and resources were regularly distributed to those who enjoyed close party connections. In short, the young and impoverished suffered most under this system, since they enjoyed little access to circuits of patronage and distribution.[55]

Exacerbated by structural adjustment austerity policies in the 1980s, a "crisis of youth" reached unprecedented proportions in the early years of the civil war. During the conflict some young people had so few opportunities to realize their social and economic aspirations that they quickly embraced the prospect of taking up arms.[56] For volunteers, joining the RUF was seen both as a means to accumulate wealth and prestige and a response to perceived injustices.[57] Though multiple forces shaped the choices and actions of combatants, by the late 1990s most combatants, both volunteer and conscript, sought redress for the physical, social, or psychological violence they had suffered. Perhaps even more importantly, both initiates and volunteers of every faction, whether the RUF, the Armed Forces Revolutionary Council (AFRC), the SLA, or local self-defense militias (groups corporately termed the Civil Defense Forces, or CDF), believed that their actions were justifiable.

The RUF and AFRC painted their victims as "collaborators", supporters of the system. They came to believe that attacking all authority figures was just, since, in the words of many ex-combatants who testified to the TRC, this served the larger goal of "bringing down the system."[58] The desire to destroy the symbols of a hierarchy in which young combatants had little stake was made manifest in the humiliation of authority figures, government representatives, or anyone socially respectable. This desire also explains why the RUF and AFRC mutilated, raped, and killed the elderly. Anger directed at anyone imagined to possess social authority became a regular expression of a deeper desire to invert the dominant social order.[59] In the combined pain and zeal of perpetrators' actions, looting was justified as redistribution while killing and maiming were imagined as legitimate forms of retribution.[60]

Combatants created and reinforced their own moral universes, hinging for every faction on presumptions of the righteousness of their actions. Whether as a response to government injustices or rebel atrocities, combatants saw their own perpetrations of violence as essentially defensive.[61] Rebels, for instance, believed that the system they would usher in would be more virtuous specifically because it would upend the old social order. As a result, they claimed a position above pre-established law.[62] This perception of righteous violence and the evocation of a higher justice explain why Tupac Shakur's track "Only God Can Judge Me" (1996) became a mantra for RUF and AFRC fighters in the late 1990s. Anticipating the sentiments of the rebels, Tupac asks, "Is it a crime to fight for what is mine?" The lyrics then build on themes of fatalism and historic injustice: "Everybody's dyin', tell me what's the use of tryin'/I've been trapped since birth, cautious, cause I'm cursed." "Only God can judge me now," the chorus concludes, appealing to a transcendent reckoning that might weigh the rapper's actions against the world he inherited.

The violence Tupac narrated in "Only God Can Judge Me" was reactive, and this aligned neatly with how combatants perceived their own actions: violence as self-protection, either in retaliation or as means of restitution for systemic injustice. Shakur's lyrics depict young men devoid, indeed robbed, of opportunity by a corrupt system that leaves few choices other than violence. At the same time, Tupac's lyrics paint a picture of internal torment and the myriad reverberations of the violence exacted on young people. This narration particularly reflected the self-perceptions of young combatants in late 1990s Sierra Leone. "Secretz of War", from the posthumous album *Still I Rise* (1999), offers another example of the way Tupac articulated the conflicting emotional frames of defensiveness, aggression, and anguish. The verse describes the experience of "seeing demons" and self-medicating with cannabis, but the chorus offers an ideal of fearlessness, of overcoming these anxieties through violent action and empowerment by possession of the secrets of war. Tupac's lyrics thus found parallels in Sierra Leone, and young combatants listened to and repeated his words as a reflection of the psychology of the war consuming them.

# ME AGAINST THE WORLD

*Translating Tupac Shakur in Sierra Leone*

For young Sierra Leoneans who suffered physical and psychological abuses, who felt that they had nothing to gain from the perpetuation of the pre-war political system, and who imagined that violence could bring them a more ideal existence, Tupac offered a mythical anchor for their desires. He not only seemed to understand and sympathize with combatants, but he also represented the kind of invincibility to which most combatants aspired.

As I suggested above, Shakur was not the only symbolic reference popular among combatants. Rather, he was part of a pantheon of trans-national icons. These icons, from Rambo to Bob Marley, were elements of a symbolic idiom that had preceded the war but gained new dimensions in the 1990s. Like Tupac, each was malleable. For instance, young Sierra Leoneans perceived Bob Marley to represent critiques of injustice, general rebelliousness, or, given the fact that reggae was not popular among older Sierra Leoneans, generic youthfulness. These meanings contributed to the RUF's use of Bob Marley T-shirts in the early years of the war. Soon, the shirts became so closely associated with the rebels that people seen wearing Marley's image were often presumed to be affiliated with the RUF. Figures such as Rambo and Chuck Norris also appealed to combatants. When the TRC asked ex-child soldiers what they imagined to be the ideal qualities of a "commando" (the preferred RUF terminology for combatants), they commonly responded with terms such as "tough", "fearsome", and "brave".[63] The everyday rhetoric of military factions emphasized fearlessness above all other character traits. Both the RUF and SLA revered Rambo and Chuck Norris because they exemplified the kinds of fearlessness to which many young people aspired.

Commanders and conscripts alike took names such as Rambo and First Blood.[64] One child recruit-turned-commander testified to the TRC that "I was feared by most of my colleague commandos because of my bravery and attacking skills. That was why my colleagues called me Young Rambo."[65] From the beginning of the war, the RUF used the Rambo film *First Blood* (1982) as a training video of sorts. As early as 1993 the SLA simiarly screened Rambo movies to prepare its combatants for offensives. Rambo offered practical instruction in guerrilla warfare and inspiration to young combatants. Moreover, as Paul Richards has demonstrated, the image of one man fighting a superior force and living by his wits in the forest resonated with combatant experiences and aspirations. Of his time with the SLA, Ishmael Beah recalled, "We all wanted to be like Rambo."[66] Rambo accorded well with the worldviews of combatants, in part because the underlying tension of *First Blood* was reactive. Like Rambo, combatants rationalized their actions as a response to the figurative first blood drawn by systemic oppression or, for SLA conscripts, rebel attacks.

Rambo was an official icon of the RUF in the early years of the war. Tupac became something of an organic icon, what Marc Sommers referred to as a "patron saint", for multiple factions in the war's final years.[67] Tupac's image and rhetoric of fearlessness and invincibility, like that of Rambo, stood as an ideal for combatants. So it is no surprise that RUF, AFRC, and other combatants, including Baimba Bompa-Turay's comrade, also chose Tupac as a nom de guerre. Shakur offered a symbolic package more complex than Rambo's. While he appealed to young combatants' desires for courageousness, his critiques of corruption and justifications of violence were more compelling than those of action film characters. Additionally, Tupac offered an idealized image of black masculinity, embodying much of what young Sierra Leoneans dreamed of: strength, wisdom, self-direction, and wealth.

Alongside Tupac Shakur, a great many African American references were part of Sierra Leone's symbolic idiom before and during the war. Hip-hop, R&B, and other musical genres were prominent in Sierra Leone youth culture, but some references were more surprising. For instance, in 1997 Sierra Leone's Ministry of Social Welfare identified Freetown gangs named the Crips and the Bloods.[68] The Crips (or Krips), painted a larger-than-life mural of Tupac, flanked by an eagle clutching a skull in its talons. Much as in Cape Town, the muralist painted the words "West Side" on a scroll stretched between the eagle's wings. Young Sierra Leoneans' familiarity with hip-hop and a wide range of African American youth cultural references was both an indication of the global preeminence of American culture and a manifestation of deeper currents that have joined the reaches of the Black Atlantic over centuries.

Since Freetown's founding by diasporic Africans from North America, Jamaica, and the UK, many Sierra Leoneans have remained

7. Mural of Tupac Shakur featuring the words "West Side" and "Krips." Freetown, Sierra Leone, May 2000. © TeunVoeten.

connected to cultural, political, discursive, and other trends across the ocean. This depth of connection in part accounts for a notorious RUF commander's nom de guerre, Black Jesus—a reference with complex historical connotations of redemption and liberation across the African diaspora. Black Jesus references illustrated a kind of "ideological trans-nationalism" (to borrow a phrase from J. Lorand Matory) that informed the dreamscapes of many young Sierra Leoneans before and during the war.[69] The fact that Tupac likewise referenced the figure of Black Jesus in his music, describing him as a savior sympathetic to a racialized experience of degradation, suggests that Tupac and his Sierra Leonean audiences shared a number of politicocultural references.

The attack on Kukuna in 1998 was one of the first to see the RUF using Tupac T-shirts as fatigues. However, references to Tupac in the war can be traced to at least a year earlier, in the months following his murder. In April 1997, only weeks before a military coup that ousted the newly elected president Ahmed Tejan Kabbah, police in Makeni detained a secondary school student for possessing rifles, grenades, and explosives. His nickname was Tupac and he was presumed to be work-ing with the RUF.[70] Soon after Tupac's arrest in Makeni, Sierra Leonean military officers, frustrated with the government's lack of support for frontline troops and perceived favoring of the CDF self-defense mili-tias, overthrew the Kabbah government. In place of the elected govern-ment, the conspirators established a military junta under Major Johnny Paul Koroma that called itself the Armed Forces Revolutionary Council (AFRC). The coup would lead to a cascade of events that briefly brought the RUF to the capital, spurred the intervention of multiple foreign military forces, and intensified violence against civilians. The targeting of civilians reached a climax during the 1999 RUF invasion of Freetown. The atrocities that the RUF committed in this campaign shocked the world, focusing significant international attention on the war in Sierra Leone for the first time. In the midst of these events, combatants' references to Tupac multiplied, and the words of the slain rapper gained greater gravity.

After taking control of Freetown in 1997, the AFRC called on the RUF to join the Koroma junta. For the AFRC this overture was the most expedient way to bring an end to the war. RUF leader Foday Sankoh, then detained in Nigeria, gave the AFRC his blessing and called on the RUF to join the junta. Soon RUF fighters marched into Freetown and exacted revenge on a populace that had shown no interest in their cause. Fortunately for Freetown's residents, AFRC/RUF control of Freetown did not last. The Kabbah government-in-exile gained the support of the Economic Community of West Africa's military force, the Economic Community Monitoring Group (ECOMOG), a conglomeration of primarily Nigerian units. In February 1998, ECOMOG drove the AFRC/RUF coalition out of Freetown and reinstated President Kabbah. In their retreat, AFRC/RUF combatants vented their anger on civilian populations. Towns along their escape routes from Freetown such as Bombali, Koinadugu, and Kono suffered a horrible fate at the hands of the embittered retreating combatants.

In the autumn of 1998, the AFRC launched an offensive from the north to retake Freetown. The RUF joined them in a scorched earth push towards the capital, ominously dubbed Operation No Living Thing. The campaign was the horrific apex of indifference to the suffering of civilians and processes of miltary conscription. Determined to reclaim Freetown and nursing feelings of betrayal, AFRC forces took the lead in a campaign that was more vengeful and brutal than any to date. They sought to intimidate the ECOMOG/SLA coalition and exact revenge on civilians who they imagined had supported the ECOMOG invasion. As AFRC and RUF forces pushed towards Freetown, other young people, including Freetown and provincial youth seizing the opportunity to loot, began swelling their ranks.[71] In early January 1999, this reinvigorated force broke through ECOMOG/SLA positions and entered the capital once again. The invasion would demonstrate the rebels' great capacity for brutality, and it would reveal that Tupac Shakur had become a lodestar for the RUF rank and file.

Residents reported that the AFRC/RUF forces that streamed into Freetown had Tupac song titles and lyrics painted on their vehicles, with references such as "All Eyez on Me", "Hit 'em Up", "Only God can Judge", and "Death Row" adorning pick-up trucks.[72] Many of the invaders wore Tupac T-shirts designed to intimidate. For example, one T-shirt worn by RUF combatants during the 1999 invasion featured the word "2PAC" flanked by piles of skulls.[73] Much like the RUF noms de guerre Commander Cut Hands or Colonel Bloodshed, the shirts were intended to induce fear, in no small measure because they represented a figure renowned for his invincibility. One resident of Freetown recalled that the rebels took Tupac's words "very seriously" and even tried "to apply the lyrics." According to many eyewitnesses, during breaks in the fighting AFRC/RUF combatants listened and danced to Tupac's music as well as that of other rap stars.[74]

The RUF's use of Tupac iconography had come at a critical juncture in the war and at a moment when Shakur's transnational popularity was increasing exponentially. The RUF had long forsaken a clear ideology and engaged in violent conscription. Now combatants had tasted power, faced international military coalitions, been humiliated in defeat, and retaken Freetown. Moreover, references to Shakur during the AFRC/RUF occupation of Freetown shed light on the psychology of the invaders. For example, the slogans that the AFRC/RUF painted on their vehicles reflected their experiences and worldviews, particularly if we accept that they took these lyrics seriously. After the 1997 ECOMOG counteroffensive, the concept of "Me Against the World" had become particularly apropos for the rebels. The lyrics, listing horrors similar to those both witnessed and committed by combatants in Freetown, make clear why this song gained special relevance. Like many of Tupac's tracks, it offered a palimpsest of isolation and pain, and a response in violence as the only way for the young and marginalized to be "seen" by the world. Though the context and references of Tupac's words were different from the readings young combatants took from the track, the dual subjectivity of victim-perpetrator narrated in "Me Against the World" captured the psychology of many young rebels at the time of the 1999 invasion. In this way, Shakur's music offered a kind of soundtrack to the war.

As the AFRC/RUF captured more of Freetown, violence against civilians reached a fevered pitch. The number of murders, rapes, and mutilations committed during the 1999 occupation of Freetown surpassed that of any other point in the previous nine years of civil war. Rebel atrocities made headlines around the world. The AFRC/RUF coalition targeted professionals, government functionaries, journalists, and any Nigerian in the city. Anyone the rebels deemed to have supported the Kabbah government was beaten or killed. As the AFRC/RUF became increasingly entrenched in the capital, ECOMOG turned to its tactical trump card: airpower. It began a bombing campaign that forced the rebels into a handful of fortified locations. The tide quickly turned against the AFRC/RUF forces and within days ECOMOG pushed them out of Freetown once again.

In the summer of 2000 the intersections of the Sierra Leone civil war and Tupac iconography were once again in clear view. Instead of the horrors that had gained the world's attention during the 1999 invasion, the exploits of a motley faction of AFRC soldiers became front-page news when they captured several British military advisors. The faction called itself the West Side Boys (WSB) in reference to Tupac's West Coast record label and the rapper's identification with the "West Side" of the American hip-hop scene. While the faction's name was an unambiguous reference to Shakur, exactly where the WSB's allegiances lay was less clear. This liminality ultimately contributed to the group's demise and thus to the end of the civil war.

The WSB's origins stretched back to the tumultuous months following the rebels' 1998 expulsion from Freetown.[75] A "West Side" identity emerged among AFRC loyalists in Tumbodu, Kono District. Junior Lion, the commander of the Dark Angel Battalion, was particularly fond of Tupac, and his enthusiasm for Shakur's music spread. Soon, other units based in Tumbodu were regularly listening to Tupac's tracks and repeating his lyrics. AFRC soldiers camped at Tumbodu also began to incorporate Tupac imagery into their shared narratives. They saw their retreat from the east of Sierra Leone as analogous to Shakur's flight from America's East Coast hip-hop scene to the West Coast. According to Mats Utas and Magnus Jörgel, from 1998 Tupac imagery helped to create a mythology that increased the cohesion of AFRC units near Tumbodu.[76] Later, members of the group would paint "2PAC" on their rifle butts, wear Tupac T-shirts, and reportedly concentrate on the rap star's more violent lyrics.[77] In early 1999, the West Side Boys emerged from the AFRC units near Tumbodu as a distinct sub-faction.

In the weeks following the January 1999 rebel defeat in Freetown, some former AFRC combatants established bases in Magbeni and Gberi Bana under the leadership of Ibrahim Kamara. These camps became known as "West Side" and people in the area began referring to the units as the West Side Boys. In 2000 the WSB joined forces with the SLA and CDF, receiving weapons and support from the government. In May, WSB forces successfully repelled RUF units marching on

Freetown. In recognition of this, and because of their stated interest to be incorporated into the national army, the president's chief of defense staff and several SLA commanders continued to aid the WSB. Some of the WSB even acted as government-hired mercenaries. Nonetheless, the WSB maintained an autonomous base and served as a virtual private militia for former AFRC junta leader Johnny Paul Koroma.[78]

After repelling the RUF in mid-2000, many WSB commanders joined the SLA or found posts in Freetown. This both weakened the faction and drained its external support. Excluded from the Lomé peace accords between the state, the RUF, and the AFRC, by the summer of 2000 the remaining WSB occupied an increasingly marginal political space. Surviving units constructed checkpoints on the road to Masiaka, preyed on passing vehicles, and took hostages. To make matters worse, in negotiations with the government, remaining WSB combatants demanded to be integrated into the national army and allowed to retain the vainglorious ranks they had given themselves, including brigadier and commander. Retaining such titles was important for the WSB because these signified respect, the kind of respect they desperately wanted from the SLA and broader society.[79] When government forces refused to recognize the fictive ranks, negotiations to absorb the militia foundered.

Frustrated by the government's inflexibility, in late August 2000 the WSB ambushed eleven British military advisors to the SLA. The WSB then attempted to use the hostages to leverage their demands. Their plan backfired. Humiliated by the hostage crisis—a "ragtag" teenage militia capturing and holding British paratroopers did not sit well with the British public—in early September a British strike force attacked the WSB base. In twenty minutes the hostages were freed and the WSB had been dealt a deathblow. In a matter of days, most of the remaining West Side Boys capitulated.[80] The rise of the WSB would be the most dramatic evocation of Tupac Shakur during the war, and their decline would clear the path towards peace. Though sporadic violence continued, UN-sponsored demobilization and disarmament programs gained traction. In January 2002, the war was officially declared over.

The defeat of the WSB did not signal the end of Tupac's prominence in Sierra Leone. Years after the end of the war, Shakur remained an important figure in the imagination of young Sierra Leoneans. When I arrived in Sierra Leone in 2004, Tupac's tapes and CDs were readily available on the streets of Freetown. Public transport minivans were decorated with references such as "All Eyez on Me" and "2PAC". A local junior league football club had taken the name Tupac. Young people hawked Tupac posters on the street; one gild-framed image of Tupac for sale near the High Court read "Amerikaz Most Wanted". I spoke with a group of Freetown boys aged eleven to fourteen who, on learning that I was from the US, immediately beamed, "Tupac!" When I asked what they admired most about the rapper, they answered almost in unison: "His lifestyle." Tupac's defiant posture, personal extravagance, and courage were as appealing to young men in post-war Sierra Leone as they had been in the 1990s.

8. Framed picture of Tupac Shakur sold in Freetown, Sierra Leone, 2004. The image is captioned "Amerikaz Most Wanted" in reference to the track "2 Of Amerikaz Most Wanted" from Shakur's 1996 album *All Eyez on Me*.

A few weeks after the defeat of the WSB, a two-part article appeared in Freetown's popular *Concord Times* newspaper. A testament to the importance of Tupac among Sierra Leonean youth, the series asked the pregnant question: is Tupac alive?[81] The author's conclusion was an unequivocal "yes". This opinion was still common after the war. "I don't believe that he's dead," Amadu Seyah, a Freetown barber, explained in 2004. "We haven't seen any proof. Biggie is dead, but Tupac? *Never*. Tupac will come back again!"[82] Other young Freetowners were of a different mind. Ali, a teenage poster salesman, told me in 2004 that Tupac was indeed dead, but that he would come back to life. "When he comes back, do you think he'll come to Freetown?" I asked. Ali looked uncomfortable with the idea. "I hope not," he answered, "because we've seen enough violence here. If Tupac comes to Sierra Leone the war might start again." This was one way of seeing the pain and suffering of the war, the aspirations of young people in postwar Sierra Leone, and the multiple dimensions of Tupac's afterlives: he was a popular icon that transcended the horrors of the war, but he also stood as a reminder of its traumas and the potential for renewed violence. More than two years after the end of the civil war, Tupac Shakur was symbolically loaded with hope as well as danger.

## Conclusion

Tupac Shakur did return, at least fleetingly. In 2012 he appeared as a ghostly aura on stage at California's Coachella Music Festival. He had been resurrected to perform with his one-time companions Snoop Dogg and Dr. Dre. Though the Tupac of Coachella was mere computer-generated projection, popularly referred to as a hologram, the lifelike performance engendered incredible excitement. His stage "appearance", however fleeting, both demonstrated interest in Tupac from a new generation and enhanced his legacy by returning him to the international limelight. It also raised questions: to what other uses might the resurrected Tupac be put? How might the hologram Tupac affect our perception of the deceased rap star?[83]

The resurrected Tupac of Coachella was the culmination of a decade and a half of reimagining the fallen performer. For many of Shakur's listeners, his death was a symbolic death of fearlessness and resilience, traits that so many young people covet. As a result, in the late 1990s many claimed that Tupac was not dead. To accept his death was to accept, in some small way, the end of one's aspiration to the invincibility and lifestyle he represented. At the same time, much of the controversy that dogged Tupac during his life began to fall away after his death. He even came to represent reconciliation. His furious battle of words with Biggie Smalls in the final year of his life might make such a reinterpretation seem implausible. Yet, just before his murder, Tupac worked towards détente with his enemies. His last video (from the final album he produced, *The Don Killuminati*) offered imagery that departed from the ferocity of "Hit 'em Up". "I Ain't Mad at 'Cha" depicted an angelic Tupac mingling with famous personalities in heaven and then returning to earth as an apparition. The song and video were both conciliatory and forgiving. While this rapprochement drew little interest during the war in Sierra Leone, it gained relevance in the conflict's aftermath. For instance, it was this message of reconciliation that drew crowds to the *Ris op Bak* (Krio: "resurrection") concert in Freetown in 2004. Moreover, the concert, which featured a number of Sierra Leonean MCs, was scheduled not long after the international release of *Resurrection*, a high-budget American documentary about Tupac's life.

As this chapter has demonstrated, Tupac's iconography and music gained profound meaning well beyond the United States. In its global circulation we can discern comparable rationales for attraction that point to a broad, albeit disjointed, community of sentiment. In the first decade after the end of the Cold War Tupac offered an expression of the alienation acutely felt by many young people around the world, a voice of dissent made all the more accessible by hip-hop as a musical vessel and its ease of replication on cassette and CD. In war-torn Sierra Leone, Tupac's messages resonated with those looking for courage and meaning in a violent world. In image and word, Tupac offered a compelling anchor for the aspirations and sense of alienation felt by young combatants who often suffered horrible violence and, in turn, exercised extreme cruelty.

Tupac's enduring, perhaps increasing, popularity is a barometer of the desire to derive meaning from a globalized life and death that seemed much larger than life. Much like other icons of dissent, Tupac Shakur railed against the injustices of the contemporary world and the forces allied against him.[84] Yet, the celebration of Tupac is also a testament to the complexity of his messages as well as the malleability of his image. In 2014 the Broadway musical *Holler If Ya Hear Me* grappled with these resonances. Though the production enjoyed limited success, it reminded viewers that Tupac's words speak across decades and generations to address many of the social ills, including poverty, inequality, and injustice, that still affect his audiences. It is for these reasons that Occupy demonstrators in New York and anti-Gaddafi militias in Libya, for instance, evoked Tupac's words and image. In the United States and Libya, and across the post-Cold War world, Tupac Shakur has been ceaselessly revived to address contemporary social ills and desires for political change.

While the depth of shared fields of meaning are often limited, Tupac's music and image have offered an idiom to a great spectrum of political thinking in the post-Cold War era. Across this spectrum, in circumstances of violence as well as reconciliation, Tupac's short life has offered a frame for interpreting the world. Moreover, the desire to resurrect the fallen rapper points to one dimension of a deeper structure of feeling that emerged from the debris of the Cold War: disillusionment with the new world order. This would find voice in social movements, popular uprisings, the resurrection of historical icons such as Che Guevara (see Chapter Six), and the emergence of new antisystemic figures. However, Tupac Shakur was not the most ubiquitous of the new post-Cold War icons of dissent. That title falls to a man far more controversial and reviled. Osama bin Laden would be the most omnipresent icon of dissent to emerge at the turn of the century, in part because he was so feared and hated. At the same time, many people, particualrly in the global South, raised Osama bin Laden's visage as a symbol for their frustrations and political demands. It is to these variegated uses of bin Laden iconography that we now turn.

4

# SUPERPOWER SYMBOLIC

## OSAMA BIN LADEN AND MILLENNIAL DISCONTENT

Soon after the horrific attacks on the World Trade Center and the Pentagon in September 2001, Osama bin Laden graffiti began to appear around the world. In the favelas of Rio de Janeiro, Brazil and on the streets of Mombasa, Kenya, taggers scrawled phrases such as "Vote for Osama," "Super Power Osama," and "Osama is our hero." Bin Laden's visage later appeared on protest posters in Surabaya, Indonesia and mobile phone screens in Amsterdam. Admirers in Nigeria, the Gambia, Papua New Guinea, Malaysia, Thailand, China, Peru, and Mexico snatched up Osama bin Laden T-shirts. In Pakistan, T-shirts sold in Peshawar labeled bin Laden "World Head." In Cape Town, South Africa T-shirts were captioned "Long Live." In Caracas, Venezuela, one popular Osama bin Laden T-shirt featured the caption "The Best."

The popular media, security agencies, and many others regularly interpreted such references as indicators of support for al-Qaeda and terrorism generally. Yet, this popular veneration of bin Laden, by both Muslims and non-Muslims, was rarely a reflection of interest in al-Qaeda, let alone a desire to emulate its violent tactics. For instance, as John L. Esposito and Dalia Mogahed have demonstrated through a remarkable data set, Muslim views of the 9/11 attacks were overwhelmingly negative.[1] More often, those who lionized bin Laden uncoupled his image from his narrow political vision and militant rhetoric and harnessed him as a symbol for multifaceted discontent or engagement with an event of global relevance. In sum, the transnational popularity of bin Laden iconography evidenced a desire for a common symbol of dissent with which to identify and onto which diverse audiences could project myriad historical frustrations.

Bin Laden's global popularity proved shorter-lived than that of the other icons in this study. Nonetheless, for several years after 9/11, his iconography was a focal point that people in many global regions perceived as a symbolic link. In this sense, Osama bin Laden functioned much like earlier icons of dissent: disaffected individuals and groups used his image as a means to articulate populist frustrations and both domestic and transnational rhetorics of dissent. As with Bob Marley and Tupac Shakur, bin Laden's political and consumerist symbolism evidenced the grafting of global frictions onto diverse local tensions.[2]

A substantial body of biographical literature on Osama bin Laden has emerged since the early 2000s.[3] Yet there have been very few reflections on his global resonance beyond jihadist circles.[4] By considering many different social contexts, this chapter takes a different tack from most reflections on bin Laden. Specifically, it seeks to understand the multiple meanings that audiences projected onto bin Laden's image as well as his iconic pliability, particularly beyond the boundaries of region and religious identity. The first section explores how audiences domesticated Osama bin Laden iconography to express general frustrations and anxieties in the wake of 9/11. Central to this phenomenon was the conflation of local dissatisfaction and the transnational imagination, which fostered intense resentment not only of domestic authorities but also of US foreign policy and that of other global powers. By way of example, the second section focuses on the urban coast of Kenya in the early 2000s, a region where some young people employed bin Laden iconography to articulate a range of social and political frustrations that linked circumstances in Kenya to wider global conditions.

In Kenya, references to bin Laden after 9/11 implied neither an adherence to his ideological positions nor a desire to mimic his actions. As with Tupac Shakur, evocations of bin Laden in the early 2000s hinged on general connotations, or perceptions of the al-Qaeda leader as embodying a range of almost superhuman abilities—perceptions shared by Muslims and non-Muslims in and beyond Kenya. To appreciate such interpretations of Osama bin Laden in Kenya, I highlight the experiences of middle- and lower-class Muslim men from the 1980s to the early 2000s, including shifting currents of political thought and the consequences of Kenyan and international counterterrorism measures.

*Symbolic Convergence in the New Millennium*

"There are two superpowers in the world," a man in Mombasa, Kenya explained in 2002, "the United States and Osama bin Laden." "At the moment," he surmised, "Osama is the one with the upper hand."[5] To appreciate the logic of this equation, and by extension the circulation of bin Laden iconography, we must first consider perceptions of 9/11 as an unprecedented symbolic blow to the United States. The plotters did not only seek to attack the United States. They also attempted to marshal the dramaturgy of visual simultaneity. They targeted prominent national symbols, indeed the most recognizable signs of America's financial and military prowess. Moreover, news cameras feeding thousands of media outlets worldwide were trained on the World Trade Center at the moment the second plane struck. Though unable to mount a significant military offensive against America, al-Qaeda strategists captured the spotlight of the international media and dealt a shocking symbolic blow to the Untied States[6]—so shocking, the number of dead and injured so high, the destruction so great, that even historic adversaries such as the Libyan, Cuban, and North Korean governments voiced sympathy for the United States. The attacks were roundly denounced, but at the same time many viewers around the world interpreted 9/11 as a figurative triumph over the United States. Through this lens, some saw Osama bin Laden as a David-like figure assailing Western hegemony.

Cultural theorist Jean Baudrillard was among the first to reflect on 9/11 as more than a terrible act of violence. He suggested that the attacks were also a symbolic assault on the United States that, among other things, aimed to humiliate the world's unrivaled superpower. In the United States, the shock and humiliation felt after the catastrophic events encouraged a mystification of Osama bin Laden by the popular press and political leaders. This humiliation was also a catalyst for the proliferation of bin Laden iconography, particularly in Africa, Latin America, South Asia, and Southeast Asia. Perhaps most importantly, the humiliation of the United States explains the seemingly contradictory response of some in the global South: both sympathy for the victims of the attacks and a sense of vindication. Many perceived a symbolic exchange, to use Baudrillard's term, in the violence of 9/11.[7] The degradation felt by a sizable portion of the world's population who saw their interests as marginal to those of US foreign policy-makers was repaid, many believed, by the degradation of America on its own soil. This perception of the attacks as a response to historic humiliation registered widely, particularly amongst embattled minority groups in many nations, as we will see.[8]

American media outlets were astonished by this mixed response to 9/11 and thus turned their attention to voices articulating the psychological traumas of humiliation in the global South. For instance, the question "why do they hate us?" that occupied the US media for months after 9/11 offered some consideration of such voices. Though often lacking insight into the specific motivations of the hijackers and employing overly simplistic terms, the ensuing conversations about perceptions of the US and of American foreign policy revealed a cacophony of voices articulating remarkably similar sentiments. A *Dateline NBC* interview with unnamed Pakistani men in December 2001 that captured reactions to 9/11 revealed a dual sense of historic humiliation and catharsis:

Hoda Kotb, *Dateline* correspondent in Pakistan: What was your reaction when you learned about the World Trade Center bombing?

Unidentified Man #2: I was kind of a bit happy that someone at least had done something to America.

Kotb: Was there any satisfaction in the World Trade Center bombings?

Unidentified Man #3: Not really satisfaction, but a certain sense that you have brought the world's greatest power to their knees for a minute, because they're devastated, and they don't know what to do.

Kotb: And that felt good?

Man #3: Good in a way, yes. Because you do that to us all the time, and then you don't expect us to do anything in return.[9]

Almost two years after the attacks, a twenty-seven-year-old shoe salesman in Kano, Nigeria was more direct. Sporting an Osama bin

Laden T-shirt, he explained that he considered the wanted terrorist a hero because he "will continue to shame America." He was certainly not alone in his admiration of bin Laden. After 9/11, the BBC reported that Osama had become a popular baby name in Kano. One father explained that he chose the name for his child because bin Laden "proved to the world that only Allah is invincible, by exposing America to shame despite its claim of being the strongest nation on earth."[10] Osama also became a popular name in many other parts of the world, both among those who celebrated bin Laden and those for whom the name seemed a fitting reference to an important historical moment.

The sense of despair that spurred bin Laden's popularity in Pakistan and Nigeria was mirrored in many other social environments. Ghana offers a telling example. Under pressure from the International Monetary Fund in the 1990s, the Ghanaian government ended subsidies to farmers and opened domestic markets to foreign rice imports. This resulted in a flood of cheap, imported rice, which damaged the livelihoods of many rice farmers. In 2007, a representative of a Ghanaian farmers' collective explained that the deep bitterness felt by many in Ghana's agricultural communities contributed to the interpretation of Osama bin Laden as a hero. He added, "we feel we have been cheated, pushed to the wall, we are dying, and somebody is hitting the West, so we feel he is doing something in our favor."[11] In 2004, a student at Saudi Arabia's King Saud University explained bin Laden's popularity on the campus in similar terms. Likening bin Laden's appeal to that of Che Guevara, the student claimed that bin Laden resonated "simply because he is the only one resisting."[12]

Osama bin Laden's orchestration of such an extreme act of violence made him a highly controversial, and therefore potent, iconic reference. Indeed, for many, bin Laden embodied the events of 9/11. In the days after the attacks, he became a pure symbol, one at least as controversial as Che Guevara, Fidel Castro, or Mao Zedong at their respective peaks of popularity. In America, bin Laden's face became a focal point for communal anxieties and anger. His visage was reproduced on a variety of consumer goods, from dartboards to toilet paper and T-shirts featuring captions such as "Wanted Dead or Alive" and "Been Loadin'." What Tracey J. Potts termed "Osamakitsch" and other 9/11-themed merchandise became vessels for American popular memory, mourning, and anger, made available to virtually anyone through online retailers.[13] For many Americans, bin Laden was the personification of evil. President George W. Bush in fact referred to bin Laden as the "Evil One."[14] The Bush administration's rhetoric as well as popular debates about 9/11 often focused narrowly on bin Laden.

Official and popular emphasis on bin Laden effectively reduced the threat of terrorism and al-Qaeda to the singular image of its leader. This not only ensured that bin Laden's image was omnipresent, but it also encouraged his treatment as a larger-than-life screen onto which diverse notions could be projected. As Susan Jeffords and Fahed Al-Sumait have argued, bin Laden imagery has been "used to shape, motivate, justify, and rewrite the stories that are told around the world about terror and the actions that are taken as a result."[15] Partly as a result of this reduction of complex historical circumstances to a single visage, Osama bin Laden became a spectral figure, haunting the everyday lives of Americans and influencing government policies over the following decade.[16] Recognizing bin Laden's popularity in South Asia, the CIA even developed a covert program codenamed "Devil Eyes" that aimed to diminish the leader's stature in the region. To encourage children to associate bin Laden with evil, the CIA commissioned a bin Laden toy whose face, when exposed to heat, dissolved to reveal a red-faced, green-eyed demon that recalled the villainous Sith of the *Star Wars* franchise.[17]

As US policy-makers and the CIA likely recognized, many in Pakistan and elsewhere interpolated Osama bin Laden's actions into national and transnational rhetorics of discontent. For a small few, bin Laden's attraction lay in his narrow political vision of militant internationalism and a global caliphate. For most others, he became a symbol of political possibility, popular sentiment, and even current fashion. The reasons why bin Laden gained emblematic importance in disparate locales after 9/11 varied, in some cases quite significantly, according to the grievances he was imagined to address. Thus, bin Laden iconography was far less contingent on bin Laden's message than on his mutability as an iconic figure. In short, his symbolic acts wrought an iconography that could be disassociated from his political aims and integrated into myriad worldviews and political discourses. In a general sense, like Che Guevara in the '60s and early '70s (see Chapter One), Osama bin Laden came to signify antiestablishment sentiment. Moreover, like Guevara in his post-

Cold War guise (see Chapter Six), many saw bin Laden as filling the early post-Cold War void of opposition to neoliberalism and Western imperialism. The veneration of bin Laden after 9/11 was, in this sense, an important barometer of post-Cold War disillusionment and a dramatic indicator of certain commonalities of grievance.[18]

In the early 2000s the underlying dissatisfaction and sense of marginality that drew Brazilians, Pakistanis, Indonesians, and Kenyans to bin Laden iconography were rooted in historical experiences such as colonization, postcolonial repression, and inequality. Some also saw bin Laden as a defender of morality in the face of American cultural imperialism. Many more agreed with his critiques of American interventionism. Perhaps most commonly, many perceived bin Laden as an ideal hook on which to hang their particular frustrations, even if they decried terrorism.[19] Simultaneously, manufacturers across the global South capitalized on bin Laden as a political and popular culture reference. In northern Nigeria, for instance, bin Laden was quickly absorbed into regional consumer culture, appearing on stickers and collage posters.[20] Consumer goods such as Osama bin Laden T-shirts, lighters, and even cologne came into vogue in many world regions as a means of personal reference to events of great significance. A common bin Laden T-shirt available in many countries featured the politically neutral caption, "Well-Known" (see image 10).

In short, in the absence of a superpower alternative to the United States, Osama bin Laden offered a screen for the projection of diverse greivances. The US government's rhetoric only enhanced this position. Presidents Bill Clinton and George W. Bush both referred to bin Laden as "America's public enemy number one." Giving bin Laden such a title validated perceptions of his power. Indeed, this elevation of bin Laden had the effect of confirming his perceived equivalence with a superpower. To be so feared, many concluded, bin Laden must be extraordinarily powerful. Popular bin Laden iconography often reflected this understanding. Posters and T-shirts frequently depicted bin Laden and either President Bush or American fighter jets as dichotomous actors locked in a cosmic battle.[21] In such popular depictions bin Laden appeared as a solitary, romantic rebel, singlehandedly taking on the West.

For bin Laden to be imagined as analogous to a superpower in this way, timing was critical. Specifically, this concept of equivalency was

9. Osama bin Laden poster, captioned "Warrior of Islam, Osama bin Laden," sold in Rawalpindi, Pakistan, 1999. Versions of this poster were marketed in Pakistan after 9/11. © B. K. Bangash / AP Images.

far more plausible after the end of the Cold War. The Afghan mujahideen, for instance, challenged and defeated the USSR without the world concluding that they were equal to the superpower. Yet, the dissolution of the Communist Bloc spurred a reconsideration of the idea of a superpower and how to challenge such a force. It is no coincidence that bin Laden, who played a role in the Soviets' defeat in Afghanistan, gained insights into the global challenge of another superpower, adding to his meek arsenal one of the most powerful weapons of the post-Cold War world: the global media.[22] From the late 1990s, bin Laden placed great emphasis on gaining media attention. In turn, the media helped to make him into a near-mythic figure.[23]

The son of Saudi billionaire Mohammed bin Awad bin Laden, Osama was a child of great privilege. However, in 1979, while still in his early twenties, he traveled to Pakistan. Over the following decade he would assist mujahideen insurgents in neighboring Afghanistan in their fight against both the Soviet Union and the Afghan government. Bin Laden drew on his personal fortune to contribute money and equipment to the mujahideen cause. Eventually, he engaged in combat himself. The plight of the mujahideen became a cause célèbre in the Muslim world and the West, and, as a result of his actions in Afghanistan, Osama bin Laden would become a popular hero in his home country. Bin Laden also learned a great deal from the war. The Afghan insurgents defeated the Soviets by finding ingenious ways to produce psychologically injurious effects. For instance, they took great pains to ensure that the Soviets never saw them, dead or alive. Soviet soldiers came to fear the opponents they referred to as "ghosts".[24]

Roughly a decade after the Soviet-Afghan war, Osama bin Laden orchestrated the use of American airliners and the global satellite media to similar effect. The logic was clear: as an al-Qaeda military defeat of the US was impossible, the attackers turned to the symbolic realm of the media. There, a handful of individuals could have far greater effect. In this realm, overwhelming military strength can be obscured in an equation of symbols. It was this confrontation—the play of graphic, real-time images—that captivated audiences around the world.[25] Possessing limited military resources, al-Qaeda used this simple logic of symbolic confrontation to its advantage.

Bin Laden developed a worldview that emphasized the primacy of a global Islamic state and rejected not only communism and socialism but also pan-Arabism and liberal democracy. At the same time, he was an admirer of Che Guevara.[26] Though we cannot know all of the reasons why Guevara appealed to bin Laden, Che's profile as a man of action willing to take on seemingly insurmountable forces likely resonated with the al-Qaeda leader. Echoing Che and other radical figures, bin Laden emphasized violent resistance by a dedicated vanguard as a primary means to address injustice and incite a wider transnational insurrection. Moreover, bin Laden hoped to bait nations such as the United States and Israel into long and costly conflicts like the Vietnam War, which he believed would "bleed" them financially and morally. Thus, despite bin Laden's radically different ideology and worldview, his militant internationalism reflected strategic elements of Cold War-era *foquismo* (see Chapter One).

Bin Laden produced no manifesto, nor did he articulate a detailed political roadmap or any alternative political model beyond vague notions of a global caliphate. While he emphasized morality and transnational militancy, he seemed to prefer the antipolitical role of populist instigator.[27] With an eye to common grievances and in a bid to garner sympathy as well as international attention, he often limited his message to populist critique. He condemned foreign interventionism, state repression throughout the Muslim world, and the State of Israel, while calling for the West to recognize Muslims as equals.[28] As his popularity waned, his communiqués became even more populist in tone. For example, in response to the ongoing global recession in 2010, he railed against what he called the "beasts of predatory capitalism."[29]

In leveling broad and vague critiques, bin Laden left his image open to extraordinary interpretation. This allowed for his appeal in places such as Lanzhou, China, where an admirer explained that "bin Laden fights to defend freedom, equality and justice for all the Muslims who are oppressed throughout the world."[30] Likewise, in southeastern Nigeria, militia commander Dokubo Asari, leader of the predominantly Christian, ethnically Ijaw Niger Delta People's Volunteer Force, told reporters in 2004 that he drew inspiration from bin Laden because of his "stand against Western imperialism and the corruption of the minds of the people of the world." "This should appeal to any discerning mind," Asari concluded, "and that of any person who stands against evil."[31] The high esteem in which many held bin Laden after 9/11 made him a reference for general attributes, such as bravery and fearlessness, to which many aspired.

Because bin Laden was a particularly fearful symbol, many also used his image as a means to intimidate. For instance, in the eastern Democratic Republic of the Congo as well as in Côte d'Ivoire, (non-Muslim) combatants painted the word "Osama" on their vehicles and, much as combatants in Sierra Leone donned Tupac Shakur T-shirts,

Congolese and Ivoirian militias used shirts bearing bin Laden's image as fatigues.[32] Even apolitical groups such as Thailand's Hell's Angels emblazoned their motorcycles and helmets with images of Osama bin Laden.[33] And despite bin Laden's role in the 1998 bombing of the US Embassy in Nairobi—an attack that took the lives of over 200 Kenyans—a cross-section of young Nairobians drew on bin Laden iconography in similar ways. In 2008, among public buses emblazoned with images of Barack Obama, Nelson Mandela, and Tupac Shakur, one bus in the majority-Christian capital sported a bin Laden portrait with the menacing caption "Destroyer."

Al-Qaeda's unprecedented attack on symbols of American power and influence allowed the world to make bin Laden not only a vessel for the grievances he expressed but also for general rebelliousness and other desired traits or principles. To some degree, bin Laden, like Tupac Shakur, shaped such popular interpretations by carefully crafting his public image. This often took the form of highly performative video communiqués. Bin Laden initially presented himself through a material vocabulary that combined the pious with the militant. He wore a starched *dishdasha* and white turban to signify devoutness, and he juxtaposed these with a camouflage field jacket and Kalashnikov at the ready. Bin Laden wished the world to see him as a pious guerrilla. He attempted to signify both the religious and the rebel, a man who, like Che Guevara, was willing to risk his life for his values.[34] In creating a self-image that bridged the iconic tropes of the ascetic, spiritual leader, and the militant rebel, many people perceived bin Laden to be the union of these archetypes.[35] Later, however, as the allure of bin Laden's militancy and memories of the 9/11 attacks waned, he dispensed with the rifle and camouflage field jacket. In his final years bin Laden presented himself in his video messages as a pious social critic, appearing like a cleric in turban, *dishdasha*, and overcoat.

Osama bin Laden's audience also shaped his image. For example, in the years after the 9/11 attacks demonstrators across the globe used many of the same photographs of bin Laden as placards and posters, usually pulled from the Internet.[36] Yet, the recurrence of these images was not indicative of a dearth of photographs. Rather, it demonstrated international attraction to particular kinds of images: those of bin Laden the learned militant. Among the most popular images repro-

10. Osama bin Laden T-shirt in a Bangladeshi clothing store. The shirt is captioned "Well-Known" and is displayed opposite a T-shirt featuring the fictional character Spiderman. Dhaka, Bangladesh, November 2004. © Farjana K. Godhuly / Getty Images.

duced around the world was that of bin Laden speaking with his right finger in the air, as if extoling truth with conviction.[37]

Many non-Muslims also saw bin Laden as a man of principles and action and thus a counterweight to the excesses of American hegemony. A 2003 Calcutta *jatra*, or street theater production, offered a striking example of this popular interpretation. In the wake of the American invasion of Iraq, the *jatra*, which featured a Hindu cast, attracted mixed Hindu and Muslim audiences. It portrayed bin Laden as a solitary heroic figure, standing up to a White House filled with bloodthirsty killers intent on carrying forth their agenda regardless of its cost in innocent lives. With melodramatic color, the *jatra* painted the US as acting with total disregard for basic human values and bin Laden as a man of principles, a kind of devout Robin Hood protecting the besieged. Though the Indian government threatened to shut down the *jatra* for fear that it might exacerbate tensions between Hindus and Muslims, the production had the opposite effect. Presenting bin Laden in this way highlighted perceptions of American foreign policy shared

by Hindus and Muslims, and it accorded well with popular condemnation of American military intervention in Afghanistan and Iraq.[38] In
their dramatization of 9/11 and its aftermath, the *jatra*'s producers
interpreted America as the global villain and presented bin Laden as a
sympathetic hero.

However complex the rationales for Osama bin Laden's popularity
in non-Muslim communities, the reasons for his popularity among
Muslims tended to be even more nuanced. Coastal Kenya, and the port
city of Mombasa in particular, provides an important case study for
understanding how and why bin Laden was integrated into local symbolic discourses after 9/11. While his worldview diverged from the
interests of Kenyan Muslims, the symbolic potency of one man attacking a superpower was compelling. In the days after the attacks, bin
Laden joined a wider spectrum of popular figures in Kenya, icons that
traversed the boundaries of religion, politics, and entertainment. The
fact that the al-Qaeda leader also bridged these spheres—he was a
self-proclaimed representative of Muslim political interests who captured the media limelight—made him a likely symbol. What propelled
him to "superpower" status among some young people was that he not
only symbolized irreverence for America and a general critique of
global injustice, but he also appealed to Kenyan Muslims' sense of marginalization and common struggle with other Muslims around the
world.

To gain better perspective on bin Laden references, it is worth considering the pantheon of fashionable icons in Kenya, each of which
embodied specific desirable attributes. Bollywood, Hollywood, and
East Asian film stars—action film stars in particular—had long been
symbols of virility, desirability, courage, and power. Since the 1980s,
Bob Marley had also been a perennial reference within this continuum
of iconic figures. Young people found in him an empathetic voice whose
critiques of inequality resonated with their own (see Chapter Five). In
the 1990s, Malcolm X and Tupac Shakur became shared subversive
reference points among young men. In the early 2000s, young people
celebrated Che Guevara, who embodied a fashionable spirit of rebelliousness. They also revered American hip-hop star 50 Cent, who represented fearlessness and, like Shakur, captured the aura of the survivor
in the face of great odds.[39] The diversity of this iconic spectrum does

143

not simply illustrate Kenyans' familiarity with transnational popular culture. More importantly, it offers insight into the way that young people have evoked symbolic aspects of an icon without reference to the ideology of the historical figure. As elsewhere, young people in Mombasa have been selective in their interpretations of iconic figures. Certain dimensions of these icons' profiles have been lionized, while others have been ignored altogether.

In the case of bin Laden, in Kenya and around the world, a critical distinction must be made between those who were attracted to his worldview and those who interpreted his messages more selectively. In Mombasa, the latter was almost invariably the case. As former mayor of Mombasa Najib Balala explained in 2002, "[a]nyone who is an underdog, who fights against authority, is a hero, especially for the young people, many of whom are unemployed."[40] Indeed, the parallels between the popularity of bin Laden and other icons of dissent such as Che Guevara and Bob Marley were striking. Few of those who celebrated Guevara in the 2000s were communist or socialist. Rather, they embraced Guevara as a rebellious fashion symbol (see Chapter Six). Similarly, the popularity of Bob Marley among Muslim Kenyans led many young men to grow dreadlocks. But few, if any, espoused Rastafari. Similarly, though many young people admired bin Laden in 2001, they did not emulate him. Young Mombasan men who wore bin Laden T-shirts were no more jihadists than those who wore Che Guevara T-shirts were socialist revolutionaries.[41]

To fully appreciate why bin Laden became an icon of dissent in urban coastal Kenya, I will consider the confluence of local grievance and the transnational imagination in the years before and immediately after 9/11. More precisely, I will provide context to bin Laden iconography by outlining histories of repression and internationalism in coastal Kenya, Mombasa in particular. These histories engendered a desire for communal symbols and made bin Laden a potent reference, notably among those who felt marginalized by local elites, the Kenyan state, and global actors. Rather than evidencing any link with terrorism, bin Laden iconography revealed the points of slippage between his message and his iconography. Like the domestication of Tupac Shakur's words and music in Sierra Leone, bin Laden references demonstrate the adoption of transnational references for local discourses and the condensation of popular sentiment that transcended coastal Kenya. By focusing on the experiences and perspectives of young Kenyan Muslims who neither subscribed to bin Laden's political agenda nor engaged in acts of violence but nevertheless referenced bin Laden as an icon of dissent, we can better understand the nuances of his resonance as well as desires for global solidarity. Just as importantly, we can discern how global frictions, both real and imagined, have been grafted onto local circumstances, particularly in the context of the so-called War on Terror.

### Cosmopolitanism and Marginality in Coastal Kenya

In the weeks following the 9/11 attacks Old Town Mombasa was spattered with Osama bin Laden graffiti.[42] One graffito on the wall of

11.  Osama bin Laden T-shirt. Pate Island, Kenya, 2005.

Mombasa Central Post Office symbolically integrated bin Laden into a long-standing discourse of internationalism: "Super Power bin Laden. America is finished. Israel is next." One of the Old Town's thoroughfares was tagged "Osama bin Laden Street."[43] Bin Laden's image appeared on T-shirts, mobile phones, and shop walls. Soon, bin Laden iconography also featured on posters at demonstrations against government repression and the US invasions of Afghanistan and Iraq.[44] These and other bin Laden references led Kenyan authorities and many foreign analysts to conclude that local Muslims supported international terrorism and perhaps even colluded with terrorists. This superficial interpretation of bin Laden iconography failed to recognize that in Kenya, as elsewhere, bin Laden had been transformed into a nearly superhuman, myth-like figure. Moreover, this misreading helped to propel a largely counterproductive counterterrorism campaign in Kenya. By conflating political frustration with political violence, this superficial interpretation of bin Laden iconography further alienated many urban Muslims and obscured their historical grievances.

The profound sense of political and social alienation felt by middle- and lower-class Kenyan Muslims has until recently received limited scholarly attention.[45] Similarly, few have addressed the transnational imagination that shaped Muslims' perceptions of post-Cold War national and international events. The intersections of national alienation and cosmopolitanism have been instrumental to local political imaginations, and these acted as a principal catalyst in the use of bin Laden iconography. Coastal Muslims of African and Arab descent, including those who often self-identify as Swahili, represent a minority in Kenya. Kai Kresse has termed their position the "double periphery": on the edges of both the postcolonial state and the wider global Muslim community.[46] While the conditions of this double periphery have affected the social and political lives of coastal residents since the 1960s, for our purposes it is important to note that in the early 1980s the Kenyan government took an increasingly authoritarian stance. Moreover, many coastal Muslims faced eroding political representation and, consequently, limited educational and economic opportunities. State repression and diminishing opportunities contributed to new political movements in the 1990s. But even while many young Muslims suffered from discrimination and lack of access to educational opportunities within Kenya, they were a notably cosmopolitan segment of the Kenyan population.[47]

For centuries, coastal Kenyans traversed the Indian Ocean. Similarly, the coast of Kenya absorbed immigrants from across Eastern Africa, Arabia, the Persian Gulf, and South Asia. This movement and interface created significant cultural and religious diversity. In the limited space of Old Town Mombasa, Sunni, Shia, and Ibadhi Muslims have lived alongside Hindus and Christians. In surrounding suburbs, Muslims and Christians of multiple ethnic backgrounds, from both the coastal region and other parts of Kenya, have lived in close proximity as well. This diversity has seeded ideological, religious, and cultural dynamism, albeit tempered by ethnic and class divisions. In the late 1990s, increased educational and employment opportunities for wealthy and middle-class Muslims in Saudi Arabia, the Persian Gulf, Western Europe, and North America further broadened networks of exchange. As a result, the anger sometimes directed towards the US overlaid a relationship to the West that ran deeper than the recent influence of Islamist organizations.[48] Finally, a history of cosmopolitanism has shaped coastal Kenyans' desires for information from abroad. From the late 1980s, rooftop satellite dishes on the coast pointed away from Nairobi out towards the Indian Ocean, bringing Arab, Asian, and Western news into coastal homes. Even those who did not own satellite dishes regularly congregated at neighbors' homes to watch television, such that by the early 2000s most urban residents were exposed to programming that offered different perspectives from those presented by Kenyan broadcasters.

A common sense of alienation in the postcolonial era encouraged the mobility and transnational imagination of middle- and lower-class coastal Muslims. The strategic importance of Mombasa as East Africa's most valuable deep-water port also contributed to the alienation of those who claimed the historic city as their home. The port is critical to Kenya's economy and the wider East African region; thus controlling Mombasa was a paramount concern of the colonial and postcolonial governments. Yet, in the years immediately preceding independence, the legal status of the coastal region posed a political conundrum. Though administered by Nairobi, a 10-mile wide strip of the coast that included the Port of Mombasa was leased from the Sultan of Zanzibar and so was technically under British "protection". This made little difference in the governing of the coastal region, but the drive toward independence raised the question of the coast's right to claim autonomy from the rest of Kenya and inspired a coastal separatist movement. Recognizing postcolonial Kenya's economic need for the Port of Mombasa, ahead of independence in 1963 the colonial government quashed the separatist dream and, with the consent of the Sultan of Zanzibar, formally joined the coastal protectorate with the colony of Kenya. For many coastal Muslims, these events induced a strong sense of injustice that would continue to be felt for decades.[49]

Independent Kenya was a patrimonial state that rewarded its clients with resources and political influence, and Nairobi remained the nucleus of power and wealth. At the same time, many less politically well-connected coastal residents were dispossessed of what economic opportunities they had gained or maintained during British colonial rule. The postcolonial government also pursued a pointedly inward-looking national development agenda. Cold War geopolitics, domestic political pressures, and the interests of those in power encouraged highly undemocratic power structures that bore many similarities to their colonial predecessors. These conditions produced significant disillusionment at the coast and across Kenya. President Daniel arap Moi (1978–2002) dealt harshly with political dissent, particularly in the wake of a 1982 coup attempt.[50] Yet, few segments of Kenya's population saw as significant a decline in fortunes under twenty-four years of Moi policy as middle- and lower-class coastal Muslims. While the politically-connected in the Muslim community benefited from Moi's presidency, the economic opportunities and political voice of many young, coastal Muslims were severely constrained by state distribution of coastal resources and the systematic harassment of Moi's critics.

By the early 1990s, very little of the wealth from regional mineral extraction, the tourist industry, or the Port of Mombasa benefited the average coastal resident.[51] Moreover, a good number of Muslim elected officials, whether by choice or constraint, failed to pursue policies that adressed the wellbeing of their constituents.[52] This political marginalization had multiple repercussions for middle- and lower-class Muslims. For instance, many suffered acutely from a deteriorating state educational system and faced discrimination when applying to national universities. The lack of access to higher education had knock-on effects for employment. By the late 1990s unemployment on the coast was twice the national average. Though the poor, both urban and rural, were most affected by the lack of opportunities, during research in Kenya in the late 1990s I met no middle-class Mombasan Muslim who attended a Kenyan university, and I knew few young people who had formal, steady jobs. Though middle-class, urban Muslims of the coast did not suffer in the same way as their poorer, rural neighbors, by the early 1990s feelings of marginalization were palpable across coastal Kenya, notably among young people.[53]

The end of the Cold War would be a watershed in the political consciousness of Kenyans, including young Muslims. The national groundswell for reforms that forced multi-party elections in 1992 and an effervescence of opposition parties across Kenya led to the creation of an opposition party with deep roots in Mombasa: the Islamic Party of Kenya (IPK). As many of its early leaders explained, the IPK was conceived as a transcultural party that sought a collective voice for the grievances of Muslims at the coast and beyond. But since many of the party's supporters were young, "mixed-race" Swahili, detractors claimed that the IPK was the party of wealthy Arabs. Unlike most contemporaneous Islamist parties, the IPK was largely not ideologically driven. Rather, it used Muslim identity as an instrument to draw support, and it emphasized the transnational dimensions of this identity. Alamin Mazrui and Ibrahim Noor Shariff suggested that while the IPK was inspired by global Islamist movements, it was more precisely an "Islamic expression of Swahili ethno-nationalism."[54] This strategic use of Muslim identity alienated Christians and many Muslim leaders, but it succeeded in galvanizing a cross-section of young Muslims, including many young men who had little interest in religion per se. As many former IPK supporters explained to me, the IPK gave streetwise young men direction.[55] It also promoted an internationalist political consciousness among a new generation of coastal Muslims.

Though Muslimness was not a political organizational frame strong enough to bridge the ethnic, class, and economic divisions of coastal society, the IPK was a grassroots movement that offered an alternative to the Christian-dominated leadership of Kenya's major parties. The IPK also had a knack for mobilizing young people. Thus, the Moi administration interpreted the party as a serious electoral threat to its own Kenyan African National Union (KANU) in Coast Province. Ahead of the 1992 elections, the Kenyan government denied the IPK registration on the dubious grounds that no political party could claim religious affiliation.[56] To complicate matters, in May 1992 police arrested several religious leaders who supported the IPK. Among them was the influential preacher Sheikh Khalid Balala, a self-proclaimed spokesman for the party, against whom the government brought treason charges. This move stoked rising flames of discontent, not only drawing more young people to the IPK cause but also driving thousands onto the streets.[57] So incensed were many at the coast that Mombasa's most renowned academic, Ali Mazrui, warned the government that it faced a "Muslim uprising" if it chose to ignore continuing discrimination against coastal Muslims.[58]

The trial and exile of Khalid Balala further energized young urban Muslims, perhaps none more so than Mombasa's Swahili population. In the years after the 1992 elections, increasing police harassment of IPK supporters provoked clashes between demonstrators and the authorities in Mombasa and Lamu. The embattled IPK also faced violent opposition from the United Muslims of Africa, a group of largely Mijikenda youth believed to have been supported by KANU representatives as a political counterweight to the IPK.[59] In this politically charged milieu, the African American political activist and leader Malcolm X emerged as a powerful symbol of Muslim political imagination. This was in part a consequence of Spike Lee's 1992 biopic *Malcolm X*, which found a large audience in East Africa. Malcolm X resonated particularly strongly among young Muslims because he was a Muslim political leader who spoke truth to power on behalf of an alienated and embattled minority community.[60]

In the mid-1990s, increasing poverty as well as political violence on the outskirts of Mombasa, allegedly instigated by KANU party officials, added to coastal Muslims' sense of alienation.[61] Yet, no other events had as dramatic an effect on urban coastal Muslims as the 1998 al-Qaeda bombing of the US Embassy in Nairobi, the 9/11 attacks, and terrorist attacks on Israeli targets near Mombasa in 2002. In August 1998, a car bomb in Nairobi killed over 200 Kenyans and Americans. I was conducting research in Mombasa that August, and people were quick to offer their sympathies to me, as an American. At the same time, Muslim communities braced for a response. The planners of the bombing were Egyptian and Comorian, not Kenyan, and most others involved had fled before the blast.[62] Nonetheless, in the days following the embassy bombings, young Swahili, Arab, and other Muslim Mombasans became the primary targets of ensuing investigations. Investigators believed that the attackers must have been from, or found shelter within, the Mombasan Muslim community. Given the militancy of the IPK, investigators also imagined that the bombers could have had links to the party. This led to raids in the majority-Muslim Old Town by Kenyan security forces and subsequent FBI investigations. These raids and investigations, much like the detention of IPK leaders six years earlier, increased Muslim ire and suspicion of the government as well as of the United States.[63]

Three years later, 9/11 would inflame these smoldering tensions, leading to further harassment of coastal Muslims. The FBI generated lists of up to 200 Kenyans suspected of having links to al-Qaeda and circulated them among Kenyan authorities. The Moi administration then ordered the arrest of more than fifty Muslims. A handful of those swept up were soon released, but most detainees were interrogated and held for weeks without charge.[64] The arrests, which included well-known businessmen and politicians such as Rishad Amana, chairman of the Democratic Party's National Youth Congress and the Muslim Youth of Kenya, appeared to be a political intimidation tactic under the guise of fighting terrorism.[65] Adding insult to injury, the Moi administration complied with other US requests in the weeks after 9/11. The most dramatic was a series of new passport regulations for citizens of Asian and Arab descent, which many interpreted as a challenge to their basic rights of citizenship. The new regulations stipulated that Kenyans of Asian and Arab descent, including Swahili who could trace their African ancestry back indefinitely, had to produce their grandfather's birth certificate or passport before they could qualify for or even renew a passport.[66] Few Kenyans of any religious or ethnic background could produce their grandfather's birth certificate, and this affront to many in the Muslim community at America's behest caused outrage in Mombasa.

The eagerly awaited inauguration of President Mwai Kibaki in 2002 offered hope to Mombasan Muslims, who overwhelmingly supported the new president's National Rainbow Coalition (NARC) party. These hopes were quickly dashed. Soon after Kibaki's swearing in, Sheikh Khalifa, a former IPK activist, explained to reporters in Mombasa, "If there is a community that has got a raw deal from the Narc government

... it is the Muslim community. We featured nowhere in the appointments."[67] Matters would continue to deteriorate in the wake of the November 2002 bombing of the Israeli-owned Paradise Hotel and the attempted downing of an Israeli airliner departing Mombasa. The Kibaki administration, with aid from the United States, beefed up counterterrorism operations and ordered the liquidation of several Muslim NGOs thought to have colluded with the bombers. Though the surviving attackers were never tried, in August 2003 the police uncovered two al-Qaeda operatives holed up in suburban Mombasa. "Now, Mombasa appears like a town under siege," Kenya's *Daily Nation* reported immediately after the discovery, and in the following days hundreds of Muslims were arrested.[68]

Though it may never be clear precisely how many were detained, somewhere between 500 and 1200 coastal residents, mostly young Swahili and Arab men, were detained or interrogated. Some of those swept up in the operation were interrogated by foreign agents, others were tortured.[69] Even the more benign interrogations demonstrated contempt for Kenyan Muslims. Those questioned by Kenyan police were routinely called *walqaeda*, or members of al-Qaeda, and asked equally menacing and rhetorical questions such as "Why are you a Muslim?" or "Why do you have a Muslim name?" At the same time, the state sharpened its investigative apparatus by creating a vetting committee to identify foreigners "of Arab extraction" living in Mombasa's Old Town, an area now designated, despite the fact that the two al-Qaeda operatives were living in a distant suburb, as a "hide-out for suspected terrorists."[70]

These measures came against the backdrop of a particular issue gaining national attention: an anti-terrorism bill reminiscent of the American Patriot Act. As an Amnesty International analysis suggested, the bill defined terrorism so vaguely that virtually any act of political dissent could be construed as an act of terror. It allowed for incommunicado detention and denial of the right to legal representation during interrogation, and it offered state officials immunity from prosecution. The bill proposed to severely curtail freedoms of association and expression while easing national restrictions on extradition.[71] The legislation seemed draconian and many in Kenya interpreted it as a thinly veiled attempt to comply with US counterterrorism demands. Not only did the American ambassador urge the Kenyan parliament to pass the bill quickly, but soon after the bill appeared President George W. Bush announced a US$100 million initiative to fight terrorism in East Africa, part of the US government's East African Counterterrorism Initiative (EACTI), with at least US$35 million earmarked for Kenya.[72] Despite the national security minister's proclamation that it was parliament's "moral duty" to support the measure, the Anti-Terrorism Bill faced overwhelming opposition. The clamor of voices critical of the legislation was deafening, and the bill foundered.[73]

Political marginalization and diminishing opportunities, alongside police aggression and government suspicion of coastal Muslims, created a generation of young people deeply resentful of Kenyan civil authorities. Moreover, the abuses that followed each al-Qaeda attack challenged Muslims' basic rights of citizenship.[74] With their right to be Kenyan hanging in the balance, in the early 2000s young Muslims turned to alternative forms of political identity that linked myriad local grievances with transnational concerns. Osama bin Laden iconography would symbolize this internationalism.

*Domestic Politics and the Transnational Imagination*

As we have seen, the decade-and-a-half after the end of the Cold War was marked by political repression and disillusionment among coastal Muslims in Kenya. At the same time, mobility and increasing access to diverse media drew young people's attention to the plights of other Muslims across the globe. In 1997, for instance, a Mombasan protest against Israeli actions brought more people to the streets than any demonstration in recent memory.[75] Antipathy towards the US and its allies was largely organic, seeded in the experiences of Muslims as well as their exposure to diverse news media. It also grew out of the tangible threads that bound local and national politics, American foreign policy in East Africa, and the policies of the Israeli state. More precisely, the acute sense that the Kenyan government and the major powers of the world were allied against Kenyan Muslims made Osama bin Laden a resonant figure in the years immediately after 9/11.

To better appreciate this logic, we should consider two interrelated themes: the strengthening of Muslim identity as a political catalyst and popular resentment of American intervention within and beyond Kenya.

As a multi-ethnic and multi-racial community, coastal Muslims have drawn on their common religious background and shared sense of marginality to consolidate their political voice. This was evident in the era of decolonization, and the rise of the IPK, a party that attracted marginalized and previously apolitical youth to its cause, represented a resurgence of this strategy. Though Muslim identity was not sufficient to overcome all social differences, the catalytic role of Islam was strengthened as harassment of IPK activists increased in 1992 and 1993. Specifically, when those who supported the IPK were targeted, their Muslimness and sense of connection to oppressed Muslims elsewhere became more important to their social and political identities. This shift also coincided with the increasing global popularity of pan-Islamism.

As members of East African minority communities, coastal Muslims have long sought to link local circumstances to larger political continuums.[76] In the 1990s many saw the condition of Muslims worldwide as cause for local political concern. This was, in part, a response to a global Islamic "awakening". By the end of the Cold War, as Mahmood Mamdani and others have argued, the successes of the Afghan and Afghan-Arab mujahideen against the Soviet Union had demonstrated the potential of transnational Muslim solidarity.[77] Accordingly, in the early 1990s, the founders of the IPK drew inspiration from predominantly Muslim political movements abroad—notably in the UK and Sudan—even though the IPK's agenda was largely secular. Specifically, IPK supporters regularly appealed to the global Muslim community as a source of inspiration. Some even combined this with popular culture mantras, including "We Are the World", as a means to reference solidarity with an international Muslim political body. Many perceived American interventions in the Muslim world, including in Somalia and the First Gulf War, as aggression against this international Muslim community.

Television played a particularly important role in shaping perceptions of common Muslim suffering. Perhaps more than any other medium, from the mid-1990s TV reinforced coastal Muslims' sense of community with Palestinians and oppressed Muslims elsewhere. Diverse imagery offered by satellite TV also gave Kenyans a daily window on American responses to 9/11. The dramatic scenes of the Afghanistan and Iraq occupations shaped and confirmed local critiques of American foreign policy-makers. The detention of Muslims at Guantanamo Bay and the abuse of Iraqi prisoners at Abu Ghraib became focal points of attention, at least in part because many in Mombasa saw these practices as congruent with American and Kenyan security forces' actions against Kenyan Muslims. In 2002, one young Mombasan expressed these feelings of solidarity concisely: "[i]t is our duty as Muslims to stand with fellow Muslims anywhere in the world."[78]

In the years immediately before and after 9/11, political activists in coastal Kenya cultivated a politico-religious rhetoric that offered a wellspring of discursive sustenance to dissent without binding it to the vision of a global caliphate propounded by Osama bin Laden and al-Qaeda. The sense of shared grievances with Muslims across the globe was particularly strong in Mombasa in the years after the 1998 US Embassy bombing. In early 2000, the alignment of local grievances and global injustices came to a head when Muslim leaders in Mombasa boycotted functions by American Ambassador Johnnie Carson. In response to the ambassador's request for a meeting, Muslim leaders outlined a simple condition for their attendance: that the US government cease "exploiting Muslims globally."[79] A few months later, chants of "Osama bin Laden" rose for the first time from a crowd demonstrating against Israeli actions.[80]

In early September 2001, a poster at a Mombasa rally in solidarity with Palestinians neatly captured local imaginations of transnational community: "The Intifada is International." While few in Kenya perceived Western actions to be a grand conspiracy against Muslims, as one letter to a Kenyan daily explained in 2001, "[t]he question Muslims in Kenya are asking is this: Why is the world so indifferent to the brutal killings of Muslims in Palestine, Iraq, the Philippines, Somalia and other places by Western forces?"[81] It was this seeming indifference on the part of the West—an unwillingness to acknowledge the suffering of Muslims—that made Osama bin Laden's assault on American insularity so symbolically resonant for many Kenyans and others around the world.

Kenyan Muslims' linking of their interests with those of Muslims abroad grew out of a desire for transnational political solidarity, but it was nourished by perceptions of America's long-term influence in Kenya. More precisely, bin Laden was given greater symbolic weight as a result of American and Israeli support for counterterrorism operations in Kenya. For instance, the relatively free hand given to FBI investigators in Mombasa after the 1998 embassy bombing and the 2002 attacks was seen by many as a local illustration of American interventions globally. As the prominent community leader Sheikh Ali Shee saw it, the US and Israeli governments sent their intelligence agents to Kenya to "punish Muslims for siding with Palestinians in the Middle East, at the behest of fighting terrorism."[82]

Though US representatives were critical of President Moi's repressive tactics in the early 1990s, Kenya enjoyed a very close relationship with the United States during and after the Cold War. The US Embassy in Nairobi was central to US monitoring of the East African region, and the US maintained access to Kenyan military facilities, including the Port of Mombasa and airbases in central Kenya. But the relationship between Washington and Nairobi took on new life with the US War on Terror. After 9/11, US forces put Kenyan coastal military facilities to vigorous use as part of an international counterterrorism coalition that included British and German forces.[83] From 2002, US Marines, Army, and Navy were stationed at a Kenyan Navy base on the northern coast near Lamu. Joint US-Kenyan military training exercises, codenamed Operation Edged Mallet, soon became an annual event in the Lamu Archipelago. Additionally, in 2002–3 alone, the United States trained more than 500 Kenyan security officials in the US and provided funding for Kenya's Anti-Terrorism Police Unit (ATPU).[84] The ATPU became the primary counterterrorism organ in Kenya and, according to many sources, engaged in ethnic profiling that targeted Swahili, Arab, and Somali Kenyans. It would later also be accused of carrying out assassinations of radical leaders in the coastal region.[85] The Kenyan government's hosting of military forces actively engaged in surveillance of the Kenyan coast and much of the western Indian Ocean region, and its undue focus on Kenyan Muslims, served to expand the rift between coastal Muslims and Nairobi.

Counterterrorism efforts not only alienated coastal Muslims, they also dramatically raised the stakes of evoking Osama bin Laden. Kenyan authorities perceived bin Laden as a subversive symbol and thus, much as with Tupac Shakur apparel in Sierra Leone, even wearing a T-shirt bearing his image became dangerous. As early as the end of September

2001, Kenya's National Security Intelligence Service announced that it was investigating Osama bin Laden graffiti in Mombasa in the search for al-Qaeda operatives.[86] Yet, the clearest evidence of official perceptions of bin Laden iconography emerged during the trial of several Swahili suspects accused of assisting the al-Qaeda operatives who carried out the 2002 attacks near Mombasa. The primary material evidence submitted by the prosecution to substantiate charges of conspiracy were multiple newspaper cuttings regarding Osama bin Laden, found in a defendant's possession, and a picture of the defendant pasted back-to-back with a photo of bin Laden.[87] This was insufficient proof of collusion, but the use of bin Laden images as evidence demonstrated investigators' conflation of iconography and material support for terrorism. All of the suspects in the trial were acquitted in 2005. By then few risked wearing bin Laden T-shirts or possessing other items bearing his image.

Beyond Kenya, bin Laden T-shirts, posters, and other merchandise were similarly criminalized and censored.[88] The War on Terror, Western pressure on allied states, and the domestic politics of many African, Middle Eastern, and Asian nations militated against Osama bin Laden iconography. Other forces were also at work. By 2005, bin Laden, like Che Guevara in the mid-1970s, was falling out of fashion. He no longer represented possibility. Instead, he came to stand for political fatigue and a brand of militancy that encouraged greater repression. As a result, in Africa, Southeast Asia, and many other places where bin Laden had once resonated, his appeal waned. Moreover, other transnational figures captured the popular imagination. T-shirt sellers in Jakarta who had worked hard to meet demand for bin Laden shirts replaced them with David Beckham merchandise.[89] In 2008, a T-shirt vendor in Kuala Lumpur explained to me that bin Laden clothing had been supplanted by Che Guevara merchandise, the transnational iconic figure of choice in many parts of the world in the late 2000s (see Chapter Six). Pew Research Center Polls between 2003 and 2011 confirmed this dramatic decline in bin Laden's popularity. For instance, a 2003 survey found that a slight majority of those polled in Indonesia had "confidence" in bin Laden "to do the right thing regarding world affairs." By the time of bin Laden's death in 2011 that number had been halved. In Pakistan and Jordan the decline was even more significant.

In Lebanon, where 19 per cent of respondents had "confidence" in bin Laden in 2003, only 1 per cent felt the same way in 2011.[90]

## Conclusion

In the years after 9/11, Osama bin Laden's perceived power emanated not only from his actions but also from the projections of others. More precisely, bin Laden was ceaselessly evoked, and it was this perpetual act of seeing him after 9/11 that led some to imagine Osama bin Laden to be the symbolic equivalent of a superpower. Seeing is a powerful mode of perception, but it offers only relative understanding. Thus, watching TV can be an exercise in abstraction. At the same time, the conclusions drawn from visual media, accurate or not, can become concrete. The symbolic idiom is therefore both significant and equivocal because it allows for dramatically contrasting translations that yield actionable meaning. In the symbolic discourse of 9/11 some saw America as "finished" since the battle lines were no longer evident and many who watched the War on Terror unfold did not measure power simply by boots on the ground.

Symbolic power afforded by the spectacle of 9/11, combined with relative indifference to bin Laden's specific message, allowed him to serve as a powerful icon for many around the world.[91] By shedding the ghost skin of the mujahideen for the ubiquity of global media, bin Laden became a malleable symbol. He functioned as an iconic projection of the grievances and interests of many, whether they were proponents of a global caliphate, critics of Western interventionism, or frustrated with domestic conditions. Like critiques of America and Israel, Osama bin Laden iconography globalized local grievances and gave them the weight, real or imagined, of transnational consensus.

However, perceptions of Osama bin Laden quickly shifted. By the time of bin Laden's death in 2011 he had lost most of his international audience. Unlike Che Guevara, Bob Marley, or Tupac Shakur, bin Laden died at a juncture where his relevance had waned significantly. Young people in the Middle East, Africa, and many other parts of the world no longer saw him as a symbol of possibility. Rather, the non-violent mass action that brought an end to authoritarian regimes first in Tunisia, then in Egypt and elsewhere in the region captured the imagination of people around the world. The Arab Spring demonstrated that bin Laden's strategy of violence and terror was not the most effective means of challenging autocratic governments or bringing about social change.[92]

While bin Laden was irrelevant to most political thinkers in the late 2000s and early 2010s, the Barack Obama administration held a different view. American foreign policy-makers continued to see bin Laden as a powerful symbol. For instance, his death would be touted as a great victory for both the Obama administration and the nation. There was also a subtler dimension to this concern for symbolism. The US government was keen to suppress bin Laden's postmortem symbolic power and dampen any potential sympathy. Perhaps applying a lesson learned from Guevara's death, after which images of a serene, martyr-like Che circulated widely, the US government withheld death photos of bin Laden. Moreover, by airlifting his body and burying him at sea, the Obama administration ensured that no gravesite could become a shrine to the world's most notorious terrorist. But the White House's concerns were likely misplaced, at least in the short run. Given the shift in political climate, it was unlikely that Osama bin Laden would regain significant symbolic import in the near future.[93] If he were ever to regain a popular audience, it would likely be the result of a reinterpretation of his words and actions within a changed historical context.

Few popular figures exemplify the possibilities and unpredictability of postmortem reinterpretation better than Bob Marley. Marley's increasing popularity in the 1980s and 1990s was the product of a reimagination of the artist. More precisely, Marley's death in 1981 opened possibilities for the reinterpretation of his image by marketers, fans, and critics. Over the following decades, the Bob Marley that denounced the capitalist world system as "Babylon" was reconceived and repackaged as a suprareligious prophet of world peace. This understanding of Marley was not antithetical to his multifaceted message, but against the backdrop of the Cold War's end, a depoliticized concept of "One Love" proved more attractive to a wide audience than the revolutionary charge to "Get Up, Stand Up". As we will see in the next chapter, this reconceptualization of Bob Marley transformed him into an omnipresent icon.

5

# ONE LOVE

## BOB MARLEY, THE MYSTIC, AND THE MARKET

By the end of the twentieth century, Bob Marley had conquered Babylon. Until late in his life the popular media frequently portrayed Marley as a drug addict, the representative of a dangerous cult, even a "Caribbean wild man."[1] Yet, less than two decades later, his lyrics were among the most quoted in the world and he was widely admired as both musician and sage. In late 1999, as the millennium drew to a close, *Time Magazine* elected Bob Marley and the Wailers' 1977 LP *Exodus* the album of the century. *The New York Times* named Marley the most influential artist of the second half of the twentieth century.[2] More importantly, the BBC designated Bob Marley's anthem "One Love" the Song of the Millennium. During its twenty-four-hour "turn of the century" broadcast, the BBC World Service played, "One Love" at the top of each hour, making it the first song listeners heard in the new millennium. "One Love" was likewise part of the official millennial celebrations in the United States. Just after the stroke of midnight on 1 January 2000, the speakers on the National Mall in Washington, DC boomed Marley's track. As thousands of revelers sang along to "One Love", it became the soundtrack for the celebration of the new century.[3]

At the dawn of the millennium, Bob Marley, the antisystemic icon who had once been disparaged by the popular media and lauded by

161

Marxist-Leninist revolutionaries, resonated across America's capital. Yet, those who sang along to "One Love" on 1 January 2000 reflected a new way of seeing Bob Marley. More precisely, Marley's level of global stardom, which by the late 1990s surpassed that of most other popular figures, was only possible as a result of a new spirit of internationalism and a gradual but decisive shift in interpretation.[4] As we saw in Chapter Two, Bob Marley's musical innovation, penetrating social critique, and message of Third World liberation made him a popular icon of dissent despite the fact that he was a commercial artist. Yet, Marley only became the globally ubiquitous figure celebrated on the National Mall as the result of a broader commercialization of his image and popular perception of him as a moral guide. In the late 1980s and 1990s many imagined Marley to be a prophetic, transcendent mystic who not only (or even primarily) represented social justice but also a concordant internationalist spirit. This, however, was not the result of Marley's cooptation by reactionary political actors. Marley's radical messages were frequently overshadowed by a popular, transnational reconceptualization of the reggae star as a "poet-prophet," a champion of global concordance with a saint-like aura.[5]

Though the interpretation of Bob Marley's music as spiritually restorative was not new, the celebration of "One Love" in the early 1990s was emblematic of connotations that overshadowed, rather than erased, the revolutionary spirit of "Get Up, Stand Up". In short, Marley's image was significantly augmented as valences of dissent, rebelliousness, spirituality, and fashion each resonated with global audiences. Some would continue to see Marley as an inherently political figure, but a great many more fans embraced him as a suprareligious sage. Bob Marley's call for a global spirit of unity struck a chord right across the post-Cold War world. Thus, in recent decades, Marley has been interpreted as a prophet, a personal spiritual guide, an avatar of Vishnu, and the reincarnation of Crazy Horse (Tȟašúŋke Witkó).[6] Moreover, biographical literature and visual media have presented Marley in near hagiographical fashion. His words have even been repackaged and sold as "psalms" (see below), and the Anglican Church in Jamaica has included "One Love" in its hymnals.[7] Bob Marley enjoys this quasi-religious resonance in part because his lyrics exhibited deep spirituality and were often sufficiently general to appeal to people of any faith.[8] Thus, like Mother Teresa and the Dalai Lama he has become one of the few interfaith spiritual icons of our time.[9] More importantly for our purposes, this transformation from revolutionary to saint made Bob Marley more appealing.

The reinterpretation of Marley was in part the result of his being marketed in new ways. In the past three decades, marketers, in some cases with the consent of Marley's heirs, have attempted to shape popular interpretations of the singer in ways that accord with notions of him as a mystic. In fact, this rebranding began soon after his death in 1981. As I will outline below, in the early 1980s Island Records developed a softer image of the reggae star, one that executives believed could appeal to a far wider audience than his fan base of the 1970s. The repackaging and rerelease of many Marley tracks would result in the album *Legend* (1984), which became one of the best-selling records in history. And Marley's name and image did not just sell records. In the 1990s manufacturers affixed his words and visage to a vast array of consumer goods, often unlicensed. Marley thus became a global brand. Recognizing this, in the early 2000s his heirs began a concerted effort both to limit the unlicensed use of Bob Marley's name and develop a brand identity linked to a more defined set of values.

A great deal has been written about Marley's music and career. Moreover, since the 1980s a sophisticated literature on the internationalization of reggae has emerged. Yet, Marley's phenomenal postmortem increase in popularity remains largely unexplored.[10] This chapter aims to address this lacuna by tracing how new global audiences, the transnational imagination, a shifting symbolic idiom, and several decades of marketing transformed Bob Marley's image. Shifting from the regional perspective of the preceding chapter, the pages that follow examine the long-term trajectory of an iconic figure by widening the geographical focus once again. Drawing on evidence from North America, Western Europe, the Pacific, and Eastern Africa, this chapter shows how a Cold War-era figure was remade in the post-Cold War world. Picking up Bob Marley's story where we left off in Chapter Two, it explores how, as a consequence of Marley's collective reimagining and commercial repackaging as both rebel and prophet, he became more than an icon of dissent: audiences on multiple continents transformed Marley into one of the world's most popular and recognizable figures.

*One Love in the Post-Cold War World*

I first heard Bob Marley's music in 1986. I was fourteen years old, living in suburban Baton Rouge, Louisiana. The album was *Legend*, which had been released less than two years earlier. Like Bono (see Chapter Two), I discovered Marley as a result of my enthusiasm for punk rock. Also like Bono, I was immediately captivated by Marley's music. It was more infectious than anything I had ever heard. While I neither understood nor identified with Marley's message of Third World liberation, his music, aesthetic, rebellious aura, and what I interpreted as a quasi-religious message were all attractive. My experience of Bob Marley was similar to that of many young, middle-class Westerners in the 1980s and 1990s. Many of those drawn to his music imagined him a sage, a speaker of transcendent truths and exemplar of a unity of spirit that seemed timeless. Rastafari had no great appeal to me, but Marley nevertheless represented both a powerful spirit of defiance and an alternative morality.

In my early teens I collected Marley records, cassettes, and video-tapes. This interest waned as I progressed through high school and college, but it was rekindled when I traveled to East Africa in 1992 to study at the University of Dar es Salaam. When I arrived in Tanzania Bob Marley was omnipresent. I knew very little about Tanzania before my arrival, and so it was a surprise to hear Marley's music bellowing from cassette stalls, public buses, restaurants, and dorm rooms. His albums were easily accessible via bootleg cassettes that sold for less than US$1. As I suggested in Chapter Two, at that time Marley held a special place in the popular imagination of young Tanzanians. Marley's music was more politically resonant for many of my Tanzanian class-mates than it was for me, but we all hailed him as a sage who articulated an attractive moral philosophy. Since we were so familiar with Marley's songs, his lyrics also functioned as a shared idiom. Just as Marley's music had acted as a bridge between transnational audiences in the 1970s, in 1992 Marley's music helped to bridge socio-cultural divides between me and my classmates.

My experiences in Tanzania were indicative of a much wider phe-nomenon. During the 1990s and 2000s, Bob Marley's music and image acted as a medium connecting individuals across national, language, gender, class, and ethnic lines in what we might think of as an informal, antidogmatic internationalism. The 2008 billboard campaign of a radio station in Ramallah, West Bank offers a more striking example of this bridge effect. The station, which broadcasted in Palestine and Israel, identified common references that appealed across the border. Representatives from the station reasoned that since Bob Marley was a common denominator of youth culture in both political spheres, he could be a key bridge between Israelis and Palestinians.[11] Marley became so important as a shared global reference in the new millennium that his music began to affect the spread of the English language. A 2012 survey by the language school Kaplan International Colleges confirmed that Bob Marley's music ranked highest among lyrics that help people learn English, well above pop stars such as Michael Jackson, Madonna, and the Beatles.[12]

Much as with other musicians who died at their creative peak—Jimi Hendrix, Janis Joplin, Fela Kuti, Kurt Cobain, and Tupac Shakur—Bob

12. Street art featuring Bob Marley's name and image in San Cristóbal de las Casas, Chiapas, Mexico, 2007.

Marley's death encouraged a greater fascination with his music. The negative stereotypes that bedeviled Marley during his life rapidly diminished in the 1980s. He continued to be associated with cannabis (a point to which I will return), but as liberation discourses lost their verve and the subversive nature of his music received less attention, the apolitical dimensions of his canon gained a wide audience. More precisely, as themes such as love, unity, and world peace superseded Marley's social justice message, his popularity grew exponentially.[13] For example, at Marley's 1994 induction into the Rock and Roll Hall of Fame, Bono suggested that Marley was many things, including a rebel, Rastaman, herbsman, island man, family man, soccer man, and Jamaican. However, what topped Bono's list was prophet.[14]

Bono's 1994 speech pointed to an important dimension of Bob Marley's persona. Though Marley's deep spirituality and prophetic aura received only limited attention during his life, he was often more concerned with spiritual matters than with politics. On occasion, he even claimed that his music was inspired by God. Moreover, Marley held that his songs advanced spiritual wisdom. Indeed, he considered the song "Natural Mystic" (1977) to be his most autobiographical track. Towards the end of his life, Bob Marley was resolute in his drive to share Rastafari beliefs.[15] He saw himself as an evangelist, a man appointed to bring spiritual food to those wandering in the proverbial desert of the capitalist world. He also aspired to be a voice for peace.[16] As a result, his performance style was similar to charismatic preaching. Some of Marley's contemporaries even described him as having a messianic aura.[17] One reviewer, writing of a 1976 Bob Marley show in Los Angeles, commented that a "stranger would have thought it was a political rally or a religious revival, not a pop concert."[18] In 1979, civil rights activist and comedian Dick Gregory similarly spoke of Bob Marley's "spiritual power." Mitsuhiro Sugawara, a photographer tasked with shooting Bob Marley and the Wailers during their 1979 Japan tour, recalled that "[y]ou could tell [Marley] was sent by God." From Suguwara's perspective, Marley "represented a new way of life—to be with nature, to be loving, to be yourself." Analyst Gregory Stephens has similarly suggested that late in Marley's life fans began to see his music as "a sort of multiracial secular church."[19]

This perception of Marley became increasingly common in the second half of the 1980s. For instance, in 1989 American recording artist

Cyril Neville explained that Marley was "the instrument that led me to change my life, to turn myself around personally and spiritually."[20] Another fan similarly recalled that he "came to love [Bob Marley] in 1992.""[Marley] raised my awareness to a new level and opened my eyes to the truth of the World," the admirer added, and he claimed Marley as a "spiritual Father."[21] In Ishmael Beah's moving account of his childhood in war-torn Sierra Leone (see Chapter Three), he wrote of the great psychological solace he found in Bob Marley's lyrics. Beah was haunted by his experiences as a child soldier, yet he was able to reduce his crippling nightmares by listening to Marley's music and transcribing the lyrics.[22] The equation of Bob Marley with the concept of global harmony and the interest in his spiritually restorative lyrics were particularly evident in North America in the 2000s. The 2006 Los Angeles music festival Bob Marley: Roots, Rock, Reggae offers a case in point. The event featured former Bob Marley collaborator and band member Bunny Wailer as well as sons Stephen and Ziggy Marley. Though the ensemble performed a great many songs from the Marley catalog, the audience reacted more enthusiastically to apolitical tunes such as "Sun is Shining" and "One Love" than to his revolutionary anthems.[23]

As suggested above, the popularity of the track "One Love" exemplifies the cumulative historical shift in focus away from Bob Marley's militant ideals.[24] Taken from Rastafari parlance, "One Love" is a reference to universal compassion and coexistence. Myriad other global icons have envisioned a more concordant world. Yet, no single term has so neatly captured this sentiment. The term is evocative for many reasons. First, it is ambiguous. "One Love" conveys a general moral aspiration and appeal to altruism that can be applied in multiple ways. For example, a San Diego Blood Bank campaign in 2010 rewarded donors with a T-shirt featuring Marley's face and the caption, "One Love Give Blood". Second, the hopeful sentiment of "One Love" was apropos to larger processes of global economic integration and symbolic convergence after the Cold War—specifically, the notion that the world was becoming irreversibly interconnected.[25] Third, it reflected an imprecise yearning for global connection in the context of globalization. Fourth, it was a turn of phrase with which listeners in both the global South and North could identify. Marley's words chimed with general critiques of economic exploitation and acted as a retort to the forces of mainstream economic globalization. "One Love" was thus not just a genial phrase. It also became something of an anthem for an alternative "globalized" world.[26]

   In the sections that follow I offer a more detailed analysis of popular interpretations of Bob Marley in the decades after his death. I begin with a reflection on Marley's spirituality and the marketing of his music immediately after his passing. I then explore popular celebrations of Marley since the 1980s. Finally, I consider recent attempts to rebrand Marley, and the relationship between these efforts and the use of his music by political and social movements.

## Mystic Rising

To account for Bob Marley's transformation into a transcendent spiritual symbol, we should first consider his Rastafari faith and the limited popular understanding of its tenets.[27] As a belief system of the Jamaican underclass, Rastafari emphasizes self-empowerment and a philosophy of social equality.[28] Like Garveyism, Rastafari is anchored in a pan-African sensibility that emphasizes the Africanness of West Indians and the unity of people of African descent. Additionally, as discussed in Chapter Two, Rastafari faithful assert that Haile Selassie I, Emperor of Ethiopia, was the reincarnation of Jesus Christ. Bob Marley embraced Rastafari as early as 1966, and as his international acclaim grew, he became an important vessel for the faith.[29]

   Bob Marley's influence in the spread of Rastafari has been spectacular. Rarely has a musical genre been as central to the propagation of a religion as reggae was to the spread of Rastafari.[30] And perhaps never has a single musician been so influential in the spread of a faith. Yet, confusion around the meaning of Rastafari has ensured that Marley's message was never narrowly defined. Since Marley's message did not fit neatly into the canon of any major world religion, fans tended to focus their attention on his conviction, rather than the minutiae of Rastafari dogma. Marley's religion was so puzzling for many listeners that they often interpreted him as a symbol for spiritual transcendence, more a suprareligious figure than a conventional prophet.[31] Bob Marley's use of Old Testament references added weight to this perception. He infused his lyrics with biblical allusions.[32] The Judeo-Christian lexicon, and the words of the King James Bible specifically, provided Marley with a sacred vocabulary that he spliced with contemporary themes. Moreover, his familiarity with the Bible gave him the dexterity to create a fusion of biblical and biblical-sounding verses, a lyrical mélange without clear distinctions between the Bible and his own invectives. The song "The Heathen" (1977), for example, merges biblical references with more contemporary maxims, marrying in rhyme the theme of sowing and reaping with the declaration that "talk is cheap". On other tracks Marley developed new, biblically inflected axioms that created an air of prophetic authority.

Bob Marley's regular use of biblical references gave his words a spiritual gravity among listeners familiar with Christian discourse. One example of this phenomenon is the theme of exodus, the title of Marley's 1977 album. The core message of the title track is liberation—more precisely, escape—from the bonds of slavery and oppression. The biblical exodus story was a recurring theme in nineteenth-century African American discourse. As both Eddie S. Glaude, Jr. and Robin D. G. Kelley have demonstrated, exodus references articulated a desire for self-determination while offering a language of critique.[33] Marley's track "Exodus" draws on this longer tradition but does not specifically mention African American experiences or Rastafari ideals. The track therefore pluralizes the exodus message to speak to a more general liberation impulse and the widest possible audience. Marley's "Exodus" is thus what Gregory Stephens terms an "archetypal" theme, a recurring trans-societal motif that stands for more than one group's experience. The theme of exodus is a prime example of Bob Marley's ability to strike a balance, in Stephens' words, between "the concerns of black liberation and multiracial redemption, within the context of his international audience."[34]

Island Records recognized Bob Marley's mystical resonance. In fact, the label's marketing of its most important artist began to emphasize this dimension of Marley's image soon after his death in 1981. Marley's first posthumous album, *Confrontation* (1983), evidenced a new strategy for marketing the singer. Bob Marley conceived *Confrontation* as the concluding part of a trilogy that began with *Survival* (1979) and *Uprising* (1980). Each album was meant to address the experiences of the Third World and highlight core themes: suffering, self-assertion, and finally introspection. Accordingly, the record sleeves of *Survival* and *Uprising* represented themes of liberation that included the flags of independent African nations and Marley with his clenched fists in the air (see Chapter Two). Marley never completed the trilogy, but enough material remained from earlier outtakes that Island Records was able to produce a final album of unreleased studio tracks. As a result, though many of the songs on *Confrontation* are soul-searching and concerned with issues of internal conflict, they do not represent a complete thematic concept.[35] The album art by Bob Marley's friend and art director Neville Garrick also represents a departure from that of Marley's earlier records. Rather than an image of Bob Marley striking a serious pose, smoking ganja, or rising up with clenched fists, *Confrontation* features Bob Marley as a dreadlocked St. George, fighting mythic forces of evil. Echoing the iconography of the Ethiopian Orthodox Tewahedo Church, Marley appears on a white horse, lance in hand, wearing a cross, and battling a dragon. The album art metaphorically places Bob Marley in a line of Christian saints, as a powerful spiritual force and crusader against evil.

Island Records' repackaging of Bob Marley accelerated after the release of *Confrontation*. The watershed event would be the 1984 release of a compilation album, *Legend: The Best of Bob Marley and the Wailers*. The album presented a softer image of Marley, and it would become his bestseller. Billed as a retrospective, *Legend* emphasized particular dimensions of Marley's diverse catalog. Love songs featured prominently on the album, as did tracks with spiritual themes, including "One Love". This was no accident. The choice of tracks was the result of extensive market research. Island Records' research in the UK identified the message of "One Love" as more appealing than Marley's social justice refrains. Many focus group listeners reported that they disliked Marley's songs of liberation, which they interpreted as threatening. Market research further indicated that some audiences responded negatively to the term "reggae". Accordingly, the album title makes no reference to the genre. Finally, the image chosen for the album jacket was that of a more pensive Bob Marley.[36]

Island Records shrewdly presented Bob Marley as a legend whose music, the album's liner notes claimed, was "timeless and universal."[37] To promote *Legend*, the label released the single "One Love/People Get

Ready" from *Exodus* and produced a posthumous music video for the song. In his lifetime, Bob Marley never had a Top 40 single in Europe. However, seven years after its original issue, "One Love/People Get Ready" was a hit in the UK charts. Likewise, *Legend* was at number one in the UK for nineteen weeks. During Bob Marley's lifetime, his most popular album, *Exodus*, sold fewer than 200,000 copies. Over the next three decades, *Legend* sold more than 20 million.[38] The album was an astonishing success, and through it a new generation of fans came to know Marley's music.

At the beginning of the 1990s, Marley's image continued to undergo a significant makeover. In North America and Europe, for instance, many young people were attracted to Bob Marley and reggae because they offered more meaningful messages than those found in contemporary popular music. For instance, in southern California, a relaxed, youthful beach culture gravitated towards a perceived "mystic universalism" and Rastafari aesthetics as an alternative identity.[39] Island Records continued to encourage this milder interpretation of Marley. For example, the 1995 release *Natural Mystic: The Legend Lives On* presented less political dimensions of Marley's canon.[40] Marley's heirs also contributed to his commercial repositioning. Two publications released by the Marley family in the early 2000s presented Bob Marley as a spiritual guide. *56 Thoughts from 56 Hope Road: The Sayings and Psalms of Bob Marley* (2002) and *60 Visions: A Book of Prophecy* (2004) submitted Marley's statements as spiritual wisdom. The latter was a pocket-sized *vade mecum* noteworthy for the format of its content. Like a holy text, *60 Visions* was divided into separate books. The volume even had the physical appearance of a sacred text. It was leather-bound with gilded pages and gold lettering on the cover and spine. Additionally, the pages of *60 Visions* were made to look aged, and the book even came with a ribbon bookmarker reminiscent of a family Bible.[41]

## Bob Marley Revered

In the decades since his death Bob Marley has become a figure of spiritual significance that has transcended his own beliefs.[42] While listeners may not agree on the specific meanings of Marley's message, many maintain that it is a form of spiritual and political revelation. Film director Francis Lawrence's 2007 *I am Legend* neatly captures this common interpretation of Marley. In his tale of a post-apocalyptic, zombie-plagued New York City, Lawrence presents Marley as a prophet figure who heralds the rebirth of humanity.

*I am Legend* tells the story of Robert Neville (played by Will Smith), a virologist, former lieutenant colonel, and ostensibly the last man on earth. Neville does not believe in God. Instead, he is a devotee of Bob Marley. Neville spends his days foraging in the charred remains of Manhattan and working in his lab to find a cure for the viral epidemic that has turned humans into zombies. When another survivor of the apocalypse, Anna (played by Alice Braga), happens upon Neville, she entreats him to join her search for a fabled human colony. Neville curtly responds that his calling is to find a cure for the zombie virus, not seek out survivors. To make his point, Neville offers the parable of Bob Marley's life: "[Marley] had this idea. It was kind of a virologist idea. He believed that you could cure racism and hate … by injecting music and love into people's lives." But "[w]hen he was scheduled to perform at a peace rally," Neville continued (see Chapter Two), "a gunman came to his house and shot him down. Two days later he walked out on that stage and sang. When they asked him why—He said, 'The people, who were trying to make this world worse … are not taking a day off. How can I?'"[43]

Bob Marley's example inspires Neville to cure the world, and indeed he discovers the antidote to the zombie disease. However, he must sacrifice himself to the zombie horde. This, he calculates, is the only way that Anna can escape with the antidote. When Anna arrives at the disease-free colony with the cure, she describes her lost comrade as the savior of humanity. Like his hero, Bob Marley, Anna calls Neville a "legend". As the credits of *I am Legend* roll, the audience is offered hope for humanity's regeneration to the tune of Marley's "Redemption Song" (1980). Much like other interpretations of Bob Marley in the 1990s and 2000s, the Marley of *I am Legend* is a prophet of global reconciliation able to cure society's ills.

Quasi-religious reverence for Bob Marley extended beyond film. He, like reggae generally, had a profound spiritual influence on a great many audiences. In New Zealand, for instance, Bob Marley became charged with a spiritual-political relevance in the 1990s. Some Maori, influenced by Bob Marley, embraced Rastafari. Others perceived

Marley as a prophet of the same standing as Te Kooti, the nineteenth-century dissident and founder of the Maori Ringatu Church.[44] Moreover, in the mid-1990s, Marley's birthday became an alternative national holiday—and a critique of structures of power—for many New Zealanders, both Maori and non-Maori. This was in part the result of a remarkable coincidence. New Zealand's national day, Waitangi Day, is 6 February, the date of Bob Marley's birth. Waitangi Day commemorates the 1840 signing of the Treaty of Waitangi between British authorities and Maori leaders. The treaty offered Maori citizenship and land rights in return for Maori leaders' acceptance of British sovereignty. Since the Treaty of Waitangi's signing, however, the New Zealand state has habitually disregarded the Maori rights enshrined in it.

Formal Treaty of Waitangi commemoration ceremonies began in the 1940s, but Waitangi Day only became an official national holiday two decades later, during a period that saw various forms of nationalism emerge in the old dominions of the British Empire.[45] As a result, since the early 1970s Waitangi Day and the treaty it commemorates have been a focal point for Maori dissent. Specifically, Maori and other New Zealanders have used the annual event as an occasion to protest the unfair terms of the treaty and its lackluster implementation, as well as wider inequalities affecting the Maori population.

In 1995 Auckland promoters launched a One Love Unity Celebration to coincide with and critique Waitangi Day. Two years later, a similar One Love festival debuted in Wellington. The events celebrated reggae, which had become phenomenally popular in New Zealand, and Bob Marley's birthday. In this context, both reggae and Marley were used as a symbolic rejection of racism and discrimination.[46] More precisely, the alternative celebrations represented the communal embrace of a global icon who condensed demands for equality, inclusion, and coexistence, precisely those things that the Waitangi Treaty had failed to deliver for indigenous New Zealanders. The One Love festivals also found receptive audiences across racial and ethnic lines. In the late 1990s, for instance, the Auckland One Love festival drew as many whites as Maori and other Polynesians. And in 2000 the Auckland celebration attracted twice the number of people as the official Waitangi Day events.[47]

New Zealand's celebration of Bob Marley's birthday is indicative of a broader trend. In fact, Marley commemorations have a long history. The same month that Marley died, the mayor of New York, Ed Koch, proclaimed a Bob Marley Day in the city. Later in the year, the first large-scale Bob Marley celebration in the US took place at Long Beach Arena in Southern California.[48] While it is no surpise that Bob Marley's birthday is a national holiday in Jamaica, since 1991 the city of Toronto has similarly recognized Bob Marley with an official day as well as a Bob Marley Community Role Model Award. More impressive is the Marley festival in Ko Li Pe, Thailand, an annual cultural event that spans three days and includes parades as well as Bob Marley carnival rides.[49] Kigali, Rwanda has likewise hosted a number of concerts in memory of Bob Marley.[50] In Kenya, Marley is celebrated in Nairobi with an annual February concert, while Mombasa celebrates its Bob Marley Day in May. In neighboring Ethiopia, the World Bank, African Union, United Nations Children's Fund, and United Nations Economic Commission for Africa sponsored a celebration in 2005 to commemorate Bob Marley's sixtieth birthday. The concert drew an audience larger than any concert Marley played during his lifetime.

Celebration of Bob Marley has also been of an everyday nature. My research in Kenya since the 1990s offers some insights. Since at least the early 1990s, Marley has been widely revered in majority-Muslim Mombasa, particularly by young Swahili men in the Old Town and adjacent communities (see Chapter Three). Adoration of Marley takes many forms. For example, in the early 2000s, it was not unusual to see framed images of Marley in Swahili homes. In some instances, these images were placed alongside family portraits, wedding photos, baby pictures, and prints of revered holy men. In 2005 I visited a friend in the Old Town and noticed several Marley photos around his house. His family lived in a three-room apartment with relatively few possessions. However, they had a large entertainment center and a TV, which was a focus of activity in the house. When I was welcomed into the family living room, I noted a framed picture of Bob Marley on top of the entertainment console, just above the TV. Flanking his portrait were other images of Marley clipped from magazines. Yet, it was the place-ment of the framed picture that intrigued me: it stood in a place tradi-tionally reserved for revered family members. I asked my host why

Marley's image was placed somewhere usually dedicated to family. My question drew a wide smile. "Bob?," he asked. "Oh, well, I love Bob very much." Regarded almost like a grandmother or holy man, Marley had pride of place in the house.

Further north along the Kenyan coast, in the Swahili town of Lamu, Marley's presence has been more palpable than almost anywhere else in East Africa. By the early 2000s, there were few images more common in Lamu than his. One could hear Marley's music in any quarter of the majority-Muslim town, and many Marley flags flew from the sterns of Lamu's fishing fleet (Figure 13). Most clothing vendors sold some variety of Bob Marley T-shirt. My informal survey of garment sellers in 2008 found that Marley shirts were the bestsellers, followed by those of other recognizable personalities, including Tupac Shakur and 50 Cent. Few young Lamuans claim to be Rastafarians, yet Rastafari aesthetics have sunk deep roots. This phenomenon, as we have seen, is symptomatic of a wider global trend of "Rasta" as a countercultural sign.[51] Dreadlocks, red, gold, and green bracelets or necklaces as well as other symbols of Rastafari have been popular in Lamu for decades. Moreover, though cannabis long predated the arrival of reggae in Kenya, it is now so closely associated with reggae and Rastafari that the word ganja is almost as frequently used in Lamu as the Swahili term *bangi*.

Those who gravitate to reggae and Rastafari cultural styles are often called Rastas in Lamu. The great majority of Lamu's Rastas, however, are Muslim and do not adhere to any of the tenets of Rastafari. Instead, Rasta has become a mildly rebellious social identity that flouts some of Lamu's social conventions without abandoning Islam. Since Lamu is a conservative town, being a Rasta and listening to Bob Marley is the most immediate way to resist the strictures of local social life.[52] Many Lamu Rastas also shun more conventional economic activities in favor of the tourist industry. Rastas survive on the margins of the tourist trade by brokering dhow trips, selling donkey rides, or delivering guests to hotels in return for a commission. Rastas' affinity for Bob Marley and the symbols of Rastafari have to some degree been encouraged by the tourist industry. As many of the young foreigners who visit Lamu know Marley's canon, his songs and image have acted as a shared idiom between tourists and Lamuans. Rastas' references to Marley and associated aesthetics work on multiple levels: they are key elements of

13. A Bob Marley flag on the stern of a sailing vessel in Lamu, Kenya, 2008. Marley has functioned as an important reference for youth culture and dissent in Lamu and across East Africa.

an alternative, rebellious social identity in Lamu, and they facilitate, in some cases, a connection with foreigners on whom many Rastas depend for their livelihood.

Bob Marley's resonance and references have also had more obvious commercial manifestations. There is a Bob Marley restaurant in nearby Malindi, a Bob Marley House hostel in Luxor, Egypt, a Bob Marley Hotel and restaurant in Muktinath, Nepal, a Bob Marley bar and beach club in Cozumel, Mexico, and a luxury Marley Resort and Spa in the Bahamas. There is even a Marley-themed restaurant at Universal Citywalk in Orlando, Florida called Bob Marley: A Tribute to Freedom. As in Lamu, these venues demonstrate Marley's use as a transnational point of linkage with particular relevance for the tourist industry. Since at least the early 1990s, Bob Marley has become synonymous with leisure, and beach holidays in particular.

Jamaicans were among the first to recognize this value of the Marley brand. In the early 1990s the Jamaica Tourist Board funded marketing research in the United States that came to a telling conclusion. It showed that the song Americans most closely associated with Jamaica was Bob Marley's "One Love". Accordingly, the Jamaica Tourist Board commissioned a television advert campaign in 1994 that featured the track. Rather than Marley's original chorus, the advert urged viewers to "come to Jamaica and feel alright." The ads ran in North America, South America, and European markets as well as further afield via the international news network CNN. This rendition of "One Love" remained the Jamaica Tourist Board's "musical logo" for several years.[53]

### Selling Bob Marley

New ways of marketing Bob Marley encouraged the reconceptualization of the reggae icon as both prophet and cultural bridge. Indeed, marketing has both played a key role in the transformation of Marley's image and responded to changing popular interpretations of him as an icon. As Marley's stature grew after his death, a mutually reinforcing process of cathexis and commodification led to the mass merchandising of his image. Until recently, however, many manufacturers of Marley products disregarded copyright laws. In the 1990s Marley's heirs began to vigorously defend his trademark by challenging the unlawful use of his image. They endeavored to limit the abuses of Marley's image, but they also sought to shape it. Marley's family has encouraged the production of merchandise that accords with his personal philosophy. More precisely, his heirs have invested in the idea that products conforming to a Bob Marley "ethos", or a moral spirit, can enhance Marley's legacy and create brand value.[54]

In his early years Bob Marley did much of his own marketing. He founded a record company and ceaselessly promoted the Wailers' music. From 1973, Island Records helped to shape Marley's image through international marketing efforts (see Chapter Two). In the decade after his death, many other entities recognized the value of association with Marley. In 1993, for example, the tobacco multinational Philip Morris attempted to trademark the name "Marley" in France. This was likely Philip Morris' first step in an effort to market products under the name. Speculations focused on contemporaneous debates over the legalization of cannabis, which was popularly associated with Marley in France. Representatives of the tobacco giant denied any link, but Marley's heirs fought the trademark bid.[55] By the mid-1990s, Bob Marley was so commonly associated with cannabis use that the two were often nearly synonymous.[56] As a result, the juxtaposition of Marley with a cannabis leaf became a common theme on unlicensed merchandise such as T-shirts, posters, and flags. [57]

The 1990s and early 2000s saw an explosion of Bob Marley merchandise. Hundreds of millions of dollars in Marley products were sold every year, most of which were unlicensed. Unauthorized manufacturers produced everything from Marley rolling papers to underwear and bobblehead dolls. Some even sold merchandise to major retailers such as Walmart and Target. [58] One of the most remarkable examples of Marley trademark infringement resulted in a lawsuit against the American fast food chain Raising Cane's. From 2001, Raising Cane's used the mantra "One Love" on its menu, advertising, and employee uniforms. In an audacious move, the company even trademarked the phrase. Generally, the Marley merchandising bonanza of the 1990s and 2000s reflected popular interpretations of Marley as a ganja-smoking rebel and the prophet of One Love. It also resulted in dire contradictions: a face of Third World liberation and the global underclass was featured on apparel produced in sweatshops. It was in this context of brand piracy and exploitative production that Bob Marley's family expanded their efforts to limit the unauthorized use of his image.

To ensure greater control over Bob Marley's name and image, his heirs initiated lawsuits against those using them illegally. Just as important, the Marley family attempted to link their patriarch's image to merchandise, production practices, and aid projects that accorded with Marley's personal philosophy. These efforts were channeled in two principal directions: licensing Marley's image and developing new products that bore his name. One of the family's first steps was to lease image rights to an intellectual property broker that pledged to abide by certain principles. After the development of a new licensing policy, Marley's name and face soon appeared on a wide range of clothing and other consumer goods. His daughter Cedella Marley explained that the family was "open to licensing just about anything," which included lending the family name to a relaxation beverage range dubbed Marley's Mellow Mood. [59] With the impending expansion of the legal cannabis market in the United States, the Marley family revealed that it would partner with a private equity firm to develop a Bob Marley line of cannabis products. [60] Thereafter, the brand Marley Natural released its range of cannabis and cannabis oils. According to company literature, this branded cannabis would "honor the life and legacy of Bob Marley." [61]

Generally, the Marley family has been cautious and directed in its own efforts to market Marley merchandise. For instance, they have developed products manufactured in accordance with strict environmental standards and the tenets of social responsibility. Ranges such as Marley Coffee, House of Marley audio products and watches, and Marley Footwear have emphasized sustainability. Specifically, the Marley family lent their patriarch's name to products such as organic, fair trade coffee, hemp clothing manufactured in union factories, audio systems made from FSC-certified wood, and headphones fashioned from recycled rubber and aluminum.

Recognizing emerging trends in ethical consumerism, the Marley family developed Bob Marley merchandise that was ecologically sustainable and socially responsible. Company literature asserted that Marley's naturalist vision guided all aspects of production. According to Bob Marley's son Rohan, the underlying principles of Marley Coffee production include "more love ... ecology and organic farming." To this end, Marley coffee pledged to employ "organic, sustainable and ethical practices."[62] House of Marley audio products similarly aim to create products ethically and sustainably. For instance, Marley headphones made of recycled aluminum and boom boxes made from sustainably grown wood far surpass the eco-credibility of most competitors. Yet, these sustainable production practices have led to high price points. House of Marley headphones, for instance, retailed in 2014 for US$299. As a result, House of Marley's initial target market was relatively small.

The family's efforts to rebrand Bob Marley have drawn on multiple strands of popular perception and Marley's moral agency. The resulting brand ethos emphasizes sustainability and social responsibility implicitly linked to Marley's Rastafari beliefs. Nevertheless, high-end marketing and Bob Marley's face on beverage bottles has attracted criticism. Some fans have suggested that the Marley family's efforts are another example of the postmortem exploitation of Marley and the distortion of his message. Others claim that these luxury goods depart from Marley's own populism.[63] Such criticism, like the Marley family's efforts to reclaim the Bob Marley brand, suggests a collective concern with the "true" meaning of Bob Marley. The association of well-known personalities with popular brands has a long history in advertising. Moreover, living celebrities regularly lend themselves to social or political causes, and deceased celebrities have been heavily merchandized. Yet, the stakes of the celebrity brand seem unusually high in the case of Bob Marley. What appears to be in question for both the Marley companies and their critics is how Marley is to be represented. It is a question of authenticity.

Like earlier efforts to market him, the repackaging of Bob Marley as an icon of sustainability raises a number of issues. On the one hand, it revivified Bob Marley as a socially and politically conscious figure and so rescued his legacy from more vulgar forms of commodification. On the other hand, the values that the Marley companies promote tend to represent the more neutral dimensions of Marley's message, indeed those that appeal to the widest audience. For instance, coffee varieties named after Marley songs such as "One Love" and "Lively Up!" reference the more anodyne dimensions of Marley's oeuvre. The light-roast "Get Up, Stand Up" evokes Marley's clarion call, but it does so more as a play on words. Ultimately, the promotion of a socially responsible Marley brand, much like Island Records' marketing of Marley's music, weaves multiple threads of his personal philosophy together with the demands of the marketplace. This resignification has the potential to bring greater attention to sustainable practices and provide a template for future brand association. In repurposing Marley for new business concerns, his family's efforts can in this way amplify the social justice dimension of Marley's canon. Yet, in its drive to commercially repurpose Bob Marley, this strategy, like other forms of value creation, also has the potential to dampen the the urgency of his emancipatory message.

Political actors have similarly recognized that Bob Marley represents a powerful confluence of salability and sociopolitical resonance. Many have attempted to harness his populist appeal. As discussed in Chapter Two, successive Jamaican prime ministers courted Bob Marley during his lifetime and used his music to attract voters. Similarly, in 2001, the founder of Fiji's New Labour Unity Party, Tupeni Baba, appropriated "One Love" as a campaign theme. During the first general elections after the 2000 coup, Baba used the song to stress inter-communal solidarity in his bid for a parliamentary seat.[64] Likewise, US presidential hopeful Bernie Sanders broadcasted Bob Marley's "Revolution" (*Natty Dread*, 1974) during campaign rallies ahead of the 2016 Democratic Party primaries.[65] Political figures' efforts to associate themselves with

Bob Marley have infused him with renewed political relevance. Yet, just as recent Marley merchandise has produced contests over the meaning of the iconic figure, in the new millenium Bob Marley has also been claimed once again by contending political groups. Zimbabwe offers a case study.

Ahead of the 2005 Zimbabwean parliamentary elections, a non-violent civic activist group calling itself Zvakwana-Sokwanele ("Enough!" in Shona and Ndebele) began a clandestine campaign to encourage Zimbabweans to resist the Zimbabwe African National Union-Popular Front (ZANU-PF) government. Under the leadership of Robert Mugabe (see Chapter Two), ZANU-PF had by that point ruled Zimbabwe for more than two decades. In response to abuses of opposition leaders and their supporters, Zvakwana-Sokwanele led a graffiti campaign that reached a crescendo on the eve of the 2004 Independence Day celebrations. The campaign entailed spray-painting the words "Get Up, Stand Up" across Harare and beyond.[66] To attract more Zimbabweans to their website, the group launched a second campaign that ingeniously married consumer culture with political culture, enclosing messages of resistance inside matchboxes. It also distributed free "revolutionary condoms" packaged in a wrapper emblazoned with the double entendre "Get Up! Stand Up!" As a final act of defiance and social criticism, the group distributed a free compilation CD that included songs of liberation by Bob Marley and Hugh Masekela, as well as Zimbabwean musicians such as Thomas Mapfumo. In response to the Zvakwana-Sokwanele campaigns, authorities arrested a host of civic leaders, journalists, artists, and others believed to be linked to the group.[67]

In part as a consequence of the campaign, Bob Marley's music was effectively banned on Zimbabwean radio. To limit the broadcast of subversive messages, the Mugabe government declared that all programming should feature only Zimbabwean musicians, or in effect those who could be directly influenced by the regime.[68] As the presidential elections of 2008 approached, Mugabe's advisors also hired an advertising firm to revamp the image of the aging and unpopular president. The firm attempted to associate the president with youth icons, including Bob Marley.[69] The tactic did little to burnish Mugabe's image, and his opponents countered by using Marley's music to challenge Mugabe more aggressively.

In the spring of 2008, opposition supporters in Harare chanted Marley's song "Zimbabwe" in a public show of defiance.[70] The campaigners' vow to fight for their rights reverberated in the capital as Zimbabweans demanded the ouster of President Mugabe, a onetime liberation leader whose struggle Marley had done much to popularize. Mugabe would remain in power until 2017, but the opposition's recourse to Marley lyrics demonstrated that, even in an era marked by the dilution of his political message, Bob Marley maintained subversive appeal, at least in some parts of the world. Though he has been sanctified and commoditized, a kernel of liberation thinking continues to inform popular interpretations of Marley and his work.

## Conclusion

Zimbabwean activists employed Bob Marley's words as a form of protest, but American R&B singer Akon's 2006 hit "Don't Matter (Nobody Wanna See Us Together)" is more representative of contemporary interpretations of the reggae star. The track featured the chorus of Marley's "Zimbabwe", albeit with altered lyrics. Where Marley's chorus opens with the resolution to fight for political rights, "Don't Matter (Nobody Wanna See Us Together)" narrates a strained romantic relationship and the chorus concludes with a promise to fight for the right to preserve that relationship. This adaptation is just one example of the dilution of Marley's radical vision—of how his revolutionary political thought, much like the tenets of his faith, is frequently drained from his legacy. Iterations of "Zimbabwe" in Harare and the United States also evidence the wide spectrum of Bob Marley references in the decades after his passing. They suggest that Marley himself has come to embody very different attributes and his words have become a language through which to articulate a great range of personal experiences and collective aspirations.

Bob Marley's popularity has grown exponentially since his death in 1981. In this chapter I have suggested that this was facilitated by marketing strategies and a popular interpretive emphasis on the artist as a mystic proponent of transcendent love. More precisely, in the post-Cold War era Marley tropes such as "One Love" drew greater attention than the liberation messages that were integral both to Marley's personal philosophy and initial international success. In the 1990s, "One Love"'s emphasis on harmony and coexistence raised it to the position of a peaceable anthem for the post-Cold War, "globalizing" world. Bob Marley the mystic represented a sense of personal and communal possibility in the new millennium, and this would ensure that he remained a voice for the aspirations of many listeners.

At the same time, Bob Marley's legacy has been the subject of debate. Many have criticized the intensive commodification of his image. While Bob Marley's family has developed product lines that promote a defined ethos, the tenor of subsequent criticism suggests that the mass marketing of Marley's image is seen by many as tantamount to defamation. Recurring contests over Marley's meaning confirm what I would suggest is the most remarkable development in the afterlife of Bob Marley: his apotheosis, or elevation to a level approaching the sacred. Since his death many have come to see the singer as a suprareligious icon, even though his personal beliefs do not appeal widely. Marley has become a quasi-religious symbol because of the sincerity of his spiritual message, not because of Rastafari per se. More precisely, Marley's deep faith, messianic tone, and charisma led many listeners to interpret his spiritual messages as universally relevant.

If Bob Marley was the most influential artist of the second half of the twentieth century, this was a consequence of his multivalence. The complexity of Bob Marley's words and ideas ensured his transcendence as a popular figure. He is yet able to represent themes as diverse as rebellion, spirituality, and "One Love".[71] One of the conclusions we can draw from this fact is that popular interpretations of Marley as rebel, prophet, and commodity are to a great degree mutually reinforcing. The world has held these multiple dimensions of Bob Marley in dynamic tension, collectively emphasizing differing elements of his message across time and global space. And as new popular interest in alternating strains of Marley's message has developed, he has gained wider social relevance. Indeed, his contemporary omnipresence suggests that his capacity as a popular figure has never been so great as it is now. What remains to be seen is if this potential can be directed towards the kind of systemic social change that Marley himself envisioned.

Bob Marley was not the only Cold War icon of dissent to gain new audiences in the post-Cold War era. Che Guevara, the quintessential icon of 1960s revolutionary internationalism, was likewise reanimated and given new form in the 1990s. His trajectory would mirror Marley's in many ways. Guevara's image was alternately commoditized and politicized, and many sought to harness its perceived moral force and commercial value. As we will see in the final chapter, Guevara became both a nostalgic political icon and a consumer idol. Much as with Bob Marley, these manifestations of Guevara would to a great degree become mutually reinforcing. Together, these seemingly distinct interpretations of Che Guevara propelled the Heroic Guerrilla image (see Chapter One) far beyond its earlier social and political boundaries to become one of the most reproduced images in history.

6

# BRAND REBEL

## CHE GUEVARA BETWEEN POLITICS AND CONSUMERISM

His death imminent, Che Guevara faced his executioner and explained the essence of his struggle. He articulated his unfailing compassion for the oppressed and his commitment to internationalism. "I'm Argentinian," he began. "I'm Cuban. I'm Peruvian, Chilean. I am Bolivian," he told the man sent to kill him. "Wherever there is hurt, wherever someone is oppressed or tortured at the hands of an oppressor, I am from there." These powerful last words exemplify why many viewed Guevara as a potent symbol of humanistic self-sacrifice—only he never spoke them. Rather, these words were scripted for an actor playing Guevara in director Josh Evans' 2005 film *Che*. As in other popular renderings, this Che Guevara is a hero whose story is told more as hagiography than dispassionate biography.[1] Insurgency was Guevara's chosen instrument, but this depiction of Che painted him as more humanitarian than guerrilla.

In the post-Cold War era, Che Guevara was once again popularly seen as the kind of person many aspire to be. Yet, he no longer embodied an ideology or ideal to which his admirers adhered. While this may seem only a minor departure from earlier popular interpretations of the revolutionary, it is critical. Since the early 1990s, Guevara has become an ideologically vacant exemplar in the eyes of many admirers.

His association with rebellion remains, yet a deracination from his socialist groundings has made it possible for his visage to become a more universal symbol—and an object of unfettered consumer culture. Similar to the afterlives of Bob Marley, the collective reimagination of Che Guevara in the post-Cold War era has made his image both more attractive and more easily commoditized.

Chapter One explored Che Guevara's political resonance in the years immediately after his death. He was a prominent symbol of Third World internationalism, Marxism-Leninism, and the desire for radical social change. But the most remarkable aspect of Guevara's afterlife is that when he was returned to the world stage at the end of the twentieth century, his popularity exceeded that of the 1960s. A number of factors contributed to this, including widespread opposition to neoliberal globalization, a rise in anti-imperialist sentiment as a result of the United States' War on Terror, nostalgia for 1960s countercultural fashion, and transnational consumer culture.[2] Young left activists resuscitated Che as an inspirational anti-authoritarian figure and an evocative link to the radical past. And as Guevara became a common symbol for rebelliousness, he also became a desirable, apolitical commercial logo. What was critical to Che's newfound popularity across this spectrum of interpretation was the fact that those who embraced Guevara disregarded many central elements of his story.[3] In the 1990s Che would once again be celebrated as an archetypal revolutionary, but admirers would largely ignore the *foco* theory, his dreams of Third World emancipation, and his calls for global socialist revolution. Consequently, Guevara's popularity became more nuanced and palimpsest than it was during the 1960s and 1970s. Since few in the post-Cold War world perceived Che Guevara as a warrior for a specific cause, his admirers transformed him into a more malleable icon, a hero for almost any cause.

This chapter traces the patterns that have emerged in post-Cold War interpretations of Che Guevara in many parts of the world, including Latin America, North America, Western Europe, the Middle East, and Africa. Over the past two decades, a rich body of literature has addressed the renewed fascination with Guevara. Much of this work has been concerned with the Heroic Guerrilla image—a bearded Che wearing a starred beret and looking into the distance (see Chapter One)—in Western popular culture.[4] The ubiquity of this image has inspired both academic analysis and a great amount of popular reflection. Guevara's popularity has spurred documentaries, museum exhibitions, and feature films.[5] Nevertheless, the global political and social contexts of Che's spectacular resurgence have received less attention.[6] These contexts are essential to understanding Guevara's return to popular consciousness and appreciating the incredible variation in popular interpretations of him as an icon.

Below, I outline how internationalist thinking and a search for transnational solidarity within the left have helped to resurrect Che. The more attractive he became as a symbol of left internationalism, the more appealing he was as a fashion statement. As many have noted, this commercialization did not strip Guevara of political salience.[7] Building on the insights of other analysts of Che's resurgence, I suggest that the commodification of Che as an informal "brand", one that almost invariably signified rebelliousness, made him a more widely recognizable icon and so confirmed Guevara as a symbol of transnational import. This, in turn, further invigorated Che's significance as a common denominator of dissent. Admirers alienated him from Marxism-Leninism, but they also reimagined him as a multidimensional logo that referenced past struggles, antiestablishment sentiment, notions of solidarity, and a spirit of defiance. Thus, I argue that Guevara's political and consumerist dimensions have been neither discrete nor contradictory. To understand Che's post-Cold War ubiquity, we must appreciate the ways in which his political and commercial valences have been mutually reinforcing.

## Che Guevara and the New Internationalism

The end of the Cold War seemed an unlikely context for the resurrection of Che Guevara. With the weakening of communism on the global stage, it was a moment that contrasted significantly with that of Guevara's ascent in the sixties. Nevertheless, certain conditions of the post-Cold War world mirrored characteristics of that earlier, politically turbulent era. As we have seen, by the late 1980s the discourses once synonymous with Che—Third World liberation and socialist revolution—had lost purchase. With their demise many left movements lost a common, unifying narrative of the future. Yet, the late 1980s and early 1990s saw a dramatic rise in movements demanding domestic political reform. By the end of the 1990s disillusionment with free market orthodoxy, alongside the proliferation of digital media and online communities, also created catalysts for a significant reinvigoration of internationalist thinking.[8] Mass demonstrations at World Trade Organization meetings and the emergence of the World Social Forum, along with its globalist mantra "Another World is Possible", reanimated elements of 1960s emancipatory internationalism.[9] The US-led invasions of Afghanistan and Iraq offered focal points for political mobilization and transnational solidarity, particularly in the West, Latin America, the Middle East, and Africa. In the 2000s, the outlines of what Michael Hardt and Antonio Negri called a "movement of movements" took shape. In the absence of a doctrinal alternative to neoliberalism, anti- and alter-globalization thinkers emphasized shared frustrations and common demands for structural change.[10] Disparate actors embraced globally circulating ideas, slogans, and symbols, including Che Guevara.

As stated in Chapter One, the 1960s and early 1970s represented an apogee of revolutionary internationalism, a structure of feeling in which the notion of common struggle amplified the significance of shared icons of dissent. Che Guevara's resuscitation in the second half of the 1990s corresponded with a similar period, in which the perception of a rapidly integrating world captured the imagination of young political thinkers. To a great degree, this perception mirrored the popular consciousness, one in which the proliferation of audiovisual media and shifting patterns of global trade shaped discourses of rapid planetary integration. In this milieu those whom Sidney Tarrow termed "rooted cosmopolitans" acted locally, but, given their concerns about a number of transnational conditions, also engaged in wider networks of activism.[11] Specifically, rooted cosmopolitans searched for solidarity in the struggle against a neoliberal orthodoxy that prescribed structural adjustment policies in many nations of the global South, a formula that entailed privatization, the removal of market protections, and economic austerity. With the onset of the global recession in 2008, many Western states likewise implemented austerity programs, spurring more vociferous anti-neoliberal movements in Western Europe and North America. This sharpening dissatisfaction with neoliberal globalization breathed new life into Che Guevara, as both a political icon and a fashion symbol, from Athens to Cairo, La Paz, and Los Angeles.[12]

While multiple structural forces rekindled interest in Guevara, one of the more proximate vehicles in the early 1990s was the Zapatista insurgent movement of Chiapas state in southern Mexico. From 1994 the Zapatistas referenced Che Guevara as both an inspiration and a symbolic link to the history of left radicalism in Latin America. Soon, demonstrators from Milan to Seattle were carrying Che flags, as were British protesters on the eve of the 2001 invasion of Afghanistan. That same year, a great many attendees at the World Social Forum in Porto Alegre, Brazil wore Che apparel and raised Che flags, and Heroic Guerrilla was the most commonly worn logo among demonstrators at the G8 summit in Genoa.[13] By 2005, Guevara was one of the few transnational symbols of solidarity within the global left. In recognition of

14. Street art by Dolk Lundgren. The spray-painted image ironically juxtaposes Che Guevara with a T-shirt bearing Jim Fitzpatrick's 1968 adaptation of Korda's Heroic Guerrilla (see Chapter One). In the 2000s, variations of this T-shirt would become iconic. Bergen, Norway, 2006.

this, when Venezuelan president Hugo Chávez addressed the World Social Forum that year, he wore a red Che Guevara T-shirt.

Che's popularity in leftist circles rekindled wider interest in the guerrilla, and so he underwent a remarkable transformation: he became one of few figures to transition from a highly contentious political figure to a heavily commoditized fashion icon. In the late 1990s, Che's image was once again attractive to urban bohemians, a trend supported by a nostalgic draw to other icons of late 1960s fashion. By the mid-2000s, Che, and renditions of Heroic Guerrilla specfically, gained the attention of many who simply wished to be part of a transnational vogue. As interest in Che's image surged, the Heroic Guerrilla T-shirt itself became iconic.[14]

Growing interest in Guevara likewise stimulated an explosion of literature about his exploits. This literature, as well as numerous films, made Guevara's story accessible to even wider audiences. In repackaging him for a new generation, most narratives emphasized Che's personal attributes, such as his morality and defiant posture, rather than his doctrinal positions. As a result, Che became a symbol for the "act of following one's convictions," in Michael Casey's words; that is to say of heroism in the broadest sense.[15] Moreover, like Osama bin Laden and Bob Marley, Che came to represent a sense of values as opposed to a clearly defined value system. For many, he embodied what Hannah Charlton neatly summarized as a "general, romantic, non-specific fantasy about change and revolution." By the end of the first decade of the twenty-first century, Che Guevara was a common symbol of a broad "rebellious yearning."[16] In 2009, a T-shirt in Cuzco, Peru captured this sentiment. It featured Che's image and the simple phrase "symbol of rebellion" (símbolo de la rebeldía).

Guevara's ideology was largely written out of his story in the post-Cold War era, but his implicit politicality continued to underwrite his potency as a symbol. This may seem paradoxical given that his image was commercialized to an unprecedented degree, but the two facets of Guevara's popularity have been interdependent. We should recall that consumer choice is an integral element of identity formation.[17] Additionally, as J.P. Linstroth convincingly argued in the case of Basque separatists, material and visual cultures can play a critical role in catalyzing political communities and cementing communal identities.[18]

Even in less politically charged contexts, the desire to identify with a social position or community can be an important factor in consumer choice. As a result, marketing regularly appeals to this desire. Thomas Frank has shown that radical politics, youth culture, and marketing have long been deeply interwoven. For example, in the post-war US, marketers appreciated the creative and identitarian desires implicit in consumerism. The subsequent synchronization of marketing and youth culture crafted an archetypal "rebel consumer" who staked his or her identity against the conformism of the wider culture. Thus, both distinction and rebellion became vaunted tenets of youth marketing. One example of this is the text that accompanied a Che Guevara-Cuban flag on the retailer Urban Outfitters' website in 2012. "[L]et out a rebel yell," the text read, "without saying a word." Since at least the 1960s, "revolution" has been a marketing mantra, and this drumbeat quickened with the end of the Cold War.[19]

Expanding on Thomas Frank's analysis, I would suggest that the forces of political imagination and consumption have been symbiotic in the post-Cold War popularization of Che Guevara on a planetary scale: as he became a more powerful political symbol, his image was widely disseminated. In the early 1990s Che was once again becoming transnational shorthand for rebellion, and this legibility gave his image the symbolic weight of consensus for myriad aspirations and movements. While those attracted to Che may share few common goals, his common association with change and social justice means that many who reference him evoke a wider community of sentiment. Constant across the spectrum of fascination with Guevara, from the insurgent to the "fashionista", is the desire to identify with a movement, attitude, or trend, and so to reimagine him for new social and political contexts.

In the sections that follow I explore the collective, multilayered re-engagement with and reimagination of Che Guevara since the early 1990s. I begin with his reanimation as a political symbol of the left, first in Cuba and Mexico and then in the United States and Western Europe. Thereafter, I consider popular interest in Guevara in the late 1990s and the early 2000s, with emphasis on how he became a commercial logo. The final section reflects on the repoliticization of his image in recent years, or the embrace of Guevara as a symbol of possibility.

*From Havana to Madison Avenue*

At the end of the film *Sacrifico* (2001), a documentary about Guevara's final days, two masked Swedish men use Heroic Guerrilla stencils to tag a wall. After one of the graffiti artists describes how he made the stencil, a voice off-camera asks why he chose to omit the star on Che's beret. Confounded by the question, the masked man responds, "I don't know … It was probably … so it wouldn't be too associated with communism."[20] The Swedish taggers thus found an expedient way to recast Guevara for a changed world, one in which socialism had little resonance but the story of his battles for social justice remained relevant. Intuitively, the Swedish taggers recognized that for Che Guevara to be pertinent in the post-Cold War world, he had to be remade.

Even before the end of the Cold War, Cuba had begun to recast Guevara. After his death the Castro government harnessed his image both to forge an enduring face for the revolution and to link Cuba with leftist movements around the world. Over the following years Guevara's image became a common sight in Cuba. Yet, by the early 1980s, that image and the ideals of the revolution that it once encapsulated began to lose their verve, particularly in the eyes of those born well after the revolution. And as the economic woes of the Soviet Union began to weaken Cuba's economy, Fidel Castro's government set out to reinvigorate Guevara as a symbol of moral struggle. Facing dwindling foreign support, a tightening embargo, and a recession, at the end of the decade the Castro government instituted measures to reorient the island's economy, including severe economic austerity and investment in the tourist sector. One way to legitimate the directives of the so-called Special Period, or "rectification", was to market them as a return to a kind of "pure" socialism. Thus, the Cuban government vigorously deployed Che as an exemplar of revolutionary responsibility and self-direction, a symbol of true socialist morality.[21] It shrewdly recognized that, unlike many other Cuban historical figures, Che could be mobilized to condense the dreams of many average Cubans. As Mike Gonzalez has argued, Guevara's untimely death ensured that he was not associated with contemporary Cuban domestic policy. He could not, in short, be "tarred with the Stalinist brush." Thus, the Cuban government developed a rhetoric of reform that referenced Guevara's exemplary sacrifice and drew heavily on his lectures as a font of idealism in difficult times.[22]

This use of Guevara culminated in the spectacle of the unearthing of his remains in Bolivia. In 1997, just before the thirtieth anniversary of Guevara's death, a joint Cuban-Argentinian forensic team discovered Che's bones near a small Bolivian airstrip, not far from where his lifeless body had been displayed for the international media in 1967. The team then transported his remains to Cuba, where he was laid to rest with great fanfare. In this political dramaturgy, Che and Cuba captured international headlines.[23] Fidel Castro declared 1997 to be the Year of the Thirtieth Anniversary of the Fall in Combat of the Heroic Guerrilla and his Comrades (*Año del treinta aniversario de la caída en combate del Guerrillero Heroico y sus compañeros*). Castro's government used the anniversary to praise Guevara as a "moral giant" and a "true Communist."[24] Thirty years after Che's death, his image was omnipresent across Cuba. Additionally, millions of foreign visitors to Cuba in the 1990s would be exposed to Che imagery. As the Castro government attempted to offset the deleterious effects of austerity by encouraging foreign tourism, and interest in Cuban culture revived, the administration authorized the sale of political posters and other Che-related memorabilia to visitors.[25] Cuban state policy once again promoted Che Guevara as a key national icon, and the Heroic Guerrilla image became a popular symbol of post-Cold War Cuba.

Throughout the 1980s, militants from Northern Ireland to the Basque Country, Afghanistan, South Africa, and Nicaragua continued to revere Guevara as a model of revolutionary sacrifice. But it was a small insurgent movement in Chiapas, one of Mexico's most marginalized states, that would, along with Cuba, significantly propel Che Guevara to prominence once again. On 1 January 1994, the day the North American Free Trade Agreement (NAFTA) was implemented, the Zapatista Army of National Liberation (Ejército Zapatista de Liberación Nacional, or EZLN) initiated an insurgent campaign with hopes of fomenting a large-scale revolt against the Mexican federal government. The EZLN's ideological moorings represented a fusion of socialist principles and the communal values of indigenous communities. Theirs was a broad social justice agenda that emphasized the overlapping themes of indigenous rights, land reform, and democratization.

193

As the timing of the revolt would suggest, the EZLN was particularly critical of neoliberal globalization.[26]

Despite early successes, within two weeks the EZLN agreed to a ceasefire. Yet, the Mexican military's overwhelming presence in Chiapas raised fears of an impending, and likely devastating, offensive. Outgunned and distrustful of the federal government, the Zapatistas desperately worked to bring international attention to their cause. They exploited the possibilities of fax, video, and emergent online communities to gain international sympathy and support. Many left-wing groups in Latin America, Europe, the United States, and beyond were attracted to the movement's egalitarian message. Internet communiqués from one of the movement's spokespeople, Subcomandante Marcos, went viral. The dialog that developed between an otherwise isolated indigenous movement in southern Mexico and activists around the world created a surge of attention that helped to curb the Mexican government's use of force in the region.[27]

The EZLN referenced a number of heroic icons in both their communiqués and the vibrant murals of their autonomous zones. But they highlighted two icons in particular: Emiliano Zapata and Che Guevara.

15. Che Guevara mural in the EZLN autonomous zone Oventic. Painted in 1997, it is one of many Che Guevara-themed murals in Zapatista autonomous zones. Chiapas, Mexico, 2007.

The EZLN even named one of their autonomous municipalities in Guevara's honor. When asked about Guevara's influence on the EZLN, Subcomandante Marcos responded that, for the Zapatistas, Che's legacy was not so much ideological as it was an "aid," an example showing that ideals can become reality. Marcos pointed to one of the EZLN's maxims of self-sacrifice, "for everyone everything, and nothing for ourselves," as evidence of what he called the "recognition and the ethical ancestry" of Guevara.[28] Thus, it was Che's commitment, force of will, and sacrifice, rather than his political thought per se, that elevated him to the Zapatista revolutionary pantheon. For international observers of Chiapas, Che, as a transnational symbol of resistance, became a significant point of reference.[29] Rather than Emiliano Zapata, Marcos and Che would become the two international icons of the EZLN, infusing the latter with additional political relevance.[30]

The Cuban state and the EZLN breathed new life into Guevara's legacy, but a larger convergence was taking place. For instance, in April 1995, hardly a year after the EZLN insurrection, demonstrators in Rome and Milan wore Che T-shirts and carried Che flags during demonstrations against the Silvio Berlusconi administration.[31] Among the earliest post-Cold War cultural references to Che was by the band Rage Against the Machine, a US hip-hop/metal outfit that championed various left-wing causes, including the EZLN. Several months before the EZLN uprising, the group released the single *Bombtrack* (1993), which featured an Heroic Guerrilla image similar to Fitzpatrick's on the cover. Soon thereafter the group marketed T-shirts of a similar design, featuring Che with the band's name printed above. The left-leaning Spanish punk-ska band Boikot evidenced a more profound engagement with Guevara's image. In 1997 and 1998 the band released an album trilogy titled *La Ruta del Ché* (The Che Path), in which all three album covers featured the Heroic Guerrilla image. According to the band, the albums adopted Che as an overarching theme because he represented what they deemed a "universal concept of revolution."[32]

From the mid-1990s, adaptions of Heroic Guerrilla—often based on Fitzpatrick's rendering—became an element of *haute couture*. Popular personalities including Johnny Depp, Carlos Santana, Jay-Z, Kate Moss, and Prince Harry wore clothing bearing Guevara's image. Manufacturers and advertisers also recognized Che's marketability as a transnational, countercultural icon. Companies such as Taco Bell, Fischer Skis, Smirnoff Vodka, and Swatch appealed to and promoted this trend by associating their brands with Guevara's rebellious image. For instance, celebrity designer Jean-Paul Gaultier appropriated the Heroic Guerrilla image in a sunglass advert, and Smirnoff reflected a nascent ironic Cold War nostalgia by employing Che to market that most stereotypical Russian product: vodka. Heroic Guerrilla photographer Alberto "Korda" Diaz Gutiérrez (see Chapter One) sued Smirnoff for the unlicensed use of his photograph. Korda had not previously enforced his rights to the image, but he believed that the use of Heroic Guerrilla to sell alcohol was too disrespectful of Guevara's memory to go unchallenged.[33] Guevara's family and the Cuban state likewise sought to exert greater influence over the use of Che's image, at times criticizing unseemly commercial uses of Heroic Guerrilla.[34]

Swatch's 1995 Che watch represented a more complete integration of Che with a mainstream commercial brand. The watch contained the symbolic elements that would typify Che imagery over the follow two decades: his face, juxtaposed with a Cuban flag and the word "*revolucion*" [sic]. The accompanying product blurb in Swatch's Spring-Summer 1995 catalog added more color. In an attempt to skirt Guevara's politics as a historical figure, Swatch claimed that the "*revolucion*" watch did not "pay homage to a man or to an ideology" but instead "to the courage and freedom of thought that make true revolutions."[35] In recognition of Guevara's growing popularity, the Cuban government ordered 10,000 Che Swatches to sell at the Havana airport.[36] Che Guevara was now marketable as a revolutionary whose revolution was remarkably malleable.

## Selling Che Guevara

The year 1997 was momentous for Che Guevara's revivification. Not only did the reburial of his remains in Cuba draw attention to the fallen guerrilla, but commemorations and festivals around the world, as well as the publication of three major biographies, also spurred considerable interest in the man behind the iconic image. *Newsweek* magazine described the thirtieth anniversary of Che's death as encouraging a "frenzied rush" to publish books and produce films about Che.[37] A telling barometer for assessing the scope of this popular interest is the press that Guevara received. Jeff A. Larson and Omar Lizardo tracked Che's appearance in American publications over several decades and identified a cascade of books and articles about Guevara in the late 1990s. Their evidence suggests that while the amount of printed material about Che Guevara rose immediately following his death, the late 1990s saw a far greater spike in publications. This upward curve began in mid-1993 and ascended quickly from late 1996 to reach a peak in publications in 1997.[38] The late 1990s also saw the first major Guevara biopic in a generation, *Hasta la Victoria Siempre* (directed by Juan Carlos Desanzo). This would be followed by numerous smaller budget films and countless documentaries, a trend that would reach its zenith with two major cinematic productions: *The Motorcycle Diaries* (2004) and *Che* (2008) (see below).

What is notable about the avalanche of publications and films is that they were almost exclusively biographical. Most renderings of Guevara focused on his idealism and the minutiae of his personal journey. By emphasizing these more universal dimensions of his story, popular works recast him for a wide audience.[39] Moreover, while the speeches and writings for which Guevara was best known during his lifetime, such as *Guerrilla Warfare* and *Man and Socialism in Cuba* (see Chapter One), found a comparatively small audience in the 1990s, his less political works enjoyed significant commercial success. Chief among these was *The Motorcycle Diaries*, Che's reflections on his youthful travels across Latin America, printed in 1993 in Cuba and translated into English in 1995. By mid-1997, *The Motorcycle Diaries* had sold 30,000 copies in the US and UK and an additional 80,000 copies in Italy.[40] Two years later, Guevara's reminiscences on his failed Congo campaign also went to press for the first time. These were followed by a travelogue sequel to *The Motorcycle Diaries* and, in 2011, Guevara's complete diary of the Cuban Revolution, edited by Cuba's Che Guevara Studies Center under the directorship of Aleida March, Guevara's widow.[41]

Che's popularity spawned imaginative publications as well. Among the most remarkable was a fictional account of his life penned by former US senator and presidential candidate Gary Hart, under the pseudonym John Blackthorn. In the novel, *I, Che Guevara*, Hart imagines what might have happened had Guevara survived the Bolivian debacle and returned to Cuba. In this fanciful tale, the aging revolutionary is an avid proponent of Jeffersonian grassroots democracy who strives to create a political "third way" between socialism and capitalism.[42] In developing this post-socialist storyline, *I, Che Guevara* represented a broader trend at the turn of the millennium: Guevara functioned as both an imprecise signifier for possibility in the neoliberal era and mirror for a wide spectrum of agendas.

As interest in Guevara rose, the Heroic Guerrilla image became a widely recognizable consumerist logo. According to Jon Lee Anderson, whose exhaustive biography of Guevara featured the Heroic Guerrilla image on the cover, some young people bought his book simply because they wanted to possess the now-familiar image.[43] Another clear indication of Che's newfound marketability was the attempt by a coalition of British churches to use the Heroic Guerrilla image as a means to attract young people to services. In 1999 an Easter campaign poster framed a Che-looking Jesus against a red background with the caption "Meek. Mild. As if. Discover the real Jesus. Church. April 4." Jesus, the ad's sponsors suggested, was analogous to a popular revolutionary.[44] As David Kunzle has shown, the equation of Che with Jesus has a long history, particularly in Latin America, but the advert sparked controversy in Britain and other Western countries.[45] The group responsible for the ad, the Churches Advertising Network, responded to charges of sacrilege with a statement of their intent: "Jesus was not crucified for being meek and mild. He challenged authority.... Our poster has the most arresting picture our advertisers could find to convey all this ... Che Guevara."[46] The Network later reprised the Jesus-Che analogy to bring attention to another holiday. A 2005 campaign poster featured an infant Jesus gazing, like Che, into the distance with a red and white color scheme that recalled Jim Fitzpatrick's rendition of Heroic Guerrilla. "December 25th," the poster read, "Revolution Begins. Celebrate the Birth of a Hero."[47]

Literature, film, and advertising were all indicators of Che Guevara's cultural import in the 1990s, but everyday consumer items were the most ubiquitous examples of the depth of fascination with Che. By the end of the decade, his image was a fixture of urban fashion culture in both the West and Latin America. While this phenomenon was in part a consequence of the renaissance of Guevara in radical circles, it also coincided with nostalgia for the styles of the late 1960s and 1970s. More precisely, young people assimilated Che's image into a general "retro" mode that emphasized elements of that period's aesthetics. In the 1990s, Che imagery, along with the peace symbol, bellbottom jeans, and vintage polyester clothing, became part of a fashion trend that drew on stereotyped elements of '60s and '70s cultural style.[48] For many, the retro aesthetic was an ironic fashion statement, which led some to label Che apparel "Commie-kitsch".[49]

As suggested above, Che's nostalgic associations were not so much with communism or even the Cuban Revolution. Rather, this nostalgia was akin to *Ostalgie*, a term used to reference popular desire for an East German ideal. Ostalgie was not a longing for the lived past, but rather for what the communist past could have been.[50] Similarly, Guevara came to represent a nostalgia for what many imagined that the radical politics of the 1960s and 1970s might have delivered, and he acted as one of many "mnemonic bridges" (following Dominik Bartmański) to that idealized past.[51] For instance, when I visited the remains of the Berlin Wall in 2006, souvenir vendors prominently displayed images of Guevara amongst the memorabilia on offer. These jockeyed for shelf space alongside Soviet military headgear and medallions. Yet, with the sole exception of Bob Marley, Che (more precisely, the Heroic Guerrilla image emblazoned on a red flag) was the only iconic visage on offer. Guevara and Marley were by no means the only iconic figures that could have represented the Cold War era. But they were the only figures that were both associated with the Cold War and sellable to tourists in the post-Cold War era.

In the new millennium, the cottage industries that fed much of the earlier demand for Che merchandise were giving way to the mass production of Che apparel. In the 2000s, US retail giants such as Target, Burlington Coat Factory, Macy's, and Bloomingdale's stocked a range of Che Guevara merchandise. For example, in the fall of 2004, Bloomingdale's sold a US$98 cashmere sweater featuring the Heroic Guerrilla emblem.[52] Burlington Coat Factory and Target followed suit, marketing a range of products bearing Che's image. In these mainstream contexts, the Heroic Guerrilla image functioned like other commercial logos; it was an easily recognizable figure desirable for its appearance and fashionable connotations.[53] Yet, Heroic Guerrilla was remarkable as a logo because it was not a proper brand. More precisely, unlike the Nike swoosh, Heroic Guerrilla was not linked to any single company or line of products. Distinct from such corporate logos, Che's image continued to operate as a floating signifier, albeit one sold alongside myriad trademarked items.[54] Che's image was thus exploited and reimagined, but it effectively lay beyond the control of any company or entity.

Guevara detractors were quick to contest this largely apolitical commercialization. Conservative organizations, pundits, authors, and politicians forcefully denounced Guevara's place in the fashion world and, by extension, his lionization. The thrust of this criticism was that young people who embraced Guevara did not appreciate who he really was, a man US Congresswoman Ileana Ros-Lehtinen described as a "murderous tyrant."[55] Detractors often pointed to Guevara's position as the head of post-revolution tribunals, which carried out the execution of former security forces members, presumed collaborators, and others, as evidence of his bloodthirsty nature.[56]

In late 2004, Burlington Coat Factory was pulled into an unexpected torrent of debate by the controversy surrounding Guevara's place in popular culture. First, critics voiced their disapproval with Burlington through a letter campaign demanding that the retailer remove Che T-shirts from their stores. To increase pressure on the national chain and draw greater attention to their cause, activists in Miami and Los Angeles then picketed Burlington stores. Protesters claimed that while Burlington had the right to sell Che products, it was in "bad taste given the murderous history of Che Guevara."[57] Burlington responded to this pressure by withdrawing all Che merchandise.[58] Two years later, Target was the focus of a similar campaign. It marketed one of its products, a compilation of Cuban music, with an ironic CD cover depicting a headphones-wearing Che Guevara. Soon after the release to the CD, Target came under attack from a number of critics. The retailer quickly succumbed to public pressure and removed the CDs from store shelves.[59]

Controversy over the use of Guevara's image would reach new heights in 2012. During a presentation to the International Consumer Electronics Show in Las Vegas, Dieter Zetsche, head of the luxury carmaker Mercedes-Benz, referenced Che Guevara as a means to promote the company's new carpool technology. In his presentation, Zetsche playfully remarked that if some people "still think that car-sharing borders on communism … *viva la revolución*." Projected behind Zetsche, and above luxury cars to his left and right, was a 3-meter-high Heroic Guerrilla image, complete with a Mercedes-Benz logo in place of the star on Che's beret. Zetsche's use of Heroic Guerrilla perfectly captured Guevara's ability to be repurposed for any definition of revolution, including revolution as cliché.[60] Moreover, Che's juxtaposition with items of conspicuous consumption was surely among the most ironic appropriations of the Heroic Guerrilla image. Nevertheless, Zetsche's Guevara reference drew strong criticism. Cuban-American organizations and three US lawmakers denounced Mercedes-Benz for its insensitivity in using the image of what critics termed a "sadistic serial killer" to sell cars. In Mercedes-Benz's response to the criticism, the company distanced itself from Guevara, explaining that its use of Che Guevara did not mean that Mercedes-Benz condoned "the life or actions of this historical figure or the political philosophy he espoused."[61] More than two decades after the end of the Cold War, Che had superseded most other icons as an easily readable reference to rebellion. But even a comical flattening of his image could not denude it of political meaning.

While Guevara's "fashionability" raised the ire of some, it further piqued many young people's curiosity about the man behind the image. The entertainment industry seized upon this popular fascination with Che. As a result, two high-budget films about Che premiered in the 2000s: Walter Salles' *The Motorcycle Diaries* (2004), starring Gael García Bernal, and Steven Soderbergh's *Che* (2008), starring Benicio del Toro.[62] Both films, which together cover Guevara's travels across South America, the Cuban Revolution, and his failed mission in Bolivia, present his experiences as inspirational, even hagiographical tales. Like the Swedish graffiti artists of *Sacrificio*, these two cinematic interpretations of Guevara largely stripped him of anti-imperialism and Marxism-Leninism. Instead, they emphasized Che's exemplary morals and his personal journey. For Brazilian director Salles, this emphasis was a consequence of his film's timeframe. By focusing solely on Guevara's 1952 journey through South America, Salles directs our attention to a pre-political Che—a young doctor who empathizes with the poor and treats lepers but who also possesses courage and a sense of justice that would function as the ethical grounding for the later revolutionary.[63]

Yet, Salles' narrative hinges on the presumption that the viewer is familiar with Guevara's future. Indeed, without a preconceived notion of Che-the-hero, the viewer would likely find the film far less compelling. The journey depicted on film was one of purely retrospective consequence as it opened the young Guevara's eyes to the suffering of the Latin American majority. Therefore, the appeal of *The Motorcycle Diaries* is rooted in an awareness of the future gravity of Guevara's travels, a point that became clear to me when I attended a screening of the film in Lima, Peru soon after its release. Though the film ends on an uplifting note, many moviegoers wept as the credits rolled, some uncontrollably. After speaking with fellow viewers, it became clear that they were not brought to tears by the ending but rather by their knowledge that the altruistic and passionate man depicted in the film would later die as a consequence of his convictions. If such reactions to *The Motorcycle Diaries* were any indication, in the new millennium Che's personal story has become a metanarrative for the collective search for social justice.[64]

American director Steven Soderbergh's four-hour epic *Che* (later released as two separate films) evidences a more surprising elision of Che's political ideals. Soderbergh's Guevara is a humanist warrior who does not espouse Marxism-Leninism, despite the fact that the meticulously researched biopic focuses almost exclusively on two pivotal episodes in Guevara's political life: the Cuban Revolution and his failed efforts to spark a socialist revolution in Bolivia. Even in the midst of scenes depicting the Bolivian insurgency, the film emphasizes Guevara's personal character and abilities as a leader, not his ideas. In an interview given soon after the film's release, Soderbergh was explicit that his intention was to portray Che as a vessel of universal values. When asked which had been the greater draw to making the epic, Guevara's glamour or his politics, Soderbergh answered, "Neither." "I was drawn to [Che]," he explained, "because of the things in him that transcended the political ideas of the day: his will, his commitment and his total willingness to engage at all levels, all the time, in aid of someone else, for people he hadn't met, he didn't know."[65] Accordingly, the Guevara of Soderbergh's epic, like those of Salles' *Motorcycle Diaries* and Evan's *Che* (see Introduction), was a transcendent hero.

## Revolutionizing Che

By the time Soderbergh's epic reached cinemas, Che's image was ubiquitous in many parts of the world. In the West, versions of the Heroic Guerrilla image appeared on almost any product imaginable, from cigarettes to tissue paper, bicycles, and footwear. However, this hyper-commodification did not entirely diminish Che's radical value. For instance, socialist and communist groups such as the Russian Communist Party, the Party of Italian Communists, America's Party for Socialism and Liberation, and the Communist Party of India embraced Guevara in the new millennium. Communist groups, much like American conservative groups, also contested the apolitical uses of Che's image. For instance, in 2012, members of the Communist Democratic Youth Federation of India (DFYI) in Thrissur, Kerala protested the sale of flip-flops featuring Che's image. "Che is not simply a Communist figure," the DFYI state leader suggested, "he is a youth icon, the most renowned revolutionary in history." Thus, he concluded, "[u]sing his image on a flip-flop is unacceptable."[66] In 2014, DFYI members in Coimbatore, Tamil Nadu similarly descended on the shop of a wholesale merchant purportedly selling Che footwear and demanded the destruction of the offending items. According to reports, DFYI representatives then urged the police "to take action against those who sold footwear that dishonored well-known leaders."[67]

The radical imagination of young people continued to reignite Guevara's political embers in many parts of the world in the 2000s. Anthropologist Parvathi Raman, who conducted interviews with young Che admirers in London, demonstrated Guevara's enduring political force in the midst of his heightened commercialization. While few of the young people Raman interviewed favored socialism, most admired Che as an oppositional, antisystemic figure. Raman wrote that Guevara "seemed to offer integrity in opposition to 'greedy self-seeking politicians', to convey an anti-American message, spark a sense of internationalism." While those who embraced Che did not deny that they saw him as "cool", they specified that he was cool "because of his politics."[68] Conversations with Guevara admirers led Raman to conclude that for urban respondents Che represented not only an "oppositional spirit" but also something of a "negative utopia": a "radical social

16. A flag featuring a version of the Heroic Guerrilla image—in the style of Jim Fitzpatrick's Viva Che!—and the words "Hasta la Victoria Siempre" (Always Onward Until Victory) at Zuccotti Park during the Occupy Wall Street protests. New York City, 14 October 2011. © Ramin Talaie / Corbis via Getty Images.

criticism" of the neoliberal era *sans* an alternative vision.[69] Raman's interviewees gravitated towards Che as a symbol of disillusionment, and they dreamed of change even though they did not envision an alternative to capitalism. Che Guevara was an attractive vessel for such oppositional sentiment.

This general oppositional spirit mounted in many Western nations with the onset of the global recession in 2008. In this climate, young people injected Che with even stronger anti-neoliberal overtones. For instance, in 2011 Che became part of a package of symbols and slogans common amongst Occupy activists from Wall Street to Los Angeles and London. Yet, it was in Latin America and the Middle East that Che's image gained the most secure grounding in the rhetoric of populist revolution. As we saw in Chapter One, in the '60s and '70s many Latin American radicals embraced Che as a revolutionary role model. As a militant symbol within factional leftist circles, Che also proved divisive.[70] By the end of the 1980s, however, the doctrinal divisions that once plagued the Latin American left were no longer so stark. In the 1990s, lagging growth and the repercussions of neoliberal policies contributed to a revival of social democratic movements, a political renaissance that emphasized reform rather than revolution. In this new political context, Che less commonly resonated as a lodestar for revolutionary violence. Instead, he became a popular symbol of democracy and social justice for what Eduardo Elena termed a "socially aware Pan-Americanism." He was also transformed into an object of mainstream consumer culture.[71]

Nicaragua offers a telling example of Guevara's post-Cold War political and cultural resonances. During the Cold War, the Sandinista National Liberation Front (FSLN) resolutely embraced Che's vision of revolutionary socialism. The FSLN seized power in 1979 and, though it had abandoned doctrinal Guevarism by that time, Che continued to be one of the movement's primary inspirational figures. Notably, Nicaraguan president Daniel Ortega (1985–90) was a former FSLN insurgent inspired by Che's example and ideas. Though Ortega and the FSLN were defeated at the polls in 1990, Che endured as an aspirational symbol among the Nicaraguan left. When Ortega was reelected on a democratic-socialist platform in 2006, he evoked Che as an inspiration. I traveled to Nicaragua during the heady days immediately following Ortega's 2007 inauguration and found Che's image to be omnipresent. Much as in the EZLN autonomous zones, Che murals were common sights. Some dated to the 1980s, but most were new. Heroic Guerrilla T-shirts sold alongside those of national heroes of the left such as Augusto Nicolás Sandino and Carlos Fonseca.

To be sure, Che's image continued to evoke the egalitarian ideals of the FSLN, but, much as in the US, it also operated as a virtual commercial logo. In clothing shops and open markets, Guevara baseball caps sold next to similar wares bearing the logos of Puma, Ralph Lauren, Adidas, Billabong, and Quicksilver.[72] Che enjoyed a prominent place among Christian-themed merchandise as well. For example, during Semana Santa (Holy Week) in the western city of Granada, vendors who had positioned themselves in front of churches in a shrewd effort to draw the attention of exiting worshippers were selling both Che Guevara posters and key chains and near-identical trinkets featuring Jesus and the Virgin Mary. As elsewhere in Latin America, Che had a pseudo-religious aura. Many Nicaraguans saw him as a moral agent who recalled the self-sacrificing figure of Christ.[73] Thus, as left sentiment surged in Nicaragua, Che represented both political optimism and an ideal morality while appealing as an object of fashion. In short, he offered a container for many Nicaraguans' aspirations—a means through which to articulate political, social, and consumer identities.

Political figures across Latin America have been inspired by and harnessed the symbolic potency of Che's image. As suggested above, Hugo Chavez regularly evoked Che's vision of socialist revolution and antiimperialism during his tenure as president of Venezuela, famously referring to Che as an "infinite revolutionary."[74] As the Pink Tide of democratic socialism washed over many South American nations in the 2000s, other heads of state, including Ecuador's Rafael Correa, Suriname's Dési Bouterse, and Bolivia's Evo Morales, articulated their fondness for Guevara.[75] Morales' 2005 presidential campaign represented one of the most sustained uses of Che's image in South American popular politics. As in Nicaragua, Che gained significant appeal among Bolivians in the years leading up to Morales' election. There was an annual Che festival in Vallegrande near the site of Guevara's execution, and Che became a popular consumer item.[76] In the run up to Morales' victory, many of his campaign offices were adorned with posters and flags bearing Guevara's visage—even Bolivian flags were splashed with the Heroic Guerrilla image. At campaign rallies, supporters greeted Morales' populist message with Che T-shirts and placards.

Just before the 2005 election, Morales offered a personal reflection on Che's meaning that emphasized his morality. "I like Che," Morales explained, "because he fought for equality, for justice." "He did not just care for ordinary people," the future president continued, "he made their struggle his own."[77] In a richly symbolic gesture, soon after assuming office Morales hung a Heroic Guerrilla portrait made of coca leaves in the presidential palace. This work of art fused a prominent symbol of indigenous rights with Che's revolutionary character. Evo Morales was neither a militant nor a communist, but his vision for a more egalitarian Bolivia was nonetheless inspired by Che's example. As "humanists," Morales explained at a 2007 commemoration of Che's death, "[we are] followers of the example of Guevara."[78] In short, more than a decade and a half after the end of the Cold War, Che remained a highly politicized symbol of popular idealism across Latin America, one that had come to occupy halls of power not by force, but by way of the ballot.

In the Middle East, too, Che Guevara's popularity as a political icon expanded significantly in the new millennium. His resonance within Palestinian militant circles dates to the late 1960s (see Chapter One), but the Second Intifada (2000–5) invigorated Guevara as a wider symbol of defiance. At the beginning of the 2000s, Che appealed most immediately to leftist militants such as members of the Popular Front for the Liberation of Palestine (PFLP). Yet, during the Second Intifada, Che's synonymity with revolution also made him a popular figure among many who did not support the PFLP.[79] From 2011, Che's political import would grow even more pervasive during the regional uprisings known collectively as the Arab Spring. Mohamed Bouazizi was a martyr for the struggle against authoritarianism in Tunisia, protesters in Yemen marched under posters of former president Ibrahim al-Hamdi, and many demonstrators in Egypt waved placards of Gamal Abdel Nasser. But Che Guevara was one of the few common symbolic denominators for protest movements across the region. Che flags, T-shirts, posters, and graffiti reproduced Guevara as an international anti-authoritarian icon that communicated largely nationalist demands for democratic reform.[80]

In Morocco, Tunisia, Egypt, Jordan, and Yemen, demonstrators waved red Che flags alongside their national standards. By the summer of 2013, Guevara's was also one of the most noticeable visages held aloft by protesters in Istanbul's Taksim Square. Indeed, Che's audience in Turkey was substantial. Not only was Che merchandise widely available, but the revolutionary icon also become associated with radical politics and the evocative phrase "Be realistic, demand the impossible." Websites and other media encouraged protesters to take up this charge. However, like the dying words scripted for Evan's 2005 biopic, this phrase likely was not Guevara's. While variants have been attributed to Che since at least the early 1970s, I have been unable to identify a speech or document in which he used this phrase.

Yet, the phrase was a prominent rallying cry of French Situationists in 1968, and it was widely repeated during the May protests in Paris that year (see Chapter One). From the vantage point of 2013, the Situationists' message harkened back to a moment of possibility in which political thinkers similarly drew upon Che's image as an emotive reference to possible worlds in the making. The Turkish demonstrators have not been alone in their conflation of Che's image and left ideals of the late 1960s. The phrase "demand the impossible" continues to appear in association with Che in many countries and on many consumer goods. In each instance Che has functioned as a symbol of possibility, a symbol of change. Just as important, by placing the Situationists' words in Guevara's mouth, admirers reimagined him for the needs and spirit of the moment.

From 2011, Guevara's revolutionary aura also gained appeal among a cross-section of Libyan rebels, some of whom wore Che T-shirts into battle. After Muammar Gaddafi's regime was deposed, Che posters and graffiti appeared throughout Tripoli. In late 2011 one rebel expressed his hope that Guevara's rebellious spirit would continue to guide militants throughout the region. "With the help of Allah," he explained, "we can all be like Che Guevara, fighting for peace and freedom around the world."[81] Guevara therefore held a distinctly revolutionary connotation in the midst of Libya's political upheaval, one whose domestic gravity was linked to an appreciation for his transnational import. Thus, while young people may have been exposed to Che through a number of channels—film, literature, the Internet, and fashion—they perceived him to encapsulate a collective desire for change. In other words, Guevara may be malleable, but he is rarely an empty signifier. Phrases such as "be like Che" may no longer resonate beyond Cuba as they did in the 1960s and 1970s, yet the desire to emulate him, to show both courage and morality, endures among many young people around the world.[82]

Che has regained revolutionary political connotations in Latin American, Middle Eastern, and North African contexts, but his resurgence in many other African nations followed a trajectory more akin to that seen in the West in the post-Cold War era. In the 1960s and 1970s, Guevara was a popular symbol within a number of leftist movements in sub-Saharan Africa. For instance, in South Africa many African National Congress members, particularly those of its uMkhonto we Sizwe (MK) armed wing, read Guevara's *Guerrilla Warfare*. Yet, Che's association with revolution and the left did not end in the 1960s. Soon after his release from prison in 1990, Nelson Mandela, co-founder of MK and future president of South Africa, called Che "an inspiration to all those who love freedom."[83] Similarly, in the 1980s, Burkina Faso's president, Thomas Sankara, drew inspiration from Guevara and Fidel Castro for his Marxist-Leninist "Democratic and Popular Revolution," referring to Che as "an embodiment of revolutionary ideas and self-sacrifice." Throughout the 1980s, Che remained a symbol of resistance in other African nations. In Kenya, for instance, the use of Che's visage to protest the Daniel arap Moi government led to the effective banning of his image.[84]

Generally, however, the disintegration or political transformation of African liberation movements slowly denuded Guevara of strong political meaning. When his popularity in many African nations began to surge again in the 2000s, it was to a degree a consequence of his fashionability. For instance, in late 2006, Uganda's *Monitor* newspaper reported that Che had become "one of the hottest fashion labels." The article added that in Uganda the Heroic Guerrilla image was so closely associated with fashion that some young people presumed that the famous face on the T-shirt was that of a clothing designer.[85] In neighboring Kenya, Guevara's popularity soared while I was conducting fieldwork there in the 2000s. Che's popularity coincided with that of Tupac Shakur and Osama bin Laden (see Chapters Three and Four). As in the US, the Heroic Guerrilla image was a fashionable logo in Kenya, a symbol of rebellion for some but also an icon commonly associated with Western brands. This equivalence was clear in the 2005 marketing efforts of a popular clothing shop in Mombasa (Figure 17). Situated on one of the Old Town's main thoroughfares, the shop commissioned a mural in which Heroic Guerrilla appeared next to brand logos such as Puma, Adidas, and Nike.

Guevara's popularity, however, was not always superficial. In 2005 and again in 2008, I asked urban Kenyans who wore Che clothing about their consumer choices. In most instances respondents readily admitted their attraction to Che products as fashionable items. But many also echoed the sentiments of the young people Parvathi Raman interviewed in the UK. Young Kenyans saw Che as a symbol of possibility, through his association with the Cuban Revolution. Though none who wore Che merchandise were socialists, or saw themselves as political radicals, many gravitated toward Guevara for the same reasons other young Kenyans have revered Bob Marley, Tupac Shakur, or Osama bin Laden: he was a transnational symbol of defiance and political change—a common (if imprecise) desire in urban Kenya.[86]

In South Africa, Che's association with indistinct rebelliousness helped to make him an attractive reference while heightening his political appeal. By the 2000s even the most ironic Che references, such as a whimsical Cuba-themed restaurant in Cape Town where servers dressed in Che T-shirts and jaunty Che-like berets, emphasized the popular equivalence of Guevara and revolution. Perhaps the most telling example of this association was merchandise sold by the South African apparel chain Identity. In 2006 Identity marketed a T-shirt featuring a rendition of Heroic Guerrilla superimposed over a map of Cuba. The collage also featured a Cuban flag and the words "ANTI-IMPERIALISTA" and "Viva Freedom." These were imprecise sentiments, but they recalled the Swatch design of the 1990s and evoked Che's association with counterhegemonic struggles. Two years later, in 2008, the same apparel chain introduced another Che Guevara T-shirt featuring a slightly different design. The T-shirt bore text that read:

17. A version of Fitzpatrick's rendering of Heroic Guerrilla used as an advertisement for a popular clothing store in Mombasa, Kenya, 2005. Guevara, who was reemerging as both a popular icon and item of fashion in Kenya, appears alongside the logos of sportswear companies such as Adidas, Nike, and Puma.

CHE REVOLUTION

viva la revolution ID [Identity Clothing Co.]
cinco di [sic] mayo Revolution
our hope in the party
and prepartion [sic] for
peace of the imperialistas

Though decontextualized and offered as nothing more than a fashion item, Che's image here remained tethered to a concept of revolution, one now more catholic and confused in its reference to Mexico. Nevertheless, the retailer had compressed Guevara and his most common connotation into one simplified code: "Che Revolution".[87] As in Uganda and Kenya, in South Africa Guevara had become so closely associated with fashion that he was often conflated with brand logos. For instance, a Cape Town man interviewed for the documentary *Sea Point Days* (2009) referred to the image of Che printed on his Identity T-shirt as "that FUBU guy"—a reference to the popular US sportswear company.[88]

South Africans embraced Che Guevara as an object of fashionable apparel, but legacies of political struggle nonetheless continued to fire his popularity. For example, in 2009—not long after Identity brought out its "Che Revolution" shirt—eThekwini Municipality renamed one of Durban's major thoroughfares Che Guevara Road. The deputy mayor of Durban, Logie Naidoo, explained the move in this way: by renaming the road "we are expressing our sincere gratitude for the sacrifice [Che Guevara] made to bring about revolutionary changes in all countries that suffered under colonialism and injustice."[89] In South Africa, therefore, both Che's political valences and his commercial value have in recent years depended on his rebel aura and his malleability as the eternal, international revolutionary.

## Conclusion

In 2012 I visited La Feltrinelli bookstore in Milan's central rail station. As soon as I entered the store my eyes were drawn to a two-meter-high Heroic Guerrilla image towering above the bookshelves. Accompanying the image was a quote from Guevara's 1960 speech "On Revolutionary Medicine": "The *life* of a *single human being* is worth a *million times more* than *all* the *property* of the *richest man* on *earth*" [emphasis in the artwork].

La Feltrinelli, owned by Giangiacomo Feltrinelli's son (see Chapter One), is one of the largest book and music store chains in Italy. Giangiacomo Feltrinelli was a complex man. He was heir to a family fortune, but he was also a staunch communist, friend to Fidel Castro, and militant who died attempting an act of revolutionary sabotage.[90] As we saw in Chapter One, Feltrinelli printed thousands of Heroic Guerrilla posters in late 1967 and published Guevara's *Bolivian Diaries*. In short, he did more to promote Che's image and program for armed struggle than almost anyone else. Forty-five years later, the Feltrinelli store in Milan's central station articulated Che's populist message, not his vision for proletarian revolution. Looking down from above, this saintly Che was more visionary humanist than insurgent. Looking up at Che from the ground floor of La Feltrinelli, it struck me just how much he had been transformed in the decades since his death. In La Feltrinelli and across the planet, Che has become largely mute on the specific convictions for which he gave his life: Marxism-Leninism and the global proletarian revolution. But global audiences have filled his silence by amplifying other dimensions of his message and worldview. Many have embraced Guevara as a signifier for morality, social justice, and similar values.

Half a century ago, the revolutionary philosopher and psychiatrist Frantz Fanon declared that Che Guevara was the "world symbol of the possibilities of one man."[91] In the new millennium, Che has become a phenomenon linked to those extraordinary possibilities, but he is also something more. He has become an example of the possibilities of a common planetary reference. Guevara has not remained transcendent in spite of a changing world. Rather, many regard his rebellious spirit and personal ethics as transcendent precisely because the world is such a different place—because communism has little meaning for younger generations and because Guevara's ethics seem more all-embracing. Indeed, the most remarkable aspect of Che's afterlife is that when he returned to the global stage in the 1990s, his popularity exceeded that of the 1960s.

To a degree, Che's post-Cold War ubiquity is the result of the kind of commercialization evident in books, film, and apparel. Through this commercial replication, Guevara was introduced as an icon to young people simultaneously desirous of fresh styles and exemplars. In the process, Che, like his two-dimensional Heroic Guerrilla likeness, has been flattened, the nuances of his ideas and beliefs pressed out. Taggers removed the star from his beret to disassociate him from communism. Mercedes-Benz brazenly replaced the star with its own company logo. Che has been co-opted, diluted, and drained of revolutionary meaning. At the same time, he has been filled with new meaning, raised to stand for things he himself never spoke of. As a result, Che Guevara has become a lodestar for myriad revolutions, movements, and trends regardless of their relation to his ideals.[92]

Increased global interdependence since the end of the Cold War has encouraged new permutations of the transnational imagination. As we have seen in previous chapters, these ways of seeing are linked to sentiment, interpretation, and the symbolic idiom. They demonstrate the possibilities of the imagination in a world desirous of shared iconic references. Increasingly stripped of ideological moorings, Che Guevara has become the epitome of revolution while reflecting the diverse values of his admirers. The fact that many depend on Che to represent political vision, general rebelliousness, and individual style suggests that global audiences have developed an incredible appetite for (perhaps a dependence on) shared images to articulate different subject positions, aspirations, and collective possibilities. Released from the ideological matrix of the Cold War, Che, like the other icons in this book, now serves to focus disparate energies on single causes, a set of causes, or, sometimes, no cause in particular. Guevara's revolutionary meaning can be ignored, repressed, or unleashed, but his symbolic potential is almost limitless.

Interpretations of Che may be diverse, but the ability of his image to capture the imagination of people around the world remains central to his omnipresence. I would suggest that there has been one common denominator among Guevara admirers from Subcomandante Marcos to London university students, demonstrators in Cairo, and youthful Mombasan consumers: an eagerness to clothe themselves in Che's rebellious aura. His image may be little more than a signifier of current fashion for some young people, but his dramatic resurgence in the post-Cold War era has hinged on this shared interest. In an interfaced world where we see each other incessantly on television, online, and in print, Che Guevara is one of only a few communal signifiers of possibility.

Moreover, while the notion that one can represent Che's revolutionary essence through a T-shirt may seem naïve, it frequently evidences something more profound than any consumer choice or individual political movement; it shows an acute desire to be part of a larger community. Like a flag or group emblem, Che is a means of linking the individual with something greater than themself. This community may have no more gravity than a diffuse consumer trend, but we should not discount the fact that the popular desire for shared symbols is arguably stronger than it has ever been, and Che's image has offered one means for activists to create symbolic linkages and solidarities. Nearly a half-century after his death, Che was the only icon of dissent simultaneously championed by Greek anti-austerity demonstrators, Yemeni critics of the Saleh government, and US Occupy activists. In these contexts Che's resurgence highlighted a shared idealism, a sense of hope for the future that found many outlets despite the lack of common direction.

In Cuzco, Peru in 2004, a man named Cosmi explained to me that Che Guevara was a hero because he was a "real" revolutionary. Cosmi confided that he loved him as a man who acted on his conscience. He even had a large Che poster at home, which he often pondered. The more Cosmi spoke about Che, the more animated he became. Then he relayed this anecdote: "I was once watching news coverage of the war in Iraq. And though the story was about American soldiers, at one point Iraqis wearing Che T-shirts walked in front of the camera." Cosmi added with great relish that he was delighted to see his love for Guevara reflected in people half a world away, people whom he had presumed knew nothing of the revolutionary. The community of sentiment that Cosmi once thought to be limited to Latin America was, much to his satisfaction, far larger. For him, Che was a symbol of the politics of possibility, and so he was comforted by the fact that this politics was not simply Peruvian or Latin American but global. We cannot know if the Iraqis Cosmi saw on television invested Guevara with the same meanings as he did, but Cosmi's presumption that they too loved Che offers insight into Guevara's potency as an icon in the twenty-first century. Che Guevara is a vessel for the articulation of a yearning for connection and change, one that encourages us to imagine, from our own diverse vantage points, patterns of transnational convergence and consensus.

# CONCLUSION

This book began with questions. Why do particular figures appeal to diverse audiences at specific historical moments? What social roles do icons play in an interfaced world? Tracing the history of global icons over the past half-century demonstrates that the answers to these questions lie not only in the form and connotations of icons, but also in their significant malleability across space and time.

Global icons put flesh on the bones of popular sentiment. Icons such as Che Guevara, Bob Marley, Tupac Shakur, and Osama bin Laden give human form to grievance and aspiration. They crystallize thought, channel ideas, foster real or imagined linkages, and focus communal energies. In short, audiences transform iconic figures into the dynamic products of the transnational imagination and collective interpretation. The appearance and content of icons are both critical to their appeal. They represent imagination beyond the state, political party, or movement. Seemingly timeless, they symbolize transcendence and communal ideals while remaining malleable. As we have seen, in the post-Cold War era Che Guevara became a ready-made symbol of revolution regardless of the rebellious act he was meant to stand for. Attraction to icons is therefore not the idolization of the individual per se. Rather, it is the idolization of possibility, of the visions and values that audiences imagine such figures to represent. Evocative form and profound content thus invest the icon of dissent with extraordinary power, a power particularly attractive to the marginalized and voiceless.

Ultimately, global icons are what audiences make of them. The history of icons in the past half-century is the story of how certain person-

217

ages, images, and objects have come to represent greater ideals, often in concert with political movements and consumer culture. The trajectory of icons evidences at once the fragility and the endurance of meaning. Global icons are greatly malleable and have recognizable transnational connotations. As we have seen throughout this book, it is this combination of malleability and incontrovertibility, or icons' ability to be vessels of shared and unique meaning, that ensures their long-term popularity. Moreover, icons of dissent are intrinsically aspirational products of the collective imagination. They can reflect sentiments shared among the disenfranchised and they can even foster horizontal connections and a sense of dignity on the part of those who embrace them. Though diverse audiences perceive icons differently, their appeal is at least in part based on the fact that they are also important to others: they appear to have universal relevance. By referencing icons, individuals place themselves within a larger collective. Thus, the recognition, appreciation, and mutual citation of the iconic messenger are in many instances just as important as the message itself.[1] And the desire to be connected has become a potent social force in transforming socioeconomic relations as well as the symbolic idiom.

Since the 1960s, the global symbolic idiom has expanded significantly. As elements of this idiom, icons of dissent have been imbued with and divested of political meaning. Indeed, interpretations of icons have changed over time, sometimes dramatically. For instance, after the Cold War, Che Guevara's popularity increased exponentially. This was not only a consequence of the commoditization of his image. Guevara's ubiquity as a consumer object and political reference was also a result of the fact that he was no longer imagined to reflect an overarching ideology. Thus, he was reconceptualized to connote the practice of solidarity in the dream of a more egalitarian world, regardless of the differing political views of his audiences. The Guy Fawkes mask offers another recent example of shared iconography and abstraction.

Since its adoption by members of Anonymous in the late 2000s, the Guy Fawkes mask has functioned much like images of Che Guevara did in the late 1960s: a common symbol with a general antiestablishment connotation but a wide range of specific associations. The mask of V, antihero and revolutionary of the *V for Vendetta* comic book series and 2005 cult classic film, has become popular amongst diverse political activists around the world. Despite the mask's reference to Guy

18. A replica of the Guy Fawkes mask featured in the 2005 film *V for Vendetta*. Since the late 2000s, the mask has become a powerful symbol of dissent used by groups and individuals around the world.

Fawkes, demonstrators in London, Nairobi, Los Angeles, and elsewhere have not worn it in homage to the Gunpowder Plot of 1605 per se but rather in reference to others who have worn the mask, including the fictional character V. The Guy Fawkes mask thus represents something only indirectly related to Fawkes the historical figure.[2] Much like the iconography considered in the preceding chapters, the Guy Fawkes mask is a symbol of dissent albeit one largely alienated from Fawkes and his cause.

If, as I have argued, decontextualized imagery is a defining characteristic of the Information Age, the distance between what we see and what we understand provides fertile ground for the development of myth-like figures. In this way, the power of antisystemic iconography is both charged and limited by the imagination. There is a significant difference between political thought in the long sixties and in the present;

during the former, many leftist political thinkers believed that history was moving in a direction favorable to their interests, even if those interests were diverse. History, they held, was advancing towards liberation, socialism, communism, or other forms of structural change. World historical change appeared possible, perhaps inevitable, such that some spoke of "the revolution" and its vanguards. This concept of historical direction may seem naïve, perhaps dangerously so in hindsight, but it was a powerful catalyst for collective action.

The contrast with the present offers a yardstick by which to measure the shift in popular consciousness over the past fifty years. We live in a moment in which incremental changes are possible, but overturning the dominant political economy is almost unimaginable to most people. The post-Cold War world lacks neither hope nor outrage, but there is an important distinction between the claim that another world is possible and a belief that "the revolution" is imminent. At the same time, the Latin American Pink Tide and the popularity of democratic-socialist and social-democratic politicians such as US Senator Bernie Sanders and UK Labour leader Jeremy Corbyn, suggests increased popular interest in stronger left ideological platforms. Additionally, the lack of a shared utopian vision has in no way diminished the importance of symbols of possibility and solidarity. If, as Branko Milanović has suggested, inequality is rising faster within nations than among them, national dissent is poised to increase across the globe.[3] Moreover, trans-border communication and the cross-fertilization of ideas show no signs of abating. Under these conditions, icons may become even more attractive as symbols of international solidarity, even in the absence of a shared vision or global hegemonic focus.

The history of icons over the past half-century also suggests that politics and consumerism have become more interdependent. Ideas are increasingly conflated with logos, and political imagination has become more contingent on the logic of consumerism. As we have seen, advertising and the arts of dissent have long been mutually influential. This has mirrored and encouraged the convergence of politics and consumer culture. Yet, the structural forces of the last quarter-century have fortified the notion that there is no alternative to capitalism. Thus, consumerism, as the everyday expression of the free market, has become a totalizing mode of interface. Consumerist aspirations gained significant political force in the late Cold War Communist bloc, and many yet view

CONCLUSION

consumerism as a liberating force. Specifically, in the West we commonly imagine routes to social change as lying squarely within consumer culture. We are told that social change can be affected by consuming organic foods, buying fair trade products, and building with FSC-certified wood. In this way, as Michelle Micheletti, Andreas Follesdal, and Dietlind Stolle have argued, the market has become deeply politicized as a site for action and the realization of individual ethics.[4]

The reverse is also true: politics has been shaped by the logics of consumerism. As we have seen with the conflation of image and idea in the icon of dissent, both politics and consumerism act as tools for identity construction. Political affiliation is often as culturally determined as consumer choice. Strategies for marketing political candidates have increasingly depended on the psychology of brand development. There is nothing new about the commodification of political campaigns, whether in the form of T-shirts, bumper stickers, or posters. Nor is there anything novel about "buying" influence. But the association of candidates and parties with broad sentiments via iconography, or the crafting of candidates' "brand identities", has become a central pillar of democratic politics around the world. As we saw in Chapter Six, President Evo Morales's supporters marshaled Che's image in his 2005 campaign. Yet, one of the most profound examples of the intersection of a political contest and the icon-making logic of contemporary consumer culture was Barack Obama's 2008 presidential campaign. In 2007, artist Shepard Fairey produced the now iconic poster of Barack Obama peering into the distance with intent, a tableau inspired by Korda's Heroic Guerrilla. Fairey wanted to portray the presidential candidate as both strong and wise, and thus he chose an image that seemed to say, as the artist recalled, "I can guide you." Channeling popular nostalgia for the lost dreams of the masses who marched under Guevara's visage in the long sixties, Fairey astutely captioned the image "HOPE".[5]

How should we understand this adaptation of the Heroic Guerrilla template for an American presidential campaign? It is remarkable that the iconography of the world's most recognizable revolutionary socialist became a model for the campaign poster of the world's most influential elected official. Some of Obama's critics surely imagined this confluence as a sign of a veiled radical agenda. The reality, however, was quite different. Through the global mediascape and the work of Shepard Fairey, the Heroic Guerrilla template transcended the political controversy that long plagued Che Guevara to become a more universal signifier of hope and change. Fairey's earlier work carried forward a tradition of blurring the lines between advertising and rebellious sentiment, often in a mode of postmodern pastiche. He conceived his most influential project, the social experiment and critique dubbed "OBEY" (which featured the image of the deceased wrestler André the Giant), as a heuristic device. Through "OBEY", Fairey encouraged viewers to question the messages produced by marketing culture.

"OBEY" was an empty signifier, and so it gained diverse meanings. But it also transmuted into precisely that which it critiqued: a consumer brand, one now largely shorn of its intended irony. "OBEY" became a desirable element of a youth fashion code and was to a great degree subsumed by it. Similarly, the Heroic Guerrilla template gained maximum resonance among American audiences because of the excision of socialism from popular interpretations of Che Guevara. In this new guise, Che could represent possibility and rebelliousness, while younger audiences could also infuse him with social meanings relevant to the present. Shepard Fairey ingeniously harnessed this connotation of possibility in recognizable form for the Obama campaign image. With "HOPE", Fairey and those who embraced the image linked Barack Obama to a history of popular iconography. With Fairey's assistance, candidate Obama's team marketed him as a heroic icon, deftly wedding political art with advertising.[6]

Like the four icons of dissent in this book, Barack Obama's "HOPE" image resonated widely. T-shirts, posters, and other consumer products bearing the design appeared across the globe. While Obama gave cynical American voters greater optimism, in Africa, the Middle East, East Asia, and elsewhere he became an even greater symbol for possibility. For those who saw many of the world's ills personified in George W. Bush and other former US presidents (see Chapter Four), Barack Obama seemed to offer redemption. It is no surprise that in London, Nairobi, and many other places T-shirts featuring Obama's image appeared along-side those of Che Guevara. Though ideologically distant, Guevara and Obama both encapsulated the perceived power of the antisystemic figure, even if Obama did not pose a challenge to the world order.

Popular imagination would also to a degree undo the power of the Obama icon. The world filled Barack Obama's image with political dreams that no politician could realize. Accordingly, during his tenure in office, President Obama was unable to maintain the same level of symbolic potency, despite efforts to shape his image.[7] Yet, as further evidence of the historical contingency of iconic resonance, Obama's popularity would see a sustained resurgence beginning late in his second term, particularly after the election of Donald Trump in 2016. The longer iconic arc of another president, Nelson Mandela, offers an illuminating comparison with Obama's trajectory. Nelson Mandela's rise to global iconic status was a consequence of both his actions as co-founder of the African National Congress's militant wing and the success of the "Free Mandela" campaign, particularly in the late 1970s and 1980s. Since Mandela was imprisoned and largely incommunicado, the ANC and anti-Apartheid organizations around the world molded his image into that of the archetypal prisoner of conscience. For many audiences, the fight for his freedom encapsulated the larger, global struggle for racial equality and social justice. After Mandela's 1990 release and subsequent election as president of South Africa in 1994, his image began to connote peace and reconciliation. In the years after his single-term presidency, Mandela's profile remained that of the popular diplomat and a symbol of racial reconciliation. By the time of his death in 2013, only traces of Mandela's militant aura remained. Rather, audiences beyond (and to a degree within) South Africa embraced him as a global statesman and human rights advocate, revered for his vision of a concordant world.[8] He was also widely commoditized, nowhere more so than in South Africa.

One lesson to take from these trajectories and the case studies in this book is that the connotations and longevity of iconic figures are dependent on the myriad forces of time. The trajectories of the iconic figures addressed here conform to an inescapable logic: the dynamic process of transforming an individual into an idealized symbol, and that symbol's circulation as a superhuman sign, is difficult to predict. Simply put, the icon is beholden to social, political, and economic forces that have no direction, and thus icons have no definite future.

Nonetheless, the Che Guevara flags of EZLN autonomous zones, Checkpoint Charlie, Zuccotti Park, and Taksim Square cast long shadows of struggles past. Contemporary left movements have returned to many of the values of the new social movements of the 1960s.

Alongside these they have resurrected historical references such as the Heroic Guerrilla and the peace symbol. These are the residues of dreams, but they have not only been reanimated for the present, they have also been reimagined and refashioned. This process has the potential to open real political possibilities. As in 1968, global icons are among the few instruments for creating symbolic linkages and solidarities across space and time. As we have seen, even in highly commoditized form, Guevara and Marley have been revived as symbols for the politics of possibility and the imagination of solidarity. Global icons of dissent are a means to build and reflect communities of sentiment, but their power and flexibility has also constrained their reproduction. As we saw in Chapter Three, even references to Tupac Shakur have, under certain conditions, proven deadly. In wartime Sierra Leone, many who wore Tupac T-shirts had no link to insurgents, yet the perception among the security forces that anyone who sported Tupac apparel was a rebel necessarily limited the potential uses of Shakur's image.

Icons of dissent have been wielded to challenge structures of power because they are so symbolically resonant. In an interfaced and radically unequal world that is becoming more conscious of those inequalities, iconic figures will likely remain important as symbols of and tools for collective action. However, we should bear in mind that even though icons focus the transnational imagination, iconography does not offer answers to evolving questions. Rather, it is the dreams that iconic figures are imagined to represent, and the collective action these engender, that will affect the course of history. The most important questions, then, are of the uses of global icons: What social and political alternatives will icons of dissent represent in the future? What dreams, perhaps yet to be imagined, will global icons embody?

# NOTES

## INTRODUCTION

1. I take the term "antisystemic" from the concept of "antisystemic movements", or movements that oppose an era's dominant transnational political, economic, or social forces. Giovanni Arrighi, Terence K. Hopkins, and Immanuel Wallerstein, *Antisystemic Movements* (New York: Verso, 1989).
2. Mike Marqusee, *Redemption Song: Muhammad Ali and the Spirit of the Sixties* (New York: Verso, 2005); Michael Ezra, *Muhammad Ali: The Making of an Icon* (Philadelphia, PA: Temple University Press, 2009).
3. "Symbolic resistance" encompasses style and subculture as well as counterhegemonic actions such as critique and disregard for sociopolitical norms, measures not always aligned with formal political movements. Stuart Hall and Tony Jefferson, eds, *Resistance Through Rituals: Youth Subcultures in Post War Britain* (New York: 1993); James C. Scott, *Domination and the Arts of Resistance: Hidden Transcripts* (New Haven, CT: Yale University Press, 1990); James C. Scott, *Weapons of the Weak: Everyday Forms of Peasant Resistance* (New Haven, CT: Yale University Press, 1984); Dick Hebdige, *Subculture: The Meaning of Style* (London: Routledge, 1979).
4. Notable exceptions include Dianna C. Niebylski and Patrick O'Connor, eds, *Latin American Icons: Fame Across Borders* (Nashville, TN: Vanderbilt University Press, 2014); Bishnupriya Ghosh, *Global Icons: Apertures to the Popular* (Berkeley, CA: University of California Press, 2011); John David Ebert, *Dead Celebrities, Living Icons: Tragedy and Fame in the Age of the Multimedia Superstar* (Santa Barbara, CA: Praeger, 2010); Susan J. Drucker and Gary Gumpert, eds, *Heroes in a Global World* (Cresskill, NJ: Hampton Press, 2008); Benedikt Feldges, *American Icons: The Genesis of a National Visual Language* (New York: Routledge, 2008); Samuel Brunk and Ben Fallaw, eds, *Heroes and Hero Cults in Latin America* (Austin, TX: University of Texas Press, 2006); Susan J. Drucker and Robert S. Cathcart, eds, *American Heroes in a Media Age* (Cresskill, NJ: Hampton Press, 1994).
5. Erwin Panofsky, *Meaning in the Visual Arts: Papers in and on Art History* (Garden City, NY: Doubleday, 1955); W.J.T. Mitchell, *Iconology: Image, Text, Ideology* (Chicago, IL: University of Chicago Press, 1986); W.J.T. Mitchell, *Cloning Terror: The War of Images,*

*9/11 to the Present* (Chicago, IL: University of Chicago Press, 2011); W.J.T. Mitchell, *Image Science: Iconology, Visual Culture, and Media Aesthetics* (Chicago, IL: University of Chicago Press, 2015).

6. Jeffrey C. Alexander has argued that the power of icons "often builds up by invisible accretions, without any relation to an organized social power that plans and engineers its production and distribution…" Jeffrey C. Alexander, "Iconic Power and Performance: The Role of the Critic," in Jeffrey C. Alexander, Dominik Bartmański, and Bernhard Giesen, eds. *Iconic Power: Materiality and Meaning in Social Life* (New York: Palgrave Macmillan, 2012), p. 34.

7. Ibid., pp. 25–6; Werner Binder, "The Emergence of Iconic Depth: Secular Icons in a Comparative Perspective," in Alexander, Bartmański, and Giesen, eds. *Iconic Power*, pp. 101–18; Émile Durkheim (Karen E. Fields, trans.), *The Elementary Forms of Religious Life* (New York: Free Press, 1995); Bernhard Giesen, *Triumph and Trauma* (Boulder, CO: Paradigm, 2004); W.J.T. Mitchell, *What Do Pictures Want? The Lives and Loves of Images* (Chicago, IL: University of Chicago Press, 2005), ch. 9; David Kunzle, *Chesucristo: The Fusion in Image and Word of Che Guevara and Jesus Christ* (Berlin: De Gruyter, 2016).

8. Gilles Deleuze and Félix Guattari, *A thousand plateaus: capitalism and schizophrenia* (London: Athlone Press, 1987).

9. Roland Barthes, "Rhetoric of the Image," in Stephen Heath, ed., *Image, Music, Text* (New York: Hill and Wang, 1977), 32–51; Stuart Hall, "Encoding, decoding," in Simon During, ed., *Cultural Studies Reader* (New York: Routledge, 1999), pp. 507–17.

10. Hannah Charlton, "Introduction," in Trisha Ziff, ed., *Che Guevara: revolutionary & icon* (London: V&A Publishers, 2006), pp. 7–14.

11. Bartmański and Alexander succinctly described this process of reduction as "an aesthetic and sensuous compression of meaning." Dominik Bartmański and Jeffrey C. Alexander, "Introduction: Materiality and Meaning in Social Life: Toward an Iconic Turn in Cultural Sociology," in Alexander, Bartmański, and Giesen, eds. *Iconic Power*, p. 2.

12. Jean Baudrillard, *Simulacra and Simulation* (Ann Arbor, MI: University of Michigan Press, 1994).

13. Michel de Certeau, *The Practice of Everyday Life* (Berkeley, CA: University of California Press, 1984); John Tomlinson, *Cultural Imperialism: A Critical Introduction* (London: Pinter, 1991); Joseph Tobin, ed., *Re-made in Japan: Everyday Life and Consumer Taste in a Changing Society* (New Haven, CT: Yale University Press, 1992); Karen Tranberg Hansen, *Salaula: The World of Secondhand Clothing and Zambia* (Chicago, IL: University of Chicago Press, 2000); Angelique Haugerud, M. Priscilla Stone, and Peter D. Little, eds, *Commodities and Globalization: Anthropological Perspectives* (Oxford: Rowman and Littlefield, 2000); Kelly Askew and Richard R. Wilk, *The Anthropology of Media: A Reader* (Malden, MA: Blackwell, 2002); Jeremy Prestholdt, *Domesticating the World: African Consumerism and the Genealogies of Globalization* (Berkeley, CA: University of California Press, 2008).

14. Thomas Frank, et. al., *Commodify your Dissent* (New York: W.W. Norton, 1997);

Thomas Frank, *The Conquest of Cool: Business Culture, Counterculture, and the Rise of Hip Consumerism* (Chicago, IL: University of Chicago Press, 1997).

15. Graeme Abernethy, *The Iconography of Malcolm X* (Lawrence, KS: University of Kansas Press, 2013).

16. Marie-José Mondzain, *Image, Icon, Economy: The Byzantine Origins of the Contemporary Imaginary* (Stanford, CA: Stanford University Press, 2005).

17. Mitchell, *Cloning Terror*, p. xvii.

18. In C.S. Peirce's typology of signs, the icon similarly retains its earlier parameters, i.e. the likeness of another thing. In Peirce's lexicon popular figures are represented as "icons"—photographs or artistic renderings—but they also act as "symbols", or signs that are repositories of complex, learned, and changing meanings. T.L. Short, *Peirce's Theory of Signs* (Cambridge: Cambridge University Press, 2007).

19. Daniel Herwitz, *The Star as Icon: Celebrity in the Age of Mass Consumption* (New York: Columbia University Press, 2008), pp. 37–8; Jeffrey C. Alexander, "The Celebrity-Icon," *Journal of Sociology* 4, 3 (2010): 323–36; Keyan G. Tomaselli and David H. T. Scott, eds, *Cultural Icons* (Walnut Creek, CA: Left Coast Press, 2009). On the national icon see, for instance, Ilene V. O'Malley, *The Myth of the Revolution: Hero Cults and the Institutionalization of the Mexican State, 1920–1940* (New York: Greenwood Press, 1986); Richard Grossman, "Augusto Sandino of Nicaragua: The Hero Never Dies," in Brunk and Fallaw, eds, *Heroes and Hero Cults in Latin America*, pp. 148–70.

20. Jeffrey C. Alexander, "Iconic Consciousness: The Material Feeling of Meaning," *Thesis Eleven* 103, 1 (2010): 10–25.

21. As Bronislaw Szerszynski and John Urry have argued, "moral agents" are "exemplars" of virtues and abstract notions that have social resonance, such as freedom and equality. Bronislaw Szerszynski and John Urry, "Cultures of Cosmopolitanism," *The Sociological Review* 50, 4 (2002): 475–6.Robert A. Segal, ed., *Hero myths: a reader* (Malden, MA: Blackwell, 2000); Celeste-Marie Bernier, *Characters of Blood: Black Heroism in the Transatlantic Imagination* (Charlottesville, VA: University of Virginia Press, 2012).

22. Claude Lévi-Strauss, "The Structural Study of Myth," *The Journal of American Folklore* 68, 270 (1955): 428–44; Allen F. Roberts, Mary Nooter Roberts, et al., eds, *A Saint in the City: Sufi Arts of Urban Senegal* (Los Angeles, CA: UCLA Fowler Museum of Cultural History, 2003); Joseph Campbell, *The Hero with a Thousand Faces* (New York: Pantheon Books, 1949); Ghosh, *Global Icons*, p. 182.

23. Alexander, "Iconic Power and Performance," p. 32; Alexander, "Iconic Consciousness." The "iconic experience" therefore represents popular engagement with both dimensions of the icon. Jeffrey C. Alexander, "Iconic Experience in Art and Life: Surface/Depth Beginning with Giacometti's *Standing Women*," *Theory, Culture & Society* 25, 5 (2008): 1–19.

24. Bartmański and Alexander, "Introduction," p. 10. On iconicity and the "iconic turn" see also Marco Solaroli, "Iconicity: A Category for Social and Cultural Theory," *Sociologica* 1 (2015) and Dominik Bartmański, "Modes of Seeing, or, Iconicity as Explanatory Notion: Cultural Research and Criticism After the Iconic Turn in

Social Sciences," 1 (2015), both avalable at http://www.sociologica.mulino.it/journal/issue/index/Issue/Journal:ISSUE:26.

25. Douglas B. Holt, *How Brands Become Icons: The Principles of Cultural Branding* (Boston, MA: Harvard Business Review Press, 2004), p. 4.

26. For a seminal analysis of this process as it relates to Che Guevara see Kunzle, *Chesucristo*.

27. Giesen, *Triumph and Trauma*.

28. Robert Hariman and John Louis Lucaites, *No Caption Needed: iconic photographs, public culture, and liberal democracy* (Chicago, IL: University of Chicago Press, 2007); Dominik Bartmański, "Inconspicuous Revolutions of 1989: Culture and Contingency in the Making of Political Icons," in Alexander, Bartmański, and Giesen, eds. *Iconic Power*, pp. 39–66.

29. Pierre Halen and János Riesz, *Patrice Lumumba entre Dieu et Diable: un héros africain dans ses images* (Paris: L'Harmattan, 1997); Bogumil Jewsiewicki, ed., *A Congo Chronicle: Patrice Lumumba in Urban Art* (New York, NY: Museum for African Art, 1999); Isabelle de Rezende, "Visuality and Colonialism in the Congo: From the 'Arab War' to Patrice Lumumba, c.1880s to 1960" (PhD Thesis, University of Michigan, 2012).

30. Maria Carolina-Cambre aptly termed this process "inter-animation". Maria Carolina-Cambre, "Virtual Resurrections: Che Guevara's Image as Place of Hope," in Tonya Davidson, Ondine Park, and Rob Shields, eds, *Ecologies of Affect: Placing Nostalgia, Desire, and Hope* (Waterloo, ON: Wilfrid Laurier University Press, 2011), p. 233; Alfred Gell, *Art and Agency: An Anthropological Theory* (Oxford: Oxford University Press, 1998).

31. Resa Aslan, *Zealot: The Life and Times of Jesus of Nazareth* (New York: Random House, 2013), p. xxx. See also Stephen Prothero, *American Jesus: How the Son of God Became a National Icon* (New York: Farrar, Straus and Giroux, 2003); Martin Kemp, *Christ to Coke: How Image becomes Icon* (New York: Oxford University Press, 2012).

32. Bartmański and Alexander, "Introduction," pp. 3–4; Arjun Appadurai, ed., *The Social Lives of Things: Commodities in Cultural Perspective* (Cambridge: Cambridge University Press, 1986); Mitchell, *What Do Pictures Want?*

33. Ghosh, *Global Icons*, pp. 177, 3.

34. Durkheim, *The Elementary Forms of the Religious Life*.

35. Stephen Howe, "Transnationalisms Good, Bad, Real, Imagined, Thick and Thin," *Interventions* 4, 1 (2002): 87–8; Benedict Anderson, *Imagined Communities: Reflections on the Origin and Spread of Nationalism* (New York: Verso, 1991). See also Pheng Cheah and Bruce Robbins, eds, *Cosmopolitics: Thinking and Feeling Beyond the Nation* (Minneapolis, MN: University of Minnesota Press, 1998).

36. In this sense, they function much like brands offering "identity myths" that express social aspirations. Holt, *How Brands Become Icons*, p. 8; Ahmed Gurnah, "Elvis in Zanzibar," in Alan Scott, ed., *The Limits of Globalization* (London: Routledge, 1997), pp. 116–42.

37. Brad Weiss, *Street Dreams and Hip Hop Barbershops: Global Fantasy in Urban Tanzania* (Bloomington, IN: Indiana University Press, 2009), p. 126; Stuart Hall, "What is this 'Black' in Black Popular Culture?," *Social Justice* 20, 1–2 (1993): 104–14.

38. Joan Fayer, "Are Heroes Always Men?," in Drucker and Cathcart, eds. *American Heroes*, pp. 24–35. "If only masculine qualities are considered heroic," Fayer succinctly noted (p. 35), "women will continue to be excluded [from the category of the hero]." Sara Evans, "Sons, Daughters, and Patriarchy: Gender and the 1968 Generation," *American Historical Review* 114, 2 (April 2009): 331–47. On gender as performance see Judith Butler, *Gender Trouble: Feminism and the Subversion of Identity* (New York: Routledge, 1990).

39. Jeffrey C. Alexander has shown that celebrity-icons often reproduce "archetypically gendered forms." Alexander, "The Celebrity-Icon," p. 330. See also Diane Negra and Su Holmes, eds, *In the Limelight and Under the Microscope: Forms and Functions of Female Celebrity* (London: Bloomsbury, 2011).

40. Ghosh, *Global Icons*; María Claudia André, ed., *Latina Icons: Iconos Femininos Latinos e Hispanoamericanos* (Mountain View, CA: Floricanto, 2006); Linda B. Hall, "Evita Peron: Beauty, Resonance, and Heroism," in Brunk and Fallaw, eds, *Heroes and Hero Cults in Latin America*, 229–63. On the relation of the mother figure to conflict and nationalism see Julie Peteet, "Icons and Militants: Mothering in the Danger Zone," *Signs* 23, 1 (1997): 103–27.

41. Dean Reynolds, "Representations of Youth and Political Consciousness in the Music of Bob Marley," *Review: Literature and Arts of the Americas* 43, 2 (2010): 241. On charisma see Tony Waters and Dagmar Waters, trans and eds, *Weber's Rationalism and Modern Society: New Translations on Politics, Bureaucracy, and Social Stratification* (New York: Palgrave Macmillan, 2015); Edward A. Shils, "Charisma, Order, and Status," *American Sociological Review* 30 (1965): 199–213; Philip Smith, "Culture and Charisma: Outline of a Theory," *Acta Sociologica* 43, 2 (2000): 101–111.

42. Osama bin Laden's communiqués contained many religious references, but in some instances he emphasized antisystemic messages as well. See for instance Osama bin Laden, "The Way to Save the Earth," 17 February 2010, available at http://thesis.haverford.edu/dspace/bitstream/handle/10066/5053/OBL20100217.pdf?sequence =4 (accessed 28 October 2016).

43. For the case of Bob Marley, see Eileen Moyer, "Street-Corner Justice in the Name of Jah: Imperatives for Peace among Dar es Salaam Street Youth," *Africa Today* 51, 3 (2005): 36–7.

44. As we will see in Chapter Two, Bob Marley was not the progenitor of this Rastafari aesthetic, but he was closely associated with it and did more than any other figure to popularize it beyond the Caribbean. The physical emulation of Marley took a controversial new form in 2016 when Snapchat developed an app that allowed smartphone users to merge pictures of themselves with Bob Marley's visage. The resulting images were widely denounced as 'digital blackface'. Alex Fitzpatrick, "Snapchat is Getting Blasted Over this Controversial 'Bob Marley' Filter," *Time.com*, 20 April 2016 http://time.com/4300726/snapchat-bob-marley-filter-blackface/ (accessed 20 July 2016).

45. See, for instance, Sven Beckert, *Empire of Cotton: A Global History* (New York: Vintage, 2015); Robert B. Marks, *The Origins of the Modern World: A Global and Environmental Narrative from the Fifteenth to the Twenty-First Century* (Lanham, MD: Rowman & Littlefield, 2015); Giorgio Riello, *Cotton: The Fabric that Made the*

*Modern World* (Cambridge: Cambridge University Press, 2013); Jürgen Osterhammel and Niels Petersson, *Globalization: A Short History* (Princeton, NJ: Princeton University Press, 2009); Patrick Manning, *Navigating World History: Historians Create a Global Past* (New York: Palgrave Macmillan, 2003); Christopher Bayly, *The Birth of the Modern World, 1780–1914: Global Connections and Comparisons* (Malden, MA: Blackwell, 2004); Kenneth Pomeranz, *The Great Divergence: China, Europe, and the making of the modern world economy* (Princeton, NJ: Princeton University Press, 2000); Michael Geyer and Charles Bright, "World History in a Global Age," *The American Historical Review* 100, 4 (1995); Sidney W. Mintz, *Sweetness and Power: The Place of Sugar in Modern History* (New York: Penguin, 1986).

46. Notable exceptions include Martin W. Lewis and Kären Wigen, *Myth of Continents: A Critique of Metageography* (Berkeley, CA: University of California Press, 1997); John Gillis, *Islands of the Mind: How the Human Imagination Created the Atlantic World* (New York: Palgrave Macmillan, 2004); Benjamin Lazier, "Earthrise; or, the Globalization of the World Picture," *American Historical Review* 116, 3 (2011): 602–30; Mark Mazower, *Governing the World: The History of an Idea* (New York: Penguin, 2012); Lynn Hunt, *Writing History in the Global Era* (New York: W.W. Norton, 2015).

47. Marshall McLuhan with Louis Forsdale, "Technology and the Human Dimension," in George Sanderson and Frank Macdonald, eds, *Marshall McLuhan, the Man and His Message* (Golden, CO: Fulcrum, 1989), p. 24; Asa Briggs and Peter Burke, *A Social History of the Media* (Malden, MA: Polity Press, 2009); John Durham Peters, *Speaking into the Air: A History of the Idea of Communication* (Chicago, IL: University of Chicago Press, 2001).

48. Kishori Mahbubani theorized a "great convergence" in reference to the shared interests and lifestyles of an emergent global middle class. The symbolic convergence that concerns us is an element of this broader convergence, but not a strictly class-oriented phenomenon. Mahbubani, *The Great Convergence: Asia, the West, and the Logic of One World* (New York: Public Affairs, 2013) Michael Kackman et. al., eds, *Television in the Age of Media Convergence* (New York: Routledge, 2011).

49. Scholars have employed the term "transnational imagination" to describe popular strategies for representing distant societies. More commonly, however, the term functions as a relatively amorphous reference to the effects of travel, education, and media exposure on collective perceptions of global interrelation. Meaghan Morris, Siu Leung Li, and Stephen Ching-kiu Chan, eds, *Hong Kong Connections: transnational imagination in action cinema* (Durham, NC: Duke University Press, 2005); Wanning Sun, *Leaving China: media, migration, and the transnational imagination* (Lanham, MD: Rowman & Littlefield, 2002), pp. 5–6; Emanuela Guano, "Spectacles of Modernity: Transnational Imagination and Local Hegemonies in Neoliberal Buenos Aires," *Cultural Anthropology* 17, 2 (2002): 181–209.

50. See, for instance, Manfred B. Steger, *Rise of the Global Imaginary: political ideologies from the French Revolution to the global war on terror* (New York: Oxford University Press, 2008); Patrick Manning, "1789–1792 and 1989–1992: Global Interactions of Social Movements," *World History Connected* 3, 1 (2005) http://worldhistory-connected.press.illinois.edu/3.1/manning.html (accessed 6 June 2011).

51. James L. Gelvin and Nile Green, eds, *Global Muslims in the Age of Steam and Print* (Berkeley, CA: University of California Press, 2013); Jeffrey C. Alexander, *Trauma: A Social Theory* (Malden, MA: Polity Press, 2012); Joanne Pemberton, *Global Metaphors: Modernity and the Quest for One World* (London: Pluto Press, 2001); Edward Said, *Culture and Imperialism* (New York: A.A. Knopf, 1993).

52. Arjun Appadurai, *Modernity at Large: Cultural Dimensions of Globalization* (Minneapolis, MN: University of Minnesota Press, 1996); David Singh Grewal, *Network Power: The Social Dynamics of Globalization* (New Haven, CT: Yale University Press, 2008); Minkah Makalani, *In the Cause of Freedom: Radical Black Internationalism from Harlem to London, 1917–1939* (Chapel Hill, NC: University of North Carolina Press, 2011).

53. Manuel Castells, *Networks of Outrage and Hope: Social Movements in the Internet Age* (Malden, MA: Polity Press, 2012); Merlyna Lim, "Clicks, Cabs, and Coffeehouses: Social Media and Oppositional Movements in Egypt, 2004–2011," *Journal of Communication* 62 (2012): 231–48; Alain Badiou, *The Rebirth of History* (London: Verso, 2012).

54. See, for instance, Eric J. Hobsbawm, *Revolutionaries: Contemporary Essays* (New York: Pantheon, 1973); Eric J. Hobsbawm, *Bandits* (New York: New Press, 2000); Campbell, *The Hero*.

55. Brunk and Fallaw, "Introduction," in Brunk and Fallaw, eds, *Heroes and Hero Cults in Latin America*, p. 3. Shakespeare's global influence would only arise later, notably with the expansion of the British Empire and the wider use of the English language. Andrew Dickson, *Worlds Elsewhere: Journeys Around Shakespeare's Globe* (New York: Henry Holt and Co., 2016).

56. See, for instance, Barry Schwartz, *George Washington: The Making of an American Symbol* (New York: Free Press, 1987).

57. Jürgen Osterhammel, *The Transformation of the World: A History of the Nineteenth Century* (Princeton, NJ: Princeton University Press, 2014); Bayly, *Birth of the Modern World*; Eric J. Hobsbawm, *The Age of Empire: 1875–1914* (New York: Pantheon, 1987).

58. John Lonsdale, "The Moral Economy of Mau Mau," in Bruce Berman and John Lonsdale, *Unhappy Valley: Conflict in Kenya and Africa* (Athens, OH: Ohio University Press, 1992), p. 347.

59. Edward Said evocatively described these technologies as "knitting the world together." Said, *Culture and Imperialism*, p. 309. Richard Ohmann, *Selling Culture: Magazines, Markets, and Class at the Turn of the Century* (New York: Verso, 1996); Jonathan Crary, *Techniques of the Observer: On Vision and Modernity in the Nineteenth Century* (Cambridge, MA: MIT Press, 1992).

60. Isabel Hofmeyr, *Gandhi's Printing Press: Experiments in Slow Reading* (Cambridge, MA: Harvard University Press, 2013); Ilham Khuri-Makdisi, *The Eastern Mediterranean and the Making of Global Radicalism, 1860–1914* (Berkeley, CA: University of California Press, 2010); Benedict Anderson, *Under Three Flags: Anarchism and the Anti-colonial Imagination* (New York: Verso, 2007); Maia Ramnath, *Haj to Utopia: How the Ghadar Movement Charted Global Radicalism and Attempted to Overthrow the British Empire* (Berkeley, CA: University of California Press, 2012).

61. Stephen Kern, *The Culture of Time and Space, 1880–1918* (Cambridge, MA: Harvard University Press, 2003), pp. 313–14.

62. Walter Benjamin, "The Work of Art in the Age of Mechanical Reproduction" in Walter Benjamin and Hannah Arendt, eds. *Illuminations* (New York: Schocken Books, 2007); Paul Virilio, *The Vision Machine* (Bloomington, IN: Indiana University Press, 1994); Guy Dubord, *The Society of the Spectacle* (New York: Zone Books, 1994); Feldges, *American Icons*; W.J.T. Mitchell, *Picture Theory: Essays on Verbal and Visual Representation* (Chicago, IL: University of Chicago Press, 1995).

63. Quoted in Kern, *Culture of Time and Space*, p. 67; Bill Kovarik, *Revolutions in Communication: Media History from Gutenberg to the Digital Age* (New York: Continuum, 2011).

64. Mitchell, *What Do Pictures Want?*, p. 47.

65. Jeffrey T. Schnapp, *Revolutionary Tides: The Art of the Political Poster, 1914–1989* (Milan: Skira, 2005); Jay W. Baird, *To Die for Germany: Heroes in the Nazi Pantheon* (Bloomington, IN: Indiana University Press, 1990); Susan Buck-Morss, "Visual Empire," *Diacritics* 37, 2/3 (2007): 171–98.

66. Faisal Devji, *The Impossible Indian: Gandhi and the Temptation of Violence* (Cambridge, MA: Harvard University Press, 2012); Claude Markovits, *The UnGandhian Gandhi: The Life and Afterlife of the Mahatma* (New York: Anthem, 2006).

67. David King, *Russian Revolutionary Posters: From Civil War to Socialist Realism, from Bolshevism to the End of Stalin* (London: Tate Publishing, 2012); Steven Heller, *Iron Fists: Branding the Totalitarian State* (New York: Phaidon, 2008); Victoria E. Bonnell, *Iconography of Power: Soviet Political Posters under Lenin and Stalin* (Berkeley, CA: University of California Press, 1999); Nina Tumarkin, *Lenin Lives!: The Lenin Cult in Soviet Russia* (Cambridge, MA: Harvard University Press, 1997).

68. Robin D.G. Kelley, *Africa Speaks, America Answers: Modern Jazz in Revolutionary Times* (Cambridge, MA: Harvard University Press, 2012). On the role of the international recording industry see Damon J. Phillips, *Shaping Jazz: Cities, Labels, and the Global Emergence of an Art Form* (Princeton, NJ: Princeton University Press, 2013); Bob W. White, "Congolese Rumba and Other Cosmopolitanisms," *Cahiers d'Études africaines* 168 (2002): 663–86; Paul Gilroy, *The Black Atlantic: Modernity and Double Consciousness* (Cambridge, MA: Harvard University Press, 1993).

69. John Shelton Lawrence and Robert Jewett, *Myth of the American Superhero* (Grand Rapids, MI: W.B. Eerdmans, 2002); Robin S. Rosenberg and Peter Coogan, eds, *What is a Superhero?* (New York: Oxford University Press, 2013); Aldo J. Regalado, *Bending Steel: Modernity and the American Superhero* (Jackson, MS: University of Mississippi Press, 2015).

70. Christopher Pinney, *'Photos of the Gods': The Printed Image and Political Struggle in India* (London: Reaktion, 2004).

71. Vijay Prashad, *The Darker Nations: A People's History of the Third World* (New York: W.W. Norton, 2007); Darryl C. Thomas, *The Theory and Practice of Third World Solidarity* (Westport, CT: Praeger, 2001); Mark T. Berger, "After the Third World? History, destiny and the fate of Third Worldism," *Third World Quarterly* 25, 1 (2004): 9–39; Quinn Slobodian, ed, *Comrades of Color: East Germany in the Cold War World* (New York: Berghahn, 2015).

72. Daniel J. Boorstin, *The Image: A Guide to Pseudo-events in America* (New York: Vintage, 1992); Roland Barthes, *Mythologies* (London: Paladin, 1972); Scott Lash and Celia Lury, *Global Culture Industry: The Mediation of Things* (Cambridge: Polity, 2007); Raymond Williams, *Television: Technology and Cultural Form* (New York: Schocken Books, 1975).

73. Maurice Rickards, *Posters of Protest and Revolution* (New York: Walker and Company, 1970); Susan Martin, ed, *Decade of Protest: Political Posters from the United States, Viet Nam, Cuba, 1965–1975* (Santa Monica, CA: Smart Art Press, 1996); Russ Davidson, *Latin American Posters: Public Aesthetics and Mass Politics* (Santa Fe, NM: Museum of New Mexico Press, 2006); Sam Durant, ed, *Black Panther: The Revolutionary Art of Emory Douglas* (New York: Rizzoli, 2007); Dugald Sterner, *The Art of Revolution. Castro's Cuba: 1959–1970* (New York: McGraw-Hill, 1970).

74. Richard Frick, Ulises Estrada, OSPAAL, et al., eds, *The Tricontinental Solidarity Poster* (Bern: Commedia-Verlag, 2003).

75. Alexander C. Cook, ed, *Mao's Little Red Book: A Global History* (Cambridge: Cambridge University Press, 2014); Wini Breines, *Community and Organization in the New Left, 1962–1968: The Great Refusal* (New York: Praeger, 1982).

76. Mary Blume, "50 Million Frenchmen Can't Be Wrong—Posters Sell," *Los Angeles Times*, 10 December 1967; Susan Sontag, "Posters: Advertisement, Art, Political Artifact, Commodity," in Michael Bierut, ed, *Looking Closer 3* (New York: Allworth Press, 1999), pp. 196–218; Leerom Medovoi, *Rebels: Youth and the Cold War Origins of Identity* (Durham, NC: Duke University Press, 2005).

77. Miguel "Mickey" Melendez, *We took the streets: Fighting for Latino rights with the Young Lords* (New York: St. Martin's Press, 2003), pp. 7, 113, 119–20; "Communists: The Cult of Che," *Time Magazine*, 17 May 1968. The style of Cuban revolutionaries resonated widely. For example, in early 1960s Zanzibar, Cuban-style fatigues and beards became popular accouterments for Zanzibar Nationalist Party stalwarts. Michael F. Lofchie, "Was Okello's Revolution a Conspiracy?," *Transition* 33 (1967): 37.

78. Lazier, "Earthrise"; James Schwoch, *Global TV: New Media and the Cold War, 1946–69* (Urbana, IL: University of Illinois Press, 2009), p. 154; Paddy Scannell, *Radio, Television, and Modern Life: A Phenomenological Approach* (Cambridge, MA: Blackwell, 1996). On the tensions between social movements and media coverage see Todd Gitlin, *The Whole World is Watching: Mass Media in the Making and Unmaking of the New Left* (Berkeley, CA: University of California Press, 2003).

79. Jeff Goodwin, *No Other Way Out: States and Revolutionary Movements, 1945–1991* (Cambridge: Cambridge University Press, 2001); Immanuel Wallerstein, "New Revolts Against the System," *New Left Review* 18 (November–December 2002): 29–39; Sidney G. Tarrow, *Power in Movement: Social Movements and Contentious Politics* (Cambridge: Cambridge University Press, 2011); Charles Tilly, *Social Movements 1768–2012* (Boulder, CO: Paradigm, 2012).

80. Sohail Daulatzai, "War at 33 1/3: Hip Hop, the Language of the Unheard, and the Afro-Asian Atlantic," in Dipannita Basu and Sidney J. Lemelle, eds, *The Vinyl Ain't Final: Hip Hop and the Globalization of Black Popular Culture* (London: Pluto Press, 2006), pp. 100–16; Kevin Mattson, "Did Punk Matter? Analyzing the

Practices of a Youth Subculture During the 1980s," *American Studies* 42, 1 (2001): 69–97; Stephen A. King, "International reggae, democratic socialism, and the secularization of the Rastafarian movement, 1972–1980," *Popular Music and Society* 22, 3 (1998): 39–60.

81. Francis Fukuyama, *The End of History and the Last Man* (New York: Free Press, 1992); Peter Geschiere, *The Perils of Belonging: Autochthony, Citizenship, and Exclusion in Africa and Europe* (Chicago, IL: University of Chicago Press, 2009).

82. Ernesto Laclau, *New reflections on the revolution of our time* (London: Verso, 1990); Ernest Mandel, *Late Capitalism* (London: Verso, 1998); Joseph Stiglitz, *Globalization and its Discontents* (New York: Norton, 2002).

83. Lawrence Wright, *The Looming Tower: Al Qaeda and the Road to 9/11* (New York: Knopf, 2006). For a wider perspective on the growing importance of religion, see Roland Robertson and JoAnn Chirico, "Humanity, Globalization, and Worldwide Religious Resurgence: A Theoretical Explanation," *Sociology of Religion* 46, 3 (1985): 219–42.

84. David Harvey, *A Brief History of Neoliberalism* (New York: Oxford University Press, 2005).

85. Sandra Ponzanesi, *The Postcolonial Cultural Industry: Icons, Markets, Mythologies* (New York: Palgrave Macmillan, 2014); Faye D. Ginsburg, Lila Abu-Lughod, and Brian Larkin, eds, *Media Worlds: Anthropology on New Terrain* (Berkeley, CA: University of California Press, 2002); Douglas Kellner, *Media Culture: Cultural Studies, Identity, and Politics Between the Modern and the Postmodern* (London: Routledge, 1995).

86. Anthony Giddens, *Runaway World* (New York: Routledge, 1999); P. David Marshall, *Celebrity and Power: Fame in Contemporary Culture* (Minneapolis, MN: University of Minnesota Press, 1997); Bronislaw Szerszynski and John Urry, "Cultures of Cosmopolitanism," *The Sociological Review* 50, 4 (2002): 461–481. See also, Sarah Franklin, Ceha Lury, and Jackie Stacey, *Global Nature, Global Culture* (London: Routledge, 2000).

87. Sanderson and Macdonald, eds, *Marshall McLuhan*.

88. Jeffrey Richards, Scott Wilson, and Linda Woodhead, eds, *Diana, The Making of a Media Saint* (London: I.B.Tauris, 1999); John Urry, *Global Complexity* (London: Polity, 2002), pp. 134–5. See also Brian Larkin, *Signal and Noise: Media, Infrastructure, and Urban Culture in Nigeria* (Durham, NC: Duke University Press, 2008).

89. Douglas Kellner, "September 11, Spectacles of Terror, and Media Manipulation: A Critique of Jihadist and Bush Media Politics," *Logos* 2, 1 (2003): 86–102. According to CBS News, 9/11 proved the "most memorable moment" in US television history. "TV's Most Memorable Moments: 9/11 Tops the List," *CBS News.com*, 11 July 2012 http://www.cbsnews.com/news/tvs-most-memorable-moments-9-11-tops-the-list/ (accessed 15 August 2016).

90. Vijay Prashad, *The Poorer Nations: A Possible History of the Global South* (New York: Verso, 2012); David Harvey, *A Brief History of Neoliberalism* (Oxford: Oxford University Press, 2007); Naomi Klein, *The Shock Doctrine: The Rise of Disaster Capitalism* (New York: Metropolitan Books, 2007); Stiglitz, *Globalization and its discontents*; Terence K. Hopkins and Immanuel Wallerstein, *The Age of Transition: Trajectory of the World-System, 1945–2025* (Bedford: St. Martin's Press, 1996).

91. Richard Kahn and Douglas Kellner estimate that there were at least fifty-six riots globally in direct response to International Monetary Fund policies between 1985 and 1992. Richard Kahn and Douglas Kellner, "Resisting Globalization," in George Ritzer, ed, *The Blackwell Companion to Globalization* (Oxford: Wiley-Blackwell, 2007), p. 664.

92. Jeffrey S. Juris, *Networking Futures: The Movements against Corporate Globalization* (Durham, NC: Duke University Press, 2008); Michael Hardt and Antonio Negri, *Multitude: War and Democracy in the Age of Empire* (New York: Penguin Press, 2004).

93. Frederic Jameson, *Postmodernity, or the cultural logic of late capitalism* (Durham, NC: Duke University Press, 1992); Slavoj Žižek, *Welcome to the Desert of the Real!: Five Essays on September 11 and other Important Dates* (New York: Verso, 2002), pp. 23–4; T.V. Reed, *The Art of Protest: Culture and Activism from the Civil Rights Movement to the Streets of Seattle* (Minneapolis, MN: University of Minnesota Press, 2005).

94. Marshall, *Celebrity and Power*; Joshua Gamson, *Claims to Fame: Celebrity in Contemporary America* (Berkeley, CA: University of California Press, 1994); Su Holmes and Sean Redmond, eds, *Framing Celebrity: New Directions in Celebrity Culture* (New York: Routledge, 2006); Sharrona Pearl and Dana Polan, "Bodies of Digital Celebrity," *Public Culture* 27, 1 (2015): 185–92.

95. Jeff Chang, *Can't Stop, Won't Stop: A History of the Hip-Hop Generation* (New York: St. Martin's Press, 2005); Jeffrey O.G. Ogbar, *Hip-Hop Revolution: The Culture and Politics of Rap* (Lawrence, KS: University Press of Kansas, 2007); Andreana Clay, *The Hip-Hop Generation Fights Back: Youth, Activism, and Post-Civil Right Politics* (New York: NYU Press, 2012); Murray Forman and Mark Anthony Neal, eds, *That's the Joint! The Hip-Hop Studies Reader* (London: Routledge, 2012).

96. Paul Gilroy, *Darker than Blue: On the Moral Economies of Black Atlantic Culture* (Cambridge: Belknap Press, 2010); Michael Eric Dyson, *Holler if you Hear Me: Searching for Tupac Shakur* (New York: Basic Civitas Books, 2003).

97. Faisal Devji, *Landscapes of the Jihad: Militancy, Morality, Modernity* (London: Hurst, 2005); Faisal Devji, *The Terrorist in Search of Humanity: Militant Islam and Global Politics* (London: Hurst, 2009).

98. Todd Gitlin, *Occupy Nation: The Roots, the Spirit, and the Promise of Occupy Wall Street* (New York: It Books, 2012); Slavoj Žižek, *The Year of Dreaming Dangerously* (New York: Verso, 2012); Kate Khatib, et al., *We Are Many: Reflections on Movement Strategy from Occupation to Liberation* (Oakland, CA: AK Press, 2012); Milton Glaser and Milko Ilic, *Design of Dissent* (Gloucester, MA: Rockport Publishers, 2005); Adam Branch and Zachariah Mampilly, *Africa Uprising: Popular Protest and Political Change* (London: Zed Books, 2015).

99. Angela Y. Davis, *Freedom is a Constant Struggle: Ferguson, Palestine, and the Foundations of a Movement* (Chicago, IL: Haymarket, 2016), p. 123.

## 1. UNTIL VICTORY: CHE GUEVARA AND THE REVOLUTIONARY IDEAL

1. Lewis H. Diuguid, "Survey Finds Guevara Hero of Student Left," *Los Angeles Times*, 15 January 1968; "Tribute to Guevara," Panama City Radio Aeropuerto, 24 October 1967, Foreign Broadcast Information Service Daily Reports (hereafter FBIS-DR),

FRB-67-207. Available online at http://infoweb.newsbank.com; 'Brazzaville President Praises Che Guevara,' Havana, 26 October 1967, FBIS-DR, FRB-67-209; Robert Vincent Daniels, *Year of the Heroic Guerrilla: World Revolution and Counterrevolution in 1968* (New York: Basic Books, 1989), p. 34.

2. Todd Gitlin, *The Sixties:Years of Hope, Days of Rage* (New York: Bantam Books, 1987), p. 330.

3. Gavin O'Toole, "Introduction," in Gavin O'Toole and Georgina Jiménez, eds, *Che in Verse* (Wiltshire: Aflame Books, 2007), pp. 36–7; Jeffrey L. Gould, "Solidarity Under Siege: The Latin American Left, 1968," *American Historical Review* 114, 2 (2009): 352; Robert E. Scott, "Student Political Activism in Latin America," in Seymour Martin Lipset and Philip G. Altbach, eds, *Students in Revolt* (Boston, MA: Beacon Press, 1970), pp. 403–31; "NFLSV Honors Che Guevara's Death Anniversary," Hanoi VNA International Service, 8 October 1968; FBIS-DR, FRB-68-198. The anniversary of Che Guevara's death would remain important for many years. As late as the mid-1970s, the US secretary of state sent out a warning to all US embassies that the anniversity could "stimulate local anti-US activity." US Secretary of State to All American Republic Diplomatic Posts, "Guevara Anniversary," Telegram 235364, 2 October 1975; D750343–0565 [Electronic Record]; Central Foreign Policy Files, 1973–79/D-Reel Microfilm, RG 59: General Records of the Department of State, US National Archives at College Park, College Park, MD (hereafter NACP) [retrieved from the Access to Archival Databases at www.archives. gov, 23 April 2014]. Jorge Castañeda, "Does Che Guevara Still Matter?," *Big Think*, 16 February 2010, http://bigthink.com/videos/does-che-guevara-still-matter (accessed 25 August 2013).

4. Marc Weitzman, "The Year Coca Cola Won the Cold War," in Marc Weitzman and Eric Hobsbawm, eds, *1968: Magnum Throughout the World* (Paris: Hazan, 1998), pp. 11–16; Alistair Hennessy, "The New Radicalism in Latin America," *Journal of Contemporary History* 7, 1/2 (January–April 1972): 1–26.

5. Gianni Statera, *Death of a Utopia: The Development and Decline of Student Movements in Europe* (New York: Oxford University Press, 1975); George N. Katsiaficas, *The Imagination of the New Left: A Global Analysis of 1968* (Boston, MA: South End Press, 1987); Carole Fink, Philipp Gassert, and Detlef Junker, eds, *1968, the World Transformed* (Cambridge: Cambridge University Press, 1998); Gerd Ranier-Horn, *The Spirit of '68: Rebellion in Western Europe and North America, 1956–1976* (Oxford: Oxford University Press, 2007); Geneviève Dreyfus-Armand, Robert Frank, Marie-Françoise Lévy, and Michelle Zancarini-Fournel, eds, *Les Années 68. Le temps de la contestation* (Brussels: Éditions Complexe, 2008); Martin Klimke and Joachim Scharloth, *1968 in Europe: A history of protest and activism, 1956–1977* (New York: Palgrave Macmillan, 2008); Philipp Glassert and Martin Klimke, eds, *1968: Memories and Legacies of a Global Revolt*, Bulletin of the German Historical Institute, Supplement 6 (Washington, DC: German Historical Institute, 2009); Oliver Rathkolb and Friedrich Stadler, eds, *Das Jahr 1968: Ereignis, Symbol, Chiffre* (Göttingen: Vienna University Press, 2010); Martin Klimke, Jacco Pekelder, and Joachim Scharloth, eds, *Between Prague Spring and French May: Opposition and Revolt in Europe, 1960–1980* (New York: Berghahn, 2011); Samantha Christiansen and

Zachary A. Scarlett, eds, *The Third World in the Global 1960s* (New York: Berghahn, 2012); Robert Gildea, James Mark, Anette Warring, eds, *Europe's 1968: Voices of Revolt* (Oxford: Oxford University Press, 2013); Timothy Brown and Andrew Lison, eds, *The Global Sixties in Sound and Vision: Media, Counterculture, Revolt* (New York: Palgrave Macmillan, 2014).

6. David Kunzle, ed., *Che Guevara: Icon, Myth, and Message* (Los Angeles, CA: UCLA Fowler Museum of Cultural History, 1997); Trisha Ziff, ed., *Che Guevara: Revolutionary & Icon* (London: V&A Publishers, 2006); Michael Casey, *Che's Afterlife: the legacy of an image* (New York: Vintage, 2009).

7. For a review of the effervescence of literature on Guevara see Paulo Drinot, "Introduction," in Paulo Drinot, ed., *Che's Travels: The Making of a Revolutionary in 1950s Latin America* (Durham, NC: Duke University Press, 2010), pp. 1–10. On Che's importance to protest movements, see Robert Frank, "Imaginaire politique et figures symboliques internationales: Castro, Hô, Mao et le 'Che'," in Dreyfus-Armand et al., *Les années 68*, pp. 31–47; and Carlos Soria-Galvarro, "Bolivia: Che Guevara in Global History," in Glassert and Klimke, eds, *1968*, pp. 33–8. On Che's importance to guerrilla movements, see Donald C. Hodges, ed., *The Legacy of Che Guevara: A Documentary Study* (London: Thames and Hudson, 1977); Brian Loveman and Thomas M. Davies, Jr., eds, *Che Guevara: Guerrilla Warfare* (Wilmington, DE: Scholarly Resources, 1997); Gordon H. McCormick, "Che Guevara: The Legacy of a Revolutionary Man," *World Policy Journal* 14, 4 (1997/1998): 63–79; Olivier Besancenot and Michael Löwy, *Che Guevara: His Revolutionary Legacy* (New York: Monthly Review Press, 2009).

8. Prasenjit Duara, "The Cold War as a historical period: an interpretive essay," *Journal of Global History* 6 (2011): 457–80; Katsiaficas, *The Imagination of the New Left*.

9. Raymond Williams, *Marxism and Literature* (Oxford: Oxford University Press, 1977); Alain Touraine, *The May Movement: Revolt and Reform* (New York: Random House, 1971).

10. Fredric Jameson, "Periodizing the 60s," *Social Text* 9/10 (1984): 208; Max Elbaum, *Revolution in the Air: Sixties Radicals Turn to Lenin, Mao, and Che* (New York: Verso, 2002), p. 23; Arif Dirlik, "The Third World in 1968," in Fink, Gassert and Junker, eds, *1968, The World Transformed*, p. 314.

11. Caroline Fink, Phillip Gassert, and Detlef Junker, "Introduction," in Fink, Gassert and Junker, eds, *1968, The World Transformed*, p. 21; Ingrid Gilcher-Holtey, "The Dynamic of Protest: May 1968 in France," *Critique* 36, 2 (August 2008): 210; Timothy S. Brown, "'1968' East and West: Divided Germany as a Case Study in Transnational History," *American Historical Review* 114, 1 (February 2009): 69–96; Simon Prince, "The Global Revolt of 1968 and Northern Ireland," *The Historical Journal* 49, 3 (2006): 851–75.

12. Benedict Anderson, *Under Three Flags: anarchism and the anti-colonial imagination* (New York: Verso, 2005), p. 28.

13. On the political uses of Trotsky and Mao, see A. Belden Fields, *Trotskyism and Maoism: Theory and Practice in France and the United States* (New York: Praeger, 1988); Gaël Abou-Khalil, "Image de Mao et imaginaire maoïste en France de 1965 à

1973," (thesis, University of Paris-I Panthéon-Sorbonne, 1999); Andrew Ross, "Mao Zedong's Impact on Cultural Politics in the West," *Cultural Politics* 1, 1 (2005): 5–22; Robin D.G. Kelley and Betsy Esch, "Black Like Mao: Red China and Black Revolution," in Fred Ho and Bill V. Mullen, eds, *Afro Asia: Revolutionary Political and Cultural Connections between African Americans and Asian Americans* (Durham, NC: Duke Univeristy Press, 2008), pp. 97–154; Timothy S. Brown, *West Germany and the Global Sixties: The Anti-Authoritarian Revolt, 1962–1978* (Cambridge: Cambridge University Press, 2013), pp. 207–10; Robeson Taj Frazier, *The East is Black: Cold War China in the Black Radical Imagination* (Durham, NC: Duke University Press, 2015). On Fanon, see Christopher J. Lee, *Toward a Revolutionary Humanism* (Athens, OH: Ohio University Press, 2015).

14.　On the concept of *communitas* see Victor Turner, *The Ritual Process: Structure and Anti-Structure* (Ithaca, NY: Cornell University Press, 1977); Christopher J. Lee, "Between a Moment and an Era: The Precursors and Afterlives of Bandung," in Christopher J. Lee, ed., *Making a World After Empire: The Bandung Moment and Its Political Afterlives* (Athens, OH: Ohio University Press, 2010), 1–44.

15.　John D. Martz, "Doctrine and Dilemmas of the Latin American 'New Left'", *World Politics* 22, 2 (1970): 173; Ruth Reitan, Michael L. Clemens and Charles E. Jones, "Global Solidarity: The Black Panther Party in the International Arena," *New Political Science* 21, 2 (1999): 177–203; Vijay Prashad, *The Darker Nations: A People's History of the Third World* (New York: New Press, 2008).

16.　Barbara and John Ehrenreich, *Long March, Short Spring: The Student Uprising at Home and Abroad* (New York: Monthly Review Press, 1969), p. 179; Mark T. Berger, "After the Third World? History, destiny and the fate of Third Worldism," *Third World Quarterly* 25, 1 (2004), 9–39; Leerom Medovoi, *Rebels: Youth and the Cold War Origins of Identity* (Durham, NC: Duke University Press, 2005), pp. 323–4; Karen Steller Bjerregaard, "Guerrillas and Grassroots: Danish Solidarity with the Third World 1960–79," in Klimke, Pekelder, and Scharloth, eds, *Between Prague Spring and French May*, pp. 213–32; Romain Bertrand, "May 68 et l'anticolonialisme", in Dominique Damamme et al, eds. *Mai-juin 68* (Paris: l'Atelier, 2008), pp. 89–101.

17.　Ruth Reitan, "Cuba, the Black Panther Party, and the U.S. Black Movement in the 1960s: Issues of Security," in Kathleen Cleaver and George Katsiaficas, eds, *Liberation, Imagination, and the Black Panther Party: A New Look at the Panthers and their Legacy* (Routledge: New York, 2001), pp. 164–74; Max Elbaum, "What Legacy from the Radical Internationalism of 1968?", *Radical History Review* 82 (Winter 2002): 40–1; Cynthia A. Young, *Soul Power: Culture, Radicalism, and the Making of a US Third World Left* (Durham, NC: Duke University Press, 2006).

18.　Klaus Mehnert, *Twilight of the Young: The Radical Movements of the 1960s and their Legacy* (New York: Holt, Rinehart and Winston, 1976), p. 114; Dirlik, "The Third World," pp. 296–7.

19.　Tom Hayden, "A Generation on Trial," *Ramparts* 9, 1 (July 1970): 20.

20.　Ernesto Chávez, *"¡Mi Raza Primero!" (My People First!): Nationalism, Identity, and Insurgency in the Chicano Movement in Los Angeles, 1966–1978* (Berkeley, CA: University of California Press, 2002), p. 65; Michael Seidman, *The Imaginary*

*Revolution: Parisian Students and Workers in 1968* (New York: Berghahn Books, 2004), p. 66.

21. Richard Davy, "Guevara: symbol of eternal political youth," *The Times*, 28 May 1968; Andrew Sinclair, "The Death and Life of Che Guevara," in Andrew Sinclair, ed., *Viva Che! The Strange Death and Life of Che Guevara* (Phoenix Mill: Sutton, 2006 [1968]), p. 180, quoted in Kunzle, ed, *Che Guevara*, p. 19; Frank, "p. politique," 36; Pacho O'Donnell, *Che Guevara: La vida por un mundo mejor* (Barcelona: Plaza Janés, 2003), p. 542.

22. Richard Holmes, *Footsteps: Adventures of a Romantic Biographer* (London: Hodder and Stoughton, 1985), p. 76.

23. Mary Blume, "50 Million Frenchmen Can't Be Wrong: Posters Sell," *Los Angeles Times*, 10 December 1967.

24. *Time Magazine*, "Communists: The Cult of Che," 17 May 1968.

25. Michael Bracewell, *Re-make/Re-model: Art, Pop, Fashion and the making of Roxy Music, 1953–1972* (London: Faber & Faber, 2007).

26. National Archives of the United Kingdom and Ireland (hereafter TNA), FCO 7/5 "Che Guevara: death and published diary of activities in Bolivia," 1967–8; John J. Goldman, "A University in, but not of its Time," *Los Angeles Times*, 26 May 1968.

27. *The New York Times*, "Actors and Author Of 'Che!' Arrested After Performance," 8 May 1969; *Time Magazine*, "Che: A Myth Embalmed in a Matrix of Ignorance," 12 October 1970.

28. *Chicago Tribune*, "Communists: The Cult of Che" and "Turkey Bans Diaries Left by 'Che' Guevara," 18 September 1968; O'Toole, "Introduction," pp. 17–18.

29. American Embassy Santiago to US Secretary of State, "Subversive 'Red Boomerang' Plot is Broken," Telegram 07654, 12 November 1975; D750394–0876 [Electronic Record]; Central Foreign Policy Files, 1973–79/D-Reel Microfilm, RG 59: General Records of the Department of State, NACP [retrieved from the Access to Archival Databases at www.archives.gov, 23 April 2014]. *Chicago Tribune*, "Try to Bomb Movie [Theater] Showing Guevara Film," 19 June 1969; Christine Petra Sellin, "Demythification: The Twentieth Century Fox *Che!*," in Kunzle, ed, *Che Guevara*, p. 103. *Che!* was not the first cinematic portrayal of Guevara's final months. Paolo Heusch's *El 'Che' Guevara* (later *Bloody Che Contra*) was released in 1968.

30. *Citizen Smith*, BBC (1977–80); Christopher Kenworthy, *Citizen Smith* (Cox and Wyman, 1978).

31. *Time Magazine*, "Che: A Myth Embalmed in a Matrix of Ignorance."

32. Tariq Ali, *Street Fighting Years: An autobiography of the sixties* (London: Colins, 1987), p. 204; Tariq Ali, *1968 and After: Inside the Revolution* (London: Blond & Briggs, Ltd., 1978), pp. xv-xvi, xx.

33. Karl E. Meyer, "Britain's Young Rebels Rally to Ali," *Times Herald*, 17 April 1968.

34. George Mariscal, *Brown-eyed Children of the Sun: lessons from the Chicano movement, 1965–1975* (Albuquerque, NM: University of New Mexico Press, 2005), p. 100; Thomas C. Wright, *Latin America in the Era of the Cuban Revolution* (Westport, CT: Praeger, 2001); John A. Gronbeck-Tedesco, "The Left in Transition: The Cuban Revolution in US Third World Politics," *Journal of Latin American Studies* 40 (2008):

651–73; Kepa Artaraz and Karen Luyckx, "The French New Left and the Cuban Revoltuion 1959–1971: Parallel Histories?," *Modern & Contemporary France* 17, 1 (2009): 67–82.

35. Martz, "Doctrines and Dilemmas", p. 180; Michael Löwy, *The Marxism of Che Guevara: Philosophy, Economics, Revolutionary Warfare* (Lanham, MD: Rowman & Littlefield, 2007).

36. Ernesto Guevara, "Message to the Tricontinental," reprinted in Che Guevara, *Guerrilla Warfare* (Lincoln, NE: University of Nebraska Press, 1998), pp. 161–72.

37. Che Guevara, "Vietnam Must Not Stand Alone," *New Left Review* (1967): 81. For a thorough analysis of Guevara's thought, see Samuel Farber, *The Politics of Che Guevara: Theory and Practice* (Chicago, IL: Haymarket, 2016).

38. McCormick, "Che Guevara," 70; Ernesto Guevara, "Letter of Resignation [1965]", quoted in Martz, "Doctrines and Dilemmas", p. 181.

39. Sara Evans, "Sons, Daughters, and Patriarchy: Gender and the 1968 Generation," *American Historical Review* 114, 2 (April 2009): 331–47. On masculinity and patriarchy within radical circles see also Mariscal, *Brown Eyed Children of the Sun*, pp. 100–1; María Josefina Saldaña-Portillo, *The revolutionary imagination in the Americas and the age of development* (Durham, NC: Duke University Press, 2003); Laura Pulido, *Black, Brown, Yellow, and Left: Radical Activism in Los Angeles* (Berkeley, CA: University of California Press, 2006), ch. 7; Alan Rosenfeld, "'Anarchist Amazons': The Gendering of Radicalism in 1970s West Germany," *Contemporary European History* 19, 4 (2010): 351–74.

40. Mark Rudd, "Che and Me," http://www.markrudd.com/?violence-and-non-violence/che-and-me.html (accessed 12 March 2011); Mark Rudd, "The Male Cult of Martyrdom: Saying Adios to Che," *WIN Magazine*, Spring 2010, http://www.warresisters.org/node/1012 (accessed 19 January 2012).

41. Jeremi Suri, "The Rise and Fall of the International Counterculture, 1960–1975," *American Historical Review* 114, 1 (February 2009): 47; John Berger, "Che Guevara: the Moral Factor," *Urban Review* 8, 3 (1967): 202–8; Casey, *Che's Afterlife*, p. 138; Robert S. Jansen, "Resurrection and Appropriation: Reputational Trajectories, Memory Work, and the Political Use of Historical Figures," *American Journal of Sociology* 112, 4 (January 2007): 953–1007.

42. Russ Davidson, *Latin American Posters: Public Aesthetics and Mass Politics* (Santa Fe, NM: Museum of New Mexico Press, 2006), pp. 57, 97; Ramón Favela, *The Art of Rupert García* (San Francisco, CA: Chronicle Books and the Mexican Musem, 1986). Other reproductions of the Korda image were also in circulation. In August 1967 the French weekly *Paris Match* published a version of Heroic Guerrilla, which accompanied an article on insurgents in South America. Many published memorials to Che in the US reproduced the Korda photograph as well. See, for instance, Todd Gitlin, "Che Lives. Che Dies," *Berkeley Barb* 5, 21 (November 24–30, 1967): 5. The Cuban government later used versions of Heroic Guerrilla on the national currency.

43. Trisha Ziff, "Guerrillero Heroico," in Ziff, ed, *Che Guevara: Revolutionary & Icon*. Cuban artist Alfredo Rostgaard, American artist Rupert García, and Polish artist Roman Cieslewicz produced similar renderings of Heroic Guerrilla in late 1967

and 1968. García's image, developed for the San Francisco State University student strike, juxtaposed Heroic Guerrilla with the phrase "Right On!" Maria-Carolina Cambre, *The Semiotics of Che Guevara: Affective Gateways* (New York: Bloomsbury, 2015), pp. 186–7; Davidson, *Latin American Posters*, pp. 55–6.

44. Aleksandra Mir, "Not everything is always Black or White [Interview with Jim Fitzpatrick]," 3 January 2005, http://www.aleksandramir.info/texts/fitzpatrick.html (accessed 5 April 2010). The Heroic Guerrilla composition would also inspire representations of other radical leaders. For instance, Black Panther Party graphic artist and Party Minister of Culture Emory Douglas adapted elements of the composition to frame Huey P. Newton for the masthead of *The Black Panther* news magazine. Colette Gaiter, "What Revolution Looks Like: The Work of Black Panther Artist Emory Douglas," in Sam Durant, ed, *Black Panther: The Revolutionary Art of Emory Douglas* (New York: Rizzoli, 2007), p. 108.

45. Ziff, "Guerrillero Heroico," p. 6; McCormick, "Che Guevara," p. 77; Casey, *Che's Afterlife*, pp. 100–2; Cambre, *Semiotics of Che*, p. 9.

46. Mark Kurlansky, *1968: The Year that Rocked the World* (New York: Ballantine, 2003), p. 21; Juergen Corleis, *Always on the Other Side: A Journalist's Journey from Hitler to Howard's End* (n.p., 2008), pp. 117–18; Juan de Onis, "Havana Fosters Guevara Cult With Zeal of Political Campaign," *The New York Times*, 7 January 1968.

47. Martin Ebon, *Che: The Making of a Legend* (New York: Universe Books, 1969), p. 172.

48. Mark Rudd, *Underground: My Life with SDS and the Weathermen* (New York: William Morrow, 2009), p. 42.

49. Though the foco theory was only partially inspired by Che's thinking, Guevara and the foco concept became synonymous. See Régis Debray, *Revolution in the Revolution? Armed struggle and political struggle in Latin America* (New York: MR Press, 1967); Ingrid Gilcher-Holtey, "The European 1960s–70s and the World: The Case of Régis Debray," in Klimke, Pekelder, and Scharloth, eds, *Between Prague Spring and French May*, pp. 269–80.

50. Gitlin, *The Sixties*, p. 239; Mike Gonzalez, "The Culture of the Heroic Guerrilla: The Impact of Cuba in the Sixties," *Bulletin of Latin American Research* 3, 2 (1984): 66–7; Joachim Schickel, *Guerrilleros, Partisanen: Theorie und Praxis* (Munich: C. Hanser, 1970); Kepa Artaraz and Karen Luyckx, "The French New Left and the Cuban Revolution 1959–1971: Parallel Histories?," *Modern & Contemporary France* 17, 1 (2009): 67–82.

51. Edward W. Said, *The World, The Text, and the Critic* (Cambridge, MA: Harvard University Press, 1983).

52. Sina Rahmani, "Anti-imperialism and its Discontents: An Interview with Mark Rudd, Founding Member of the Weather Underground," *Radical History Review* 95 (Spring 2006): 117–21.

53. Mark Rudd, Untitled article, *Movement* (March 1969), http://beatl.barnard.columbia.edu/ Columbia68/ (accessed 14 March 2011); Hilton Obenzinger, *Busy Dying* (Tuscon, AZ: Chax, 2008), pp. 76–7.

54. Steve Diamond et. al., "Revolution at Columbia," *The Fifth Estate* 3, 2 (May 16–31,

1968): 1; Mark Rudd, "Columbia: Notes on the Spring Rebellion," in Carl Oglesby, ed, *The New Left Reader* (New York: Grove Press, 1969), p. 311.

55. Rahmani, "Anti-imperialism and Its Discontents"; *The New York Times*, "Cubans Quote Rudd," 14 June 1968; Tom Hayden, "Two, Three, Many Columbias," *Ramparts* 15 June 1968; Joanne Grant, *Confrontation on Campus: The Columbia Pattern for the New Protest* (New York: New American Library, 1969); Eleanor Raskin, "The Occupation of Columbia University: April 1968," *Journal of American Studies* 19, 2 (1985): 260. The SAS and SDS also piqued their fellow students' curiosity about Che. After the revolt books about him became bestsellers at the Columbia University bookstore. John J. Goldman, "A University in, but Not of its Time," *Los Angeles Times*, 26 May 1968.

56. Timothy S. Brown, *West Germany and the Global Sixties: The Anti-Authoritarian Revolt, 1962–1978* (Cambridge: Cambridge University Press, 2013), p. 207.

57. Brown, *West Germany*, p. 211.

58. Gerd Poppe quoted in James Mark and Anna von der Goltz, "Encounters," in Robert Gildea, James Mark and Anette Warring, eds, *Europe's 1968: Voices of Revolt*, (Oxford: Oxford University Press, 2013), p. 145.

59. Martin Klimke, *The Other Alliance: Student Protest in West Germany and the United States in the Global Sixties* (Princeton, NJ: Princeton University Press, 2010), pp. 8, 92 and Chapter 2; Mehnert, *Twilight of the Young*, pp. 102, 114; Chris Harman, *The Fire Last Time: 1968 and after* (London: Bookmarks, 1988), p. 37; Uta G. Poiger, "Imperialism and consumption: two tropes in West German radicalism," in Axel Schildt and Detlef Siegfried, eds, *Between Marx and Coca-Cola: youth cultures in changing European societies, 1960–1980* (New York: Berghahn, 2006), pp. 161–74.

60. Ingrid Gilcher-Holtey, "Transformation by Subversion? The New Left and the Question of Violence," in Belinda Davis, Wilfried Mausback, Martin Klimke, and Carla MacDougall, eds, *Changing the World, Changing Oneself: Political Protest and Collective Identities in West Germany and the U.S. in the 1960s and 1970s* (New York: Berghahn Books, 2010), pp. 161–3; Jeremi Suri, "The Cultural Contradictions of Cold War Education: West Berlin and the Youth Revolt of the 1960s," in Jeffrey A. Engel, ed, *Local Consequences of the Global Cold War* (Washington, DC: Woodrow Wilson Center Press, 2007), pp. 57–76.

61. Klimke, *The Other Alliance*, p. 189.

62. Michael A. Schmidtke, "Cultural Revolution or Cultural Shock? Student Radicalism and 1968 in Germany," *South Central Review* 17, 1 (Winter 1999–Spring 2000): 77–89; Martin Klimke, "West Germany," in Klimke and Scharloth, *1968 in Europe*, p. 104; Nick Thomas, *Protest Movements in 1960s West Germany: A social history of dissent and democracy* (Oxford: Berg, 2003), pp. 157–9; Mark Kurlasky, *1968: The Year the Rocked the World* (New York: Ballantine, 2004), pp. 149–50; Seidman, *The Imaginary Revolution*, p. 66; Quin Slobodian, *Foreign Front: Third World Politics in Sixties West Germany* (Durham, NC: Duke University Press, 2012).

63. Maurice Brinton, "Paris: May 1968," *Solidarity Pamphlet* 30 (June 1968); Besancenot and Löwy, *Che Guevara*, p. 88; Ehrenreich and Ehrenreich, *Long March, Short Spring*, p. 89.

64. Edgar Morin and Claude Lefort, *La brèche: Premières réfléxions sur les événements*

(Paris: Fayard, 1968); Richard Davy, "New radicals are the 'babies who were picked up,'" *Times*, 29 May 1968; Gilcher-Holtey, "The Dynamic of Protest"; Robert Vincent Daniels, *Year of the Heroic Guerrilla: World Revolution and Counterrevolution in 1968* (New York: Basic Books, 1989), p. 156.

65. Daniel Singer, *Prelude to Revolution: France in May 1968* (New York: Hill and Wang, 1970), pp. 64–5; Mehnert, *Twilight of the Young*, p. 170; Bernard Lacroix, *L'utopie communautaire. Mai 68, histoire sociale d'une révolte* (Paris: PUF, 2006).

66. Quoted in Elaine Carey, *Plaza of Sacrifices: Gender, Power, and Terror in 1968 Mexico* (Albuquerque, NM: University of New Mexico Press, 2005), p. 13; Paco Ignacio Taibo, *'68* (New York: Seven Stories Press, 2004), p. 16.

67. Elena Poniatowska, *Massacre in Mexico* (Columbia, MO: Missouri University Press, 1991), p. 32.

68. Katsiaficas, *The Imagination of the New Left*, pp. 47–8; Henry Ginigers, "Mexican Students Stage Unusual Protest Against President," *The New York Times*, 14 August 1968.

69. John Spitzer and Harvey Cohen, "Shades of Berlin ['36]: In Mexico ['68]", *Ramparts* 7, 6 (26 October 1968): 42.

70. Olga Cárdenas Trueva, et. al., "Anexo: Chronología del Movimiento del Estudiantil de 1968 en México," in Fernando Solana, Mariángeles Comesaña, and Javier Barros Valero, eds. *Evocación del 68* (Mexico, D.F.: Siglo Veintiuno Editores, 2008), p. 164; Gilberto Guevara Niebla, *1968: largo camino a la democracia* (Mexico, DF: Cal y Arena, 2008). On the wider counterculture of 1960s Mexico, of which Che Guevara was a part, see Eric Zolov, *Refried Elvis: The Rise of Mexican Counterculture* (Berkeley, CA: University of California Press, 1999).

71. Jorge Tamayo, "Gestacion y Desarrollo del Movimiento del '68: Estudiantes y Profesores," in *Evocación del 68*, p. 86; Carey, *Plaza of Sacrifices*, pp. 42–3.

72. Carey, *Plaza of Sacrifices*, p. 110; Gilberto Guevara Niebla, *La democracia en la calle: crónica del movimiento estudiantil mexicano* (Mexico, D.F.: Instituto de Investigaciones Sociales, UNAM, 1988); Dolores Trevizo, "Between Zapata and Che: A Comparison of Social Movement Success and Failure in Mexico," *Social Science History* 30, 2 (2006): 212–13.

73. Michael L. Clemons and Charles E. Jones, "Global Solidarity: The Black Panther Party in the International Arena," in Kathleen Cleaver and George Katsiaficas, eds. *Liberation, Imagination, and the Black Panther Party: A New Look at the Panthers and their Legacy* (New York: Routledge, 2001), p. 27; Robin D.G. Kelley and Betsy Esch, "Black Like Mao: Red China and Black Revolution," in Fred Ho and Bill V. Mullen, eds. *Afro Asia: Revolutionary Political and Cultural Connections between African Americans and Asian Americans* (Durham, NC: Duke Univeristy Press, 2008), pp. 97–154. Ahmad A. Rahman has also suggested that Che Guevara affected the Detroit BPP's perceptions of gender. According to Rahman, Che's insistence that women could fight alongside men informed male BPP members' attempts to overcome their own internalized sexism. See Ahmad A. Rahman, "Marching Blind: The Rise and Fall of the Black Panther Party in Detroit," in Yohuru Williams and Jama Lazerow, eds. *Liberated Territory: Untold local perspectives on the Black Panther Party* (Durham, NC: Duke University Press, 2008), pp. 203–4. See also Kathleen Neal Cleaver,

"Women, Power, and Revolution," in Cleaver and Katsiaficas, eds. *Liberation, Imagination, and the Black Panther Party*, pp. 123–7.

74. Huey P. Newton, "The Founding of the Black Panther Party," in David Hilliard and Donald Weise, eds, *The Huey P. Newton Reader* (New York: Seven Stories Press, 2003), p. 50; Nikhil Pal Singh, "The Black Panthers and the 'Undeveloped Country' of the Left," in Charles E. Jones, ed., *The Black Panther Party (Reconsidered)* (Baltimore, MD: Black Classic Press, 1998), p. 67. See also Robert O. Self, "The Black Panther Party and the Long Civil Rights Era," in Jama Lazerow and Yohuru Williams, eds. *In Search of the Black Panther Party: new perspectives on a revolutionary movement* (Durham, NC: Duke University Press, 2006), pp. 15–55.

75. Jennifer B. Smith, *An International History of the Black Panther Party* (New York: Garland Publishing, 1999), pp. 67–9, 72, 78; Maria Höhn, "The Black Panther Solidarity Committee and the Trial of the Ramstein 2," in Belinda Davis, Wilfried Mausback, Martin Klimke, and Carla MacDougall, eds., *Changing the World, Changing Oneself: Political Protest and Collective Identities in West Germany and the U.S. in the 1960s and 1970s* (New York: Berghahn Books, 2010), 215–39.

76. George Katsiaficas, "Organization and Movement: The Case of the Black Panther Party and the Revolutionary People's Constitutional Convention of 1970," in Cleaver and Katsiaficas, eds, *Liberation, Imagination, and the Black Panther Party*, p. 146.

77. W.W. Rostow to the President [Lyndon B. Johnson], "Death of 'Che' Guevara," 11 October 1967, available online through the National Security Archive, The George Washington University at https://nsarchive2.gwu.edu/NSAEBB/NSAEBB5/docs/doc07.pdf (accessed 12 September 2016).

78. TNA FCO 95/1108, "'Che Guevarist' insurgency in Ceylon; supply of material to Ceylon on counter-insurgency measures and the rehabilitation of detainees," 1971.

79. Ernesto Guevara, *Guerrilla Warfare* (New York: MR Press, 1961), p. 1; see also José A Moreno, "Che Guevara on Guerrilla Warfare: Doctrine, Practice and Evaluation," *Comparative Studies in Society and History* 12, 2 (April 1970): 114–33; Martz, "Doctrine and Dilemmas"; Matt D. Childs, "An Historical Critique of the Emergence and Evolution of Ernesto Che Guevara's *Foco* Theory," *Journal of Latin American Studies* 27, 3 (October 1995): 593–624.

80. Gonzalez, "The Culture of the Heroic Guerrilla," p. 67; Brian Loveman and Thomas M. Davies, Jr, "Preface," in Loveman and Davies, Jr, eds, *Che Guevara: Guerrilla Warfare*, p. x; Schickel, *Guerrilleros, Partisanen; Chicago Tribune*, "Students Majoring in Revolution," 20 April 1968.

81. Donald C. Hodges, "Introduction," in Hodges, ed., *The Legacy of Che Guevara*, pp. 43, 48, 100.

82. John Follain, *Jackal: The complete story of the legendary terrorist, Carlos the Jackal* (New York: Arcade, 1998) p. 18.

83. Ibid., p. 14.

84. Karen Asbley, et. al., "You Don't Need a Weatherman to Know Which Way the Wind Blows," *New Left Notes* (June 18, 1969), 28; Ron Jacobs, *The Way the Wind Blew: A History of the Weather Underground* (London: Verso, 1997); Jeremy Varon,

*Bringing The War Home: The Weather Underground, the Red Army Faction, and revolutionary violence in the sixties and seventies* (Berkeley, CA: University of California Press, 2004).

85. William Ayers, *Fugitive Days: A Memoir* (Boston, MA: Beacon, 2001), p. 169; Jeff Jones, "From the Suburbs to Saigon," in Mary Susannah Robbins, ed. *Against the Vietnam War: Writings by Activists* (Syracuse, NY: Syracuse University Press, 1999), p. 145; Mark Rudd, *Underground*, p. 173; Thai Jones, *From the labor movement to the Weather Underground, one family's century of conscience* (New York: Free Press, 2004), p. 177.

86. Rahmani, "Anti-imperialism and Its Discontents," p. 122; Maurice Isserman, "You Don't Need a Weatherman but a Postman Can Be Helpful: Thoughts on the SDS and the Antiwar Movement," in Melvin Small, William D. Hoover, and Charles DeBennedetti, eds. *Give Peace a Chance: Exploring the Vietnam Antiwar Movement* (Syracuse, NY: Syracuse University Press, 1992), pp. 22–34.

87. Cathy Wilkerson, *Flying Close to the Sun: My Life and Times As a Weatherman* (New York: Seven Stories Press, 2007), pp. 206–7; Hodges, *Legacy of Che Guevara*, p. 69; Ayers, *Fugitive Days*, p. 262.

88. Katsiaficas, *The Imagination of the New Left*, p. 144; "Fall Offensive," *The Water Tunnel* 4, 3 (October 26, 1970): 4.

89. Besancenot and Löwy, *Che Guevara*, pp. 84–85; Norman Gall, "Guerrilla Saint," *The New York Times*, 5 May 1968.

90. Carlos Marighella, *Mini-manual do Guerrilheiro Urbano* (n.p., 1969). See also Abraham Guillén, *Estrategia de la guerrilla urbana: Principios básicos de guerra revolucionaria* (Montevideo: Ediciones Liberacion, 1969).

91. "Brazilian Priest Praises Che, Condemns U.S.," 4 December 1967, FBIS-DR; FBIS-FRB-67-235.

92. Diuguid, "Survey Finds Guevara Hero of Student Left"; Hodges, "Introduction," *Legacy of Che Guevara*, pp. 63–5. On this convergence see Giullio Girardi, *Che Guevara visto da un Cristiano: Il significato etico della su scelta rivoluzionaria* (Milan: Sperling & Kupfer, 2005); David Kunzle, *Chesucristo: The Fusion in Image and Word of Che Guevara and Jesus Christ* (Berlin: De Gruyter, 2016).

93. Maria Riberio do Valle, *1968, o diálogo e a violência: movimento estudantil e ditadura militar no Brasil* (Campinas: Editora da Unicamp, 1999); Joseph Novitski, "Rebels in Brazil, Shifting Attacks to Cities, Denounce Costa on Seized Radio," *The New York Times*, 16 August 1969; Besancenot and Löwy, *Che Guevara*, p. 85.

94. "30 preguntas a un tupamaro," *Punto Final*, 2 June 1968, reprinted in Hodges ed, *Legacy of Che Guevara*, p. 112; Leopoldo Madruga, "Tupamaros y gobierno: dos poderes en pugna," *Granma* 6, 241 (1970): 6–7, reprinted in Ernesto Mayans, ed, *Tupamaros: Antologia Documental* (Cuernavaca, Mexico: Centro Intercultural de Documentacion, 1971), 5/7–5/24.

95. Antonio Mercader and Jorge de Vera, *Tupamaros: Estrategia y Acción* (Montevideo: Editorial Alfa, 1969); Marysa Gerassi, "Uruguay's Urban Guerrillas," *New Left Review* 1 (62) July–August 1970: 22–9.

96. *Chile Hoy*, interview with two official spokesmen of the ERP, 11–17 May 1973, reprinted in Hodges, ed, *Legacy of Che Guevara*, p. 175. See also Daniel de Santis,

ed. *A Vencer o Morir: Historia del PRT-ERP, Documentos, Tomo 1 Volume 2* (Buenos Aires: Nuestra América, 2006).

97. Besancenot and Löwy, *Che Guevara*, pp. 85–6.

98. Loveman and Davies, "Guerrilla Warfare, Revolutionary Theory, and Revolutionary Movements in Latin America," in *Che Guevara*, p. 29; Hal Brands, *Latin America's Cold War* (Cambridge, MA: Harvard University Press, 2010), pp. 55–6.

99. Leila Khaled, *My People Will Live: The Autobiography of a Revolutionary* (London: Hodder and Stoughton, 1973), pp. 93–4.

100. Ibid.

101. Peter Snow and David Phillips, *Leila's Hijack War: The True Story of 25 Days in September* (London: Pan Books, 1970); Jesse W. Lewis, Jr., "Arab World Backs 'Heroic' Hijackers," *Washington Post* 12 September 1970; William J. Coughlin, "Palestinian Heroine," *Los Angeles Times* 11 October 1970; Bassam Abu Sharif, *Arafat and the Dream of Palestine* (London: Palgrave Macmillan, 2009), pp. 45–7.

102. Brands, *Latin America's Cold War*, pp. 52–8; Loveman and Davies, "Preface," in *Che Guevara: Guerrilla Warfare*, p. x; Luis Alberto Flores, "Las Enseñanzas Revolucionarias del 'Che' y la Revolucion Salvadoreña," in (no ed.) *El pensamiento revolucionario del comandante 'Che' Guevara* (Buenos Aires: Dialectica, 1988), pp. 289–94; Malcolm Deas, "'Putting Up with Violence': Ernesto Guevara, Guevarismo, and Colombia," in Paulo Drinot, ed., *Che's Travels: The Making of a Revolutionary in 1950s Latin America* (Durham, NC: Duke University Press, 2010), pp. 127–47; McCormick, "Che Guevara," p. 78. Another militant group of note inspired by Guevara was the "Che Guevara Brigades", which operated in France in the mid-1970s. "Che Guevara Brigades Claim Credit," 11 May 1976, FBIS-DR; FBIS-LAT-76-093.

## 2. REBEL MUSIC: BOB MARLEY AND THE CULTURAL POLITICS OF LIBERATION

1. TNA PREM 16/2080 "Grenada. Coup d'etat 1979." The Bishop government initially embraced Grenadian Rastas and integrated them into the Provisional Revolutionary Army. Horace Campbell, *Rasta and Resistance: From Marcus Garvey to Walter Rodney* (Trenton, NJ: Africa World Press, 1987), pp. 163–5; Charles Reavis Price, "Political and Radical Aspects of the Rastafarian Movement in Jamaica," *Nature, Society, and Thought* 13, 2 (2000): 155–80.

2. Paul Gilroy, *Darker than Blue: On the Moral Economies of Black Atlantic Culture* (Cambridge, MA: Belknap Press, 2010).

3. Jon Bradshaw, "The Reggae Way to 'Salvation'," *New York Times Magazine* 14 August 1977.

4. Gregory Stephens, *On Racial Frontiers: The New Culture of Frederick Douglass, Ralph Ellison, and Bob Marley* (New York: Cambridge University Press, 1999), p. 214; *The Beat*, "Voices: Bob Marley's Worldwide Impact," 14, 3 (1995): 59.

5. Eusi Kwayana suggested that Bob Marley had more success in bringing popular attention to African liberation movements than the efforts of grassroots movements around the world. Eusi Kwayana, "Preface," in Horace Campbell, *Rasta and*

*Resistance: From Marcus Garvey to Walter Rodney* (Trenton, NJ: Africa World Press, 1987), p. xii.

6. Gilroy, *Darker than Blue*, p. 114.

7. "Ask Obama Live: An MTV Interview with The President," *MTV*, 26 October 2012 available at http://www.mtv.com/videos/news/851721/barack-obama-is-a-bob-marley-fan.jhtml#id=1696102 (accessed 29 July 2014).

8. Don Snowden, "Marley's Ghost," *Los Angeles Times*, 9 October 1988.

9. Rex Nettleford, "Greetings on behalf of the University of the West Indies," in Eleanor Wint and Carolyn Cooper, eds. *Bob Marley: The Man and his Music* (Kingston: Arawak Publications, 1995), pp. xiv-xv.

10. Catherine Sampson, "Nothing But a Revolution," *The Times* (London) 18 May 1989; Lena Williams, "Americans Sense a New Patriotism," *The New York Times* 4 July 1990.

11. *Rolling Stone* magazine even asserted that Marley looked like Guevara. Ed McCormack, "Bob Marley with a Bullet," *Rolling Stone*, 12 August 1976.

12. Bob Marley's refrain of universal liberation drew on a much longer tradition, one traceable to the Age of Revolution. See Michael O. West and William G. Martin, "Introduction: Contours of the Black International," in Michael O. West, William G. Martin, and Fanon Che Wilkins, eds, *From Toussaint to Tupac: The Black International since the Age of Revolution* (Chapel Hill, NC: University of North Carolina Press, 2009), p. 5; Brenda Gayle Plummer, *In Search of Power: African Americans in the era of decolonization, 1956–1974* (Cambridge: Cambridge University Press, 2013).

13. Rob Kenner, "The Business of Bob," *Billboard Magazine*, 12 February 2011.

14. Mark T. Berger, "After the Third World? History, destiny and the fate of Third Worldism," *Third World Quarterly* 25, 1 (2004): 9–39; Samantha Christiansen and Zachary A. Scarlett, eds, *The Third World in the Global 1960s* (New York: Berghahn, 2012).

15. Henderson Dalrymple, *Bob Marley: Music, Myth & the Rastas* (Sudbury: Carib-Arawak Publishers, 1976), p. 23.

16. Kwame Dawes, *Bob Marley: Lyrical Genius* (London: Sanctuary, 2002), p. 128.

17. Don Snowden, "Marley's Ghost," *Los Angeles Times*, 9 October 1988.

18. Gilroy, *Darker than Blue*, p. 112. Gilroy likewise offered a sustained analysis of Marley's antipolitics.

19. Stephen Davis, "The Marley Legacy," *Reggae and African Beat* 6, 3 (1987): 13.

20. Bob Marley also refuted Cold War geopolitical divisions with the notion of "One Love", a hopeful statement that would become his most repeated refrain after the end of the Cold War (see Chapter Five).

21. On the Black Power movement in Jamaica and its influence on reggae, see James Bradford, "Brother Wally and De Burnin' of Babylon: Walter Rodney's Impact on the Reawakening of Black Power, the Birth of Reggae, and Resistance to Global Imperialism," in Christiansen and Scarlett, eds, *The Third World in the Global 1960s*, pp. 142–56.

22. John Rockwell, "Reggae: Bob Marley," *The New York Times*, 19 June 1978.

23. Michael Witter, "Soul Rebel: Bob Marley and the Caribbean Revolution," *The Beat* 13, 3 (1992): 38.

24. Keisha Lindsay and Louis Lindsay, "Bob Marley and the Politics of Subversion," in Eleanor Wint and Carolyn Cooper, eds, *Bob Marley: The Man and his Music* (Kingston: Arawak Publications, 1995), pp. 77, 78.

25. Dawes, *Bob Marley*.

26. Rupert Lewis, "The African renaissance and the Caribbean," *South African Journal of International Affairs* 8, 1 (2001): 60.

27. Jon Bradshaw, "The Reggae Way to 'Salvation'," *New York Times Magazine*, 14 August 1977.

28. Dawes, *Bob Marley*, p. 151.

29. As confidant Allan 'Skill' Cole explained soon after Bob Marley's death, "[s]ome people in Africa tell me when Bob sing is like is them him [speaking] to." Quoted in Malika Lee Whitney and Dermott Hussey, *Bob Marley: Reggae King of the World* (New York: E.P. Dutton), p. 191.

30. *The Beat*, "Voices," 59. For similar sentiments in war-ravaged Lebanon, see Mark LeVine, *Heavy Metal Islam: Rock, resistance, and the struggle for the soul of Islam* (New York: Three Rivers, 2008), 146. As a Rwandan DJ succinctly explained, in contexts of political repression, "Marley says for us what we can't say." Quoted in Terisa E. Turner, "Rastafari and the New Society: Caribbean and East African feminist roots of a popular movement to reclaim the earthly commons," in Terisa E. Turner with Bryan J. Ferguson, *Arise Ye Mighty People!: Gender, class, and race in popular struggles* (Trenton, NJ: Africa World Press, 1994), p. 45.

31. Though scant information is available about Bob Marley's attitude towards contemporary leftist political currents, in 1978 a reporter asked Bob Marley what he thought of former collaborator Peter Tosh's interest in Marxism and Che Guevara. Marley responded that he was "a Rasta" not a Marxist. Interview after receiving the United Nations Medal of Peace in 1978, available at https://www.youtube.com/watch?v=HQFIU6nQJoo (accessed 23 September 2016).

32. George Lipsitz, *Dangerous Crossroads: Popular Music, Postmodernism and the Poetics of Place* (New York: Verso, 1997), p. 34.

33. Paul James, "Arguing globalizations: Propositions towards an investigation of global formation," *Globalizations* 2, 2 (2005): 193–209. On music as a catalyst for constructing communities of interest, see also Alex Perullo, "Hooligans and Heroes: Youth Identity and Hip-Hop in Dar es Salaam, Tanzania," *Africa Today* 51, 4 (2005): 75–101; Mark LeVine, "Music and the Aura of Revolution," *International Journal of Middle Eastern Studies* 44 (2012): pp. 794–7.

34. Neil J. Savishinsky, "Rastafari in the Promised Land: The Spread of a Jamaican Socioreligious Movement among the Youth of West Africa," *African Studies Review* 37, 3 (1994): 27.

35. Daniel Widener, *Black Arts West: Culture and Struggle in Postwar Los Angeles* (Durham, NC: Duke University Press, 2010).

36. Gary MacEoin, *Revolution Next Door: Latin America in the 1970s* (New York: Holt, Reinhart and Winston, 1971), p. 16; S. P. Ramat, ed. *Rocking the State: Rock Music and Politics in Eastern Europe and Russia* (Boulder, CO: Westview Press, 1994). See

also Neferti X.M. Tadiar, "Popular Laments: Affective literacy, democratization, and war," *Cultural Studies* 23, 1 (2009): 1–26; Timothy Brown, "Music as a Weapon? Ton Steine Scherben and the Politics of Rock in Cold War Berlin," *German Studies Review* 32, 1 (2009): 1–22.

37. Mark LeVine has similarly demonstrated the social and political force of rock, reggae, and hip hop in the Middle East. Mark LeVine, *Heavy Metal Islam*. See also Titus Hjelm, Keith Kahn-Harris, and Mark LeVine, eds, *Heavy Metal: Controversies and Countercultures* (Sheffield: Equinox Books, 2013).

38. Lisa Barg, "Paul Robeson's *Ballad for Americans*: Race and the Cultural Politics of 'People's Music'," *Journal of the Society for American Music* 2, 1 (2008): 27–70.

39. Gilroy, *Darker than Blue*, p. 108; Richard Williams, "Marley Mutes his Anger," *The Sunday Times* 5 June 1977.

40. Bob Marley researcher, archivist, and biographer Roger Steffens likened Marley's lyrics to haiku for their ability to strip elaborate concepts down to raw kernels of insight. Steffens, "Bob Marley: Rasta Warrior," Nathaniel Samuel Murrell et al., eds, *Chanting Down Babylon: the Rastafari Reader* (Philadelphia, PA: Temple University Press, 1998), p. 257.

41. Dawes, *Bob Marley*, pp. 187–8.

42. Gregory Stephens, *On Racial Frontiers: The New Culture of Frederick Douglass, Ralph Ellison, and Bob Marley* (New York: Cambridge University Press, 1999), p. 149.

43. Jason Toynbee, *Bob Marley: Herald of a Postcolonial World?* (Malden, MA: Polity Press, 2007), p. 220; Brent Hagerman, "Everywhere Is War: Peace and Violence in the Life and Songs of Bob Marley," *Journal of Religion and Popular Culture* 24, 3 (2012): 380–92. Marley's keyboardist, Earl "Wia" Lindo, who co-wrote many lyrics with Marley, explained that they drafted songs "from a kind of high universal … plane of ideas." Of their songwriting sessions, Lindo recalled feeling "the whole world in your consciousness…" Klaus Ludes, "The Wailers' Earl 'Wia' Lindo," in Hank Bordowitz, ed, *Every Little Thing Gonna Be Alright: The Bob Marley Reader* (Cambridge, MA: De Capo Press, 2004), p. 295 (reprinted from *Classical Reggae Interviews*, 29 May 1998).

44. See for instance Bruce E. Levine, *Get Up, Stand Up: Uniting Populists, Energizing the Defeated, and Battling the Corporate Elite* (White River Junction, VT: Chelsea Green Publishing, 2011); Jim Elmslie and Camellia Webb Gannon with Peter King, *Get Up, Stand Up: West Papua stands for its rights*, report prepared for the West Papua Project at the Centre for Peace and Conflict Studies, University of Sydney, July 2010.

45. Robert Hilburn, "Marley Sends his Message Through Special Delivery," *Los Angeles Times* 27 November 1979.

46. Steed V. Davidson, "Leave Babylon: The Trope of Babylon in Rastafarian Discourse," *Black Theology: An International Journal* 6, 1 (2008): 46–60.

47. Ennis B. Edmonds, "Dread 'I' In-a-Babylon: Ideological Resistance and Cultural Revitalization," in Murrell et al., eds, *Chanting Down Babylon*, pp. 24–5, 27.

48. Peter Walshe, "The Evolution of Liberation Theology in South Africa," *Journal of Law and Religion* 5, 2 (1987): 299–311.

49. Erna Brodber, "Black Consciousness and Popular Music in Jamaica in the 1960s

and 1970s," *Caribbean Quarterly* 31, 2 (1985): 53–66; Price, "Political and Radical Aspects of the Rastafarian Movement."

50. Derek Jewell, "Reggae for Revolution," *The Sunday Times* 20 June 1976.

51. Stephens, *On Racial Frontiers*, p. 191.

52. See also Randal L. Hepner, "Chanting Down Babylon in the Belly of the Beast: The Rastafarian Movement in the Metropolitan United States," in Murrell et al., eds, *Chanting Down Babylon*, p. 199.

53. Dalrymple, *Bob Marley*, p. 30.

54. Chris Blackwell, "Bob Marley: Absolutely, Truly Natural", *Review: Literature and Arts of the Americas* 43, 2 (2010): 152–3.

55. Simon Jones, *Black Culture, White Youth: The Reggae Tradition from JA to UK* (London: Macmillan, 1988), p. 42; Gilroy, *Darker than Blue*, p. 112.

56. Dick Hebdige, *Subculture: The Meaning of Style* (London: Routledge, 1979).

57. Journalist Colin Campbell surmised that by the late 1970s Bob Marley was likely the most recognized "contemporary folk hero." "Reggae Rebels," *60 Minutes* (Australia), 1979; Horace Campbell, "Rastafari as Pan Africanism in the Caribbean and Africa," *African Journal of Political Economy* 2, 1 (1988): 75–88; Anita M. Waters, *Race, Class, and Political Symbols: Rastafari and Reggae in Jamaican Politics* (New Brunswick, NJ: Transaction Books, 1985), pp. 187–8.

58. Quoted in Ed McCormack, "Bob Marley with a Bullet," *Rolling Stone* 12 August 1976.

59. Dan Sewell, "A Calypso Beat in Politics," *Philadelphia Inquirer* 2 December 1984. See also Stephen A. King, *Reggae, Rastafari, and the Rhetoric of Social Control* (Jackson, MS: University of Mississippi Press, 2002). Bob Marley's guitarist, Al Anderson, later relayed that security agents warned him that the entire band was the object of an assassination plot. Larson Sutton interview of Al Anderson, "The Infamous Al Anderson Interview," 20 May 2012, http://midnightraverblog.com/2012/05/30/the-infamous-al-anderson-interview/ (accessed 26 April 2014).

60. On the elections and the historical intersections of politics and reggae in Jamaica, see Waters, *Race, Class, and Political Symbols*.

61. A commentary on the attempt on his life, the 1979 track "Ambush in the Night" (*Survival*) addressed the fraught politics of Jamaica, and specifically how the politics of socioeconomic distribution turned citizens against one another.

62. "Marley Shot," *The Jamaica Daily News* 4 December 1976; Roger Steffens, "The Night They Shot Bob Marley: The Untold Story. Interview by Roger Steffens," *Reggae and African Beat* 4, 3 (June 1985), 19–25; Stephen Davis, *Bob Marley* (Garden City, NY: Doubleday, 1985), pp. 172–80.

63. Chris May, "Bob Marley: Return of the Native," *Black Music and Jazz Review* (April 1978).

64. Vivienne Goldman, *The Book of Exodus: The Making and Meaning of Bob Marley and the Wailers' Album of the Century* (New York: Three Rivers Press), p. 281.

65. Dawes, *Bob Marley*, p. 249. The *Los Angeles Times* called *Survival* "uncompromisingly militant." Don Snowden, "Marley: A Matter of 'Survival'", *Los Angeles Times* 11 November 1979.

66. Simon Jones, *Black Culture, White Youth: The Reggae Tradition from JA to UK* (London: Macmillan, 1988), pp. 94–5.
67. "Bono Inducts Bob Marley into Rock and Roll Hall of Fame," (1994) http://www. youtube.com/watch?v=L3Hb5qM4ldg (accessed 10 January 2014).
68. Hebdige, *Subculture*. John Rockwell wrote that during his time with the Sex Pistols in the late 1970s the group listened exclusively to reggae between shows. John Rockwell, "They Flavor their Rock with Reggae," *The New York Times* 11 November 1979. By 1981 punk bands in Eastern Europe had also embraced Marley. For instance, the Gdansk outfit Tilt incorporated "Get Up, Stand Up" into their live performances. Andrzej Jakubowicz, "Dread inna Polan," *The Beat* 3, 2 (1984): 9–10.
69. Jones, *Black Culture, White Youth*, p. 161.
70. Ibid.; Toynbee, *Bob Marley*, p. 218.
71. Jones, *Black Culture*, pp. 161–2.
72. Jones suggested that even groups on the far right incorporated Marley's words into their political rhetoric. For example, the ultra-right National Front's newspaper called on its white, working-class readers to "stand up for their rights." Quoted in Jones, *Black Culture*, pp. 101–2; Hebdige, *Subculture*.
73. Bruno Blum, "Marley International: Reggae's Impact on France," *The Beat* 26, 2 (2007): 30–1.
74. Michel Marriott, "Marley and his Message," *Washington Post* 11 February 1985.
75. On this intersection see Kevin Mattson, "Did Punk Matter?: Analyzing the Practices of a Youth Subculture During the 1980s," *American Studies* 42, 1 (2001): 69–97.
76. *Bad Brains: Band in DC*, directed by Mandy Stein and Benjamen Logan (2012).
77. Eric Moore quoted in David Maraniss, *Barack Obama: The Story* (New York: Simon & Schuster, 2013), pp. 370–1.
78. Marriott, "Marley and His Message".
79. Alice Walker, "Redemption Day," *Mother Jones* December 1986.
80. Bruce Weber, "Reggae Rhythms Speak to an Insular Tribe," *The New York Times* 19 September 1999.
81. Neil J. Savishinsky, "Transnational Popular Culture and the Global Spread of the Jamaican Rastafarian Movement," *New West Indian Guide* 8, 3–4 (1994): 264–5. "Bob Marley shouted across the ocean at us," explained a Havasupai woman interviewed in the early 1980s. See "Cedella Marley at Havasupai Reservation" (1982), available at http://www.youtube.com/watch?v=dcZ2iIbLwyU (accessed 25 April 2014). The video features Marley's mother, Cedella Booker, during her visit to the Grand Canyon with keyboardist Tyrone Downey. See also Roger Steffens, "Rastas of the Canyon," *High Times* February 1993, 46–51; Richard Grant, "Dread Indians," *The Age* (Australia) 14 January 1995; Matt Golosinski, "Rastas on the Res," *Phoenix New Times* 18 January 1996.
82. Whitney and Hussey, *Bob Marley*, p. 128; Arnold Shaw, *Black Popular Music in America* (New York: Schirmer Books, 1986), p. 265. For a more complete analysis of reggae's resonance among Native American listeners in the Southwestern US, see Luis Alvarez, "Reggae Rhythms in Dignity's Diaspora: Globalization, Indigenous Identity, and the Circulation of Cultural Struggle," *Popular Music and Society* 31, 5 (2008): pp. 575–97.

83. Gary Okihiro, "Afterward: Toward a Black Pacific," in Heike Raphael-Hernandez and Shannon Steen, eds, *AfroAsian Encounters: Culture, History, Politics* (New York: New York University Press, 2006), p. 325; quoting Ku'ualoha Ho'omanawanui, "Yo, Brah, It's Hip Hop Jawaiian Style: The Influence of Reggae and Rap on Contemporary Hawaiian Music," *Hawaii Review* 56 (2001): 153.

84. West and Martin, "Introduction: Contours of the Black International," in West, Martin, and Wilkins, eds, *From Toussaint to Tupac*, p. 37.

85. Toynbee, *Bob Marley*, pp. 216–17; John Castles, "'*Tjungaringanyi*: Aboriginal Rock," in Philip Hayward, ed, *From Pop to Punk to Postmodernism: Popular Music and Australian Culture from the 1960s to the 1990s* (Sydney: Allen and Unwin, 1992), p. 30. See also Okihiro, "Afterward: Toward a Black Pacific," in Raphael-Hernandez and Steen, eds, *AfroAsian Encounters*, pp. 313–30.

86. Brent Clough, "Jamming Down Under: Bob Marley's Legacy and Reggae Culture in Australia and New Zealand," in Eleanor Wint and Carolyn Cooper, eds, *Bob Marley: The Man and his Music* (Kingston: Arawak Publications, 1995), p. 30.

87. Martin Flanagan, "A Legend of the Land," *The Age* (Australia) 15 November 2008.

88. Refining his point, Yunupingu reflected that "[s]ome of the things I feel about my life, our country" were similar to those "Marley would have felt." Quoted in Timothy White, *Catch a Fire: The Life of Bob Marley* (New York: Henry Holt and Company, 2000), p. 414.

89. Frank Jan van Dijk, "JAHmaica: Rastafari and Jamaican Society, 1930–1990" (PhD thesis, Utrecht University, 1998), p. 264; Frank Jan Van Dijk, "Chanting Down Babylon Outernational: The Rise of Rastafari in Europe, the Caribbean, and the Pacific," in Murrell et al., eds, *Chanting Down Babylon*, p. 194.

90. Savishinsky, "Transnational Popular Culture," pp. 273–4. See also William G. Hawkeswood, "I'N'I Ras Tafari: Identity and the Rasta Movement in Auckland" (MA thesis, Department of Anthropology, University of Auckland, 1983).

91. Clough, "Jamming Down Under," pp. 26–9; Alvarez, "Reggae Rhythms in Dignity's Diaspora."

92. Helen Bain, "Bob's still stirring it up", *The Dominion* (Wellington) 20 January 2001.

93. Anita M. Waters, "Bob Marley: A Final Interview," available at http://webby. cc.denison.edu/~waters/marley.html (accessed 27 April 2014).

94. In Ghana, for instance, Marley's *Rastaman Vibration* established his popularity as early as 1976. George Zowonu, "Ghana Pumps along to Reggae," *The Reggae & African Beat* 3, 2 (1984): 8–9. A 1989 survey of young people in the Ghanaian cities of Accra and Kumasi found that Marley ranked as most popular among a dozen well-known Ghanaian and international musicians. Surveys conducted in Francophone West Africa produced similar results. See Savishinsky, "Rastafari in the Promised Land" 24–5. Marley resonated so strongly in Nigeria that when the state renamed a street in the federal capital Abuja "Bob Marley Street" in 2009, a government spokesperson described him as an "African Reggae Icon." See the Federal Capital Territory Administration, "Renaming of Streets in the Federal Capital City," http://fct.gov.ng/fcta/index.php?option=com_content&task=view &id=119&Itemid=73 (accessed 28 July 2009).

95. Kone Baru Oman, "Fan Mail: Letter from the Ivory Coast [September 1981]", in Whitney and Hussey, *Bob Marley*, p. 135.

96. White, *Catch a Fire*, p. 328.

97. Roger Steffens, "Zimbabwe Victorious: Bob Marley's African Triumph," *The Beat* 17, 3 (1998): 48–55.

98. Curiously, according to the British Broadcasting Corporation, Prime Minister Robert Mugabe was not interested in Marley performing at Zimbabwe's independence ceremony. Rather, Mugabe preferred British pop singer Cliff Richard. Lucy Fleming, "Mugabe Turns 90," *BBC News* 14 February 2014 http://www.bbc.com/news/world-africa-26257237 (accessed 15 February 2014).

99. One of the most compelling accounts of this event is Horace Campbell, *Rasta and Resistance: From Marcus Garvey to Walter Rodney* (Trenton, NJ: Africa World Press, 1987), pp. 144–7. See also Horace Campbell, "The Night the British Flag was Lowered in Rhodesia," *Westindian Digest* (June 1980): 64–66; Timothy White, "Rebel Music," in Stephen Davis and Peter Simon, eds, *Reggae International* (New York: R&B, 1982), p. 82; Adrian Boot, Rita Marley, and Chris Salewicz, *Bob Marley: Songs of Freedom* (New York: Viking Studio Books, 1995).

100. "Recording of Zimbabwe's independence celebrations at the Rufaro Stadium, 1980," 18 April 1980, Baseler Afrika Bibliographien (Basel), Ruth Weiss Sound Archives, 1 TPA.43 142. In one of his final interviews Marley reflected on the joy he experienced in meeting commanders of the Zimbabwean liberation forces. Waters, "Bob Marley: A Final Interview." In 1990 Bob Marley's son Ziggy similarly headlined Namibia's independence celebrations.

101. National Archives of South Africa, Cape Town Archives Repository (hereafter KAB), Cape Town, IDP 3/398, P82/2/81 "Aansoek om 'n Beslissing—Survival," 13 January 1982. James Smith, "South Africa sees Body Heat but not the end of censorship," *The Globe and Mail* (Canada) 4 May 1982; Fraser G. McNeill, "Rural Reggae: The Politics of Performance in the Former 'Homeland' of Venda," *South African Historical Journal* 64, 1 (2012): 84.

102. McNeill, "Rural Reggae," 93.

103. KAB IDP 3/398, P/92/07/36 Application for Review, "Survival," 1 July 1992.

104. *Correire Della Sera*, "Centomila allo stadio: Bob Marley batte gli 'europei'," 28 June 1980; Daniele Caroli, "Top Crowds in Italy for Marley Concerts," *Billboard* 19 July 1980; Steffens, "Bob Marley: Rasta Warrior," p. 262.

105. Paul Hofmann, "The Swiss Malaise," *The New York Times* 8 February 1981.

106. Francesca Polletta, "Politicizing Childhood: The 1980 Zurich Burns Movement," *Social Text* 33 (1992): 83, 92.

107. *Tages-Anzeiger*, "Der Sänger, der zum Heiligen wurde Bob Marley, der bekannteste Musiker der Dritten Welt, lebte für seine Musik und in seinen Widersprüchen," 8 May 2012.

108. Quoted in Heinz Nigg, "Violence and Symbolic Resistance in the Youth Unrest of the Eighties," in Sønke Gau and Katharina Schlieben, eds, *Spektakel, Lustprinzin oder das Karnivaleske? Ein Reader über Möglichkeiten, Differenzerfahrungen und Strategien des Karnevalesken in kultureller/politischer Praxis* (Berlin: B_Books, 2008), p. 153.

109. Waters, *Race, Class, and Political Symbols*, pp. 238–40; Jo Thomas, "With Pride and Music, Jamaicans Bury Bob Marley," *New York Times* 22 May 1981.

110. Thomas, "With Pride and Music."

111. White, *Catch a Fire*, pp. 317–18.

112. Pamela Constable, "US Troops in Grenada Remain on the Alert," *Boston Globe* 19 November 1981. For a comprehensive account of the US invasion, see TNA PREM 19/1048, "Grenada. Power struggle. US-led invasion; position of Governor-General; attitude of UK Government; part 1," 1983; TNA PREM 19/1049, "Grenada. Power struggle. US-led invasion; position of Governor-General; attitude of UK Government; part 2," 1983.

113. Michel Marriott, "Marley and His Message," *Washington Post* 11 February 1985.

114. Jennifer Genevieve, "Amnesty Tour Praised for Artists' Quiet Dignity," *Toronto Star* 5 September 1988; Barbara Jaeger, "Human Rights Now: Music Issues Call to Action," *The Record* (New Jersey) 21 September 1988; idem, "A Glittering End to Amnesty's Tour for Human Rights," *The Record* 17 October 1988.

115. Maria-Carolina Cambre, *The Semiotics of Che: Affective Gateways* (New York: Bloomsbury, 2015), ch. 5.

116. Henri Myrttinen, "Masculinities, Violence, and Power in Timor Leste," *Revue Lusotopie* 12, 1–2 (2005): 240, 241. Moreover, graffiti and other forms of iconography that demonstrated support for the rebels frequently referenced Bob Marley. Henri Myrttinen, "Histories of violence, states of denial: militias, martial arts and masculinities in Timor-Leste" (PhD thesis, University of KwaZulu-Natal, 2010), p. 295.

117. Henri Myrttinen, "Histories of Violence: Occupation, Resistance, and Masculinities in Timor-Leste," in Christine De Matos and Rowena Ward, eds., *Gender, Power, and Military Occupations: Asia Pacific and the Middle East since 1945* (New York: Routledge, 2012), p. 63. In neighboring Malaysia, a Bob Marley gang developed in Petaling Jaya. Shamsul Akmar, "Battle Continues on Use of Islam in Party Names and Malay Divide," *New Straits Times* (Malaysia) 1 April 2000.

118. As testament to the controversy surrounding Bob Marley in the 1990s, Freetown resident Bockarie Kamara burned his Marley T-shirts after seeing a boy with a Marley T-shirt badly beaten by authorities. Lansana Fofana, "Sierra Leone—Politics: Bob Marley Joins the War," *IPS-Inter Press Service* 6 June 1995; UN Office for the Coordination of Humanitarian Affairs, *Sierra Leone: Humanitarian situation report*, May (New York: United Nations, 2003).

119. Eileen Moyer found that Bob Marley's regular evocation of Africa contributed to his popularity in Tanzania. In fact, many young people spoke of Marley's 1980 Zimbabwe performance as a sign of his commitment to African concerns. Eileen Moyer, "Street-Corner Justice in the Name of Jah: Imperatives for Peace among Dar es Salaam Street Youth," *Africa Today* 51, 3 (2005): 36–7. See also Pieter Remes, "Global Popular Musics and Changing Awareness of Urban Tanzanian Youth," *Yearbook for Traditional Music* 31 (1999): 1–26.

120. Paul Daley, "Coup in the Pacific: 'Rasta rebels' who sing war's praises," *The Age* (Australia) 10 June 2000. Other militants in Guadalcanal wore Che Guevara T-shirts as impromptu uniforms.

121. Hank Bordowitz, ed, *Every Little Thing Gonna Be Alright: The Bob Marley Reader* (Cambridge, MA: De Capo Press, 2004), p. 239.

## 3. ME AGAINST THE WORLD: TUPAC SHAKUR AND POST-COLD WAR ALIENATION

1. Lasana Fofana, "Sierra Leone: Rap star's T-shirt a major factor in conflict," *Inter Press Service* 8 October 1998, http://www.ipsnews.net/1998/10/sierra-leone-rap-stars-t-shirt-a-major-factor-in-conflict/ (accessed 26 September 2016).

2. On the particular meanings of Tupac in Tanzania, see Brad Weiss, *Street Dreams and Hip Hop Barbershops: Global Fantasy in Urban Tanzania* (Bloomington, IN: Indiana University Press, 2009).

3. On the politics of post-Cold War Africa, see, for instance, M. Anne Pitcher and Kelly M. Askew, "African Socialisms and Postsocialisms," *Africa* 76, 1 (2006): 1–14; Stephen Ellis, "Africa After the Cold War: New Patterns of Government and Politics," *Development and Change* 27, 1 (1996): 1–28.

4. Bernard-Henri Lévy (Charlotte Mitchell, trans.), *War, Evil, and the End of History* (Hoboken, NJ: Melville House Publishing, 2003), p. 1.

5. Arjun Appadurai, *Modernity at Large: Cultural Dimensions of Globalization* (Minneapolis, MN: University of Minnesota Press, 1996).

6. See for instance Pieter Remes, "Global Popular Musics and Changing Awareness of Urban Tanzanian Youth," *Yearbook for Traditional Music* 31 (1999): 1–26.

7. On Túpac Amaru's rebellion, its legacy, and other adoptions of his name, see Charles F. Walker, *The Tupac Amaru Rebellion* (Cambridge, MA: Belknap Press, 2014). Two left-wing insurgent groups also took the name of the eighteenth-century rebel: Uruguay's Tupamaros (see Chapter One) and Peru's Túpac Amaru Revolutionary Movement.

8. Joshua Bloom and Waldo E. Martin, Jr., *Black Against Empire: The History and Politics of the Black Panther Party* (Berkeley, CA: University of California Press, 2014); Assata Shakur, *Assata: An Autobiography* (Westport, CT: L. Hill, 1987); Murray Kempton, *The Briar Patch: The People of the State of New York v. Lumumba Shakur, et al* (New York: E.P. Dutton, 1973).

9. Michael Eric Dyson, *Holler if you hear me: Searching for Tupac Shakur* (New York: Basic Civitas Books, 2003); Tayannah Lee McQuillar and Fred L. Johnson, *Tupac Shakur: The Life and Times of an American Icon* (Boston, MA: Da Capo Press, 2010); Candace Sandy and Dawn Marie Daniels, *How Long Will They Mourn Me?: The Life and Legacy of Tupac Shakur* (New York: One World/Ballantine, 2006).

10. On hip-hop and masculinity see Imani Perry, *Prophets Of The Hood: Politics And Poetics In Hip Hop* (Durham, NC: Duke University Press, 2004).

11. Eithne Quinn, *Nuthin' but a "G" Thang: The Culture and Commerce Of Gangsta Rap.* (New York: Columbia University Press, 2005).

12. John Broder, "Quayle Calls for Pulling Rap Album Tied to Murder Case," *Los Angeles Times* 23 September 1992. For an analysis of the racialized criticism of Shakur during his life and the dismissive ways in which media outlets reflected on his death, see Robin D.G. Kelley and Philip Brian Harper, "Representin' What?:

Black popular culture, image politics, and the death of Tupac Shakur," *Frieze* 31 November-December (1996), https://frieze.com/article/representin-what? language=de (accessed 22 August 2018).

13. Jamal Joseph, *Tupac Legacy* (New York: Atria, 2006).

14. Mikal Gilmore, "Tupac redeemed," *Rolling Stone* 16 November 2006, p. 104.

15. Tupac Shakur, *The Rose that Grew from Concrete* (New York: MTV/Pocket Books, 1999).

16. Carlos D. Morrison, "Death narratives from the killing fields: Narrative criticism and the case of Tupac Shakur," in Ronald L. Jackson II and Elaine B. Richardson, eds, *Understanding African American Rhetoric: Classical Origins to Contemporary Innovations* (New York: Routledge, 2003), p. 202.

17. Greg Dimitriadis, *Performing identity/performing culture: Hip hop as text, pedagogy, and lived practice* (New York: Peter Lang, 2001); Dyson, *Holler if you hear me*.

18. Eithne Quinn, "'All eyez on me': The paranoid style of Tupac Shakur," in Peter Knight, ed., *Conspiracy nation: The politics of paranoia in postwar America* (New York: New York University Press, 2002), p. 188.

19. Dyson, *Holler if you hear me*, p. 25.

20. Dipannita Basu and Sidney J. Lemelle, eds, *The Vinyl Ain't Final: Hip Hop and the Globalization of Black Popular Culture* (London: Pluto Press, 2006), pp. 100–16.

21. Sara Terry, "Hip hop leaps into world youth culture," *Christian Science Monitor* 5 May 1999. See also Adam Cooper, "'Gevaarlike transitions': Negotiating hegemonic masculinity and rites of passage amongst Coloured boys awaiting trial on the Cape Flats," *Psychology in Society* 37 (2009): 5; Bongani Madondo, "Thug Messiah," *Sunday Times* (South Africa) 7 September 2003.

22. Ginger Thompson, "Young, hopeless and violent in the New South Africa," *The New York Times* 21 March 2003, p. 6; South African Press Association, "Two allegedly kill themselves after policemen's murder," 5 September 2000; Don Melvin, "Special report: South African elections: Crime mars ANC's political record," *The Atlanta Journal-Constitution* 29 May 1999.

23. Rowan Philip, "To live and die in SA," *Sunday Times* (South Africa) 11 January 2004.

24. Theresa Smith, "Staggie Keeps Peace at Clash over Murals," *Cape Argus* 20 February 2004; David Lurie, *Cape Town Fringe: Manenberg Avenue is where it's happening* (Cape Town: Double Storey Books, 2004).

25. IRIN, "In-depth: Youth in Crisis: Coming of Age in the 21st Century, South Africa: Gang culture in Cape Town," 27 February 2007, http://pictures.irinnews.org/in-depth/70038/28/south-africa-gang-culture-in-cape-town (accessed 28 October 2016).

26. Stephen Haw, "Shaking up the global village," *Sunday Times* (South Africa), 19 April 2000.

27. Cooper, "*Gevaarlike* transitions."

28. George Wehrfritz and Dorothy Wickham, "The Tupac Uprising: Outlaws With a Cause," *Newsweek* 16 August 1999.

29. Asger Leth, dir., *Ghosts of Cité Soleil* (2006); Somini Sengupta, "Mortal combat

rages but 'mortal kombat' rules," *The New York Times* 10 June 2003; *The Namibian* "Congo Kinshasa: In the heart of war," 9 April 1999.

30. Emsie Ferreira, "Strife-torn Ivory Coast bans camouflage as fashion statement," *Agence France Presse* 13 November 2002.

31. George Packer, "Gangsta war: Young fighters take their lead from American pop culture," *The New Yorker* 3 November 2003, p. 73; Halifu Osumare, "Global hip-hop and the African diaspora," in Harry J. Elam and Kennell Jackson, eds, *Black cultural traffic: Crossroads in global performance and popular culture* (Ann Arbor, MI: University of Michigan Press, 2005), pp. 266–88.

32. George Gittoes, dir., "Soundtrack of War," *VH1* 18 August 2005. Many other US soldiers also found solace in Tupac's music. See Gina Damron, "More Marines Head Out: Painful Partings," *Detroit Free Press* 17 December 2006.

33. Paul Rogers, "African Rebel Soldiers and Their Eerie Obsession With Tupac Shakur," *LA Weekly* 12 September 2011 http://blogs.laweekly.com/westcoastsound/2011/09/tupac_week_african_rebel_soldi.php (accessed 26 September 2016).

34. Sebastian Abbot, "Rap Music Inspires Libyan Rebels To Defeat Gaddafi," *Associated Press*, 24 April 2011; Mercy Corps, "Libyan Youth Rap for Freedom", 2011 https://www.youtube.com/watch?v=nIObt5iq8aU (accessed 26 September 2011). See also Hishaam Aidi, "The Grand (Hip-Hop) Chessboard: Race, Rap and Raison d'État," *Middle East Report* 260 (2011): 25–39.

35. Omar Hammami later claimed that the voice on the track was not his. Spencer Ackerman, "There's no turning back: my interview with a hunted American jihadist," *Wired* 4 April 2013 http://www.wired.com/dangerroom/2013/04/omar-hammami/all/ (accessed 9 May 2013).

36. Michael Hainley, "All Eyez *on* Him," *GQ Magazine* December 2012, http://www.gq.com/news-politics/politics/201212/marco-rubio-interview-gq-december-2012?currentPage=1 (accessed 1 March 2015).

37. Danna Harman, "Sierra Leone: The path from pariah to peace," *Christian Science Monitor* 18 September 2002.

38. For an incisive account of the life worlds of combatants, see Danny Hoffman, *The War Machines: Young Men and Violence in Sierra Leone and Liberia* (Durham, NC: Duke University Press, 2011).

39. Yusuf Bangura, "Comments," in Special Issue: "Lumpen youth culture and political violence: Sierra Leoneans debate the RUF and the civil war", *African Development* 20, 3/4 (1997): 185; Julie Maxted, "Youth and war in Sierra Leone," *African Identities* 1, 1 (2003): 69–78.

40. Ibrahim Abdullah, "Bush path to destruction: The origin and character of the Revolutionary United Front (RUF/SL)," in Ibrahim Abdullah, ed, *Between democracy and terror: The Sierra Leone civil war* (Dakar: Council for the Development of Social Science Research in Africa, 2004); Yusuf Bangara, "The political and cultural dynamics of the Sierra Leone war: A critique of Paul Richards," in *Between democracy and terror*, pp. 13–40; Lansana Gberie, *A Dirty War in West Africa: The RUF and the destruction of Sierra Leone* (Bloomington, IN: Indiana University Press, 2006); Hoffman, *The War Machines*; David Keen, *Conflict and Collusion in Sierra Leone* (New

York: Palgrave Macmillan, 2005); Kieran Mitton, *Rebels in a Rotten State: Understanding atrocity in the Sierra Leone civil war* (Oxford: Oxford University Press, 2015).

41. Ibrahim Abdullah and Ismail Rashid, "'Smallest victims; youngest killers': Juvenile combatants in Sierra Leone's civil war," in *Between democracy and terror*, p. 243.

42. Weiss, *Street Dreams*, p. 126.

43. Revolutionary United Front of Sierra Leone (RUF/SL), *Footpaths to democracy: Toward a new Sierra Leone* (n.p., 1995). In the words of the Sierra Leone TRC, the conflict was a war "without rules." Sierra Leone Truth and Reconciliation Commission, "Truth and Reconciliation Commission Report" (hereafter "TRC") (Freetown: Government Printers, 2004), 3A, ch.4: 15; Lansana Gberie typified the RUF as an amorphous "mercenary enterprise." Gberie, *A Dirty War*, p. 153.

44. Danny Hoffman, "The Civilian Target in Sierra Leone and Liberia: Political Power, Military Strategy, and Humanitarian Intervention," *African Affairs* 103 (2004): 21–226; Sierra Leone TRC, "TRC", ch.4: 73.

45. Ishmael Beah, *A long way gone: Memoirs of a boy soldier* (New York: Farrar, Straus, Giroux, 2007), p. 124. As Yusuf Bangura put it plainly, '[g]uns have an empowering effect on the socially estranged," Bangura, "Comments," p. 185.

46. Danny Hoffman, "Disagreement: Dissent Politics and the War in Sierra Leone," *Africa Today* 52, 3 (2006): 3–22; Keen, *Conflict and Collusion*, pp. 56, 79.

47. Achille Mbembe, "Necropolitics," *Public Culture* 15, 1 (2003): 15–20; Mats Utas and Magnus Jörgel, "The West Side Boys: military navigation in the Sierra Leone civil war," *Journal of Modern African Studies* 46, 3 (2003): 487–511. For a more complete analysis of the psychodynamics of violence during the Sierra Leone civil war, see Mitton, *Rebels in a Rotten State*.

48. PRIDE, *Ex-combatants' views of the Truth and Reconciliation Commission and the Special Court for Sierra Leone* (n.p., 2002). On rationales for using children as soldiers, see Bernd Beber and Christopher Blattman, "The Logic of Child Soldiering and Coercion," *International Organization* 67, 1 (2013): 65–104.

49. Keen, *Conflict and Collusion*.

50. William P. Murphy, "Military patrimonialism and child soldier clientelism in the Liberian and Sierra Leonean civil wars," *African Studies Review* 46, 2 (2003): 61–87; Krijn Peters, "Reintegrating young ex-combatants in Sierra Leone: Accommodating indigenous and wartime value systems," in Jon Abbink and Ineke van Kessel, eds., *Vanguard or vandals: Youth, politics, and conflict in Africa* (Leiden: Brill, 2005), pp. 277–8.

51. Henrik E. Vigh, "Social death and violent life chances," in Catrine Christiansen, Mats Utas & Henrik E. Vigh, eds, *Navigating youth, generating adulthood: social becoming in an African context* (Uppsala: Nordic Africa Institute, 2006), pp. 31–60. In the TRC's words a "new human" was born of the initiation process. Sierra Leone TRC, "TRC", 3A, ch.4: 120.

52. Beah, *Long way gone*, p. 136; Mitton, *Rebels in a Rotten State*.

53. Sierra Leone TRC, "TRC", 3A, ch.4: 77. This phenomenon of victim-turned-perpetrator creates a conundrum of analysis, as Slavoj Žižek has suggested, since it denies the simple dichotomies with which we are often more comfortable: soldier/civilian, victim/perpetrator, good child/bad child. Slavoj Žižek, *The Fragile*

*Absolute* (London: Verso, 2000), p. 60; Mahmoud Mamdani, *When victims become killers: Colonialism, nativism, and the genocide in Rwanda* (Princeton, NJ: Princeton University Press, 2002).

54. Krijn Peters, *Re-examining voluntarism: Youth combatants in Sierra Leone* (Pretoria: Institute for Security Studies, 2004).
55. Earl Conteh-Morgan and Mac Dixon-Fyle, *Sierra Leone at the end of the twentieth century: History, politics, and society* (New York: Peter Lang, 1999), p. 144.
56. Bangura, "The Political and Cultural Dynamics," p. 33; Danny Hoffman, "Like beasts in the bush: Synonyms of childhood and youth in Sierra Leone," *Postcolonial Studies* 6, 3 (2003): 295–308; Krijn Peters, *War and the Crisis of Youth in Sierra Leone* (Cambridge: Cambridge University Press, 2011); Sierra Leone TRC, "TRC", 3A, ch.3: 43.
57. Sierra Leone TRC, "TRC", ch.4: 106; Beah, *Long way gone*, p. 199.
58. Sierra Leone TRC, "TRC", 3A, ch.4: 47, 56; Caspar Fithen and Paul Richards, "Making war, crafting peace: Militia solidarities & demobilisation in Sierra Leone," in Paul Richards, ed, *No peace, no war: An anthropology of contemporary armed conflicts* (Athens, OH: Ohio University Press, 2005), pp. 117–36.
59. Keen, *Conflict and Collusion*, p. 245.
60. Abdullah and Rashid, "Smallest Victims," p. 243.
61. On this notion of aggressive violence as born of a defensive psychology, see Michael Jackson, *In Sierra Leone* (Durham, NC: Duke University Press), p. 38.
62. Keen, *Conflict and Collusion*, p. 75.
63. Sierra Leone TRC, "TRC", 3A, ch.4: 78, fn.141.
64. See, for instance, the testimony of Commanders Boston Flomoh (RUF) and Idrissa Kamara (WSB). Ibid., 3A, ch.3: 93. An RUF base in Northern Province, near Mabang, Tonkolili District, was also under the command of a man nicknamed First Blood.
65. Ibid., 3A, ch.4: 119, 78, fn. 141.
66. Paul Richards, *Fighting for the rainforest: War, youth, and resources in Sierra Leone* (Portsmouth, NH: Heinemann, 1996); Beah, *Long way gone*, p. 121.
67. Marc Sommers, "Youth, war, and urban Africa: Challenges, misunderstandings, and opportunities," in Blair A. Ruble, Joseph S. Tulchin, Diana H. Varat, with Lisa M. Hanley, eds, *Youth explosion in developing world cities: Approaches to reducing poverty and conflict in an urban age* (Washington, DC: Woodrow Wilson International Center for Scholars, 2003), pp. 25–46.
68. Lansana Fofana, "U.S. influences blamed for delinquency in Sierra Leone," *Inter Press Service News Wire* 6 May 1997. For a detailed analysis of pre-war youth cultures in Sierra Leone, see Ibrahim Abdullah, "Youth culture and rebellion: Understanding Sierra Leone's wasted decade," *Critical Arts* 16, 2 (2002): 19–37.
69. J. Lorand Matory, *Black Atlantic Religion: Tradition, transnationalism, and matriarchy in the Afro-Brazilian candomblé* (Princeton, NJ: Princeton University Press, 2005).
70. Fofana, "U.S. influences".
71. Sierra Leone TRC, "TRC", 3A, ch.3: 212.
72. Marc Sommers, "Urbanization, war, and Africa's youth at risk: Towards understanding and addressing future challenges," paper prepared for USAID and Creative

Associates International, 2003, http://www.beps.net/crisis_situation/africa.htm (accessed 11 January 2007), pp. 12–13. In 2000 Sommers interviewed refugees in the Gambia who had been in Freetown during Operation No Living Thing. Residents also reported seeing the vehicles of the attackers painted with the words "Missing in Action", a reference to the famous Chuck Norris film (*Missing in Action*, 1984).

73. See, for instance, photos taken in Freetown by the Italian photographer A. Raffaelle Ciriello, "Postcards from Hell" (1999), http://www.raffaeleciriello.com/site/56main.html (accessed 29 September 2016); and Sebastian Junger, "The terror of Sierra Leone," *Vanity Fair* August 2000, p. 116.

74. Sommers, "Youth, war, and urban Africa"; Sommers, "Urbanization, war, and Africa's youth," pp. 12–13.

75. David Keen suggested that the West Side Boys emerged from a particular coalition of AFRC/RUF combatants who controlled the Okra Hills immediately before the 1999 invasion of Freetown and, in fact, led the invasion. *Conflict and Collusion*, p. 222.

76. Utas and Jörgel, "West Side Boys," pp. 493–4, 498.

77. Dom Phillips, "Death becomes him," *The Guardian* 14 April 2001.

78. Utas and Jörgel, "West Side Boys," pp. 495, 503; Sierra Leone TRC, "TRC", 3A, ch.3: 121, 217–8, 250–1; ibid., 3A, ch.4: 71–2; William Reno, "Political networks in a failing state: The roots and future of violent conflict in Sierra Leone," *Internationale Politik und Gesellschaft/International Politics and Society* 10, 2 (2003): 60–1.

79. Keen, *Conflict and Collusion*, p. 234.

80. Ibid, pp. 284–5. See also Damien Lewis, *Operation Certain Death: The Inside Story of the SAS's Greatest Battle* (London: Century, 2004).

81. Osman Benk Sankoh, "Is Tupac alive?," *Concord Times* (Sierra Leone) 11 & 18 November 2000.

82. Eric Pape, "Shook ones," *Spin* July 2004, p. 97. On hip-hop and the wider experiences of postwar young people, see Boima Tucker, *Musical Violence: Gangsta Rap and Politics in Sierra Leone* (Current African Issues 52) (Uppsala: Nordic Africa Institute, 2013); Krijn Peters, "The Crisis of Youth in Postwar Sierra Leone: Problem Solved?," *Africa Today* 58, 2 (2011): 129–53; Susan Shepler, "Youth Music and Politics in Post-War Sierra Leone," *Journal of Modern African Studies* 48, 4 (2010): 627–42.

83. In 2015 the sports beverage Powerade also used Tupac's voice in a television advert. Rupert Neate, "How celebrities can make millions after death: meet the man with the formula," *The Guardian* 22 November 2014.

84. Al Letson, "Tupac Shakur: Hip Hop Immortal," *BBC The Documentary* 31 December 2014, http://www.bbc.co.uk/programmes/p02fdmlc?ocid=socialflow_twitter (accessed 31 December 2014).

## 4. SUPERPOWER SYMBOLIC: OSAMA BIN LADEN AND MILLENNIAL DISCONTENT

1. John L. Esposito and Dalia Mogahed, *Who Speaks for Islam? What a Billion Muslims Really Think* (New York: Gallup Press, 2007).

2. Matthias Krings, "Marke 'Osama'. Über Kommunikation und Kommerz mit Bin-Laden-Bildern in Nigeria," *Peripherie* 113/29 (2009): 32.

3. See for example Michael Scheuer, *Osama bin Laden* (New York: Oxford University Press, 2011); Peter L. Bergen, *The Osama bin Laden I Know: An Oral History of al Qaeda's Leader* (New York: Free Press, 2006); Lawrence Wright, *The Looming Tower: Al Qaeda and the Road to 9/11* (New York: Knopf, 2006); Yossef Bodansky, *Bin Laden: The Man Who Declared War on America* (Roseville, CA: Forum, 2001).

4. The most significant and comprehensive work addressing the meaning and resonances of Osama bin Laden is the pioneering volume edited by Susan Jeffords and Fahed Al-Sumait, *Covering Bin Laden: Global Media and the World's Most Wanted Man* (Urbana-Champaign, IL: University of Illinois Press, 2015).

5. Manoah Esipisu, "Mombasa Bombings," *The Independent* 22 November 2002.

6. Mark Danner argued that the hijackers used television to attack America "at its point of greatest vulnerability: at the level of spectacle." Mark Danner, "Is He Winning? Taking Stock of the Forever War," *The New York Times Magazine* 11 September 2005, p. 50. On the symbolism of the World Trade Center and the September 11 attacks, see W.J.T. Mitchell, *What Do Pictures Want? The Lives and Loves of Images* (Chicago, IL: University of Chicago Press, 2005). See also Wendy Bowler, "Seeing Tragedy in the News Images of September 11," in Jeffrey C. Alexander, Dominik Bartmański, and Bernhard Giesen, eds, *Iconic Power: Materiality and Meaning in Social Life* (New York: Palgrave Macmillan, 2012), pp. 85–99.

7. Jean Baudrillard, *The Spirit of Terrorism, and Requiem for the Twin Towers* (New York: W.W. Norton & Co., 2003). See also Elemer Hankiss, "Symbols of Destruction," *After September 11* http://essays.ssrc.org/sept11/essays/hankiss.htm (accessed 5 May 2005); Retort (Iain Boal, T.J. Clark, Joseph Matthews, and Michael Watts), *Afflicted Powers: Capital and Spectacle in a New Age of War* (New York: Verso, 2005), pp. 24–37.

8. Jeffrey N. Wasserstrom, "Anti-Americanisms, Thick Description, and Collective Action," *After September 11*, http://essays.ssrc.org/sept11/essays/wasserstrom.htm (accessed 29 September 2016); Achin Vanaik, "The Ethics and Efficacy of Political Terrorism," in Eric Hershberg and Kevin W. Moore, eds., *Critical Views of September 11: Analyses from Around the World* (New York: W.W. Norton & Co., 2002).

9. *Dateline NBC* 7 December 2001.

10. Aminu Abubakar, "Bin Laden still dear to Nigerian Muslims on eve of Bush visit," *Agence France-Presse* 10 July 2003; BBC News, "Osama Baby Craze Hits Nigeria," 3 January 2002, http://news.bbc.co.uk/1/hi/world/africa/1741171.stm (accessed 29 September 2016). In Northern Nigeria, 9/11 became intertwined with local political and ethnic tensions. Krings, "Marke 'Osama'," pp. 34–5; Umar Habila, Dadem Danfulani, and Sati U. Fwatshak, "Briefing: September 2001 Events in Jos, Nigeria," *African Affairs* 101 (2002), 251–2.

11. Ken Kirby, dir., *The Great African Scandal* (2007).

12. Neil MacFarquhar, "Saudis support a jihad in Iraq, not back home," *The New York Times* 23 April 2004. See also Sandra Jordan, "Inca Rebels Flex Their Muscles," *Observer* 12 June 2005.

13. Tracey J. Potts, "'Dark tourism' and the 'kitschification' of 9/11," *Tourist Studies* 12, 3 (2012): 232–49; Kevin Merida, "Osama bin Laden, Capitalist Tool," *Washington Post* 6 October 2001; Dana Heller, ed., *The Selling of 9/11: How a National Tragedy became a Commodity* (New York: Palgrave Macmillan, 2005).

14. Mahmoud Eid, "The Two Faces of Osama bin Laden: Mass Media Representations as a Force for Evil and Arabic Hero," in Susan J. Drucker and Gary Gumpert, eds, *Heroes in a Global World* (Cresskill, NJ: Hampton Press, 2008), pp. 177–8.

15. Susan Jeffords and Fahed Al-Sumait, "Introduction: After bin Laden," in Jeffords and Al-Sumait, eds, *Covering Bin Laden*, p. xiii.

16. American foreign policy-makers invested Osama bin Laden's image with great significance. For instance, in a 2004 congressional hearing on terrorism in Africa, the chairman of the Subcommittee on Africa of the Committee on International Relations (House of Representatives) raised the issue of bin Laden T-shirts in Nigeria. "Fighting Terrorism in Africa: Hearing before the Subcommittee on Africa of the Committee on International Relations, United States House of Representatives," 2004, available at http://commdocs.house.gov/committees/intl-rel/hfa92870.000/hfa92870_0f.htm (accessed 12 January 2010).

17. Adam Goldman, "CIA Hatched Plan to Make Demon Toy to Counter Osama bin Laden's Influence," *Washington Post* 19 June 2014.

18. Eid, "The Two Faces of Osama bin Laden."

19. On the confluence of social and political forces that attracted audiences to Osama bin Laden iconography see Farish A. Noor's analysis of the repercussions of 9/11 in Malaysia. Noor, "When Osama and friends came a-calling: the political deployment of the overdetermined image of Osama ben Laden in the contestation for Islamic symbols in Malaysia," in Peter Van Der Veer and Shoma Munshi, eds, *Media, war, and terrorism: responses from the Middle East and Asia* (New York: Routledge, 2004), 197–223.

20. Krings, "Marke 'Osama'."

21. Aditi Bhatia, "The Discursive Portrayals of Osama bin Laden," in Jeffords and Al-Sumait, eds, *Covering Bin Laden*, pp. 20–34. In an image printed on T-shirts in Indonesia in 2002, bin Laden was depicted taking on an star-spangled elephant as it attempted to squash a scorpion. Bin Laden, the image seemed to suggest, was as a defender of the weak against the strong. Rory Callinan, "Bali, Terror on our Doorstep," *The Advertiser* 26 October 2002.

22. Melani McAlister, "Television, Terrorism, and the Making of Incomprehension," *The Chronicle of Higher Education* 7 December 2001, p. 13.

23. Jeffords and Al-Sumait, "Introduction: After bin Laden."

24. Artyom Borovik, *The Hidden War* (New York: Atlantic Monthly Press, 1990).

25. Mark Danner, "The Battlefield in the American Mind," *The New York Times* 16 October 2001; Marc Howard Ross, "The Political Psychology of Competing Narratives: September 11 and Beyond," *After September 11, 2001* http://essays.ssrc.org/sept11/essays/ross.htm (accessed 29 September 2016); Retort, *Afflicted Powers*.

26. Reuters, "Bin Laden was a Che Guevara Fan," *Dawn* (Pakistan) 25 May 2012 avail-

able at http://dawn.com/2012/05/25/bin-laden-was-che-guevara-fan-wife-tells-pakistani-interrogator/ (accessed 26 May 2012).

27. On this ethical and transnational emphasis see Faisal Devji, *Landscapes of the Jihad: Militancy, Morality, Modernity* (London: Hurst, 2005).

28. Faisal Devji, "Al Qaeda, Spectre of Globalisation," *Soundings* 32 (2006): 27. *Observer*, Osama bin Laden's "Letter to America," 24 November 2002. Martin Walker, "Brand Osama has widespread appeal," *United Press International* 21 September 2001; Anonymous, *Through Our Enemies' Eyes: Osama bin Laden, Radical Islam, and the Future of America* (Washington, DC: Brassey's, Inc., 2003).

29. Osama bin Laden, "The Way to Save the Earth," 17 February 2010 http://triceratops.brynmawr.edu:8080/dspace/handle/10066/5053.

30. "Since September 11 (2001)," Wenke added, "Muslims have lifted up their heads." Boris Cambreleng, "Young Chinese Muslims look up to 'hero' bin Laden," *Agence France-Presse* 25 February 2003.

31. *The News* (Nigeria), "Our Links with Biafra," 20 September 2004. This sentiment was shared by a prisoner in Cape Town's Pollsmoor maximum-security prison, interviewed by Jonny Steinberg. "People misunderstand what [Osama bin Laden] has done…" he explained. "In the US, they make male prostitution legal. They have gambling and alcohol. They make abortion legal … And they are trying to force Western doctrine on Afghanistan." Jonny Steinberg, "Walls of mental prisons soar ever higher in wake of polarising September 11," *Business Day* (South Africa) 12 June 2004.

32. George Packer, "Gangsta War: Young Fighters Take their Lead from American Pop Culture," *The New Yorker* 3 November 2003, pp. 76–7.

33. Jason Burke, *Al-Qaeda: The True Story of Radical Islam* (London: Penguin Books, 2004), p. 39.

34. Begoña Aretxaga, "Terror as Thrill: First Thoughts on the 'War on Terrorism,'" *Anthropological Quarterly* 75, 1 (2002): 143–4.

35. Krings, "Marke 'Osama'," pp. 49–51.

36. One of the most noteworthy web-based images to be reproduced by demonstrators appeared in Dhaka in October 2001. The image ironically juxtaposed Osama bin Laden with Bert, a puppet featured on the American children's television program *Sesame Street*. On the layered meanings of this juxtaposition and its reproduction, see David Pedersen, "As Irrational as Bert and Bin Laden: The Production of Categories, Commodities, and Commensurability in the Era of Globalization," *Public Culture* 15, 2 (2003): 238–59.

37. Krings, "Marke 'Osama'," p. 40.

38. Arun Rath, "INDIA—Starring Osama bin Laden," *Frontline World* http://www.pbs.org/frontlineworld/stories/india205/thestory.html (accessed 29 September 2016); "Interview with Arun Rath: Confronting New Myths," www.pbs.org/frontlineworld/stories/india205/rath.html (accessed 29 June 2003).

39. For a wider perspective on popular culture in coastal Kenya, see Andrew J. Eisenberg, "Hip-Hop and Cultural Citizenship on Kenya's 'Swahili Coast,'" *Africa* 82 (2012): 556–78.

40. Declan Walsh, "Imam warns of 'undeclared war' between US, Israel," *Independent on Sunday* 1 December 2002.

41. In a similar vein, many analysts have interpreted veiling in coastal East Africa as intrinsically political and conservative. However, Laura Fair's work in Zanzibar has shown that for a great many women who choose the veil (*niqāb*), fashion is more important than piety. Laura Fair, "Veiling, Fashion, and Social Mobility: A Century of Change in Zanzibar," in Elisha P. Renne, ed, *Veiling in Africa* (Bloomington, IN: Indiana University Press, 2013), pp. 15–33.

42. *The Nation*, "Muslims Stormed the Streets Over Military Actions," 13 October 2001.

43. Agence France-Presse, "Ferry company orders removal of bin Laden portrait," 8 November 2001.

44. Agence France-Presse, "Investigators probe pro-bin Laden graffiti in Kenyan city," 25 September 2001; "Muslims protest in Kenya, police involved in Mombasa," 12 October 2001; Associated Press, "Kenya's Muslims Debate bin Laden's Role," 3 December 2002. Matthias Krings showed that similar sentiments and consumer goods appeared in northern Nigeria immediately after 9/11. Krings, "Marke 'Osama'."

45. Efforts to address this lacuna include Alamin Mazrui and Ibrahim Noor Shariff, *The Swahili: Idiom and Identity of an African People* (Trenton, NJ: Africa World Press, 1994); Rüdiger Seesemann, "Kenyan Muslims, the aftermath of 9/11, and the 'war on terror'", in Benjamin F. Soares and Rene Otayek, eds, *Islam and Muslim Politics in Africa* (London: Palgrave Macmillan, 2007), pp. 157–76; Kai Kresse, "Muslim Politics in Postcolonial Kenya: Negotiating Knowledge on the Double-Periphery," *Journal of the Royal Anthropological Institute* 15, 1 (2009): 76–94; Jeremy Prestholdt, "Kenya, the United States, and Counterterrorism," *Africa Today* 57, 4 (2011): 3–27; Hassan Mwakimako and Justin Willis, 'Islam, Politics, and Violence on the Kenyan Coast', *Observatoire des Enjeux Politiques et Sécuritaires dans la Corne de l'Afrique*, Note 4, July 2014, http://www.lam.sciencespobordeaux.fr/sites/lam/files/note4_observatoire.pdf (accessed 4 December 2014); Hassan J. Ndzovu, *Muslims in Kenyan Politics: Political Involvement, Marginalization, and Minority Status* (Evanston: Northwestern University Press, 2014).

46. Kresse, "Muslim Politics." See also Edward Simpson and Kai Kresse, "Introduction," in Edward Simpson and Kai Kresse, eds, *Struggling with History: Islam and Cosmopolitanism in the Western Indian Ocean* (London: Hurst, 2007).

47. This phenomenon was not unique to Mombasa. See Jean and John L. Comaroff, "Réflexions sur la jeunesse, du passé à la postcolonie," *Politique Africaine* 80 (2000): 90–110; Mamadou Diouf, "Engaging Postcolonial Culture: African Youth and Public Space," *African Studies Review* 46, no. 2 (2003): 1–12.

48. Ali Mazrui, "Stages of Globalization in the African Context: Mombasa," in Nezar Al Sayyad, ed, *Hybrid Urbanism: On the Identity Discourse and the Built Environment* (Westport, CT: Praeger, 2001), pp. 111–30.

49. Jeremy Prestholdt, "Politics of the Soil: Separatism, Autochthony, and Decolonization at the Kenyan Coast," *Journal of African History* 55, 2 (2014): 249–70; Justin Willis and George Gona, "*Pwani C Kenya?* memory, documents and seces-

sionist politics in coastal Kenya," *African Affairs* 112, 446 (2013): 48–71; James R. Brennan, "Lowering the Sultan's Flag: Sovereignty and Decolonization in Coastal Kenya," *Comparative Studies in Society and History* 50, 4 (2008): 831–61; Ahmed I. Salim, "The movement for 'Mwambao' or coast autonomy in Kenya, 1956–1963," *Hadith* 2 (1970): 212–28.

50. Daniel Branch, *Kenya: Between Hope and Despair* (New Haven, CT: Yale University Press, 2011).

51. Carole Rakodi, et. al., "Poverty and Political Conflict in Mombasa," *Environment and Urbanization* 12, 1 (2000): 153–170; *Coast Express*, "Upcountry People also have Vast Interests," 14 November 2003.

52. Chege Mbitiru, "Radicalization of Islam Feared As Muslim Activism Increases," *Associated Press Wire Service* 17 September 1993.

53. Janet McIntosh, *The Edge of Islam: Power, Personhood, and Ethnoreligious Boundaries on the Kenya Coast* (Durham, NC: Duke University Press, 2009).

54. Mazrui and Shariff, *The Swahili*, p. 153.

55. For the protection of my informants, all remain anonymous. Anonymous interviewee, Mombasa, 30 May 2005; anonymous interviewee, Mombasa, 26 July 2008.

56. Hassan Juma Ndzovu, "The Politicization of Muslim Organizations and the Future of Islamic-Oriented Politics in Kenya," *Islamic Africa* 3, 1 (2012): 25–53; Thomas P. Wolf, "Contemporary Politics," in Jan Hoorweg, Dick Foeken, and R.A. Obudho, eds, *Kenya Coast Handbook: Culture, Resources and Development in the East African Littoral* (New Brunswick, NJ: Transaction Publishers, 2000); US Department of State, "Kenya Human Rights Practices, 1994," Washington, DC, February 1995.

57. Human Rights Watch, *Kenya: Human Rights Developments, 1992* www.hrw.org/reports/1993/WR93/Afw-02.htm (accessed 3 October 2016).

58. Xinhua General Overseas News Service, "Kenya warned of Muslim uprising," 6 June 1992. Ali Mazrui has elsewhere suggested that in the early 1990s the coast seemed poised for a "black *intifadah*." See Ali A. Mazrui, "The black intifadah? Religion and rage at the Kenyan coast," *Journal of Asian and African Affairs* 4, (1993): 87–93; and Mazrui, "Preface," in *Kenya Coast Handbook*, p. xxvi.

59. Wolf, "Contemporary Politics," p. 142.

60. On the resurgent popularity of Malcolm X in the 1990s, see William W. Sales, Jr., *From Civil Rights to Black Liberation: Malcolm X and the Organization of Afro-American Unity* (Boston, MA: South End Press, 1994), ch. 1; Jacqueline Urla, "'We Are All Malcolm X!': Negu Gorriak, Hip-Hop, and the Basque Political Imaginary," in Tony Mitchell, ed, *Global Noise: Rap and Hip-Hop Outside the USA* (Middletown, CT: Wesleyan University Press, 2001), pp. 171–93; Graeme Abernethy, *The Iconography of Malcolm X* (Lawrence, KS: University of Kansas Press, 2013). On Malcolm X and Muslim internationalism, see Sohail Daulatzai, *Black Star, Crescent Moon: The Muslim International and Black Freedom beyond America* (Minneapolis, MN: University of Minnesota Press, 2012).

61. Human Rights Watch, *Violence as a Political Weapon*, New York, 2002, www.hrw.org/reports/2002/kenya/Kenya0502–04.htm (accessed 3 October 2016).

62. Jeremy Prestholdt, "Phantom of the Forever War: Fazul Abdullah Mohammed and the Terrorist Imaginary," *Public Culture* 21, 3 (2009): 451–64.

NOTES

63. Njuguna Mutonya, "Kenya: FBI Men Quiz Muslims," *Daily Nation* 29 May 2000 http://allafrica.com/stories/200005290053.html (accessed 28 October 2016).
64. Francis Thoya, "Suspects Go to Court to Halt FBI Extradition Bid," *Daily Nation* 13 November 2001.
65. *The Indian Ocean Newsletter*, "Dismay at Police Roundup of Muslims," 17 November 2001; Hervé Maupeu, "East African Muslims and the 11 September Crisis," *Mambo!* 2, 1 (2002): 5.
66. Timothy Kalyegira, "Kenya's Muslims protest new passport laws," *United Press International* 26 September 2001; "Split over Coast Muslim demo," *Daily Nation* 7 June 2001.
67. Karim Rajan, Mwakera Mwajefa, and Jonathan Manyindo, "Imams criticise anti-terror drive," *Coast Express* 11 April 2003.
68. Ngumbao Kithi, "Threat hovering over coastal region as security forces step up surveillance," *Sunday Nation* 31 August 2003.
69. Amnesty International found that at least one of the detainees interrogated by foreign agents was threatened with internment at Guantanamo Bay. Another was tortured with electric shocks. Amnesty International, "Kenya: The impact of 'anti-terrorism' operations on human rights," 23 March 2005, http://www.refworld. org/docid/42ae982b0.html (accessed 3 October 2016); Agence France-Presse, "Sixth suspect charged over deadly Kenya blasts," 18 September 2003; Agence France-Presse, "500 imigrantes ilegais são detidos no Quênia," 31 August 2003.
70. Stephen Mbogo, "Arrests May Have Prevented Attack on Anniversary of US Embassy Bombing," *CNSNews.com* 6 August 2003.
71. Amnesty International, "Memorandum to the Kenyan Government on the Suppression of Terrorism Bill 2003," https://www.amnesty.org/en/documents/ afr32/003/2004/en/ (accessed 3 October 2016); Harrison Kinyanjui, "Opinion: Anti-Terror Law Will Roll Back Kenya's Civil Liberties," *The East African* 30 June 2003; Francis Thoya, "Imam's fury over new anti-terror Bill," *Coast Express* 20 June 2003.
72. These monies were part of America's East Africa Counter-Terrorism Initiative. Sandra T. Barnes, "Global Flows: Terror, Oil, and Strategic Philanthropy," *African Studies Review* 48, 1 (2005): 1–22; "Letter: Terrorism: Ambassador spelled out US demands," *Daily Nation* 19 June 2003.
73. Nation Team, "Suspected terrorist, 24, is arrested," *Daily Nation* 30 June 2003; Muslim Civic Education Trust (Kenya), *Toleo #213: Suppression of Human Rights Bill?*, 9 January 2004; Samwell Siringi, "Threats of mass action over Bill on terrorism," *Daily Nation* 16 July 2003; Issa Hussein, David Mugonyi, Adan Mohamed, Patrick Mathangani and Onesmus Kilonzo, "Suspected terrorist, 24, is arrested," *Daily Nation* 30 June 2003.
74. Seesemann, "Kenyan Muslims."
75. Shabbir Versi, "Mombasa throbs with anti-blasphemy rally," *Muslim Media.com* 16–31 August 1997.
76. Prestholdt, "Politics of the Soil"; Nathaniel Mathews, "Imaging Arab Communities: Colonialism, Islamic Reform, and Arab Identity in Mombasa, Kenya, 1897–1933," *Islamic Africa* 4, 2 (2013): 135–63.

77. Mahmood Mamdani, *Good Muslim, Bad Muslim: America, the Cold War, and the Roots of Terror* (New York: Pantheon Books, 2004).
78. Tom Osanjo, "The Kenyan Town where Arafat is a Hero," *Panafrican News Agency Daily Newswire* 14 April 2002; Fuad Nahdi, "A cocktail of grievances in paradise: Tourism, US swagger and a new Islam have transformed Mombasa," *The Guardian*, 29 November 2002; Ndzovu, *Muslims in Kenyan Politics*, 119–20.
79. Nation Correspondent, "Imams Warn the US Over 'Misuse,'" *Daily Nation* 29 February 2000.
80. *Times of India*, "Anti-Israel protests rock Mombasa," 21 October 2000.
81. N.S. Bakari, "Letters: Shed No Tear for Osama Friends," *Nation* 27 October 2001.
82. Bogonko Bosire, "Kenyan Muslims claim harassment over blast probe," Agence France-Presse 5 March 2003. US investigators may not have seen their work as retribution, but presumed local connections with radical movements were the central concern of foreign investigators and counterterrorism agencies in Kenya. See Prestholdt, "Kenya, the United States, and Counterterrorism"; Jeremy Prestholdt, "Fighting Phantoms: The United States and Counterterrorism in Eastern Africa," in Gershon Shafir, Everard Meade, and William J. Aceves, eds, *From Moral Manic to Permanent War: Lessons and Legacies of the War on Terror* (London: Routledge, 2013), pp. 127–56.
83. Patrick Mayoyo, "US Warns of Missile Attacks in Nairobi," *The East African* 17 March 2003.
84. Emily Wax, "Fearing Attack, Kenya Searches for Al Qaeda Suspect," *Washington Post* 16 May 2003.
85. "Inside Kenya's Death Squads," *Al Jazeera* 8 December 2014, http://interactive. aljazeera.com/aje/KenyaDeathSquads/#film (accessed 18 April 2016); "Kenya to Investigate Al Jazeera Allegations of 'Death Squads'," *Reuters* 10 December 2014, http://www.reuters.com/article/us-kenya-security-media-idUSKBN-0JO1OV20141210 (accessed 3 October 2016). For additional cases of alleged police abuse, including extrajudicial executions, see the Open Society Justice Initiative and Muslims for Human Rights, *"We're Tired of Taking You to the Court": Human Rights Abuses by Kenya's Anti-Terrorism Police Unit* (New York: Open Society Foundations, 2013).
86. Agence France-Presse, "Investigators Probe Pro-Bin Laden Graffiti in Kenyan City," 25 September 2001; "Hunt for Bin Laden Links in Kenya," *BBC News* 25 September 2001 http://news.bbc.co.uk/2/hi/africa/1560952.stm (accessed 28 March 2004).
87. Jillo Kadida, "Lawyer Calls Case 'Ploy to get Cash for Terror Squad,'" *The Nation* 26 April 2005; *East African Standard*, "Bomb Suspect 'Had Osama Cuttings'," 28 July 2004.
88. Agence France-Presse, "President warns Liberians not to wear Osama bin Laden T-shirts," 12 November 2002; *Toronto Star*, "Canada taking steps back to sanity," 16 February 2007; *Times of India*, "History-sheeter who put up posters nabbed," 2 May 2010.
89. Paul Dillon, "Worries grow, Indonesia ripe to become al Qaeda base," *Globe and Mail* 25 September 2002.
90. Pew Research Center, "On Anniversary of bin Laden's Death, Little Backing of al

Qaeda: Survey Report," *Pew Research Center: Global Attitudes & Trends* 30 April 2012, available at http://www.pewglobal.org/2012/04/30/on-anniversary-of-bin-ladens-death-little-backing-of-al-qaeda/ (accessed 3 Feburary 2015). See also Eid, "The Two Faces of Osama bin Laden," p. 174.

91. Douglas Kellner, "September 11, Spectacles of Terror, and Media Manipulation: A Critique of Jihadist and Bush Media Politics," *Logos* 2, 1 (2003): 86–102.

92. Jeffrey Fleishman, "Osama bin Laden's Appeal had Waned in the Arab World," *Los Angeles Times* 2 May 2011.

93. Andrew Hill, "The bin Laden Tapes," in Jeffords and Al-Sumait, eds, *Covering Bin Laden*, pp. 35–52.

## 5.  ONE LOVE: BOB MARLEY, THE MYSTIC, AND THE MARKET

1. Jon Bradshaw, "The Reggae Way to 'Salvation'," *The New York Times Magazine* 14 August 1977; "Bob Marley and the Reggae Rebellion," *Crawdaddy* August 1975.

2. *Time Magazine*, "Best Album Exodus by Bob Marley & the Wailers (1977)," 31 December 1999, http://www.time.com/time/magazine/article/0,9171,993039-2,00.html (accessed 28 June 2009).

3. E.R. Shipp, "In millennial hype self-interest overwhelmed religious meaning of day", *Daily News* (New York) 6 January 2000.

4. Guy Garcia, "Marley's Ghost," *Time Magazine* 24 June 2001. The year 2001 saw an uptick in Bob Marley's popularity, likely in part because of the millennial attention and his reception of a star on the Hollywood Walk of Fame. If we measure interest in Marley by the number of Google searches including his name, his popularity remained relatively steady between 2004 and 2014, though it began to decrease thereafter. See Google Trends, "Web Search Bob Marley. Worldwide, 2004—present", https://trends.google.com/trends/explore?date=all&q=%2Fm%2F0bkf4 (accessed 23 August 2018).

5. Brent Clough, "Jamming Down Under: Bob Marley's Legacy and Reggae Culture in Australia and New Zealand," in Eleanor Wint and Carolyn Cooper, eds, *Bob Marley: The Man and his Music* (Kingston: Arawak Publications, 1995), p. 27.

6. Anoop Pandey, "The Raja of Rasta and Reggae: Bob Marley is not Dead, he's just not here with me or you," *Nepali Times* 28 January–3 February 2005; Gregory Stephens, *On Racial Frontiers: The New Culture of Frederick Douglass, Ralph Ellison, and Bob Marley* (New York: Cambridge University Press, 1999), p. 214; Francesco Mastalia and Alfonse Pagano, *Dreads* (New York: Artisan, 1999), p. 56.

7. Episocpal News Service, "Jamaica: Anglican hymnals to include reggae songs," 6 August 2007, http://archive.episcopalchurch.org/81808_88829_ENG_HTM.htm (accessed 28 April 2014).

8. See Stephens, *On Racial Frontiers*, pp. 215–16.

9. On Mother Teresa as a suprareligious figure hailed by Christians, Muslims, and Hindus, see Bishnupriya Ghosh, *Global Icons: Apertures to the Popular* (Berkeley, CA: University of California Press, 2011).

10. Roger Steffens offered a valuable overview of the complex meanings of Bob Marley in "Forward: Bob Marley: Artist of the Century," in Hank Bordowitz, ed, *Every*

*Little Thing Gonna Be Alright: The Bob Marley Reader* (Cambridge, MA: De Capo Press, 2004). For a comprehensive list of publications related to Bob Marley see Joe Jurgensen, *Bob Marley: The Complete Annotated Bibliography* (Prospect, KY: Haras Publishing, 2009). For an authoritative oral history of Marley's life see Roger Steffens, *So Much Things to Say: The Oral History of Bob Marley* (New York: W.W. Norton, 2017).

11. David Wainer, "Ramallah-based radio station appeals to Israelis and Palestinians via common language," *Jerusalem Post* 24 March 2008.

12. The survey further determined that "One Love", "No Woman, No Cry", and "Stir it Up" were the Marley tracks most useful for students keen to augment their English skills. *Marketwire*, "Bob Marley Tops the Charts for Helping Music Lovers to Learn English," 23 October 2012, http://www.marketwired.com/press-release/bob-marley-tops-the-charts-for-helping-music-lovers-to-learn-english-1716832.htm (accessed 20 March 2014).

13. Critic Don Snowden contended that as early as 1988 a "personality cult" was developing around Bob Marley. Don Snowden, "Marley's Ghost," *Los Angeles Times* 9 October 1988.

14. Quoted in Janet L. DeCosmo, "Bob Marley: Religious Prophet?," in Eleanor Wint and Carolyn Cooper, eds, *Bob Marley: The Man and his Music* (Kingston: Arawak Publications, 1995), p. 59.

15. Bob Marley's eldest son, Ziggy, explained that his father's message was one of "love, peace, and unity through music." David Alexanian, dir., *Marley Africa Road Trip*, Discovery Channel, 2011, Episode 1. Love, peace, and unity were common refrains in Marley's music. In the 1970s, when a reporter from a Norwegian broadcasting company asked Bob Marley what his "special message" was, he replied: "Truth, peace, and love, and music, ya know, an livity." "Bob Marley Interview Norway," https://www.youtube.com/watch?v=wh2TUiCMbYU (accessed 19 January 2014).

16. Roger Steffens, "Bob Marley: Rasta Warrior," in Nathaniel Samuel Murrell, William David Spencer, and Adrian Anthony McFarlane, eds, *Chanting Down Babylon: the Rastafari Reader* (Philadelphia, PN: Temple University Press, 1998), pp. 253, 259. This was likely reinforced by the fact that Rastafari elders often referred to Marley as a latter-day Joseph. Timothy White, *Catch a Fire: The Life of Bob Marley* (New York: Henry Holt and Company, 2000), p. 419.

17. Hugh Hodges, "Walk Good: West Indian Oratorical Traditions in Bob Marley's *Uprising*," *The Journal of Commonwealth Literature* 40, 2 (2005): 43–63.

18. Larry Rohter, "Bob Marley: Reggae from a 'Rastaman'," *Washington Post* 26 April 1976. Rohter dubbed Marley a "cult figure" in the United States, or a "prophet in the eyes of his fans."

19. Dick Gregory, AMANDLA—Festival of Unity, Cambridge, MA, 21 July 1979, http:// www.youtube.com/watch?v=C2ZASLnuwlk (accessed 14 October 2013); Hiroshi Hiyama, "Bob Marley remains hero for the down and out … of Japan," Agence France Presse 9 February 2005; Stephens, *On Racial Frontiers*, p. 149.

20. Timothy White, "Give Thanks and Praise: The Music Community Remembers Bob

Marley," *The Beat* 8, 3 (1989): 29; Dawta Jamaka, "Bob the Prophet," *Reggae and African Beat* 3, 3 (1984): 27, 33.

21. Comment posted by peace2012ization on the YouTube video of Marley's performance at AMANDLA—Festival of Unity, Cambridge, MA, 21 July 1979, http://www.youtube.com/watch?v=C2ZASLnuwIk (accessed 14 October 2013). See also BBC World Service, "One Love—The Legacy of Bob Marley," 16 May 2011, http://www.bbc.co.uk/programmes/p00gk5kz (accessed 19 April 2013).

22. Ishmael Beah, *A Long Way Gone: Memoirs of a Boy Soldier* (New York: Farrar, Straus and Giroux, 2007), pp. 163–4.

23. Steve Mirkin, "Bob Marley Festival: Roots Rock Reggae," *Daily Variety* (Los Angeles) 15 August 2006, p. 9. See also Stevenson Jacobs, "Jamaica Marks Bob Marley's 59th Birthday," Associated Press Online 6 February 2004.

24. President Barack Obama was even symbolically linked to Bob Marley via the phrase "One Love". For instance, T-shirts produced by Concrete Roots featured images of Obama in red, gold, and green, blanketed by peace signs and captioned with the words "One Love." The Obama White House similarly promoted this association during the 2009 inauguration, when Herbie Hancock, Will.I.Am, and Sheryl Crow performed "One Love" on the National Mall.

25. Michelle A. Stephens, "Babylon's 'Natural Mystic': The North American Music Industry, the Legend of Bob Marley, and the Incorporation of Transnationalism," *Cultural Studies* 12, 2 (1998): 141.

26. Richard Salter, "Rastafari in a Global Context: Affinities of 'Orthognosy' and 'Oneness' in the Expanding World," *Ideaz* 7 (2008): 10–27. In 2009 the website Playing for Change produced a virtual concert in an effort to promote grassroots transnational cultural exchange. Its "song around the world" featured musicians from South Africa, Italy, India, Nepal, Spain, the Democratic Republic of the Congo, Israel, and the United States playing Bob Marley's "One Love". Playing for Change, http://playingforchange.com/episodes/3 (accessed 26 July 2013). This sentiment has realized other tangible forms through the Marley family's non-profit organization 1Love: http://www.1love.org.

27. Clough, "Jamming Down Under", p. 27.

28. Stephen King, *Reggae, Rastafari, and the Rhetoric of Social Control* (Jackson, MS: University Press of Mississippi, 2002).

29. Stephens, *On Racial Frontiers*, p. 191.

30. Neil J. Savishinsky, "Transnational Popular Culture and the Global Spread of the Jamaican Rastafarian Movement," *New West Indian Guide* 8, 3–4 (1994): 260; Dean MacNeil, *The Bible and Bob Marley: Half the Story Has Never Been Told* (Eugene, OR: Cascade Books, 2013); Marvin Sterling, *Babylon East: Performing Dancehall, Roots Reggae, and Rastafari in Japan* (Durham, NC: Duke University Press, 2010).

31. Kwame Dawes, *Bob Marley: Lyrical Genius* (London: Sanctuary, 2002), p. 19.

32. Neil J. Savishinsky, "Rastafari in the Promised Land: The Spread of a Jamaican Socioreligious Movement among the Youth of West Africa," *African Studies Review* 37, 3 (1994): 31.

33. Eddie S. Glaude, Jr, *Exodus!: Religion, Race, and Nation in Early Nineteenth-Century Black America* (Chicago, IL: University of Chicago Press, 2000); Robin D.G. Kelley,

*Freedom Dreams: The Black Radical Imagination* (Boston, MA: Beacon, 2003), pp. 16–17.

34. Stephens, *On Racial Frontiers*, pp. 149, 215.
35. Ben Apatoff, "25 years of 'Confrontation': Posthumous epic marks silver anniversary," *BobMarley.com* 23 May 2008, available at https://weroad.wordpress.com/2008/06/04/25-years-of-confrontation/ (accessed 3 October 2016).
36. Stephens, "Babylon's 'Natural Mystic'," pp. 145–6; Paul Gilroy, *Small Acts: Thoughts on the Politics of Black Cultures* (London: Serpent's Tail, 1993), pp. 237–57; Chris Salewicz, *Bob Marley: The Untold Story* (New York: Faber and Faber, 2009), pp. 401–2; Chris Kornelis, "How Bob Marley Was Sold to the Suburbs," *Phoenix New Times* 2 July 2014.
37. Adverts for *Legend* proclaimed, "the legend lives on." Simon Jones, *Black Culture, White Youth: The Reggae Tradition from JA to UK* (London: Macmillan, 1988), p. 68. The perceived timelessness of Marley's music may also stem from the fact that his brand of roots reggae differed from mainstream music outside of the Caribbean. Marley's sound was thus not easily framed within the parameters of a clearly defined cultural moment.
38. This number does not include the pirated versions of *Legend* sold in Africa, Latin America, Asia, and elsewhere, which may account for the majority of albums circulatied. Edna Gundersen, "'Legend,' Bob Marley's best-of album, lands on a milestone," *USA Today* 30 July 2009; Salewicz, *Bob Marley*, p. 402; Kornelis, "How Bob Marley Was Sold". According to other sources, Marley has sold over 75 million albums since the mid-1990s. "How the Bob Marley Estate Still Makes Millions Every Year—Even Though He Died More Than 30 Years Ago," *Black Business.org* 9 April 2014, http://blog.blackbusiness.org/2014/04/how-bob-marley-estate-still-makes-millions.html#.VQaAUhYapGM (accessed 16 March 2015). According to Island Records, Bob Marley's sales had only reached about US$20 million at the time of his death. Roger Steffens, "Bob Marley: 10 Years After," *The Beat* 10, 3 (1991): 35.
39. Nikke Finke, "Bibles, Blond Locks: the New Rastafarians," *Los Angeles Times* 15 March 1987; Michelle A. Stephens, "Babylon's Natural Mystic", p. 163. Stephens argued that "mystic universalism is not revolutionary internationalism, and the cultural politics of transnationalism as transcendence is a politics that typically erases the postcolonial racial other in order to reconstitute a pluralistic liberal nationalism." See also Mario Vargas Llosa, "My Son the Rastafarian," *San Francisco Chronicle* 30 March 1986.
40. Stephens, "Babylon's Natural Mystic," pp. 148–9.
41. Promotional material billed the slim volume as "a welcome companion for all who value the wisdom of a true poet of peace." "Description," Tuff Gong Books.com http://www.tuffgongbooks.com/60visions.html (accessed 25 April 2014). Roger Steffens has similarly referred to Marley's songs as "psalms". Roger Steffens, "Bob Marley: 10 Years After," *The Beat* 10, 3 (1991): 35.
42. Eileen Moyer wrote that young men in Dar es Salaam likewise spoke of Marley as a "prophet or a saint of the Rastafari faith." "Street-Corner Justice in the Name

of Jah: Imperatives for Peace among Dar es Salaam Street Youth," *Africa Today* 51, 3 (2005): 46–7.

43. Francis Lawrence, dir., *I Am Legend*, 2007. In the film, Robert Neville's daughter is fittingly named "Marley".

44. Helen Bain, "Bob's still stirring it up", *The Dominion* (New Zealand) 20 January 2001. On reggae and Rastafari in New Zealand, and interest on the part of Maori audiences specifically, see Luis Alvarez, "Reggae Rhythms in Dignity's Diaspora: Globalization, Indigenous Identity, and the Circulation of Cultural Struggle," *Popular Music and Society* 31, 5 (2008): 575–97; Neil J. Savishinsky, "Transnational Popular Culture and the Global Spread of the Jamaican Rastafarian Movement," *New West Indian Guide* 8, 3–4 (1994): 272–4.

45. A.G. Hopkins, "Rethinking Decolonization," *Past and Present* 200 (2008): 211–47.

46. By 2000 the per capita consumption of reggae music in New Zealand rivaled anywhere outside of the Caribbean. Vanessa Bidois, "With love but no drink," *The New Zealand Herald*, 12 January 2000.

47. Graham Reid, "Positive vibration," *The New Zealand Herald* 6 February 1999. In 2001, Will 'Ilolahia, the Tongan organizer of the Wellington One Love festival, explained that "Bob Marley talked a lot about bringing people together, so that is really relevant to what we are trying to achieve on Waitangi Day." Bain, "Bob's still stirring it up." Reggae festivals in the US, Kenya, and elsewhere have similarly used the "One Love" moniker.

48. *The New York Times*, "Koch Proclaims Bob Marley Day," 31 May 1981; Tom Cheyney, "L.A. Salutes Bob Marley," *The Beat* 9, 2 (1990): 8–9. Organizers have often scheduled Marley commemorations in February or May to coincide with Marley's birthday or the anniversary of his death.

49. Robert Lalah, "Bob Marley: A Prophet without honour in his homeland—Allison," *Jamaican Gleaner* 29 January 2008. Washington, DC has hosted a Bob Marley Commemorative Weekend and Filmfest, and in 2012 Los Angeles declared 7 August its Bob Marley Day. In 2009, the port city of Kochin in Kerala, India held its inaugural Bob Marley Fest.

50. Hrvoje Hranjski, "Rwandans celebrate Bob Marley and message of African unity," *Associated Press Worldstream* 11 May 1998.

51. Salter, "Rastafari in a Global Context," p. 10.

52. This, in part, is why a Lamu council assembly member voiced her intention to introduce a bill that would ban dreadlocks in Lamu. Kalume Kazungu, "Now Lamu Proposes to Outlaw Dreadlocks," *Daily Nation* 16 April 2014.

53. Jamaica Tourist Board, "One Love (1994–2003)," Tourism Information Publishing Site, no date, http://www.jtbonline.org/JTB/Pages/OneLove.aspx (accessed 25 April 2013).

54. Sara Kettler, "Bob Marley's Empire," *Biography.com* 11 May 2016, http://www.biography.com/news/bob-marley-products-estate (accessed 25 October 2016). See also "Marley Natural: Home," https://www.marleynaturaltheherb.com/ (accessed 25 October 2016).

55. *The Independent*, "Marley Family Defends Name," 4 November 1993. At roughly the same time, Philip Morris hired the research firm Market Insight to assist with

Marlboro advertising in Ivory Coast. The firm identified Marley as an important musical figure among young people. Market Insight (Vienna), "Marlboro: Image Dynamics Study in the Ivory Coast," March 1994, p. 28, available at http://legacy.library.ucsf.edu/tid/jws19e00/pdf (accessed 28 April 2014).

56. According to Brent Hagerman, tourists and pilgrims who enter Bob Marley's mausoleum in Jamaica are encouraged to ritually smoke ganja in his presence. Brent Hagerman, "Buried above the Ground: Between Babylon and Zion at the Bob Marley Mausoleum," *Wadabagei* 13, 2 (2010): 74.

57. Bob Marley's music and image has offered a longstanding alternative identity for Western young people. So common was Marley's popularity among American college students by 2005 that the satirical newspaper *The Onion* lampooned the phenomenon with an article titled "Bob Marley Rises from the Grave to Free Frat Boys from Bonds of Oppression," *The Onion* 5 October 2005, http://www.theonion.com/content/node/41242 (accessed 2 August 2009).

58. Rob Kenner, "The Business of Bob Marley," *VNU Entertainment News Wire* 4 February 2011.

59. Katia Dunn, "Bob Marley: The Man, The Myth, The Brand," *Morning Edition* (NPR) 11 March 2009, http://www.npr.org/templates/story/story.php?storyId=101 674745 (accessed 10 October 2016); David Usborne, "For sale: Bob Marley," *The Independent* 12 February 2009.

60. Privateer Holdings, "Family of Bob Marley and Privateer Holdings Unveil World's First Cannabis Brand," 18 November 2014, http://www.privateerholdings.com/blogmaster/2015/11/17/family-of-bob-marley-and-privateer-holdings-unveil-worlds-first-global-cannabis-brand (accessed 22 October 2016); Shannon Bond, "Bob Marley: Marlboro Man of Marijuana?," *Financial Times* 18 November 2014, http://www.ft.com/cms/s/2/01da3e7e-6e81-11e4-a65a-00144feabdc0.html (accessed 16 March 2015).

61. MarleyNatural.com, "Marley Natural: Press," 18 November 2014, http://www.marleynatural.com/press/#releases (accessed 15 March 2015; no longer available); Bond, "Bob Marley: Marlboro Man of Marijuana?"

62. Jason Kirby, "One Smokin' Brand," *Maclean's* 2 March 2009; "Our Story" http://marleycoffee.com/ (accessed 27 April 2013).

63. Rob Kenner, "The Business of Bob," *Billboard Magazine* 12 February 2011; Danielle and Andy Mayoras, "Are Bob Marley's Heirs Destroying his Legacy?", *Forbes* 5 December 2011, http://www.forbes.com/sites/trialandheirs/2011/12/05/are-bob-marley-heirs-destroying-his-legacy/ (accessed 16 March 2015); Dotun Adebayo, "Bob Marley's legacy is going up in cannabis smoke," *The Guardian* 20 November 2014, http://www.theguardian.com/commentisfree/2014/nov/20/bob-marley-legacy-cannabis-smoke-reggae-dopeheads (accessed 17 March 2015).

64. Frank Robson, "International man of mischief," *Sydney Morning Herald* 22 March 2003; S. Chandrasekharan, "Election in Fiji from 25th August: will it make a dent on the racial fault lines?", South Asia Analysis Group, Paper No. 301, 23 August 2001.

65. John Wagner, "Songs of 'revolution' and others that make Bernie Sanders's playlist," *The Washington Post* 8 February 2016.

66. *Business Day* (South Africa), "Voices for freedom heard in Zimbabwe," 14 March 2005.
67. Andrew Meldrum, "Mugabe is Spooked by the Letter Z," *Observer* 20 June 2004; IPS Correspondents, "ZIMBABWE: 'We are Everywhere' Says Shadowy Pro-Democracy Group," IPS News Agency 10 October 2004, http://www.ipsnews. net/2004/05/zimbabwe-we-are-everywhere-says-shadowy-pro-democracy-group/ (accessed 10 October 2016); "Zvakwana: Interview with Zvakwana," *New Internationalist* 376 (March 2005), http://newint.org/features/2005/03/01/waves/#sthash.zXO9XhLj.dpuf (accessed 16 August 2009).
68. Banning Eyre, "Postscript Added to Freemuse Report no. 3, 'Playing with Fire: Fear and Self-Censorship in Zimbabwean Music.' Second edition, 2005," *Freemuse Report* 5 January 2005, http://www.freemuse.org/sw8663.asp (accessed 16 August 2009).
69. Diane Farsetta, "Image and Reality in Zimbabwe," *PR Watch.com* 25 June 2008 (originally published in *The Times* (Johannesburg)), http://www.prwatch.org/spin/2008/06/7485/image-and-reality-zimbabwe (accessed 15 March 2015).
70. Joshua Jelly-Schapiro, "The Bob Marley Story," *New York Review of Books* 9 April 2009.
71. Reggae expert Roger Steffens astutely described Bob Marley as a "rebel for all reasons." Roger Steffens, "Bob Marley: Cultural Icon," in Hank Bordowitz, ed, *Every Little Thing Gonna Be Alright: The Bob Marley Reader* (Cambridge, MA: De Capo Press, 2004), p. xx.

6. BRAND REBEL: CHE GUEVARA BETWEEN POLITICS AND CONSUMERISM

1. This was not the first time that last words were put in Che Guevara's mouth. In 1970, a play by Rolf Hochhuth titled *The Guerrillas* had Che speak the similarly romantic line, "My death here [in Bolivia]—in a calculated sense—is the only possible victory." *Time Magazine*, "Che: A Myth Embalmed in a Matrix of Ignorance," 12 October 1970.
2. Paul J. Dosal, "San Ernesto de la Higuera: The Resurrection of Che Guevara," in Lyman L. Johnson, ed, *Death, dismemberment, and memory: body politics in Latin America* (Albuquerque, NM: University of New Mexico Press, 2004), pp. 317–41; Gary Cross, *Consumed Nostalgia: Memory in the Age of Fast Capitalism* (New Haven, CT: Yale University Press, 2015). On the development of a post-Cold War global consumer culture, see Emily S. Rosenberg, "Consumer Capitalism and the End of the Cold War," in Melvyn P. Leffler and Odd Arne Welstad, eds, *The Cambridge History of the Cold War, Volume III, Endings* (Cambridge: Cambridge University Press, 2010), pp. 489–512; Frank Trentmann, *Empire of Things: How We Became a World of Consumers, from the Fifteenth Century to the Twenty-First* (New York: Harper Collins, 2016).
3. Che Guevara became so distanced from ideology that some in early twenty-first-century East Timor saw his image as according with anti-Communist sentiment. Henri Myrttinen, "Histories of violence, states of denial: militias, martial arts and masculinities in Timor-Leste" (PhD Thesis, University of KwaZulu-Natal, 2010), pp. 264–5.

NOTES pp. [186–189]

4. The most important works include David Kunzle, ed, *Che Guevara: Icon, Myth, and Message* (Los Angeles, CA: UCLA Fowler Museum of Cultural History and Center for the Study of Political Graphics, 1997); Trisha Ziff, ed, *Che Guevara: Revolutionary & Icon* (London: V&A Publishers, 2006); Michael Casey, *Che's Afterlife: the legacy of an image* (New York: Vintage, 2009); Maria-Carolina Cambre, *The Semiotics of Che Guevara: Affective Gateways* (New York: Bloomsbury Publishers, 2015).

5. UCLA's Fowler Museum of Cultural History staged a major exhibition (with an accompanying publication, see above) as early as 1997: "Che Guevara: Icon, Myth, and Message." Kunzle, ed. *Che Guevara*; idem, "Che Guevara: Icon, Myth and Message: Seeing Che as Icon through Artists' Eyes," *UCLA Today* 10 October 1997. The University of California, Riverside staged an exhibition in 2005 focused on the Heroic Guerrilla image, *Revolution and Commerce: The Legacy of Korda's Portrait of Che Guevara*, which was followed in 2006 by a similar exhibition at London's V&A Museum, *Che Guevara: Revolutionary and Icon*. The resulting volume was edited by Trisha Ziff (see above).

6. Historically grounded accounts include Kunzle, ed. *Che Guevara*; Mike Gonzalez, "The Resurrections of Che Guevara", *International Socialism* 77 (December 1997); Olivier Besancenot and Michael Löwy, *Che Guevara: His Revolutionary Legacy* (New York: Monthly Review Press, 2009); Maria Carolina-Cambre, "Virtual Resurrections: Che Guevara's Image as Place of Hope," in Tonya Davidson, Ondine Park, and Rob Shields, eds, *Ecologies of Affect: Placing Nostalgia, Desire, and Hope* (Waterloo, ON: Wilfrid Laurier University Press, 2011) pp. 217–43. Jeff A. Larson and Omar Lizardo, "Generations, Identities, and the Collective Memory of Che Guevara," *Sociological Forum* 22, 4 (2007): 425–51.

7. Cambre, *Semiotics of Che Guevara*; Parvathi Raman, "Signifying Something: Che Guevara and Neoliberal Alienation in London," in Harry G. West and Parvathi Raman, eds, *Enduring Socialism: Explorations of Revolution and Transformation, Restoration and Continuation* (New York: Berghahn, 2009) pp. 250–70. Larson and Lizardo, "Generations".

8. Anthony Giddens, *Runaway World* (New York: New Press, 1999); Arjun Appadurai, *Modernity at Large: Cultural Dimensions of Globalization* (Minneapolis, MN: University of Minnesota Press, 1999).

9. Manuel Castells, *Networks of Outrage and Hope: Social Movements in the Internet Age* (London: Polity, 2012); Jai Sen and Peter Waterman, eds, *World Social Forum: Challenging Empires* (New Delhi: Viveka Foundation, 2004).

10. Michael Hardt and Antonio Negri, *Multitude: War and Democracy in the Age of Empire* (New York: Penguin Press, 2004); Geoffrey Pleyers and Alain Touraine, *Alterglobalization: Becoming actors in the global age* (Malden, MA: Polity, 2010); Heather Gautney, *Protest and Organization in the Alternative Globalization Era* (New York: Palgrave 2010); Joss Hands, *@ is for Activism: Dissent, Resistance, and Rebellion in a Digital Culture* (New York: Pluto Press, 2011).

11. Sidney Tarrow, *The New Transnational Activism* (Cambridge: Cambridge University Press, 2005).

12. Vijay Prashad, *The Poorer Nations: A Possible History of the Global South* (New York: Verso, 2013), p. 9; Donatella della Porta and Sidney Tarrow, eds, *Transnational*

275

Protest and Global Activism (Lanham, MD: Rowman and Littlefield, 2004); Giovanni Arrighi, Terence Hopkins, and Immanuel Wallerstein, *Antisystemic Movements* (London: Verso, 1989).

13. Frank Lechner and John Boli, *World Culture: Origins and Consequences* (Malden, MA: Blackwell Publishers, 2005), p. 153; *Canberra Times*, "Che's Face Still Stirs Rage on Injustice," 4 January 2005; Larson and Lizardo, "Generations."

14. Heroic Guerrilla became a template for those who wished to equate or ironically juxtapose themselves with Che as a symbol of rebellion. For example, the cover of Madonna's album *American Life* (2003) featured the vocalist wearing a beret and striking a pose similar to that of Che in the Heroic Guerrilla image. Figures from Margaret Thatcher and Mahatma Gandhi to Jesus and James Dean have been equated with Che's revolutionary character through the adaptation of the Heroic Guerrilla template.

15. Casey, *Che's Afterlife*, p. 262; Brian Wallis, "Che Lives!," in Ziff, ed, *Che Guevara*, pp. 30–1.

16. Hannah Charlton, "Introduction," in *Che Guevara: Revolutionary and Icon*, p. 12; Brook Larmer, "Che Chic," *Newsweek* 21 July 1997, pp. 38–9; Gonzalez, "The Resurrections of Che Guevara."

17. Jonathan Friedman, *Consumption and Identity* (Chur, Switzerland: Harwood, 1994).

18. J.P. Linstroth, "The Basque Conflict Global Speaking: Material Culture, Media and Basque Identity in the Wider World," *Oxford Development Studies* 30, 2 (2002): 205–22; Leerom Medovoi, *Rebels: Youth and the Cold War Origins of Identity* (Durham, NC: Duke University Press, 2005).

19. Thomas Frank, et. al., *Commodify your Dissent* (New York: W.W. Norton, 1997); Thomas Frank, *The Conquest of Cool: Business Culture, Counterculture, and the Rise of Hip Consumerism* (Chicago, IL: University of Chicago Press, 1997); Joseph Heath and Andrew Potter, *Nation of Rebels* (New York: Harper, 2004); Adrian Carrasquillo, "Urban Outfitters removes Che Guevara merchandise after outrage," *NBCLatino. com*, 29 October 2012, http://nbclatino.com/2012/10/29/ urban-out tters-removes-che-guevara (accessed 23 May 2014).

20. Erik Gandini and Tarik Saleh, dir. *Sacrificio (Who Betrayed Che Guevara?)*, 2001. The star on Guevara's beret gained popular relevance as a reference to socialism immediately following his death, but this was not its initial meaning. Rather, it symbolized his rank as commander during and immediately after the Cuban Revolution.

21. Susan Eva Eckstein, *Back from the Future* (Princeton, NJ: Princeton University Press, 1995); Gonzalez, "The Resurrections of Che Guevara." Guevara's economic initiatives also continued to have relevance for Cuba. Helen Yaffe, "Che Guevara's Enduring Legacy: Not the *Foco* But the Theory of Socialist Construction," *Latin American Perspectives* 36, 2 (2009): 49–65.

22. J.P. Spicer-Escalante, "From Korda's Guerrillero Heroico to Global Brand: Ernesto 'Che' Guevara," in Dianna C. Niebylski and Patrick O'Connor, eds, *Latin American Icons: Fame Across Borders* (Nashville, TN: Vanderbilt University Press, 2014), pp. 50–2; Gonzalez, "The Resurrections of Che Guevara"; Hanno Hardt, Luis Rivera-Perez, and Jorge A. Calles-Santillana, "The death and resurrection of

Ernesto Che Guevara: US media and the deconstruction of a revolutionary life," *International Journal of Cultural Studies* 1, 3 (1998): 351–72.

23. Servando Serrano Torrico, ed. *El Che después de 28 años: documental* (Cochabomba, Bolivia: Editorial Serrano, 1999); Larry Rohter, "Cuba Buries Che, the Man, but Keeps the Myth Alive," *The New York Times* 17 October 1997.

24. Radio Havana Cuba, "Fidel Castro's Speech at Funeral Ceremony Honoring Che & Companions," 17 October 1997.

25. Ariana Hernández-Reguant, "Copyrighting Che: Art and Authorship Under Cuban Late Socialism," *Public Culture* 16, 1 (2004): pp. 1–29; Cambre, *Semiotics of Che*, pp. 17–18.

26. Gloria Muñoz Ramírez, *The fire and the word: a history of the Zapatista movement* (San Francisco, CA: City Lights Books, 2008).

27. One of the groups inspired by the Zapatistas was People's Global Action, which would become a central force in the organization of the WTO protests in Seattle. David Graeber, *Direct Action: An Ethnography* (Oakland, CA: AK Press, 2009), p. 227. Clifford Bob, *The Marketing of Rebellion: Insurgents, Media, and International Activism* (Cambridge: Cambridge University Press, 2005); Henry James Morello, "e-(re)volution: Zapatistas and the Emancipatory Internet," *A Contracorriente* 4, 2 (2007): pp. 54–76; Naomi Klein, "The Unknown Icon," *The Guardian* 3 March 2001; Alex Khasnabish, *Zapatistas: Rebellion from the Grassroots to the Global* (New York: Zed Books, 2010); Nicholas Henck, *Broadening the Struggle and Winning the Media War: 'Marcos Mystique', 'Guerrilla Chic', and Zapatista P.R.* (Montreal: Kersplebedeb, 2002).

28. Pacificar.com, "El Che sigue vivo, está con nosotros y con muchos más," 13 April 2003 (accessed 27 March 2009).

29. Nick Henck, *Subcommander Marcos: The Man and the Mask* (Durham, NC: Duke University Press, 2007), p. 361; J.P. Linstroth outlines this phenomenon of international symbols as important modes of representing nationalist identity in "The Basque Conflict". See also Jacqueline Urla, "'We Are All Malcolm X!': Negu Gorriak, Hip-Hop, and the Basque Political Imaginary," in Tony Mitchell, ed, *Global Noise: Rap and Hip-Hop Outside the USA* (Middletown, CT: Wesleyan University Press, 2001), pp. 171–93.

30. M. Clint McCowan, "Imagining the Zapatistas: Rebellion, Representation and Popular Culture," *International Third World Studies Journal and Review* 14 (2003): 29–34; Andres Oppenheimer, *Bordering on Chaos: Mexico's Roller-Coaster Journey Toward Prosperity* (Boston, MA: Little, Brown and Co., 1996).

31. My thanks to Erica Baffelli for her personal reflections on these demonstrations. Gonzalez, "The Resurrections of Che Guevara." Similarly, in 1990 a militant group calling itself the "Che Brigade" operated in Argentina. In 1994 Argentine president Carlos Menem publicly criticized young people who celebrated Che Guevara. "Menem Warns Against Rebirth of Old Conflicts," 2 May 1994, FBIS-DR; FBIS LAT-94-084.

32. Doreen Carvajal, "30 Years After His Death, Che Guevara Has New Charisma," *The New York Times* 30 April 1997.

33. Hernández-Reguant, "Copyrighting Che".

34. Cambre, *Semiotics of Che*, pp. 18–19.
35. Quoted in Kunzle, *Che Guevara*, p. 106. As a means to emphasize their product's relationship to a rebellious concept, the makers of Mexico's El Che cola similarly printed the word *revolución* above Che's image on the bottle's label.
36. Tina Rosenberg, "The World Resurrects Che," *The New York Times* 20 July 1997; Casey, *Che's Afterlife*, p. 306.
37. Juan Carlos Rocha, "30 Years Later, Che Draws Admirers from Around the World," Inter Press Service 7 October 1997, http://www.ipsnews.net/1997/10/bolivia-30-years-later-che-draws-admirers-from-around-the-world/ (accessed 10 October 2016); Brook Larmer, "Che Chic," *Newsweek* 21 July 1997, pp. 38–9. Three major biographies were published around the thirtieth anniversary of Che's death: Paco Ignacio Taibo II, *Ernesto Guevara: también conocido como el Che* (Planeta: Benito Juárez, 1996, trans. 1997); Jon Lee Anderson, *Che Guevara: A Revolutionary Life* (New York: Grove Press, 1997); Jorge G. Castañeda, *Compañero: vida y muerte del Che Guevara* (New York: Vintage, 1997, trans. 1998).
38. Jeff A. Larson and Omar Lizardo's research shows two additional, if lesser, peaks in US publications related to Che: the first in mid-2000 and the second in late 2002. Newspaper articles about Che followed a similar trajectory during the mid-1990s but began a general upward trajectory from 1998. Evidence from Spain likewise reveals an up-tick around 1997 but records a significant increase in newspaper articles about Che from 2002, a surge that in 2004 outpaced even the 1997 coverage. Larson and Lizardo, "Generations," p. 430. The volume of artistic production related to Che, including poetry and film, has taken a similar direction. According to Gavin O'Toole and Georgina Jimenez, Che reemerged as a poetic muse in the mid-1990s. Gavin O'Toole and Georgina Jiménez, eds, *Che in Verse* (Wiltshire: Aflame Books, 2007). More comprehensive data based on Internet searches related to Che augments this picture. Though such statistics only go back to 2004, since that year the volume of Google searches about Guevara has seen two significant peaks, the first in 2004 and the second in 2007, both around the anniversary of his death. Google Trends, Web Search Interest: Che Guevara. Worldwide, 2004—present [2013] http://www.google.com/trends/explore#q=%22che+guevara%22&cmpt=q (accessed 5 September 2013).
39. See, for instance, Jean Cormier, *Che Guevara* (Monaco: Editions du Rocher, 1995); Juan Ignacio Siles de Valle, *La guerrilla del Che ya la narrative boliviana* (La Paz: Plural Editores, 1996); Pierre Kalfon, *Che: Ernesto Guevara, une légende du siècle* (Paris: Seuil, 1997); David Sandison, *Che Guevara* (New York: St. Martin's Griffin, 1998); Henry Butterfield Ryan, *The Fall of Che Guevara: A Story of Soldiers, Spies and Diplomats* (New York: Oxford University Press, 1997). For alternative interpretations that emphasized Che's convictions and worldview, see Richard Harris, "Reflections on Che Guevara's Legacy," *Latin American Perspectives* 25, 4 (1998): 19–32; Tony Saunois, *Che Guevara: Symbol of Struggle* (London: CWI Publications, 1997); Peter McLaren, *Che Guevara, Paulo Freire, and the Pedagogy of Revolution* (Lanham, MD: Rowman & Littlefield, 1999).
40. Larmer, "Che Chic," pp. 38–9. In part as a result of this surge of interest in Che,

*Time Magazine* named him among the 100 most influential people of the twentieth century.

41. William Gálvez, *Che in Africa: Che Guevara's Congo Diary* (New York: Ocean Press, 1999). A more authoritative version of Che's diaries was published in 2000 as *The African Dream: The Diaries of the Revolutionary War in the Congo* (New York: Grove Press, 2000). Ernesto Che Guevara, *Latin American Diaries: The Sequel to Motorcycle Diaries* (Melbourne: Ocean Press, 2011); Ernesto Che Guevara, *Diary of a Combatant: The Diary of the Revolution that Made Che Guevara a Legend* (Melbourne: Ocean Press, 2013); Shasta Darlington, "50-plus years later, Cuba publishes Che diary," *CNN.com* 14 June 2011 http://www.cnn.com/2011/WORLD/americas/06/14/cuba.che.guevara/ (accessed 5 July 2016).

42. John Blackthorn, *I, Che Guevara: A Novel* (New York: William Morrow & Co., 1999).

43. NPR, "Thirty Years after his Death, Che Guevara still an Icon," *Weekend Edition Sunday* 3 October 2004, http://www.npr.org/templates/story/story.php?storyId=4058889 (accessed 10 October 2016).

44. Marjorie Miller, "Church Ads Send Revolutionary Message," *Los Angeles Times* 7 January 1999.

45. David Kunzle, *Chesucristo: The Fusion in Image and Word of Che Guevara and Jesus Christ* (Berlin: De Gruyter, 2016); Dosal, "San Ernesto de la Higuera." See also similar popular associations with Patrice Lumumba, in Bogumil Jewsiewicki, "Corps interdits. La représentation christique de Lumumba comme rédempteur du peuple zaïrois," *Cahiers d'Études Africaines* 36, 141/142 (1996): 113–42.

46. Church Ads, "Meek. Mild. As if, Easter 1999," http://www.churchads.org.uk/past/1999/index.html (accessed 10 October 2016); BBC News, "Jesus ad campaign 'not blasphemous,'" 7 January 1999. http://news.bbc.co.uk/2/hi/uk_news/250752.stm (accessed 14 May 2010). The Salvation Army later reproduced the Easter image in its official magazine, *The War Cry*.

47. David Kunzle, "Chesucristo: Fusion, Myths, and Realities," *Latin American Perspectives* 35, 2 (2008): 112–13.

48. Gary Cross, *Consumed Nostalgia: Memory in the Age of Fast Capitalism* (New Haven, CT: Yale University Press, 2015). On retro style, see Frederic Jameson, "Postmodernism and consumer society," in Hal Foster, ed, *The Anti-Aesthetic: essays on postmodern culture* (Port Townsend, WA: Bay Press, 1983), pp. 111–25.

49. Tina Rosenberg, "The World Resurrects Che," *The New York Times* 20 July 1997; Shannon Smiley, "Germany Debates 'Terrorist Chic,'" *The Washington Post* 20 February 2005.

50. Slavoj Žižek, *Welcome to the Desert of the Real!: Five Essays on September 11 and Related Dates* (New York: Verso, 2002), pp. 23–4; Jonathan Bach, "'The Taste Remains': Consumption, (N)ostalgia, and the Production of East Germany," *Public Culture* 14, 3 (2002): 545–56; Dominic Boyer, "*Ostalgie* and the Politics of the Future in Eastern Germany," *Public Culture* 18, 2 (2006): 361–81.

51. Dominik Bartmański, "Successful icons of failed time: Rethinking post-communist nostalgia," *Acta Sociologica* 53, 4 (2011): 213–31.

52. Karen Thomas, "Guevara re-emerges to lead a cultural revolution," *USA Today* 15 April 2004.

53. Mark Scheerer, "Marxist Revolutionary Seizes Market Place from Beyond the Grave," *CNN.com* 14 July 1997.

54. Cambre, *Semiotics of Che*, ch. 2.

55. *C-Span2*, "Exposing the Real Che Guevara," 1 August 2007.

56. Humberto Fontova, *Exposing the Real Che Guevara and the Useful Idiots Who Idolize Him* (New York: Penguin, 2008); Alvaro Vargas Llosa, "The Killing Machine: Che Guevara, from Communist Firebrand to Capitalist Brand," *The Independent Institute* 11 July 2005, http://www.independent.org/newsroom/article.asp?id=1535 (accessed 10 October 2016).

57. Free Star Media, "Miami and Los Angeles Residents Protest Burlington Coat Factory for Promoting Che Guevara," http://www.freestarmedia.com/burlingtonchefactory.html (accessed 28 March 2009); *National Review*, "Cuban Americans are angry at the Burlington Coat Factory for marketing a line of Che Guevara T-shirts, just in time for Christmas," 27 December 2004.

58. UPI.com, "Che Guevara backlash grows," 13 December 2004, http://www.upi.com/Top_News/2004/12/13/Che_Guevara_backlash_grows/UPI-3272110 2955493/ (accessed 12 October 2016).

59. Michele Gershberg, "Target Pulls Che Guevara CD Case," *Reuters* 26 December 2006, http://www.reuters.com/article/us-target-guevara-idUSNCM3830252006 1226 (accessed 28 October 2016). Macy's likewise removed Che products in its Miami-area stores in response to a letter-writing campaign. Chuck Strouse, "Che Guevara Who?," *Miami New Times* 3 April 2008, http://www.miaminewtimes.com/2008–04–03/news/che-guevara-who/2. In 2012, Urban Outfitters also succumbed to public pressure to discontinue the sale of a Cuban flag featuring the Heroic Guerrilla image. Carrasquillo, "Urban Outfitters removes Che Guevara merchandise after outrage."

60. Similarly, Mahatma Gandhi featured in a late 1990s Apple Computer, Inc. ad campaign.

61. Beth Stebner, "Viva la gaffe," *Daily Mail* 13 January 2012; Cristina Corbin, "Mercedes' apology for use of Che Guevara photo to promote luxury cars does little to quiet outcry," *Fox News.com* 13 January 2012, http://www.foxnews.comhttp://www.foxnews.com/us/2012/01/13/mercedes-benz-apologizes-for-use-che-guevara-photo-to-promote-its-vehicles (accessed 2 September 2012).

62. If there had been any doubt about the intent of the film to cater to the public's appetite for Che, the film's trailer explained that *Che* was the "true story of the man behind the icon."

63. Rebecca Carte, "Trickster, Traveler, Cultural Hero: Ernesto 'Che' Guevara," *Studies in Latin American Popular Culture* 27 (2008): 167–83.

64. For instance, the play *Che Guevara*, which debuted in Beijing in April 2000, used Che's life as a metaphor for the struggle for social justice in contemporary China. Liu Yuan, "Enter, Stage Left," *Asia Week.com* 21, 1 (12 January 2001). http://www.asiaweek.com/asiaweek/magazine/2001/0112/as.theatre.html (accessed 8 September 2004). See also Aleida Guevara, "On the motorcycle behind my father, Che Guevara," *The New York Times* 12 October 2004.

65. Stuart Jeffries, "Rebel without a pause," *The Guardian* 16 December 2008.

66. Rohit Raj, "DYFI Stir to Stamp Out Che Guevara Slippers," *The Asian Age* 29 November 2012, http://www.pressreader.com/india/the-asian-age/20121129/ textview (accessed 18 October 2016).

67. A. Sabburaj, "Guevara image on footwear sparks protests in Coimbatore," *Times of India* 26 September 2014, http://timesofindia.indiatimes.com/City/Coimbatore/ Guevara-image-on-footwear-sparks-protests-in-Coimbatore/articleshow/43464486. cms (accessed 18 February 2015). Concern with inappropriate uses of Che's image in India has not been limited to communists. In 2011 Bahujan Samaj Party (BSP) members in Coimbatore also demonstrated against the sale of Guevara flip-flops. In that instance, both the manager of the shop and an employee were arrested on charges of dishonoring Guevara. *New Indian Express*, "Che Guevara Slippers Lands Fashion Shop in Row," 24 August 2011, http://www.newindianexpress.com/ states/tamil_nadu/article306632.ece (accessed 16 July 2016). The following year, flip-flops sold in Vijayawada, Andhra Pradesh also drew condemnation from the Organisation for Protection of Democratic Rights. *The Hindu*, "Printing of Che Pictures on Slippers Decried," 21 April 2012, http://www.thehindu.com/news/ cities/Vijayawada/printing-of-che-pictures-on-slippers-decried/article3338980.ece (accessed 16 July 2016).

68. Raman, "Signifying Something," pp. 264–7, 268–9.

69. Ibid., p. 268.

70. Hal Brands, *Latin America's Cold War* (Cambridge, MA: Harvard University Press, 2010).

71. Eduardo Elena, "Point of Departure: Travel and Nationalism in Ernesto Guevara's Argentina," in Paulo Drinot, ed, *Che's Travels: The Making of a Revolutionary in 1950s Latin America* (Durham, NC: Duke University Press, 2010), p. 47. On the tension between politics and consumerism in Colombia, see Carolina Cambre, "Revolution Within the Revolution: A Caracas Collective and the Face of Che Guevara", *Review of Education, Pedagogy, and Cultural Studies* 31, 4 (2009): 338–64; Bernie Becker, "Six Questions for Greg Crandin on Che's Legacy," *Harper's* 30 September 2007.

72. See also Casey, *Che's Afterlife*, p. 211.

73. Equivalence of Jesus and Che in Nicaragua dates to at least the early 1980s. Giulio Girardi, *Faith and Revolution in Nicaragua: Convergence and Contradictions* (Maryknoll, NY: Orbis Books, 1989); David Kunzle, *The Murals of Revolutionary Nicaragua, 1979–1992* (Berkeley, CA: University of California Press, 1995); Kunzle, *Chesucristo*. On the colloquial canonization of Che in central Bolivia, see Andres Schipani, "The Final Triumph of Saint Che," *Observer* 22 September 2007.

74. BBC News, "Cuba pays tribute to Che Guevara," 9 October 2007, http://news. bbc.co.uk/2/hi/americas/7033880.stm (accessed 28 August 2013). Judith Ewell, "Che Guevara and Venezuela: Tourist, Guerrilla Mentor, and Revolutionary Spirit," in Drinot, ed, *Che's Travels*, pp. 148–80. For a detailed study of the multiple meanings of Che in Chavez's Venezuela see Carolina Cambre, "Revolution Within the Revolution: A Caracas Collective and the Face of Che Guevara," *Review of Education, Pedagogy, and Cultural Studies* 31, 4 (2009): 338–64. Through close examination of the uses of Che's image by the Colectivo Alexis Gonzáles Vive Carajo in Caracas,

Cambre concluded that Che acts as a central figure in efforts to tell communal stories, bolster relationships within the community, and inspire alternative agendas; see pp. 351, 353.

75. On Dési Bouterse, see Ranu Abhelakh, "Suriname lawmakers elect ex-dictator as president," *Agence France Presse* 19 July 2010.

76. Álex Ayala Ugarte, "Che Sat Here," *The Virginia Quarterly Review* 85, 1 (2009): 71–81.

77. David Rieff, "Che's Second Coming?," *The New York Times Magazine* 20 November 2005. Morales' inauguration speech of 2006 also referenced Che as an ancestor "who fought for a new world in equality." Quoted in Besancenot and Löwy, *Che Guevara*, p. 82.

78. "Evo Morales Praises Example of Ernesto Che Guevara," *Agencia Cubana de Noticias* 9 October 2007, available at http://energy-net.org/NUZ/SAM/07O098.TXT.' (accessed 28 October 2016).

79. Reuters, "Che Guevara: For Some Palestinians an Intifada Hero," *GulfNews.com* 2 July 2001, http://gulfnews.com/news/uae/general/che-guevara-for-some-palestinians-an-intifada-hero-1.420195 (accessed 28 October 2016).

80. Guevara-related web searches reveal a surging interest in Che during 2011–12. Data compiled by Google Trends suggests that web interest in Guevara increased significantly in several North African nations from late 2011 until early 2013. Google Trends, "Web Search Interest: Che Guevara. Worldwide, 2004—present", http://www.google.com/trends/explore#q=%22che+guevara%22&cmpt=q (accessed 5 September 2013).

81. RT, "From Tripoli to Damascus," 26 December 2011, http://rt.com/news/syria-libya-gunmen-mercenaries-643/ (accessed 18 October 2016).

82. Similarly, a Canadian website used a quiz game called "What's Your Che Factor?" to determine how closely visitors' responses to various scenarios "match up with Che Guevara's." See http://cheguevara.ca/whats-your-che-factor/ (accessed 10 July 2016).

83. Interview with Mac Maharaj, *SABC News* 8 December 2013; "Mandela Addresses Event," 30 July 1991; FBIS-DR; FBIS-LAT-91-146

84. Thomas Sankara, *We Are the Heirs of the World's Revolutions: Speeches from the Burkina Faso Revolution, 1984–1987* (New York: Pathfinder, 2007), p. 101; "Burkina's Compoare Speaks," 18 October 1987; FBIS-DR; FBIS-AFR-87-196; Cambre, *Semiotics of Che*, p. 53.

85. *The Monitor* (Uganda), "Che Guevara Lives On As a Fashion Icon," 1 December 2006.

86. In the words of a clothes dealer in downtown Nairobi, some young people gravitated to Che because of a desire to be associated with "revolutionary symbols of rebellion." Kamau Mutunga, "Symbols of Radical Change," *The Nation* (Kenya) 14 October 2005. In the late 2000s, a unit of insurgents in the eastern Democratic Republic of the Congo called the "Group of Che" used Guevara T-shirts as fatigues. Stephanie McCrummen, "For Tutsis of Eastern Congo, Protector, Exploiter or Both?," Washington Post Foreign Service 6 August 2007; David McDougall,

"Encounter with a Rebel," *CBC News* 17 November 2008, http://www.cbc.ca/world/story/2008/11/17/f-mcdougall-nkunda.html (accessed 5 April 2010).

87. In 2013 Identity marketed a similar Che T-shirt with the word "attitude" replacing "revolution". Many of South Africa's other major retailers, including Truworths and Edgars, likewise stocked Che T-shirts.

88. François Verster, dir., *Sea Point Days*, 2009.

89. Derrick Dlamini and Swazi Dlamini, "Che's Streets Ahead," *ezaseGagasini Metro* (South Africa) 23 October 2009, http://www.durban.gov.za/Documents/City_Government/Media_Publications/Ezasegagasini_Metro_Gazette/2009/23%20October%202009%20Ezasegagasini%20Page%201.pdf (accessed 28 October 2016); Sinegugu Ndlovu, "Remember Guevara's Virtues—daughter," *Independent Online* (South Africa) 21 October 2009, http://www.iol.co.za/news/south-africa/remember-guevaras-virtues—daughter-462271 (accessed 28 October 2016).

90. Carlo Feltrinelli, *Feltrinelli: A Story of Riches, Revolution, and Violent Death* (San Diego, CA: Harcourt Trade, 2002).

91. Quoted in Kunzle, ed, *Che Guevara*, p. 19.

92. See, for instance, Lahav Harkov, "Viva la revolucion? Zionist Union uses Che in campaign materials," *Jerusalem Post* 9 March 2015, http://www.jpost.com/Israel-Elections/Viva-la-revolucion-Zionist-Union-uses-Che-in-campaign-materials-393366 (accessed 1 August 2016).

CONCLUSION

1. As Werner Binder summed up, icons act as "common points of reference for a global civil discourse." Werner Binder, "The Emergence of Iconic Depth: Secular Icons in a Comparative Perspective," in Jeffrey C. Alexander, Dominik Bartmański, and Bernhard Giesen, eds, *Iconic Power: Materiality and Meaning in Social Life* (New York: Palgrave Macmillan, 2012), p. 113.

2. Oliver Kohns, "Guy Fawkes in the 21st Century: A Contribution to the Political Iconography of Revolt," *Image and Narrative* 14, 1 (2013): 89–104; Tamara Lush and Verena Dobnik, "Occupy Wall Street: Vendetta Masks Become Symbol of the Movement," *Huffington Post* 4 November 2011, http://www.huffingtonpost.com/2011/11/04/occupy-wall-street-vendetta-mask_n_1076038.html (accessed 4 November 2016).

3. Branko Milanović, *Global Inequality: A New Approach for the Age of Globalization* (Cambridge, MA: Harvard University Press, 2016).

4. Michele Micheletti, Andreas Follesdal, and Dietlind Stolle, "Introduction," in Michele Micheletti, Andreas Follesdal, and Dietlind Stolle, eds, *Politics, Products, and Markets: Exploring Political Consumerism Past and Present* (New Brunswick, NJ: Transaction Publishers, 2003), pp. ix-xxvi.

5. William Booth, "Obama's On-the-Wall Endorsement," *The Washington Post* 18 May 2008; Lisa Cartwright and Stephen Mandiberg, "Obama and Shepard Fairey: The Copy and Political Iconography in the Age of the Demake," *Journal of Visual Culture* 8, 2 (2009): 172–6.

6. Jeffrey C. Alexander, "Heroes, Presidents, and Politics," *Contexts* 9, 4 (2010): 16–21;

idem, *The Performance of Politics: Obama's Victory and the Democratic Struggle for Power* (New York: Oxford University Press, 2010). On the related realm of "guerrilla marketing", see Michael Serazio, *Your Ad Here: The Cool Sell of Guerrilla Marketing* (New York: New York University Press, 2013).

7. Jeffrey C. Alexander and Bernadette N. Jaworsky, *Obama Power* (Cambridge: Polity Press, 2014).

8. Rob Nixon, "Mandela, Messianism, and the Media," *Transition* 51 (1991): 42–55; Xolela Mangcu, "Retracing Nelson Mandela through the Lineage of Black Political Thought," *Transition* 112 (2013): 101–16; Steven Nelson, "Nelson Mandela's Two Bodies," *Transition* 116 (2014): 130–421.

# SELECTED SOURCES

*Archives*

South Africa

National Archives of South Africa, Cape Town Archives Repository, Cape Town, Film and Publication Board (1975–1996), IDP 3/398

Switzerland

Baseler Afrika Bibliographien, Basel, Ruth Weiss Sound Archives

United Kingdom

National Archives of the United Kingdom and Ireland, Kew, Foreign and Commonwealth Office, FCO 7 American and Latin American Departments; FCO 95 Information Research Department; Records of the Prime Minister's Office, PREM 16 Correspondence and Papers, 1974–1979; PREM 19 Correspondence and Papers, 1979–1997

United States

Foreign Broadcast Information Service Daily Reports, 1967–1996; available at http://infoweb.newsbank.com

National Archives at College Park, College Park, Maryland, Records of the Department of State, Central Foreign Policy Files, 1973-79/D-Reel Microfilm, RG 59; available from the Access to Archival Databases at www.archives.gov

*Published Sources*

Newspapers and Wire Services

*Age* (Australia)
*Agence France-Presse*
*Agencia Cubana de Noticias*
*Asian Age* (India)
*Associated Press*

# SELECTED SOURCES

Atlanta Journal-Constitution
Berkeley Barb (US)
Boston Globe
British Broadcasting Corporation News
Business Day (South Africa)
Canadian Broadcasting Corporation News
Canberra Times
Chicago Tribune
Christian Science Monitor
Coast Express (Kenya)
Concord Times (Sierra Leone)
Corriere Della Sera (Italy)
Daily Nation (Kenya)
Daily News (US)
Daily Variety (US)
Dawn (Pakistan)
Dominion (New Zealand)
East African (Kenya)
East African Standard (Kenya)
Episcopal News Service
Globe and Mail (Canada)
Guardian (UK)
Hindu (India)
Independent (UK)
Independent online (South Africa)
Inter Press Service
Jamaica Daily News
Jamaica Gleaner
Jerusalem Post
Los Angeles Times
Marketwire
Miami New Times
Monitor (Uganda)
Moscow Times
Namibian
National Review (US)
Nepali Times
New Indian Express
New Straits Times (Malaysia)
New York Times
New York Times Magazine
New Zealand Herald
News (Nigeria)
Observer (UK)
Pan-African NewsWire

# SELECTED SOURCES

*Philadelphia Inquirer*
*Phoenix New Times*
*Record* (New Jersey)
*San Francisco Chronicle*
*South African Press Association*
*Sunday Times* (South Africa)
*Sydney Morning Herald*
*Tages-Anzeiger* (Switzerland)
*Times* (UK)
*Times of India*
*Toronto Star*
*UCLA Today*
*United Press International*
*USA Today*
*Washington Post*
*Xinhua General Overseas News Service* (China)

Periodicals

*Beat* (also *Reggae and African Beat*)
*Billboard*
*Black Music and Jazz Review*
*Crawdaddy*
*Fifth Estate*
*Gig*
*Harper's*
*High Times*
*LA Weekly*
*Maclean's*
*Melody Maker*
*Mother Jones*
*Movement*
*Music Pulse*
*New Left Notes*
*Newsweek*
*New York Times Review of Books*
*New Yorker*
*Ramparts*
*Rolling Stone*
*Solidarity Pamphlet*
*Source*
*Spin*
*Staunch*
*Time*
*Vanity Fair*
*Water Tunnel*

# SELECTED SOURCES

*Westindian Digest*

*Books, Papers, and Journal Articles*

Abdullah, Ibrahim, ed., *Between Democracy and Terror: The Sierra Leone Civil War* (Dakar: Council for the Development of Social Science Research in Africa, 2004).

Abernethy, Graeme, *The Iconography of Malcolm X* (Lawrence, KS: University Press of Kansas, 2013).

Alexander, Jeffrey C., "Iconic Experience in Art and Life: Surface/Depth Beginning with Giacometti's *Standing Women*," *Theory, Culture & Society* 25, 5 (2008): 1–19.

———— "Iconic Consciousness: The Material Feeling of Meaning," *Thesis Eleven* 103, 1 (2010): 10–25.

———— "The Celebrity-Icon," *Journal of Sociology* 4, 3 (2010): 323–36.

———— *The Performance of Politics: Obama's Victory and the Democratic Struggle for Power* (New York: Oxford University Press, 2010).

Alexander, Jeffrey C., Dominik Bartmański and Bernhard Giesen, *Iconic Power: Materiality and Meaning in Social Life* (New York: Palgrave Macmillan, 2012).

Alvares, Luis, "Reggae Rhythms in Dignity's Diaspora: Globalization, Indigenous Identity, and the Circulation of Cultural Struggle," *Popular Music and Society* 31, 5 (2008): 575–97.

Anderson, Benedict, *Under Three Flags: Anarchism and the Anti-Colonial Imagination* (New York: Verso, 2007).

———— *Imagined Communities: Reflections on the Origin and Spread of Nationalism* (New York: Verso, 1991).

Anderson, Jon Lee, *Che Guevara: A Revolutionary Life* (New York: Grove Press, 1997).

André, María Claudia, ed., *Latina Icons: Iconos Femininos Latinos e Hispanoamericanos* (Mountain View, CA: Floricanto, 2006).

Appadurai, Arjun, *Modernity at Large: Cultural Dimensions of Globalization* (Minneapolis, MN: University of Minnesota Press, 1996).

———— ed., *The Social Lives of Things: Commodities in Cultural Perspective* (Cambridge: Cambridge University Press, 1986).

Arrighi, Giovanni, Terence K. Hopkins, and Immanuel Wallerstein, *Antisystemic Movements* (New York: Verso, 1989).

Aslan, Resa. *Zealot: The Life and Times of Jesus of Nazareth* (New York: Random House, 2013).

Ayers, William, *Fugitive Days: A Memoir* (Boston, MA: Beacon, 2001).

Badiou, Alain, *The Rebirth of History* (London: Verso, 2012).

Baird, Jay W., *To Die for Germany: Heroes in the Nazi Pantheon* (Bloomington, IN: Indiana University Press, 1990).

Barthes, Roland, *Mythologies* (London: Paladin, 1972).

———— "Rhetoric of the Image," in Stephen Heath, ed., *Image, Music, Text* (New York: Hill and Wang, 1977), pp. 32–51.

Basu, Dipannita and Sidney J. Lemelle, eds. *The Vinyl Ain't Final: Hip Hop and the Globalization of Black Popular Culture* (London: Pluto Press, 2006).

Baudrillard, Jean, *Simulacra and Simulation* (Ann Arbor, MI: University of Michigan Press, 1994).

# SELECTED SOURCES

Bayly, Christopher, *The Birth of the Modern World, 1780–1914: Global Connections and Comparisons* (Malden, MA: Blackwell, 2004).

Beah, Ishmael, *A Long Way Gone: Memoirs of a Boy Soldier* (New York: Farrar, Straus, and Giroux, 2007).

Beckert, Sven, *Empire of Cotton: A Global History* (New York: Vintage, 2015).

Benjamin, Walter and Hannah Arendt, eds. *Illuminations* (New York: Schocken Books, 2007).

Berger, Mark T., "After the Third World? History, destiny and the fate of Third Worldism," *Third World Quarterly* 25, 1 (2004): 9–39.

Berman, Bruce and John Lonsdale, *Unhappy Valley: Conflict in Kenya and Africa* (Athens, OH: Ohio University Press, 1992).

Bernier, Celeste-Marie, *Characters of Blood: Black Heroism in the Transatlantic Imagination* (Charlottesville, VA: University of Virginia Press, 2012).

Besancenot, Olivier and Michael Löwy, *Che Guevara: His Revolutionary Legacy* (New York: Monthly Review Press, 2009).

Bonnell, Victoria E., *Iconography of Power: Soviet Political Posters under Lenin and Stalin* (Berkeley, CA: University of California Press, 1999).

Boorstin, Daniel J., *The Image: A Guide to Pseudo-Events in America* (New York: Vintage, 1992).

Bordowitz, Hank, ed., *Every Little Thing Gonna Be Alright: The Bob Marley Reader* (Cambridge, MA: De Capo Press, 2004).

Branch, Adam and Zachariah Mamphilly, *Africa Uprising: Popular Protest and Political Change* (London: Zed Books, 2015).

Brands, Hal, *Latin America's Cold War* (Cambridge, MA: Harvard University Press, 2010).

Breines, Wini, *Community and Organization in the New Left, 1962–1968: The Great Refusal* (New York: Praeger, 1982).

Briggs, Asa and Peter Burke, *A Social History of the Media* (Malden, MA: Polity Press, 2009).

Brown, Timothy S., *West Germany and the Global Sixties: The Anti-Authoritarian Revolt, 1962–1978* (Cambridge: Cambridge University Press, 2013).

Brunk, Samuel and Ben Fallaw, eds. *Heroes and Hero Cults in Latin America* (Austin, TX: University of Texas Press, 2006).

Buck-Morss, Susan, "Visual Empire," *Diacritics* 37, 2/3 (2007): 171–98.

Butler, Judith, *Gender Trouble: Feminism and the Subversion of Identity* (New York: Routledge, 1990).

Cambre, Maria-Carolina, "Revolution within the Revolution: A Caracas Collective and the Face of Che Guevara," *Review of Education, Pedagogy and Cultural Studies* 31, 4 (2009): 338–64.

———— *The Semiotics of Che Guevara: Affective Gateways* (New York: Bloomsbury, 2015).

Campbell, Horace, *Rasta and Resistance: From Marcus Garvey to Walter Rodney* (Trenton, NJ: Africa World Press, 1987).

Campbell, Joseph, *The Hero with a Thousand Faces* (New York: Pantheon Books, 1949).

Carey, Elaine, *Plaza of Sacrifices: Gender, Power and Terror in 1968 Mexico* (Albuquerque, NM: University of New Mexico Press, 2005).

Cartwright, Lisa and Stephen Mandiberg, "Obama and Shepard Fairey: The Copy and

# SELECTED SOURCES

Political Iconography in the Age of the Demake," *Journal of Visual Culture* 8, 2 (2009): 172–6.

Casey, Michael, *Che's Afterlife: The Legacy of an Image* (New York: Vintage, 2009).

Castañeda, Jorge G., *Compañero: vida y muerte del Che Guevara* (New York: Vintage, 1997).

Castells, Manuel, *Networks of Outrage and Hope: Social Movements in the Internet Age* (Malden, MA: Polity Press, 2012).

Chang, Jeff, *Can't Stop, Won't Stop: A History of the Hip-Hop Generation* (New York: St. Martin's Press, 2005).

Cheah, Pheng and Bruce Robbins, eds. *Cosmopolitics: Thinking and Feeling Beyond the Nation* (Minneapolis, MN: University of Minnesota Press, 1998).

Christiansen, Samantha and Zachary A. Scarlett, eds. *The Third World in the Global 1960s* (New York: Berghahn, 2012).

Clay, Andreana, *The Hip-Hop Generation Fights Back: Youth, Activism, and Post-Civil Rights Politics* (New York: NYU Press, 2012).

Cleaver, Kathleen and George Katsiaficas, eds. *Liberation, Imagination, and the Black Panther Party: A New Look at the Panthers and their Legacy* (Routledge: New York, 2001).

Cook, Alexander C., ed., *Mao's Little Red Book: A Global History* (Cambridge: Cambridge University Press, 2014).

Cooper, Adam, "'*Gevaarlike* transitions': Negotiating hegemonic masculinity and rites of passage amongst Coloured boys awaiting trial on Cape Flats," *Psychology in Society* 37 (2009):1–17.

Crary, Jonathan, *Techniques of the Observer: On Vision and Modernity in the Nineteenth Century* (Cambridge, MA: MIT Press, 1992).

Cross, Gary, *Consumed Nostalgia: Memory in the Age of Fast Capitalism* (New Haven, CT: Yale University Press, 2015).

Daulatzai, Sohail, *Black Star, Crescent Moon: The Muslim International and Black Freedom Beyond America* (Minneapolis, MN: University of Minnesota Press, 2012).

Davidson, Russ, *Latin American Posters: Public Aesthetics and Mass Politics* (Santa Fe, NM: Museum of New Mexico Press, 2006).

Davidson, Tonya, Ondine Park, and Rob Shields, eds. *Ecologies of Affect: Placing Nostalgia, Desire, and Hope* (Waterloo, ON: Wilfrid Laurier University Press, 2011).

Davis, Angela Y., *Freedom is a Constant Struggle: Ferguson, Palestine, and the Foundations of a Movement* (Chicago, IL: Haymarket, 2016).

Davis, Stephen, *Bob Marley* (Garden City, NY: Doubleday, 1985).

Dawes, Kwame, *Bob Marley: Lyrical Genius* (London: Sanctuary, 2002).

de Rezende, Isabelle, "Visuality and Colonialism in the Congo: From the 'Arab War' to Patrice Lumumba, c.1880s to 1960" (PhD Thesis, University of Michigan, 2012).

Deleuze, Gilles and Félix Guattari, *A thousand plateaus: capitalism and schizophrenia* (London: Athlone Press, 1987).

Devji, Faisal, *Landscapes of the Jihad: Militancy, Morality, Modernity* (London: Hurst, 2005).

——— *The Terrorist in Search of Humanity: Militant Islam and Global Politics* (New York: Columbia University Press, 2009).

——— *The Impossible Indian: Gandhi and the Temptation of Violence* (Cambridge, MA: Harvard University Press, 2012).

# SELECTED SOURCES

Dickson, Andrew, *Worlds Elsewhere: Journeys Around Shakespeare's Globe* (New York: Henry Holt and Co., 2016).

Drucker, Susan J. and Robert S. Cathcart, eds. *American Heroes in a Media Age* (Cresskill, NJ: Hampton Press, 1994).

Drucker, Susan J. and Gary Gumpert, eds. *Heroes in a GlobalWorld* (Cresskill, NJ: Hampton Press, 2008).

Dubord, Guy, *The Society of the Spectacle* (New York: Zone Books, 1994).

Durant, Sam, ed., *Black Panther: The Revolutionary Art of Emory Douglas* (New York: Rizzoli, 2007).

Durkheim, Émile (Karen E. Fields, trans.), *The Elementary Forms of Religious Life* (New York: Free Press, 1995).

Dyson, Michael Eric, *Holler If You Hear Me: Searching for Tupac Shakur* (New York: Basic Civitas Books, 2003).

Ebert, John David, *Dead Celebrities, Living Icons: Tragedy and Fame in the Age of the Multimedia Superstar* (Santa Barbara, CA: Praeger, 2010).

Elbaum, Max, *Revolution in the Air: Sixties Radicals Turn to Lenin, Mao, and Che* (New York: Verso, 2002).

Evans, Sara, "Sons, Daughters, and Patriarchy: Gender and the 1968 Generation," *American Historical Review* 114, 2 (April 2009): 331–47.

Ezra, Michael, *Muhammad Ali: The Making of an Icon* (Philadelphia, PA: Temple University Press, 2009).

Fink, Carole, Philipp Gassert, and Detlef Junker, eds. *1968, The World Transformed* (Cambridge: Cambridge University Press, 1998).

Follain, John, *Jackal: The Complete Story of the Legendary Terrorist, Carlos the Jackal* (New York: Arcade, 1998).

Forman, Murray and Mark Anthony Neal, eds. *That's the Joint! The Hip-Hop Studies Reader* (London: Routledge, 2012).

Frank, Thomas, *The Conquest of Cool: Business Culture, Counterculture, and the Rise of Hip Consumerism* (Chicago, IL: University of Chicago Press, 1997).

Frank, Thomas, et. al., *Commodify your Dissent* (New York: W.W. Norton, 1997).

Franklin, Sarah, Celia Lury, and Jackie Stacey, *Global Nature, Global Culture* (London: Routledge, 2000).

Frazier, Robeson Taj, *The East is Black: Cold War China in the Black Radical Imagination* (Durham, NC: Duke University Press, 2015).

Frick, Richard, Ulises Estrada, OSPAAL, et. al., eds, *The Tricontinental Solidarity Poster* (Bern: Commedia-Verlag, 2003).

Fukuyama, Francis, *The End of History and the Last Man* (New York: Free Press, 1992).

Gamson, Joshua, *Claims to Fame: Celebrity in Contemporary America* (Berkeley, CA: University of California Press, 1994).

Gberie, Lansana, *A Dirty War in West Africa: The RUF and the Destruction of Sierra Leone.* (Bloomington, IN: Indiana University Press, 2006).

Gell, Alfred, *Art and Agency: An Anthropological Theory* (Oxford: Oxford University Press, 1998).

Gelvin, James L. and Nile Green, eds. *Global Muslims in the Age of Steam and Print* (Berkeley, CA: University of California Press, 2013).

# SELECTED SOURCES

Geyer, Michael and Charles Bright, "World History in a Global Age," *The American Historical Review* 100, 4 (1995): 1034–60.

Ghosh, Bishnupriya, *Global Icons: Apertures to the Popular* (Berkeley, CA: University of California Press, 2011).

Giddens, Anthony, *Runaway World* (New York: Routledge, 1999).

Giesen, Bernhard, *Triumph and Trauma* (Boulder, CO: Paradigm, 2004).

Gillis, John, *Islands of the Mind: How the Human Imagination Created the Atlantic World* (New York: Palgrave Macmillan, 2004).

Gilroy, Paul, *The Black Atlantic: Modernity and Double Consciousness* (Cambridge, MA: Harvard University Press, 1993).

——— *Darker than Blue: On the Moral Economies of Black Atlantic Culture* (Cambridge, MA: Belknap Press, 2010).

Ginsburg, Faye D., Lila Abu-Lughod, and Brian Larkin, eds. *Media Worlds: Anthropology on New Terrain* (Berkeley, CA: University of California Press, 2002).

Gitlin, Todd, *The Sixties: Years of Hope, Days of Rage* (New York: Bantam Books, 1987).

——— *The Whole World is Watching: Mass Media in the Making and Unmaking of the New Left* (Berkeley, CA: University of California Press, 2003).

——— *Occupy Nation: The Roots, the Spirit, and the Promise of Occupy Wall Street* (New York: It Books, 2012).

Gonzalez, Mike, "The Resurrections of Che Guevara," *International Socialism* 77 (December 1997).

Goodwin, Jeff, *No Other Way Out: States and Revolutionary Movements, 1945–1991* (Cambridge: Cambridge University Press, 2001).

Grewal, David Singh, *Network Power: The Social Dynamics of Globalization* (New Haven, CT: Yale University Press, 2008).

Guano, Emanuela, "Spectacles of Modernity: Transnational Imagination and Local Hegemonies in Neoliberal Buenos Aires," *Cultural Anthropology* 17, 2 (2002): 181–209.

Gurnah, Ahmed, "Elvis in Zanzibar," in Alan Scott, ed., *The Limits of Globalization* (London: Routledge, 1997), pp. 116–42.

Halen, P. and J. Riesz, *Patrice Lumumba entre Dieu et Diable: un héros africain dans ses images* (Paris: L'Harmattan, 1997).

Hall, Stuart, "Encoding, decoding," in Simon During, ed., *Cultural Studies Reader* (New York: Routledge, 1999), pp. 507–17.

——— "What is this 'Black' in Black Popular Culture?," *Social Justice* 20, 1–2 (1993): 104–14.

Hall, Stuart and Tony Jefferson, eds. *Resistance Through Rituals: Youth Subcultures in Post War Britain* (New York: 1993).

Hansen, Karen Tranberg, *Salaula: The World of Secondhand Clothing and Zambia* (Chicago, IL: University of Chicago Press, 2000).

Hardt, Michael and Antonio Negri, *Multitude: War and Democracy in the Age of Empire* (New York: Penguin Press, 2004).

Hariman, Robert and John Louis Lucaites, *No Caption Needed: Iconic Photographs, Public Culture, and Liberal Democracy* (Chicago, IL: University of Chicago Press, 2007).

# SELECTED SOURCES

Haugerud, Angelique, M. Priscilla Stone, and Peter D. Little, eds. *Commodities and Globalization: Anthropological Perspectives* (Oxford: Rowman and Littlefield, 2000).

Hebdige, Dick, *Subculture: The Meaning of Style* (London: Routledge, 1979).

Heller, Steven, *Iron Fists: Branding the Totalitarian State* (New York: Phaidon, 2008).

Hernández-Reguant, Ariana, "Copyrighting Che: Art and Authorship Under Cuban Late Socialism," *Public Culture* 16, 1 (2004): 1–29.

Herwitz, Daniel, *The Star as Icon: Celebrity in the Age of Mass Consumption* (New York: Columbia University Press, 2008).

Ho, Fred and Bill V. Mullen, eds. *Afro Asia: Revolutionary Political and Cultural Connections between African Americans and Asian Americans* (Durham, NC: Duke University Press, 2008).

Hobsbawm, Eric J., *Revolutionaries: Contemporary Essays* (New York: Pantheon, 1973).

———— *The Age of Empire: 1875–1914* (New York: Pantheon, 1987).

———— *Bandits* (New York: New Press, 2000).

Hodges, Donald C., ed., *The Legacy of Che Guevara: A Documentary Study* (London: Thames and Hudson, 1977).

Hoffman, Danny, *The War Machines: Young Men and Violence in Sierra Leone and Liberia* (Durham, NC: Duke University Press, 2011).

Hofmeyr, Isabel, *Gandhi's Printing Press: Experiments in Slow Reading* (Cambridge, MA: Harvard University Press, 2013).

Holt, Douglas B., *How Brands Become Icons: The Principles of Cultural Branding* (Boston, MA: Harvard Business Review Press, 2004).

Hoorweg, Jan, Dick Foeken, and R.A. Obudho, eds. *Kenya Coast Handbook: Culture, Resources and Development in the East African Littoral* (New Brunswick, NJ: Transaction Publishers, 2000).

Howe, Stephen, "Transnationalisms Good, Bad, Real, Imagined, Thick and Thin," *Interventions* 4, 1 (2002): 87–8.

Hunt, Lynn, *Writing History in the Global Era* (New York: W.W. Norton, 2015).

Jameson, Frederic, *Postmodernity, or the cultural logic of late capitalism* (Durham, NC: Duke University Press, 1992).

Jeffords, Susan and Fahed Al-Sumait, eds. *Covering Bin Laden: Global Media and the World's Most Wanted Man* (Urbana-Champaign, IL: University of Illinois Press, 2015).

Jewsiewicki, Bogumil, ed., *A Congo Chronicle: Patrice Lumumba in Urban Art* (New York: Museum for African Art, 1999).

Johnson, Lyman L., ed., *Death, Dismemberment, and Memory: Body Politics in Latin America* (Albuquerque, NM: University of New Mexico Press, 2004).

Jones, Simon, *Black Culture, White Youth: The Reggae Tradition from JA to UK* (London: Macmillan, 1988).

Juris, Jeffrey S., *Networking Futures: The Movements against Corporate Globalization* (Durham, NC: Duke University Press, 2008).

Kackman, Michael et. al., eds. *Television in the Age of Media Convergence* (New York: Routledge, 2011).

Katsiaficas, George N., *The Imagination of the New Left: A Global Analysis of 1968* (Boston, MA: South End Press, 1987).

Keen, David, *Conflict and Collusion in Sierra Leone* (New York: Palgrave Macmillan, 2005).

# SELECTED SOURCES

Kelley, Robin D.G., *Africa Speaks, America Answers: Modern Jazz in Revolutionary Times* (Cambridge, MA: Harvard University Press, 2012).

Kellner, Douglas, "September 11, Spectacles of Terror, and Media Manipulation: A Critique of Jihadist and Bush Media Politics," *Logos* 2, 1 (2003): 86–102.

——— *Media Culture: Cultural Studies, Identity, and Politics Between the Modern and the Postmodern* (London: Routledge, 1995).

Kemp, Martin, *Christ to Coke: How Image becomes Icon* (New York: Oxford, 2012).

Kern, Stephen, *The Culture of Time and Space, 1880–1918* (Cambridge, MA: Harvard University Press, 2003).

Khaled, Leila, *My People Will Live: The Autobiography of a Revolutionary* (London: Hodder and Stoughton, 1973).

Khatib, Kate, et al. *We Are Many: Reflections on Movement Strategy from Occupation to Liberation* (Oakland, CA: AK Press, 2012).

Khouri-Makdisi, Ilham, *The Eastern Mediterranean and the Making of Global Radicalism, 1860–1914* (Berkeley, CA: University of California Press, 2010).

King, David, *Russian Revolutionary Posters: From Civil War to Socialist Realism, from Bolshevism to the End of Stalin* (London: Tate Publishing, 2012).

Klimke, Martin, Jacco Pekelder, and Joachim Scharloth, eds. *Between Prague Spring and French May: Opposition and Revolt in Europe, 1960–1980* (New York: Berghahn, 2011).

Kovarik, Bill, *Revolutions in Communication: Media History from Gutenberg to the Digital Age* (New York: Continuum, 2011).

Kresse, Kai, "Muslim Politics in Postcolonial Kenya: Negotiating Knowledge on the Double-Periphery," *Journal of the Royal Anthropological Institute* 15, 1 (2009): 76–94.

Krings, Matthias, "Marke 'Osama'. Über Kommunikation und Kommerz mit Bin-Laden-Bildern in Nigeria," *Peripherie* 113/29 (2009): 31–55.

Kunzle, David, ed., *Che Guevara: Icon, Myth, and Message* (Los Angeles: UCLA Fowler Museum of Cultural History and Center for the Study of Political Graphics, Berlin 1997).

——— *Chesucristo: The Fusion in Image and Word of Che Guevara and Jesus Christ* (Berlin: De Gruyter, 2016).

Kurlansky, Mark, *1968: The Year that Rocked the World* (New York: Ballantine, 2004).

Laclau, Ernesto, *New Reflections on the Revolution of our Time* (London: Verso, 1990).

Larkin, Brian, *Signal and Noise: Media, Infrastructure, and Urban Culture in Nigeria* (Durham, NC: Duke University Press, 2008).

Larson, Jeff A. and Omar Lizardo, "Generations, Identities, and the Collective Memory of Che Guevara," *Sociological Forum* 22, 4 (2007): 425–51.

Lash, Scott and Celia Lury, *Global Culture Industry: The Mediation of Things* (Cambridge: Polity, 2007).

Lawrence, John Shelton and Robert Jewett, *Myth of the American Superhero* (Grand Rapids, MI: W.B. Eerdmans, 2002).

Lazier, Benjamin. "Earthrise; or, the Globalization of the World Picture," *American Historical Review* 116, 3 (2011): 602–30.

LeVine, Mark, *Heavy Metal Islam: Rock, Resistance, and the Struggle for the Soul of Islam* (New York: Three Rivers, 2008).

# SELECTED SOURCES

———— "Music and the Aura of Revolution," *International Journal of Middle Eastern Studies* 44 (2012): 794–7.

Lévi-Strauss, Claude, "The Structural Study of Myth," *The Journal of American Folklore* 68, 270 (1955): 428–44.

Lewis, Martin W. and Kären Wigen, *Myth of Continents: A Critique of Metageography* (Berkeley, CA: University of California Press, 1997).

Lim, Merlyna, "Clicks, Cabs, and Coffeehouses: Social Media and Oppositional Movements in Egypt, 2004–2011," *Journal of Communication* 62 (2012): 231–48.

Linstroth, J.P., "The Basque Conflict Global Speaking: Material Culture, Media and Basque Identity in the Wider World," *Oxford Development Studies* 30, 2 (2002): 205–22.

Loveman, Brian and Thomas M. Davies, Jr., eds. *Che Guevara: Guerrilla Warfare* (Wilmington, DE: Scholarly Resources, 1997).

Mabhubani, Kishori, *The Great Convergence: Asia, the West, and the Logic of One World* (New York: Public Affairs, 2013).

Makalani, Minkah, *In the Cause of Freedom: Radical Black Internationalism from Harlem to London, 1917–1939* (Chapel Hill, NC: University of North Carolina Press, 2011).

Mamdani, Mahmoud. *When Victims Become Killers: Colonialism, Nativism, and the Genocide in Rwanda* (Princeton, NJ: Princeton University Press, 2002).

———— *Good Muslim, Bad Muslim: America, the Cold War, and the Roots of Terror* (New York: Pantheon Books, 2004).

Mandel, Ernest, *Late Capitalism* (London: Verso, 1998).

Manning, Patrick, "1789–1792 and 1989–1992: Global interactions of social movements," *World History Connected* 3, 1 (2005), http://worldhistoryconnected.press.illinois. edu/3.1/manning.html (accessed 18 October 2016).

Markovits, Claude, *The UnGandhian Gandhi: The Life and Afterlife of the Mahatma* (New York: Anthem, 2006).

Marks, Robert B., *The Origins of the Modern World: A Global and Environmental Narrative from the Fifteenth to the Twenty-First Century* (Lanham, MD: Rowman & Littlefield, 2015).

Marqusee, Mike, *Redemption Song: Muhammad Ali and the Spirit of the Sixties* (New York: Verso, 2005).

Marshall, P. David, *Celebrity and Power: Fame in Contemporary Culture* (Minneapolis, MN: University of Minnesota Press, 1997).

Martin, Susan, ed., *Decade of Protest: Political Posters from the United States, Viet Nam, Cuba, 1965–1975* (Santa Monica, CA: Smart Art Press, 1996).

Mazower, Mark, *Governing the World: The History of an Idea* (New York: Penguin, 2012).

Mazrui, Alamin and Ibrahim Noor Shariff, *The Swahili: Idiom and Identity of an African People* (Trenton, NJ: Africa World Press, 1994).

McCormick, Gordon H., "Che Guevara: The Legacy of a Revolutionary Man," *World Policy Journal* 14, 4 (1997/8): 63–79.

Medovoi, Leerom, *Rebels: Youth and the Cold War Origins of Identity* (Durham, NC: Duke University Press, 2005).

Mehnert, Klaus, *Twilight of the Young: The Radical Movements of the 1960s and their Legacy* (New York: Holt, Rinehart and Winston, 1976).

# SELECTED SOURCES

Melendez, Miguel "Mickey", *We took the streets: Fighting for Latino rights with the Young Lords* (New York: St. Martin's Press, 2003).

Micheletti, Michele, Andreas Follesdal, and Dietlind Stolle, eds. *Politics, Products, and Markets: Exploring Political Consumerism Past and Present* (New Brunswick, NJ: Transaction Publishers, 2003).

Mintz, Sidney W., *Sweetness and Power: The Place of Sugar in Modern History* (New York: Penguin, 1986).

Mitchell, Tony, ed., *Global Noise: Rap and Hip-Hop Outside the USA* (Middletown, CT: Wesleyan University Press, 2001).

Mitchell, W. J. T., *Iconology: Image, Text, Ideology* (Chicago, IL: University of Chicago Press, 1986).

———— *Picture Theory: Essays on Verbal and Visual Representation* (Chicago, IL: University of Chicago Press, 1995).

———— *What Do Pictures Want? The Lives and Loves of Images* (Chicago, IL: University of Chicago Press, 2005).

———— *Cloning Terror: The War of Images, 9/11 to the Present* (Chicago: University of Chicago Press, 2011).

———— *Image Science: Iconology, Visual Culture, and Media Aesthetics* (Chicago: University of Chicago Press, 2015).

Mitchell, W. J. T., ed., *The Language of Images* (Chicago, IL: University of Chicago Press, 1980).

Mondzain, Marie-Jose, *Image, Icon, Economy: The Byzantine Origins of the Contemporary Imaginary* (Stanford, CA: Stanford University Press, 2005).

Morris, Meaghan, Siu Leung Li, and Stephen Ching-kiu Chan, eds. *Hong Kong connections: transnational imagination in action cinema* (Durham, NC: Duke University Press, 2005).

Moyer, Eileen, "Street-Corner Justice in the Name of Jah: Imperatives for Peace among Dar es Salaam Street Youth," *Africa Today* 51, 3 (2005): 31–58.

Murrell, Nathaniel Samuel, William David Spencer, and Adrian Anthony McFarlane, eds. *Chanting Down Babylon: The Rastafari Reader* (Philadelphia, PN: Temple University Press, 1998).

Negra, Diane and Su Holmes, eds. *In the Limelight and Under the Microscope: Forms and Functions of Female Celebrity* (London: Bloomsbury, 2011).

Niebylski, Dianna C. and Patrick O'Connor, eds. *Latin American Icons: Fame Across Borders* (Nashville, TN: Vanderbilt University Press, 2014).

Nixon, Rob, "Mandela, Messianism, and the Media," *Transition* 51 (1991): 42–55.

Noor, Farish A., "When Osama and friends came a-calling: the political deployment of the overdetermined image of Osama ben Laden in the contestation for Islamic symbols in Malaysia," in Peter Van Der Veer and Shoma Munshi, eds. *Media, war, and terrorism: responses from the Middle East and Asia* (New York: Routledge, 2004), 197–223.

Ogbar, Jeffrey O.G., *Hip-Hop Revolution: The Culture and Politics of Rap* (Lawrence, KS: University Press of Kansas, 2007).

Ohmann, Richard, *Selling Culture: Magazines, Markets, and Class at the Turn of the Century* (London; New York: Verso, 1996).

O'Malley, Ilene V., *The Myth of the Revolution: Hero Cults and the Institutionalization of the Mexican State, 1920–1940* (New York: Greenwood Press, 1986).

# SELECTED SOURCES

Osterhammel, Jürgen, *The Transformation of the World: A History of the Nineteenth Century* (Princeton, NJ: Princeton University Press, 2014).

Osterhammel, Jürgen and Niels Petersson, *Globalization: A Short History* (Princeton, NJ: Princeton University Press, 2009).

O'Toole, Gavin and Georgina Jiménez, eds. *Che in Verse* (Wiltshire: Aflame Books, 2007).

Panofsky, Erwin, *Meaning in the Visual Arts: Papers in and on Art History* (Garden City, NY: Doubleday, 1955).

Pearl, Sharrona and Dana Polan, "Bodies of Digital Celebrity," *Public Culture* 27, 1 (2015): 185–92.

Pedersen, David, "As Irrational as Bert and Bin Laden: The Production of Categories, Commodities, and Commensurability in the Era of Globalization," *Public Culture* 15, 2 (2003): 238–59.

Pemberton, Jo-Anne, *Global Metaphors: Modernity and the Quest for One World* (London: Pluto Press, 2001).

Peteet, Julie, "Icons and Militants: Mothering in the Danger Zone," *Signs* 23, 1 (1997): 103–27.

Peters, John Durham, *Speaking into the Air: A History of the Idea of Communication* (Chicago, IL: University of Chicago Press, 2001).

Peters, Krijn, *War and the Crisis of Youth in Sierra Leone* (Cambridge: Cambridge University Press, 2011).

Phillips, Damon J., *Shaping Jazz: Cities, Labels, and the Global Emergence of an Art Form* (Princeton, NJ: Princeton University Press, 2013).

Pinney, Christopher, *'Photos of the Gods': The Printed Image and Political Struggle in India* (London: Reaktion, 2004).

Pomeranz, Kenneth, *The Great Divergence: China, Europe, and the Making of the Modern World Economy* (Princeton. NJ: Princeton University Press, 2000).

Prashad, Vijay, *The Darker Nations: A People's History of the Third World* (New York: W.W. Norton, 2007).

——— *The Poorer Nations: A Possible History of the Global South* (New York: Verso, 2013).

Prestholdt, Jeremy, *Domesticating the World: African Consumerism and the Genealogies of Globalization* (Berkeley, CA: University of California Press, 2008).

——— "Politics of the Soil: Separatism, Autochthony, and Decolonization at the Kenyan Coast," *Journal of African History* 55, 2 (2014): 249–70.

Prothero, Stephen, *American Jesus: How the Son of God Became a National Icon* (New York: Farrar, Straus and Giroux, 2003).

Rahmani, Sina, "Anti-Imperialism and Its Discontents: An Interview with Mark Rudd, Founding Member of the Weather Underground," *Radical History Review* 95 (Spring 2006): 117–21.

Ramnath, Maia, *Haj to Utopia: How the Ghadar Movement Charted Global Radicalism and Attempted to Overthrow the British Empire* (Berkeley, CA: University of California Press, 2012).

Rancière, Jacques and T. V. Reed, *Dissensus: On Politics and Aesthetics* (New York: Continuum, 2010).

Reed, T.V., *The Art of Protest: Culture and Activism from the Civil Rights Movement to the Streets of Seattle* (Minneapolis, MN: University of Minnesota Press, 2005).

# SELECTED SOURCES

Regalado, Aldo J., *Bending Steel: Modernity and the American Superhero* (Jackson, MS: University of Mississippi Press, 2015).

Reynolds, Dean, "Representations of Youth and Political Consciousness in the Music of Bob Marley," *Review: Literature and Arts of the Americas* 43, 2 (2010): 237–42.

Richards, Jeffrey, Scott Wilson, and Linda Woodhead, eds. *Diana, The Making of a Media Saint* (London: I.B. Tauris, 1999).

Richards, Paul, *Fighting for the Rainforest: War, Youth, and Resources in Sierra Leone* (Portsmouth, NH: Heinemann, 1996).

Rickards, Maurice, *Posters of Protest and Revolution* (New York: Walker and Company, 1970).

Riello, Giorgio, *Cotton: The Fabric that Made the Modern World* (Cambridge: Cambridge University Press, 2013).

Ritzer, George, ed, *The Blackwell Companion to Globalization* (Oxford: Wiley-Blackwell, 2007).

Roberts, Allen F. and Mary Nooter Roberts, et. al., eds. *A Saint in the City: Sufi Arts of Urban Senegal* (Los Angeles: UCLA Fowler Museum of Cultural History, 2003).

Rosenberg, Robin S. and Peter Coogan, eds. *What is a Superhero?* (New York: Oxford University Press, 2013).

Rudd, Mark, *Underground: My Life with SDS and the Weathermen* (New York: William Morrow, 2009).

Said, Edward, *Culture and Imperialism* (New York: A.A. Knopf, 1993).

Salewicz, Chris, *Bob Marley: The Untold Story* (New York: Faber and Faber, 2009).

Sanderson, George and Frank Macdonald, eds. *Marshall McLuhan, the Man and His Message* (Golden, CO: Fulcrum, 1989).

Savishinsky, Neil J., "Transnational Popular Culture and the Global Spread of the Jamaican Rastafarian Movement," *New West Indian Guide* 8, 3–4 (1994): 259–81.

Scannell, Paddy, *Radio, Television, and Modern Life: A Phenomenological Approach* (Cambridge, MA: Blackwell, 1996).

Schnapp, Jeffrey T., *Revolutionary Tides: The Art of the Political Poster, 1914–1989* (Milan: Skira, 2005).

Schwoch, James, *Global TV: New Media and the Cold War, 1946–69* (Urbana, IL: University of Illinois Press, 2009).

Scott, James C., *Weapons of the Weak: Everyday Forms of Peasant Resistance* (New Haven, CT: Yale University Press, 1984).

———— *Domination and the Arts of Resistance: Hidden Transcripts* (New Haven, CT: Yale University Press, 1990).

Segal, Robert A., ed., *Hero myths: a reader* (Malden, MA: Blackwell, 2000).

Seidman, Michael, *The Imaginary Revolution: Parisian Students and Workers in 1968* (New York: Berghahn Books, 2004).

Shafir, Gershon, Everard Meade, and William J. Aceves, eds. *From Moral Manic to Permanent War: Lessons and Legacies of the War on Terror* (London: Routledge, 2013).

Shils, Edward A., "Charisma, Order, and Status," *American Sociological Review* 30 (1965): 199–213.

Short, T.L. *Peirce's Theory of Signs* (Cambridge: Cambridge University Press, 2007).

# SELECTED SOURCES

Sierra Leone Truth and Reconciliation Commission, *Truth and Reconciliation Commission Report* (Freetown: Government Printers, 2004).

Simpson, Edward and Kai Kresse, eds. *Struggling with History: Islam and Cosmopolitanism in the Western Indian Ocean* (London: Hurst, 2007).

Smith, Philip, "Culture and Charisma: Outline of a Theory," *Acta Sociologica* 43, 2 (2000): 101–11.

Soares, Benjamin F. and Rene Otayek, eds. *Islam and Muslim Politics in Africa* (London: Palgrave Macmillan, 2007).

Solana, Fernando, Mariángeles Comesaña, and Javier Barros Valero, eds. *Evocación del 68* (México, D.F.: Siglo Veintiuno Editores, 2008).

Sontag, Susan, "Posters: Advertisement, Art, Political Artifact, Commodity," in Michael Bierut, ed., *Looking Closer 3* (New York: Allworth Press, 1999), 196–218.

Steffens, Roger, *So Much Things to Say: The Oral History of Bob Marley* (New York: W.W. Norton, 2017).

Steger, Manfred B., *Rise of the global imaginary: Political ideologies from the French Revolution to the global war on terror* (New York: Oxford University Press, 2008).

Stephens, Michelle A., "Babylon's Natural Mystic: The North American Music Industry, the Legend of Bob Marley, and the Incorporation of Transnationalism," *Cultural Studies* 12, 2 (1998): 139–67.

Stiglitz, Joseph, *Globalization and its Discontents* (New York: Norton, 2002).

Sun, Wanning, *Leaving China: media, migration, and the transnational imagination* (Lanham, MD: Rowman & Littlefield, 2002).

Szerszynski, Bronislaw and John Urry, "Cultures of Cosmopolitanism," *The Sociological Review* 50, 4 (2002): 461–81.

Taibo, Paco Ignacio II, *Ernesto Guevara: también conocido como el Che* (Planeta: Benito Juárez, 1996, trans. 1997).

Tarrow, Sidney G., *Power in Movement: Social Movements and Contentious Politics* (Cambridge: Cambridge University Press, 2011).

Thomas, Darryl C., *The Theory and Practice of Third World Solidarity* (Westport, CT: Praeger, 2001).

Tilly, Charles, *Social Movements, 1768–2012* (Boulder, CO: Paradigm, 2012).

Tobin, Joseph, ed., *Re-made in Japan: Everyday Life and Consumer Taste in a Changing Society* (New Haven, CT: Yale University Press, 1992).

Tomaselli, Keyan G. and David H. T. Scott, eds. *Cultural Icons* (Walnut Creek, CA: Left Coast Press, 2009).

Tomlinson, John, *Cultural Imperialism: A Critical Introduction* (London: Pinter, 1991).

Toynbee, Jason, *Bob Marley: Herald of a Postcolonial World?* (Malden, MA: Polity Press, 2007).

Tumarkin, Nina, *Lenin Lives!: The Lenin Cult in Soviet Russia* (Cambridge, MA: Harvard University Press, 1997).

Turner, Victor, *The Ritual Process: Structure and Anti-Structure* (Ithaca, NY: Cornell University Press, 1977).

Urry, John, *Global Complexity* (London: Polity, 2002).

Utas, Mats and Magnus Jörgel, "The West Side Boys: military navigation in the Sierra Leone civil war," *Journal of Modern African Studies* 46, 3 (2003): 487–511.

# SELECTED SOURCES

Virilio, Paul, *The Vision Machine* (Bloomington, IN: Indiana University Press, 1994).

Wallerstein, Immanuel, "New Revolts Against the System," *New Left Review* 18, November–December (2002): 29–39.

Waters, Anita M., *Race, Class, and Political Symbols: Rastafari and Reggae in Jamaican Politics* (New Brunswick, NJ: Transaction Books, 1985).

Waters, Tony and Dagmar Waters, trans. and eds. *Weber's Rationalism and Modern Society: New Translations on Politics, Bureaucracy, and Social Stratification* (New York: Palgrave Macmillan, 2015).

Weiss, Brad, *Street Dreams and Hip Hop Barbershops: Global Fantasy in Urban Tanzania* (Bloomington, IN: Indiana University Press, 2009).

Weitzman, Marc and Eric Hobsbawm, eds. *1968: Magnum Throughout the World* (Paris: Hazan, 1998).

West, Harry G. and Parvathi Raman, eds. *Enduring Socialism: Explorations of Revolution and Transformation, Restoration and Continuation* (New York: Berghahn, 2009).

West, Michael O., William G. Martin, and Fanon Che Wilkins, eds. *From Toussaint to Tupac: The Black International since the Age of Revolution* (Chapel Hill, NC: University of North Caroline Press, 2009).

White, Bob W., "Congolese Rumba and Other Cosmopolitanisms," *Cahiers d'Études africaines* 168 (2002): 663–86.

White, Timothy, *Catch a Fire: The Life of Bob Marley* (New York: Henry Holt and Company, 2000).

Whitney, Malika Lee and Dermott Hussey, *Bob Marley: Reggae King of the World* (New York: E.P. Dutton).

Widener, Daniel, *Black Arts West: Culture and Struggle in Postwar Los Angeles* (Durham, NC: Duke University Press, 2010).

Williams, Raymond, *Television: Technology and Cultural Form* (New York: Schocken Books, 1975).

———— *Marxism and Literature* (Oxford: Oxford University Press, 1977).

Wint, Eleanor and Carolyn Cooper, eds. *Bob Marley: The Man and his Music* (Kingston: Arawak Publications, 1995).

Wright, Lawrence, *The Looming Tower: Al Qaeda and the Road to 9/11* (New York: Knopf, 2006).

Young, Cynthia A., *Soul Power: Culture, Radicalism, and the Making of a US Third World Left* (Durham, NC: Duke University Press, 2006).

Ziff, Trisha, ed., *Che Guevara: Revolutionary & Icon* (London: V&A Publishers, 2006).

Žižek, Slavoj, *Welcome to the Desert of the Real!: Five Essays on September 11 and other Important Dates* (New York: Verso, 2002).

———— *The Year of Dreaming Dangerously* (New York: Verso, 2012).

# INDEX

Abdullah, Ibrahim, 113
Abidjan, Ivory Coast, 89
Aboriginal Australians, 77, 87–8
Abu Ghraib prisoner abuse scandal
    (2003), 155
Abu Sharif, Bassam, 67
Action Faction, 51–2, 61
Adidas, 206, *211*
Afghanistan, 25
    and Guevara, 193
    Soviet War (1979–89), 138, 139,
        154
    US-led War (2001–14), x, 101,
        143, 146, 154–5, 188, 215
African Americans
    Black Liberation Army (BLA),
        103
    Black Panther Party (BPP), 40,
        57–8, 62, 103–4
    Black Power, 58, 62, 80, 81, 87
    Civil Rights Movement (1954–
        68), 8, 13, 22, 50, 52, 77, 81,
        87
    Marley and, 86–7
African National Congress, 223
African Union, 174
Afrocentrism, 79
agitprop, 20

Akon, 182
Alexander, Jeffrey, 10
Algeria, 21, 40, 62
Ali, Muhammad, 4
Ali, Tariq, 44–5
*All Eyez on Me* (2Pac), 103, 104,
    106, 123, 127
*All Eyez on Me* (2017 film), 100
All People's Congress (APC), 117
Allende, Salvador, 21
'Always Onward Until Victory',
    14, 42, 50, 56, 57
Amana, Rishad, 151
'Amerikaz Most Wanted' (2Pac),
    127
Amnesty International, 71, 93–4,
    152
Amsterdam, Netherlands, 131
anarchism, 48
Anderson, Benedict, 11, 39
Anderson, Jon Lee, 198
André the Giant, 222
Anglican Church, 162
Angola, 52
Ann Arbor, Michigan, 61
Anonymous, 218
'Another World is Possible', 188
antinuclear movement, 23, 87, 88

# INDEX

antirealism, 42
Anti-Terrorism Police Unit
    (ATPU), Kenya, 156
apartheid, 23, 26, 87, 90–91, 223
Apollo 11 moon landing (1969), 22
Appadurai, Arjun, 17
Aquino, Corazon, 24
Arab Spring (2011), 17, 28,
    110–11, 158–9, 207, 208
Argentina, 1, 23, 45, 46, 64, 65,
    94, 193
Aristide, Jean-Bertrand, 110
Arizona, United States, 87
Armed Forces for the National
    Liberation of East Timor
    (Falintil), 94
Armed Forces of National
    Liberation, 60, 63
Armed Forces Revolutionary
    Council (AFRC), 117, 118, 120,
    122
Army Math Research Lab,
    Madison, 62
Arusha, Tanzania, 100
Asari, Dokubo, 140
Aslan, Reza, 11
Auckland, New Zealand, 173
Aung San Suu Kyi, 12
Australia, 77, 87–8, 91
authoritarianism, 11, 23, 26, 28,
    158, 207
*Autobiography of Malcolm X, The*, 50
Ayers, Bill, 61

Baba, Tupeni, 180
'Babylon System' (Bob Marley and
    the Wailers), 79
Bad Boy Records, 104, 106
Bad Brains, 86
'Bad Card' (Bob Marley and the
    Wailers), 92
Bahamas, 176

Balala, Khalid, 150
Balala, Najib, 144
Baltimore, Maryland, 104
Bangladesh, *142*
Bangura, Yusuf, 113
Barcelona, Catalonia, 43
Bartmański, Dominik, 10, 199
Basque Country, 190, 193
Baton Rouge, Louisiana, 164
Baudrillard, Jean, 133
Beah, Ishmael, 115, 120, 167
Beatles, The, 4, 22, 42, 165
Beckham, David, 157
Ben Bella, Ahmed, 21
Bergen, Norway, *189*
Berlin Wall, 71, 199
Berlusconi, Silvio, 195
*Better Dayz* (2Pac), 106
Bible, 78, 168–9
Biggie Smalls (The Notorious
    B.I.G.), 105–6, 127, 129
Billabong, 206
Bin Laden, Mohammed bin Awad,
    139
Bin Laden, Osama, x, 1, 2, 3, 5–8,
    13, 14, 15, 25, 26, 28, 29, 31,
    131–59
    Bangladesh and, *142*
    beard, 15
    Brazil and, 131, 137
    and capitalism, 140
    camouflage jacket, 15, 141
    China and, 131, 140
    consumer goods, visage on, 132,
        135–6, 137
    Côte d'Ivoire and, 140–41
    death (2011), 15, 157, 158–9
    Democratic Republic of the
        Congo and, 140–41
    'Devil Eyes' program, 136
    *dishdasha*, 15, 141
    and foco theory, 140

Ghana and, 135
and Guevara, 139
Indonesia and, 131, 137, 157
Jordan and, 157
Kenya and, 31, 131, 132–3, 137,
  141, 143–57, 209, 210
Lebanon and, 158
Malaysia and, 131, 157
as 'man of action', 13, 142
masculinity and, 13
Nigeria and, 131, 134–5, 140
Pakistan and, 131, 134, 137,
  138, 139, 157
Saudi Arabia and, 135
South Africa and, 131
Soviet–Afghan War (1979–89),
  139
Thailand and, 131, 141
Venezuela and, 131
video communiqués, 141
Biserat, Shaku, 108
Bishop, Maurice, 69
Black Jesus, 122
Black Liberation Army (BLA), 103
Black Panther Party (BPP), 40,
  57–8, 62, 103–4
Black Power, 62, 74, 77, 80, 81,
  87, 88
Black September (1970), 61
Blackthorn, John (Gary Hart),
  197–8
Blackwell, Chris, 81–2
Blé Goudé, Charles, 110
Bloods (Freetown), 120
Bloomingdale's, 199
Blum, Bruno, 86
Bob Marley: Roots, Rock, Reggae
  festival (2006), 167
Boikot, 195
Boksburg, Johannesburg, 108
Bolívar, Simón, 18
Bolivia, 35, 46, 59, 62, 63, 65,
  193, 197–8, 202, 206–7, 221

Bolivian Diary (Guevara), 42–3, 212
Bollywood, 143
Bombali, Sierra Leone, 123
'Bombtrack' (Rage Against the
  Machine), 195
Bompa-Turay, Baimba, 111–12, 120
Bono (Paul Hewson), 85, 97, 164,
  166
Boogie Down Productions, 27
Boorstin, Daniel J., 21
Bouazizi, Mohamed, 28, 207
Bouterse, Dési, 206
Bowie, David, 15
Bravo, Douglas, 60
Brazil, 43, 63, 64, 77, 131, 137,
  189, 201
British Broadcasting Corporation
  (BBC), 135, 161
Broadway, New York City, 100, 130
Brown Berets, 40
Brown, Timothy S., 53
Bunia, Democratic Republic of the
  Congo, 110
Burkina Faso, 209
Burlington Coat Factory, 199, 200
Burnin' (Bob Marley and the
  Wailers), 82
'Burnin' and Lootin'' (Bob Marley
  and the Wailers), 75
Bush, George W., 136, 137, 153,
  222

Cable News Network (CNN), 177
Cabral, Amílcar, 21
Calcutta, India, 142
California, United States, 22, 42,
  43, 57, 100, 128, 167, 171, 174,
  189, 200, 205, 219
calypso, 89
Cameron, James, 25
Canada, 174
'Candle in the Wind' (Elton John),
  26

# INDEX

cannabis, 79–80, 84, 110, 116, 118, 166, 170, 175, 177–8
Cape Town, South Africa, 100, 108, *109*, 120, 131, 210, 212
capitalism, 4, 16, 23, 24–6, 41, 220
  Bin Laden and, 140
  JCR and, 65
  Marley and, 75
  neoliberalism, 23, 25–6, 31, 137, 186, 188, 194, 205, 220
  Occupy movement and, 17, 28
  Rastafari and, 75, 78
  socialism and, 24
  student movements and, 52, 53
  Third World and, 40
  Weather Underground Organization (WUO) and, 62
Captain America, 21
Caracas, Venezuela, 131
Carlos the Jackal (Ilich Ramírez Sánchez), 22, 60–61
Carmichael, Stokely (Kwame Ture), 52, 87
Carson, Johnnie, 155
Casey, Michael, 190
Castro, Fidel, 20, 38, 40, 41, 45, 50, 60, 192, 209
*Catch a Fire* (Bob Marley and The Wailers), 81–2
Catholicism, 24, 79, 91, 111
Central Intelligence Agency (CIA), 136
cha-cha, 89
'Changes' (2Pac), 111
Chaplin, Charlie, 20
Chapman, Tracy, 93
Charles, Prince of Wales, 90
Charlton, Hannah, 190
Chávez, Hugo, 190, 206
*Che!* (1969 film), 43
*Che* (2005 film), 185, 208

*Che* (2008 film), 197, 201, 202
Che Guevara Commando Unit, Palestine, 66–7
Che Guevara Commando Unit, Uruguay, 64
Che-Lumumba Club, 40
Checkpoint Charlie, Berlin, 223
Chiapas, Mexico, *165*, 189, 193–5, *194*
Chicago, Illinois, 61–2
  Chicago Eight, 41, 61
  Haymarket Square bombing (1969), 61
child soldiers, 111–12, 113, 115–16, 119–20, 167
Chile, 21, 43, 63, 65, 94
China
  and Bin Laden, 131, 140
  Mao Zedong, 4, 22, 38, 39, 41, 44, 54, 67, 71
  Sun Yat-sen, 20
  Tiananmen Square protests (1989), 11, 71
Christianity, 11, 13, 18
  Anglican Church, 162
  Bible, 78, 168–9
  Catholicism, 24, 79, 91, 111
  Ethiopian Orthodox Tewahedo Church, 170
  Guevara and, 63, 198, 206
  in Jamaica, 78, 162
  in Kenya, 141, 147, 149
  Maori Ringatu Church, 173
  Marley and, 78, 79, 88, 91, 162, 168–9, 170
  in Nicaragua, 206
  in Nigeria, 140
  Shakur and, 111
  in United Kingdom, 198
Churches Advertising Network, 198
Cité Soleil, Port-au-Prince, 110

# INDEX

*Citizen Smith*, 43

Civil Defense Forces (CDF), 117, 122, 125

Civil Rights Movement (1954–68), 8, 13, 22, 50, 52, 77, 81, 87

Clapton, Eric, 82–3

Clegg, Johnny, 74

Clinton, William 'Bill', 137

Coachella Music Festival, 128

Cobain, Kurt, 165

Cohn-Bendit, Daniel, 49, 54

Coimbatore, Tamil Nadu, 203

Cold War era (1947–91), 20, 23, 24–5, 35–94
    see also post-Cold War era

Colombia, 63, 67

Colonel Bloodshed, 123

Columbia University, 43, 46, 50, 51–2

'Coming in from the Cold' (Bob Marley and the Wailers), 92

Commander Cut Hands, 123

communism, 17, 24, 38, 39, 59, 138, 139, 144, 187, 192, 213, 220
    in China, 22
    in Cuba, 57, 193
    demise of, 24, 192
    in Bolivia, 59
    in France, 54
    in India, 203
    in Italy, 203
    in Russia, 203
    in South Africa, 95
    in United States, 40
    in Venezuela, 60

Communist Democratic Youth Federation of India (DFYI), 203

Communist International, 17, 39

Communist Party of Bolivia, 59

Communist Party of China, 22

Communist Party of India, 203

Communist Party of Italy, 203

Communist Party of Russia, 203

Communist Party of South Africa, 95

Communist Party of the United States, 40

Communist Party of Venezuela, 60

*communitas*, 40, 44, 57

Comoros, 150

*Concord Times*, 128

'Concrete Jungle' (Bob Marley and the Wailers), 82

*Confrontation* (Bob Marley and the Wailers), 169–70

Constructivism, 20

consumerism, xii, 1–3, 8, 10, 20, 25, 28–29, 218, 220–222
    Bin Laden and, 132, 135, 137
    Guevara and, 28, 32, 184, 186, 187, 189, 190, 191, 195–215
    Marley and, 28, 73, 177–82

Corbyn, Jeremy, 220

Correa, Rafael, 206

Côte d'Ivoire, 89, 110, 140–41

Cozumel, Mexico, 176

'Crazy Baldhead' (Bob Marley and the Wailers), 87

Crazy Horse (Thhassúŋke Witkó), 162

Crips (Freetown), 120, *121*

Cuba, 192–3
    Heroic Guerrilla image, 48, 49, 50, 193, 196
    reburial of Guevara (1997), 193, 196
    Revolution (1953–9), 1, 7, 40, 44–5, 48, 50, 51, 58, 59–60, 62, 63, 199, 201, 202, 210
    and September 11 attacks (2001), 133
    Year of the Heroic Guerrilla (1968), 50

# INDEX

Year of the 30th Anniversary of the Fall in Combat of the Heroic Guerrilla (1997), 193
Cuzco, Peru, 190, 215
Cyprus, 100
Czechoslovakia, 53

Dalai Lama, 163
Dalrymple, Henderson, 73, 81
Damar, Arif, 43
Dar es Salaam, Tanzania, 95–6, 100, 164
Dark Angel Battalion, 125
*Dateline NBC*, 134
Davis, Angela, 4, 12
Davis, Miles, 86
Dawes, Kwame, 73, 78, 84
Dawson's Field hijackings (1970), 67
Dean, James, 20
Death Row Records, 104, 123
Debray, Régis, 51, 52, 59–60
decolonization, 21, 38, 39
Delaware, United States, 81
'demand the impossible', 208
Demirtas, Metin, 43
Democratic Party of Kenya, 151
Democratic Party of the United States, 180
Democratic Republic of the Congo (Congo-Kinshasa), 110, 140–41
democratic socialism, 206, 220
Denmark, 58, 76
Depp, Johnny, 195
Desanzo, Juan Carlos, 197
Devi, Phoolan, 12
'Devil Eyes' program, 136
Dhaka, Bangladesh, *142*
Diana, Princess of Wales, 13, 26
Diaz Gutiérrez, Alberto 'Korda', 48, 65, 196, 221
Díaz Ordaz, Gustavo, 55

Digital Underground, 104
Dili, East Timor, 94
Dohrn, Bernardine, 61, 62
Dole, Robert 'Bob', 105
*Don Killuminati, The* (2Pac), 104, 106, 129
'Don't Matter' (Akon), 182
Dr. Dre, 128
dreadlocks, 15, 79, 85, 89, 144, 170, 175
Durban, South Africa, 212
Durkheim, Émile, 11, 93
Dutschke, Rudi, 52–4
Dylan, Robert 'Bob', 61, 77, 86
Dyson, Michael Eric, 107

Earthrise image, 23
East African Counterterrorism Initiative (EACTI), 153
East Germany (1949–90), 71, 97, 199
East Harlem, New York City, 103
East Timor, 73, 94
Economic Community Monitoring Group (ECOMOG), 123, 124–5
Ecuador, 206
Edmonds, Ennis, 79
Egypt, 4, 17, 21, 28, 150, 207, 208, 214
Ejército de Liberación Nacional (ELN), 63, 65
Ejército Revolucionario del Pueblo (ERP), 64, 65
Ejército Zapatista de Liberación Nacional (EZLN), 12, 189, 193–5, 214, 223
Elena, Eduardo, 205
Engels, Friedrich, 17
Esposito, John, 131
Ethiopia, 20, 74, 75, 79, 89, 168, 174

# INDEX

Ethiopian Orthodox Tewahedo
Church, 170
Evans, Josh, 185, 208
Evans, Sara, 46
'Exodus' (Bob Marley and the
Wailers), 169
*Exodus* (Bob Marley and the
Wailers), 84, 103, 161, 169, 171

Fairey, Shepard, 221–2
Fanon, Frantz, 22, 39, 42, 50, 213
Fawkes, Guy, 28, 218–19, *219*
Fayer, Joan, 13
Federal Bureau of Investigation
(FBI), 151
Feltrinelli, Giangiacomo, 48, 212
La Feltrinelli bookstore, Milan,
212–13
femininity, 13, 25
50 Cent, 143
*56 Thoughts from 56 Hope Road*
(Marley), 171
Fiji, 180
*First Blood*, 119–20
First World War (1914–18), 19, 20
Fischer Skis, 196
Fitzpatrick, Jim, 48–9, 57, 61, 65,
189, 195, 198
Flint, Michigan, 62
foco theory, 51–67, 140, 186
Follesdal, Andreas, 221
Fonda, Peter, 22
Fonseca, Carlos, 12, 206
*Footpaths to Democracy*, 114
Forças Armadas da Libertação
Nacional de Timor-Leste
(Falintil), 94
Forest Stewardship Council (FSC),
179, 221
'400 Years' (Bob Marley and the
Wailers), 87
France

BPP solidarity chapter, 58
and Guevara, 22, 42, 44, 49,
51, 53
Jeunesse communiste révolution-
naire (JCR), 54
and Marley, 80, 86, 177
May 1968 protests, 49, 54–5,
208
Situationists, 208
Franco, Francisco, 43
Frank, Thomas, 191
Frankfurt, Germany, 52, 53
free trade, 23, 25, 220
Freetown, Sierra Leone, 99, 111,
120, *121*, 122–5, 126, 127–8,
*127*, 129
Frente Sandinista de Liberación
Nacional (FSLN), 12, 64, 70,
205–6
FUBU, 212
Fuerzas Armadas de Liberación
Nacional, 60, 63
Fukuyama, Francis, 24, 101

G8, 189
Gabriel, Peter, 93
Gaddafi, Muammar, 110, 130, 208
Gairy, Eric, 69
Gall, Norman, 63
Gambia, 131
Gandhi, Indira, 90
Gandhi, Mohandas 'Mahatma', 4,
13, 20, 84
ganja (cannabis), 79–80, 84, 110,
116, 118, 166, 170, 175, 177–8
García Bernal, Gael, 201
Garvey, Marcus, 20, 75, 79, 80,
168
de Gaulle, Charles, 54, 55
Gaultier, Jean-Paul, 196
Gberi Bana, Sierra Leone, 125
Gberie, Lansana, 113

# INDEX

Genoa, Italy, 189
Germany
  and Guevara, 37, 42, 44, 46, 47,
    52–4, 199, 223
  and Marley, 71, 84, 97
  and Shakur, 100
  'Get Up, Stand Up' (Bob Marley
    and The Wailers), 30, 71, 78–9,
    82, 86, 87, 91–4, 97, 159, 162,
    180
Ghana, 21, 135
Ghosh, Bishnupriya, 11
Gilcher-Holtey, Ingrid, 53
Gilroy, Paul, 27, 70, 74, 77, 82
Ginsberg, Allen, 37
Gitlin, Todd, 51
Glaude, Eddie S., 169
global financial crisis (2008), 188,
  205
Gonzalez, Mike, 192
Gramsci, Antonio, 39
Granada, Nicaragua, 206
Grand Canyon, Arizona, 87
Great Silent March (1968), 57
Greece, 215
Gregory, Richard 'Dick', 166
Grenada, 69, 93
Guadalcanal, Solomon Islands, 96,
  110
Guantanamo Bay detention camp,
  155
Guatemala, 67
Guerrilla Warfare (Guevara), 51, 58,
  59, 63, 197, 209
Guevara, Ernesto 'Che', x, xi, 1,
  3, 5–8, 13–15, 21, 22, 28–30,
  32–3, 35–68, 185–215
  Afghanistan and, 193
  Argentina and, 64, 65, 193
  Basque Country and, 193
  beard, 14, 22, 32, 43, 186
  beret, 14, 22, 32, 43, 186, 201
  Bin Laden and, 139
  Bolivia and, 35, 46, 59, 62, 63,
    65, 193, 197–8, 202, 206–7,
    221
  Bolivian Diary, 42–3, 212
  books on, 37, 43, 190, 196–8
  Brazil and, 43, 63, 64, 189, 201
  Burkina Faso and, 209
  Chicago Eight and, 41
  Chile and, 43, 63, 65
  Colombia and, 63, 67
  Cuba and, 1, 7, 40, 44–5, 48,
    49–50, 51, 58, 59–60, 62, 63,
    191–3, 196
  death (1967), 15, 35, 58, 62, 64,
    66, 159, 185, 197–8
  Democratic Republic of the
    Congo and, 45, 46, 197
  Ecuador and, 206
  Egypt and, 207, 208, 214
  films about, 43, 185, 187, 190,
    192, 196–7, 201–2, 208
  and foco theory, 51–67, 186
  France and, 22, 42, 44, 49, 51,
    54–5
  Germany and, 37, 42, 44, 46,
    47, 52–4, 199, 223
  Guatemala and, 67
  Guerrilla Warfare, 51, 58, 59, 63,
    197, 209 'Hasta la victoria siem-
    pre', 14, 42, 50, 56, 57
  Heroic Guerrilla image, see He-
    roic Guerrilla image
  India and, 203
  and internationalism, 1, 7, 29,
    37–9, 44, 45, 48, 54, 55, 60,
    63, 65, 68, 186, 187–96
  Ireland, and, 48–9
  Italy and, 35, 43, 48, 195, 197,
    203, 212–13
  Japan and, 37
  Jordan and, 208

Kenya and, 143, 144, 209–10, *211*, 214
Libya and, 208
long hair, 14, 22, 32, 43
Malaysia and, 157
*Man and Socialism in Cuba*, 197
as 'man of action', 13, 45, 139
martyr status, 15, 37, 68
masculinity and, 13, 45, 46, 108
*Memoirs of Che Guevara, The*, 67
'Message to the Tricontinental', 45
Mexico and, 12, 37, 42, 44, 46, 55–7, 191, 193–5, 214, 223
Morocco and, 208
*Motorcycle Diaries, The*, 197
Netherlands and, 43, 48
Nicaragua and, 12, 63, 64, 67, 193, 205–6
Northern Ireland and, 193
Norway and, *189*
'On Revolutionary Medicine', 212
OSPAAAL and, 21
Palestine and, 66, 207
Panama and, 35
Peru and, 63–4, 190, 202
poetry about, 37
reburial in Cuba (1997), 193, 196
and revolutionary violence, 37, 58–67
in Russia, 203
South Africa and, 95, 193, 209, 210–12
Soviet Union and, 35
Spain and, 43, 195
Suriname and, 206
Sweden and, 192
Tunisia and, 207, 208
Turkey and, 43, 208, 223
Uganda and, 209

United Kingdom and, 35, 42, 44, 49, 197, 198, 203–5, 210, 214
United States and, 35–7, 40–46, 50–52, 57–62, 189, 191, 195–202, 203, 205
Uruguay and, 46, 63, 64, 65
'*Venceremos*', *36*, 42, 61
Venezuela and, 59, 60, 63, 190, 206
Vietnam War and, 7, 35, *36*, 37, 38, 45, 54, 57, 61, 64
'Viva Che!' image (Fitzpatrick), 48–9, *49*, 57, 61, 65, *189*, 195, 198, *204, 211*
Yemen and, 207, 208, 215
Guinea-Bissau, 21
Guinea, 100, 111
Gulf War
  First (1990–91), 25, 154
  Second (2003–11), 101, 110, 142–3, 146, 154

Habel, Janette, 54
'Hail Mary' (2Pac), 111
Haile Selassie I emperor of Ethiopia, 20, 74, 79, 168
Haiti, 18, 100, 110
Hamburg, Germany, 52
al-Hamdi, Ibrahim, 207
Hamilton Hall, Columbia University, 52
Hammami, Omar, 111
Hampton, Fred, 62
Hani, Chris, 95
Harare, Zimbabwe, 90, 180–81
*Harder They Come, The*, 81
Hardt, Michael, 188
Harry, Duke of Sussex, 195
Hart, Gary, 197–8
'*Hasta la Victoria Siempre*', 14, 42, 50, 56, 57

# INDEX

*Hasta la Victoria Siempre* (1997 film), 197

Havana, Cuba, 48, 49

Havasupai people, 87

Hawaii, 87

Hayden, Tom, 52

Haymarket Square, Chicago, 61

'Heathen, The' (Bob Marley and The Wailers), 169

heavy metal, 77

Hell's Angels, 141

Hema people, 110

Hendrix, Jimi, 165

Herbs, 88

Heroic Guerrilla image, 14, 22, 32, 42–50, *49*, 65, 184, 186, 189–215, 221–4
  in Bolivia, 206–7
  in Brazil, 43, 189
  Carlos the Jackal (Ilich Ramírez Sánchez) and, 61
  in Chile, 43
  in Cuba, 49, 193
  in France, 42, 44, 49
  in Germany, 44, *47*, 53
  in Italy, 42, 48, 189, 212
  in Kenya, 210, *211*
  in Mexico, 44, *56*, 57, 189, 194, *194*
  in Nicaragua, 206
  in Peru, 190
  in South Africa, 210–12
  in United Kingdom, 42, 43, 44, 198
  in United States, 42, 43, 44, 58, 189, 191, 195–6, 198, 199–201, *204*
  in Uganda, 209
  in Venezuela, 190

Hilburn, Robert, 79

Hinduism, 162

hip-hop, 24, 27, 77, 97–111 118, 120, 123–30

'Hit 'em Up' (2Pac), 106, 123, 129

Ho Chi Minh, 11, 21, 41, 44, *47*, 54, 67, 71

Hoffman, Danny, 113

*Holler If Ya Hear Me*, 100, 130

Hollywood, 43, 100, 143

Holmes, Richard, 42

Holt, Douglas B., 10

'HOPE' (Fairey), 222

Hopi people, 87

House of Marley, 179

Howe, Stephen, 11–12

Human Rights Now! tour (1988), 71, 93–4

Hussein Fatal, 105

Hussein, Saddam, 25

'I Ain't Mad at 'Cha' (2Pac), 129

*I am Legend*, 172

'I Shot the Sheriff' (Bob Marley and The Wailers), 82–3, 90

*I, Che Guevara* (Blackthorn), 197–8

Identity, 210–12

Ijaw people, 140

imaginative solidarities, 11–12, 39

imagined communities, 12, 39

India, 21, 90, 94, 142–3, 203

Indonesia, 94, 131, 137, 157

Institute for Defense Analysis, 52

International Monetary Fund (IMF), 135

internationalism, 26
  Bin Laden and, 136, 140, 144, 146, 149, 153
  Black Panther Party and, 58
  Guevara and, 1, 7, 29, 37–9, 44, 45, 48, 54, 55, 60, 63, 65, 68, 184, 185, 186, 187–95, 203–205, 207, 212
  Marley and, 81, 162, 165

Internet, 16–17, 25, 26, 28, 102, 141, 194, 208

Iran, 66
Iraq, 25, 101, 110, 142–3, 146, 154
   Abu Ghraib prisoner abuse scandal (2003), 155
   Gulf War I (1990–91), 25, 154
   Gulf War II (2003–11), 101, 110, 142–3, 146, 154
Ireland, 48–9
Irish Republican Army (IRA), 66
'Is This Love?' (Bob Marley and the Wailers), 90
Isatabu Freedom Movement, 96
Islam, 149, 154, 175
Islamic Party of Kenya (IPK), 149–51, 154
Island Records, 8, 30, 32, 70, 81–5, 163, 169–71
Israel, 66–7, 140, 150, 152, 153, 156, 158, 165
Istanbul, Turkey, 208, 223
Italy, 11, 23, 35, 43, 48, 58, 91, 94, 189, 195, 197, 212
Ivory Coast, 89, 110, 140–41

Jackson, Mahalia, 77
Jackson, Michael, 165
Jakarta, Indonesia, 157
Jamaica, 20, 72, 75, 78, 80–81, 83–4, 92–3, 96, 174, 180
   Christianity in, 78, 162
   Garvey, 20, 75, 79, 80, 168
   independence (1962), 81
   Labour Party, 83, 92–3
   One Love Peace Concert (1978), 84
   Order of Merit, 92
   People's National Party, 83
   Rastafari in, 78–80, 81, 168–9
   Smile Jamaica Concert (1975), 83–4, 172
   Tourist Board, 176–7

Japan, 37, 58, 91, 94, 100
jatra, 142
Jay-Z, 97, 195
Jeffords, Susan, 136
Jesse James Gang, 61
Jesus Christ, 11, 63, 168, 198, 206
Jesus, 25
Jeunesse communiste révolutionnaire (JCR), 54
Joan of Arc, 18
Johannesburg, South Africa, 100, 108
John Paul II, Pope, 24, 91
John, Elton, 26
Johnson, Lyndon B., 58–9
Jones, Simon, 82, 85–6
Joplin, Janis, 15, 165
Jordan, 61, 157, 208
Jörgel, Magnus, 125
Juárez, Benito, 57
'Judge Not' (Bob Marley and The Wailers), 81
Juice, 104
Jung, Carl, 9
Junior Lion, 125
Junta de Coordinación Revolucionaria (JCR), 65–6

Kabbah, Ahmed Tejan, 122, 123, 124
Kadafi, 105
Kamara, Ibrahim, 125
Kano, Nigeria, 134–5
Kaplan International Colleges, 165
Kastro, 105
Kaunda, Kenneth, 90
Kaya (Bob Marley and the Wailers), 84
Keen, David, 113
Kelley, Robin D.G., 169
Kennedy, John F., 15
Kensington, London, 42

# INDEX

Kenya, ix, 19, 143–57, 175–6
  Anti-Terrorism Police Unit
    (ATPU), 156
  and Bin Laden, 31, 131, 132–3,
    137, 143–57, 209, 210
  Democratic Party, 151
  and Guevara, 143, 144, 209–10,
    211, 214
  Islamic Party of Kenya (IPK),
    149–51, 154
  Kenyan African National Union
    (KANU), 149, 150
  and Marley, x, 143, 144, 174–6,
    176, 210
  Mombasa attacks (2002), 150,
    152
  Muslim community, 143–57,
    175–6
  Muslim Youth of Kenya, 151
  Nairobi US embassy bombing
    (1998), 141, 150, 155
  National Rainbow Coalition
    (NARC), 151–2
  National Security Intelligence
    Service, 157
  Operation Edged Mallet, 156
  and September 11 attacks
    (2001), 151, 154
  and Shakur, 100, 141, 143, 209,
    210
  United Muslims of Africa, 150
Kerala, India, 203
Kern, Stephen, 19
Khaled, Leila, 66
Kibaki, Mwai, 151
Kigali, Rwanda, 174
King Saud University, 135
King, Jr., Martin Luther, 13, 22
Kingston, Jamaica, 81, 83, 84
Ko Li Pe, Thailand, 174
Koch, Edward, 174
Koinadugu, Sierra Leone, 123

Kono, Sierra Leone, 95, 123, 125
Koroma, Johnny Paul, 122, 126
Kotb, Hoda, 134
Krahl, Hans-Jürgen, 53
Kresse, Kai, 146
Kuala Lumpur, Malaysia, 157
Kukuna, Sierra Leone, 99, 122
Kunzle, David, 198
Kuti, Fela, 165

Labour Party of Jamaica, 83
Labour Party of the United
  Kingdom, 44, 220
Lamarca, Carlos, 64
Lamu, Kenya, 150, 156, 175–6,
  176
Lanzhou, China, 140
Larson, Jeff, 197
Las Vegas, Nevada, 100, 200
Lawrence, Francis, 172
Lazier, Benjamin, 23
Lebanon, 158
Lee, Spike, 8, 150
Legend (Bob Marley and The
  Wailers), 163, 164, 170–71
Lenin, Vladimir, 20, 22, 39, 41, 54
Lennon, John, 4
liberation theology, 79
Libya, 110–11, 130, 133, 208
Lima, Peru, 100, 202
Lincoln Memorial, Washington,
  DC, 36
Lincoln Park, Chicago, 61
Lindsay, Keisha and Louis, 75
Linstroth, J.P., 190
Lipsitz, George, 76
Little Red Book (Mao Zedong), 22
Lizardo, Omar, 197
Lomé, Togo, 100, 126
London, England, 35, 42, 43, 44,
  80, 84, 203, 205, 214, 219, 222
London School of Economics, 60

# INDEX

Long Beach, California, 174
Lonsdale, John, 19
Los Angeles, California, 42, 43, 100, 104, 166, 167, 200, 205, 219
Louisiana, United States, 164
Louverture, Toussaint, 18
Low Library, Columbia University, 52
Lumumba, Patrice, 11
Lumumba University, Moscow, 35, 60
Lundgren, Dolk, *189*
Luxemburg, Rosa, 20, 41
Luxor, Egypt, 176

Maathai, Wangari, 12
Macy's, 199
Madison, Wisconsin, 62
Madison Square Garden, New York City, 74
Madonna, 25, 165
Magbeni, Sierra Leone, 125
Magusheni, South Africa, 108
Mahatma Gandhi Hall, London, 35
Makaveli (Tupac Shakur), 106
'Make Jihad With Me' (Hammami), 111
Makeba, Miriam, 4
Makeni, Sierra Leone, 122
Malaita, Solomon Islands, 96
Malaysia, 131, 157
Malcolm X, 8, 50, 52, 143, 150
*Malcolm X* (1992 film), 8, 150
Malindi, Kenya, 176
Mamdani, Mahmood, 154
*Man and Socialism in Cuba* (Guevara), 197
Mandela, Nelson, 4, 21, 23, 94, 141, 223
Mandela, Winnie, 12
Manenberg, Cape Town, 108, *109*

Manley, Michael, 83, 84, 92
Mao Zedong, 4, 22, 39, 41, 44, 54, 67, 71
Maoism, 38, 40, 57, 58, 60, 70, 75, 76, 89
Maori people, 88, 172–4
Maraniss, David, 87
Marcos de Oliveira, Jose, 63
Marcuse, Herbert, 39
Marighella, Carlos, 63
Marley Coffee, 179, 180
Marley Footwear, 179
Marley, Cedella, 178
Marley, Rita, 83
Marley, Robert 'Bob', x, xi, 1–2, 3, 5–8, 14, 15, 17, 24, 28–32, 69–98, 161–84, 224
    Africa and, 89–91
    Australia and, 77, 87–8, 91
    assassination attempt (1975), 83–4, 103, 172
    'Babylon System', 79
    'Bad Card', 92
    Bahamas and, 176
    beard, 15, 71
    'Burnin' and Lootin'', 75
    Canada and, 174
    cancer, 1, 91, 92–3
    *Catch a Fire*, 81–2
    clothes, 15, 71
    'Coming in from the Cold', 92
    *Confrontation*, 169
    'Crazy Baldhead', 87
    death (1981), 1, 92–3, 95, 159, 166, 171
    dreadlocks, 15, 71, 94
    East Timor and, 94
    Egypt and, 176
    English language and, 165
    Ethiopia and, 174
    'Exodus', 169
    *Exodus*, 84, 103, 161, 169, 171

# INDEX

Fiji and, 180

*56 Thoughts from 56 Hope Road* (Marley), 171

'400 Years', 87

France and, 86, 177

and cannabis (ganja), 84, 166, 175, 177–8

Germany and, 71, 84, 97

'Get Up, Stand Up', 30, 71, 78–9, 82, 86, 87, 91–4, 97, 159, 162, 180

Grenada and, 69–70, 93

'Heathen, The', 169

and human rights, 71, 93

'I Shot the Sheriff', 82, 90

'Is This Love?', 90

Island Records and, 8, 30, 32, 70, 81–5, 163, 169–71

Italy and, 91

Ivory Coast and, 89

Jamaica and, 72, 75, 80–81, 83–4, 92–3, 96, 162, 174, 176–7, 180

'Judge Not', 81

*Kaya*, 84

Kenya and, x, 143, 144, 174–6, *176*, 210

*Legend*, 163, 164, 170–71

and liberation, 30, 73, 85–91, 169, 170

marketing of, 30, 81–5, 169–71, 177–82

masculinity and, 94

merchandise, 177–9, 181

Mexico and, *165*, 176

*Natty Dread*, 82, 180

'Natural Mystic', 166

*Natural Mystic*, 171

Nepal and, 176

New Zealand and, 87, 88–9, 91, 172–4

Nicaragua and, 70, 93, 97

'No More Trouble', 74

'One Love', 2, 17, 32, 159, 161–2, 167–8, 170, 178, 182–3

One Love Peace Concert (1978), 84

Palestine and, 165

and psalms, 162, 171

Rastafari, 15, 72, 75, 78–81, 86, 92, 97, 144, 164, 166, 168, 172, 175, 179

*Rastaman Vibration*, 83

'Real Situation', 90

'Rebel Music', 83

'Redemption Song', 75

'Revolution', 75, 180

Rwanda and, 174

'She's Gone', 90

Sierra Leone and, 94–5, 96, 97, 112, 119, 167

'Simmer Down', 81

*60 Visions* (Marley), 171

'Slave Driver', 82

Smile Jamaica Concert (1975), 83–4, 172

Solomon Islands and, 96

South Africa and, 90–91, 93, 95

South Pacific and, 87, 96

as spiritual icon, 2, 11, 32, 159, 162–71, 183

'Sun is Shining', 167

*Survival*, 84, 87, 88, 89, 90, 91, 169, 170

Switzerland and, 91–2, 97

'Talkin' Blues', 83

Tanzania and, 95–6, 97, 164

Thailand and, 174

'Them Belly Full', 83, 90

United Kingdom and, 80, 84, 85–6, 161

United States and, 70, 81, 86–7, 93, 161–2, 164, 166–7, 174, 176, 180, 182

*Uprising*, 84–5, 90, 169, 170
Uprising Tour (1980), 85, 91
'War', 74
'Zimbabwe', 70, 89–90, 182
Zimbabwe and, 70, 71, 89–90,
     91, 181–2
Marley, Rohan, 179
Marley, Stephen, 167
Marley, Ziggy, 167
Marley's Mellow Mood, 178
Martí, José, 41
Martinique, 22
Marx, Karl, 17, 39, 41, 47, 52, 54
Marxism, 20, 26, 39, 40, 43, 112
  Black Panther Party and, 57
  foco theory and, 51, 59
  Guevara and, 45, 186, 187, 201,
     213
  Marley and, 70, 75, 79, 89, 97,
     162
  New Jewel Movement and, 69
  Sandinista National Liberation
     Front and, 70
  Sankara and, 209
Mary, mother of Jesus, 13, 206
masculinity, 13, 25, 46, 94, 105,
     107–8, 111, 120
  Guevara, 13, 46, 108
  Marley and, 94
  Shakur and, 2, 105, 107–8, 111,
     120
Masiaka, Sierra Leone, 126
Matory, J. Lorand, 122
Mazrui, Alamin, 149, 150
Mbembe, Achille, 115
McLuhan, Marshall, 25
'Me Against the World' (2Pac), 14,
     105, 124
*Me Against the World* (2Pac), 104
*Memoirs of Che Guevara, The*, 67
Mercedes-Benz, 200–201, 213
'Message to the Tricontinental'
     (Guevara), 45

Mexico
  and Bin Laden, 131
  Cinco de Mayo, 210–11
  and Guevara, 12, 37, 42, 44, 46,
     55–7, 189, 191, 193–5, 223
  and Marley, *165*, 176
  Olympic Games (1968), 22, 55
  Revolution (1910–20), 12, 20,
     41, 57
  and Shakur, 100
  student protests (1968), 55–7,
     *56*
  Tlatelolco massacre (1968), 57
  Zapatista Army of National
     Liberation (EZLN), 12, 189,
     193–5, 223
Miami, Florida, 200
Micheletti, Michelle, 221
Mijikenda peoples, 150
Milan, Italy, 35, 48, 91, 195, 212
Milanović, Branko, 220
Mitchell, William John Thomas,
     9, 19
Mitton, Kieran, 113
Mixed Relations, 88
uMkhonto we Sizwe (MK), 209
Mogahed, Dalia, 131
arap Moi, Daniel, 148, 151, 156,
     209
Moldova, 100
Mombasa, Kenya, 100, 131, 133,
     144–57, 210, 214
  Bob Marley Day, 174
  al-Qaeda attacks (2002), 150,
     152
*Monitor*, 209
Monroe, Marilyn, 20
Montevideo, Uruguay, 64
Morales, Evo, 206–7, 221
Morelos, José María, 57
Morningside Park, Harlem, 52
Morocco, 208

# INDEX

Morrison, Carlos, 106–7
Moscow, Russia, 35, 60
Moss, Kate, 195
Mossad, 67
Mother Teresa, 13, 163
*Motorcycle Diaries, The*, 197, 201–2
Movement of 22 March, 54
'movement of movements', 188
Movimento Revolucionário 8 de
    Outubro (MR-8), 64
Movimiento de Izquierda
    Revolucionaria, Chile, 63, 65
Movimiento de Izquierda
    Revolucionaria, Peru, 63–4
Moyer, Eileen, 95–6
Mozambique, 52
Mugabe, Robert, 70, 90, 180–81
Mujahideen (Afghanistan), 138,
    139, 154
Muktinath, Nepal, 176
Mukwevho, Colbert, 90–91
Munich, Germany, 47, 52
Musina, South Africa, 90–91
Muslim Youth of Kenya, 151
Mussolini, Benito, 11
MySpace, 111

N'Dour, Youssou, 93
Naidoo, Logie, 212
Nairobi, Kenya, 100, 141, 148,
    150, 155, 174, 219, 222
Namibia, 73
Nanterre, Paris, 42, 54
Napoleon I, emperor of the
    French, 18
Nasser, Gamal Abdel, 4, 21, 207
National Broadcasting Company
    (NBC), 134
National Liberation Army of
    Bolivia, 63, 65
National Liberation Front of
    Algeria (FLN), 40, 62

National Liberation Front of
    Vietnam (NLF), 40, 41, 53, 54,
    58, 61, 62
National Mall, Washington, DC, 35
National Rainbow Coalition
    (NARC), 151
*Natty Dread* (Bob Marley and the
    Wailers), 82–3, 180
'Natural Mystic' (Bob Marley and
    the Wailers), 166
*Natural Mystic* (Bob Marley and the
    Wailers), 171
Negri, Antonio, 188
Nehru, Jawaharlal, 21
neocolonialism, 11, 73, 94
neoliberalism, 24–6, 31, 137, 186,
    188, 194, 205, 220
Nepal, 176
Neruda, Pablo, 37
Netherlands, 43, 48, 58, 80, 131
Neville, Cyril, 167
New Afrikan Panthers, 104
New Afrikan People's
    Organization, 104
New Jewel Movement, 69, 93
New Labour Unity Party, 180
New Left, 38, 44–5, 46, 51, 59, 74
New Right, 23
New York, United States, 22, 42,
    43
    Bob Marley Day, 174
    Broadway, 100, 130
    Columbia University, 43, 46, 50,
        51–2, 61
    East Harlem, 103
    Madison Square Garden, 74
    Occupy Wall Street (2011), *204*,
        205, 215
    September 11 attacks (2001), x,
        2, 26, 31, 131–46, 150, 151,
        154, 158
    Shakur, assassination attempt on
        (1994), 105–6

# INDEX

Shakur murals, 100
*New York Times*, 19, 70, 74, 161
New Zealand, 87, 88–9, 91, 100, 172–4
*Newsweek*, 196
Newton, Huey P., 58
Nicaragua, 12, 59, 63, 64, 67, 70, 93, 97, 193, 205–6
Niger Delta People's Volunteer Force, 140
Nigeria, 122, 124, 131, 134–5, 140
Nightingale, Florence, 13
Nike, 200, *211*
Nkrumah, Kwame, 21
No Fixed Address, 88
'No More Trouble' (Bob Marley and the Wailers), 74
Non-Aligned Movement, 20, 40
Norris, Carlos 'Chuck', 112, 119
North American Free Trade Agreement (NAFTA), 193
North Korea, 133
North Vietnam (1945–75), 37
Northern Ireland, 193
Norway, 100, *189*
Notorious B.I.G., The (Biggie Smalls), 105–6, 127, 129
nuclear weapons, 23, 87, 88
Nyerere, Julius, 21, 95

Oakland, California, 35, 57, 104
Obama, Barack, 70, 87, 141, 159, 221–3
'OBEY' (Fairey), 222
Occupy movement, 17, 28, 130, *204*, 205, 215, 223
Old Left, 38, 59
Old Testament, 78, 168
Olivetti, 43
Olympic Games, 4, 22, 55
'On Revolutionary Medicine' (Guevara), 212

'One Love' (Bob Marley and the Wailers), 2, 17, 32, 159, 161–2, 167–8, 170, 178, 182–3
One Love Peace Concert (1978), 84
One Love Unity Celebration (1995), 173
'Only God Can Judge Me' (2Pac), 118, 123
Opera House riots (1980), 91–2
Operation Edged Mallet, 156
Operation No Living Thing (1998), 123
Operation Urgent Fury (1983), 93
Organization of Latin American Solidarity (OLAS), 40, 48
Organization of Solidarity for the People of Africa and Asia (OSPAA), 40
Organization of Solidarity of the People of Asia, Africa, and Latin America (OSPAAAL), 21
Organization of the Petroleum Exporting Countries (OPEC), 61
Orlando, Florida, 176
Ortega, Daniel, 205
'Osamakitsch', 135
*Ostalgie*, 199
Outlaw Immortalz, 105
Outlaws (armed group), 110

Pakistan, 131, 134, 137, *138*, 139, 157
Palestine, 60–61, 66–7, 154, 155, 156, 165, 207
Palestinian National Liberation Movement (Fatah), 66
Palm Beach, Florida, 43
pan-Africanism, 79, 81, 168
pan-Arabism, 139
Panama, 35

Pando, Uruguay, 64
Papua New Guinea, 131
Paris, France, 22, 42, 49, 54–5
Partito Socialista Italiano di Unità
    Proletaria, 53
Party for Socialism and Liberation,
    203
Party of Italian Communists, 203
Pate Island, Kenya, *145*
peace symbol, 199, 224
People's Mojahedin Organization
    of Iran, 66
People's National Party (PNP), 83,
    92
People's Revolutionary Army of
    Argentina, 64, 65
Pérez Gonzalez, Antonio 'Ñiko', 48
Perón, Isabel, 65
Peru, 18, 59, 63–4, 100, 103, 131,
    190, 202, 215
Peshawar, Pakistan, 131
Pew Research Center, 157
Philip Morris, 177
Philippines, 24, 155
Pink Tide, 206, 220
Plaza de la Revolución, Havana, 49
*Poetic Justice*, 104
Poland, 24
police brutality, 58, 104, 106, 111
Polletta, Francesa, 92
Polynesia, 88–9, 173
Popular Front for the Liberation of
    Palestine (PFLP), 60–61, 66–7,
    207
Port-au-Prince, Haiti, 100, 110
Porto Alegre, Brazil, 189
post-Cold War era (1991–), 2, 7,
    10, 24–29, 99–215
    symbolic convergence, 16–18,
        102, 133–45, 167
Potts, Tracey, 135
Prague Spring (1968), 53

Pratt, Geronimo, 103
Presley, Elvis, 20
Price, Antony, 42
Progressive Labor Party, 62
'providential self-assurance', 102,
    112
Provo movement, 48
psalms, 162, 171
psychological operations
    (PSYOPs), 93
Public Enemy, 27
Puma, 206, *211*
punk rock, 77, 85, 86, 91, 164,
    195
Pussy Riot, 12

al-Qaeda, 131, 136, 141, 151, 155,
    157
    Mombasa attacks (2002), 150,
        152
    September 11 attacks (2001), x,
        2, 26, 31, 131–46, 150, 151,
        154, 158
    US East African embassy bomb-
        ings (1998), 141, 150, 155
Quayle, James Danforth 'Dan', 105
Quicksilver, 206
Quinn, Eithne, 107
Qutb, Sayyid, 25

Radio Free Grenada, 69, 93
Rage Against the Machine, 195
Raising Cane's, 178
'Raising the Flag on Iwo Jima'
    (Rosenthal), 11
Ralph Lauren, 206
Ramadan, Yousef, 110–11
Ramallah, West Bank, 165
Raman, Parvathi, 203–5, 210
Rambo, 25, 112, 119–20
Ramírez Sánchez, Ilich (Carlos the
    Jackal), 22, 60–61

# INDEX

Rashid, Ishmail, 113

Rastafari, 15, 20, 72, 75, 78–81, 86, 92, 97, 144, 164, 166, 168, 172, 175, 179

*Rastaman Vibration* (Bob Marley and the Wailers), 83

Rawalpindi, Pakistan, *138*

'Real Situation' (Bob Marley and the Wailers), 90

'Rebel Music' (Bob Marley and the Wailers), 83

'Redemption Song' (Bob Marley and the Wailers), 75

reggae, 24, 27, 68–98 102, 119, 162–77, 180–3

religious icons, 9, 10, 11, 13, 18

Republic of the Congo (Congo-Brazzaville), 35

Republic of the Congo (Congo-Léopoldville 1960–64), 11, 46, 197

'Revolution' (Bob Marley and the Wailers), 75, 180

*Revolution in the Revolution?* (Debray), 51

Revolutionary Left Movement, 63–4

Revolutionary Movement of October 8 (MR-8), 64

Revolutionary People's Constitutional Convention, 58

Revolutionary United Front (RUF), 94–5, 99–100, 101, 108, 110, 111–28

revolutionary violence, 37, 44, 58–67, 73

Rhodesia (Zimbabwe), 70, 89–90

Richards, Paul, 120

Ringatu Church, 173

Rio de Janeiro, Brazil, 131

Robeson, Paul, 20, 77

Robin Hood, 18

Rock Against Racism, 85

Rockwell, John, 74

*Rolling Stone*, 83

Rome, Italy, 195

Romero, Óscar, 23

'rooted cosmopolitans', 188

Ros-Lehtinen, Ileana, 200

Roskilde Festival, Denmark, 76

Rostow, Walt Whitman, 58–9

Roy, Arundhati, 12

Rubio, Marco, 111

Rudd, Mark, 46, 50–52, 61

Rufaro Stadium, Harare, 90

rumba, 89

Russian Federation, 12, 100

Russian Revolution (1917), 20, 22

*Ruta del Ché, La* (Boikot), 195

Rwanda, 174

*Sacrifico*, 192, 201

Said, Edward, 51

Saint Ann Parish, Jamaica, 80

Saint Petersburg, Russia, 100

Salah-ad-Din, Sultan of Egypt and Syria, 18

Sales, Bill, 52

Salles, Walter, 201–2

El Salvador, 23

San Cristobal de las Casas, Mexico, *165*

San Diego, California, 167

San Siro stadium, Milan, 91

Sanchez, Celia, 12

Sanders, Bernard, 180, 220

Sandinista National Liberation Front (FSLN), 12, 64, 70, 205–6

Sandino, Augusto, 12, 41, 206

Sankara, Thomas, 209

Sankoh, Foday, 114, 122

Santana, Carlos, 195

Sartre, Jean-Paul, 39

satellite television, 147, 154

# INDEX

Saudi Arabia, 135
Savishinsky, Neil, 77
*Sea Point Days*, 212
Seaga, Edward, 83, 84, 92, 93
Second World, 20
Second World War (1939–45), 20
'Secretz of War' (2Pac), 118
September 11 attacks (2001), x, 2, 26, 31, 131–46, 150, 151, 154, 158
Seyah, Amadu, 128
al-Shabaab, 111
Shakespeare, William, 16
Shakur, Afeni, 103–4
Shakur, Assata, 103
Shakur, Mutulu, 103
Shakur, Tupac, xii, 1, 2, 3, 5–8, 10, 14, 27, 28, 29, 30–31, 98, 99–130, 132, 141, 143, 144, 158, 165, 209, 210, 217, 224
'Against All Odds', 106
*All Eyez on Me*, 103, 104, 106, 123, 127
assassination attempt (1994), 103, 105–6
*Better Dayz*, 106
Biggie Smalls (The Notorious B.I.G.), feud with, 105–6, 129
censorship, calls for, 105
'Changes', 111
Coachella hologram performance (2012), 128
death (1996), 100, 104, 107, 128–9
Death Row, 104, 123
*Don Killuminati, The*, 104, 106, 129
'Hail Mary', 111
'Hit 'em Up', 106, 123, 129
'I Ain't Mad at 'Cha', 129
Ivory Coast and, 110
*Juice*, 104

Kenya and, 100, 141, 143, 209, 210
legal battles, 105
Libya and, 110–11, 130
Makaveli, 106
as 'man of action', 110
masculinity and, 2, 105, 107–8, 120
'Me Against the World', 14, 105, 124
*Me Against the World*, 104
as nom de guerre, 111, 120
'Only God Can Judge Me', 118, 123
*Poetic Justice*, 104
and police brutality, 104, 106, 111
and racism, 103, 104, 107, 111
'Secretz of War', 118
Sierra Leone and, 30–31, 99–100, 101, 102, 108, 110, 111–28, 129, 224
Solomon Islands and, 110, 111
Somalia and, 111
South Africa and, 108, *109*, 111
*Still I Rise*, 106, 118
'Thug Life', 105
*Thug Life*, 105, 108
'To Live and Die in LA', 108
'Troublesome '96', 106
*2Pacalypse Now*, 104
'West Side', 108, *109*, 110, 120, *121*, 125
Shariff, Ibrahim Noor, 149
'She's Gone' (Bob Marley and the Wailers), 90
Shee, Ali, 156
Sierra Leone
Armed Forces Revolutionary Council (AFRC), 117, 118, 120, 122–6
Civil Defense Forces (CDF), 117, 122, 125

Economic Community Monitoring Group (ECOMOG), 123, 124–5
Lomé Peace Accord (1999), 126
and Marley, 94–5, 96, 97, 112, 119, 167
and Norris, 112, 119
and Rambo, 112, 119–20
Revolutionary United Front (RUF), 94–5, 99–100, 101, 108, 110, 111–28
and Shakur, 30–31, 99–100, 101, 102, 108, 110, 111–28, 129, 224
Sierra Leone Army (SLA), 113, 115, 117, 119, 120, 123, 125–6
Truth and Reconciliation Commission (TRC), 116, 119
West Side Boys (WSB), 125
'Simmer Down' (Bob Marley and The Wailers), 81
Sinclair, Andrew, 42
Situationists, 208
Six-Day War (1967), 66
60 Visions (Marley), 171
ska, 85, 86, 195
'Slave Driver' (Bob Marley and the Wailers), 82
Slovenia, 100
Smile Jamaica Concert (1975), 83–4, 172
Smirnoff Vodka, 196
Smith, Ian, 89
Snoop Dogg, 128
social media, 17, 26
socialism, 24, 101, 192
    Bin Laden and, 139
    capitalism and, 24
    Guevara and, 1, 7, 29, 32, 35, 37, 41, 43–4, 48, 50–68, 186, 187, 192, 222

OSPAAAL and, 21–2
Marley and, 71, 74, 75, 78, 83, 87, 91–2, 97
Pink Tide, 206, 220
Socialist Party of Proletarian Unity, 53
Soderbergh, Steven, 201, 202
Solomon Islands, 96, 110
Somalia, 111, 154, 155
Sommers, Marc, 120
Sorbonne, Paris, 54
South Africa, 4, 12, 21, 23, 24, 52, 223
    apartheid, 23, 26, 87, 90–91, 223
    and Bin Laden, 131
    and Guevara, 67, 193, 209, 210–12
    and Marley, 90–91, 93, 94, 95
    and Shakur, 100, 108, 109, 110
South Pacific, 87, 88–9, 173
Soviet Union, 11, 23, 35, 59, 138, 139, 154
Soweto, Johannesburg, 95
Sozialistischer Deutscher Studentenbund (SDS), 52–4
Spain, 43, 190, 193, 195
Springsteen, Bruce, 93
Sri Lanka, 59
Stalin, Joseph, 11, 192
Star Wars, 136
Steinem, Gloria, 12
Stephens, Gregory, 166, 169
Still I Rise (2Pac), 106, 118
Sting (Gordon Sumner), 93
Stolle, Dietlind, 221
Structural adjustment, 26, 117, 188
Student Afro-American Society (SAS), 52
Students for a Democratic Society (SDS), 46, 50, 51–2, 61, 62

# INDEX

Subcomandante Marcos (Rafael
  Vicente), 12, 194, 195, 214
Sudan, 25, 154
Sugawara, Mitsuhiro, 166
al-Sumait, Fahed, 136
'Sun is Shining' (Bob Marley and
  the Wailers), 167
Sun Yat-sen, 20
*Sunday Times*, 80
Superman, 21
Surabaya, Indonesia, 131
Suriname, 206
*Survival* (Bob Marley and the
  Wailers), 84, 87, 88, 89, 90, 91,
  169, 170
Swahili people, 146, 149, 150,
  151–2, 156–7, 174–6
Swatch, 196, 210
Sweden, 58, 192
Switzerland, 91–2, 97
symbolic convergence, 16–18,
  102, 133–45, 167
symbolic idiom, 18–29, 101,
  112–13, 119, 120, 158, 163,
  214, 218

Taco Bell, 196
Taibo II, Paco Ignacio, 55
Tajikistan, 100
Taksim Square, Istanbul, 208, 223
Talkin' Blues' (Bob Marley and the
  Wailers), 83
Tamil Nadu, India, 203
'Tank Man', 11
Tanzania, ix, 21, 95–6, 97, 100,
  114, 164
Target, 178, 199, 200
Tarrow, Sidney, 188
Te Kooti, 173
television, 16, 20, 21, 25, 102,
  147, 154
Temple, Shirley, 42

Thailand, 131, 141
'Them Belly Full' (Bob Marley and
  the Wailers), 83, 90
Thhassúŋke Witkó, 162
Third World, 20, 21, 40, 45, 53,
  67, 70, 73, 74, 85, 92, 96, 103,
  162, 164, 169, 178, 186, 187
Thrissur, Kerala, 203
*Thug Life* (2Pac), 105, 108
Thug Life (gang), 108
Thugs (gang), 108
Tiananmen Square protests (1989),
  11, 71
Tijuana, Mexico, 100
*Time Magazine*, 43, 83, 161
*Titanic*, 25
Tlatelolco massacre (1968), 57
'To Live and Die in LA' (2Pac), 108
Togo, 100, 126
Tokyo, Japan, 100
del Toro, Benicio, 201
Toronto, Ontario, 174
Torres, Camilo, 63
Tosh, Peter, 4, 71, 78–9, 81
Touraine, Alain, 39
transnational imagination, 16–19,
  22–3, 26, 29, 217, 224
  Bin Laden and, 132, 136, 139,
    140, 144–5, 153
  Guevara and, 39–40, 58
  Marley and, 71, 78, 95, 96, 102,
    162, 164
  Shakur and, 100–101, 112
transnational library, 39
Transworld Airlines, 66
traveling theory, 51
Treaty of Waitangi (1840), 173
Trench Town, Kingston, 81
Trotsky, Leon, 20, 22, 39, 54
'Troublesome '96', (2Pac), 106
Tubman, Harriet, 12
Tucumán Province, Argentina, 65

Tumbodu, Kono, 125
Tunisia, 28, 207, 208
Túpac Amaru II (José Gabriel
    Condorcanqui), 18, 103
Tupamaros, 62, 63, 64, 65
Ture, Kwame (Stokely
    Carmichael), 52, 87
Turkey, 43, 208, 223
Tutu, Desmond, 24
Twentieth Century Fox, 43

26th of July Movement, 40, 50,
    55, 60
*2Pacalypse Now* (2Pac), 104

U2, 85, 97
Uganda, 209
United Arab Emirates, 100
United Kingdom
    Afghanistan War (2001–14), 189
    *Citizen Smith*, 43
    Diana, Princess of Wales, 13, 26
    and Guevara, 35, 42, 43, 44–5,
        49, 197, 198, 203, 210, 214
    Islam in, 154
    Kenya, colonial (1895–1963),
        148
    and Marley, 80, 84, 85–6, 161
    Occupy movement, 205
    Treaty of Waitangi (1840), 173
    Victoria, queen of the United
        Kingdom, 18
    Vietnam Solidarity Campaign, 44
    West Side Boys hostage crisis
        (2000), 125, 126
    Zanzibar Protectorate (1890–
        1963), 147
United Muslims of Africa, 150
United Nations, 17, 84, 126, 174
United States
    Abu Ghraib prisoner abuse scan-
        dal (2003), 155

Afghanistan War (2001–14), x,
    101, 143, 146, 154, 188, 189
    and authoritarianism, 23
Apollo 11 moon landing (1969),
    22
Bin Laden, killing of (2011), 15,
    157, 158–9
Black Liberation Army (BLA),
    103
Black Panther Party (BPP), 40,
    57–8, 62, 103–4
Black Power, 58, 62, 80, 81, 87
Brazil ambassador kidnapping
    (1969), 64
Brown Berets, 40
Bush administration (2001–9),
    136, 137, 153, 222
Central Intelligence Agency
    (CIA), 136
Chicago Eight, 41
Civil Rights Movement (1954–
    68), 8, 13, 22, 50, 52, 77, 81,
    87
Communist Party, 40
Dawson's Field hijackings
    (1970), 67
East African embassy bombings
    (1998), 141, 150, 155
East African Counterterrorism
    Initiative (EACTI), 153
Federal Bureau of Investigation
    (FBI), 151
Grenada, invasion of (1983), 93
Guantanamo Bay detention
    camp, 155
    and Guevara, 35–7, 40–46,
        50–52, 57–62, 189, 191,
        195–202, 203, 205
Gulf War I (1990–91), 25, 154
Gulf War II (2003–11), 101,
    110, 142–3, 146, 154
Institute for Defense Analysis, 52

and Marley, 70, 81, 86–7, 93, 161–2, 164, 166–7, 174, 176, 180, 182
New Afrikan People's Organization, 104
North American Free Trade Agreement (NAFTA), 193
Obama administration (2009–17), 159, 221–3
Occupy movement, 204, 205, 215, 223
Operation Edged Mallet, 156
Party for Socialism and Liberation, 203
Patriot Act (2001), 152
Progressive Labor Party, 62
psychological operations (PSYOPs), 93
Revolution (1765–83), 18
September 11 attacks (2001), x, 2, 26, 31, 131–46, 150, 151, 154, 158
and Shakur, 105, 106–7, 110, 111, 112, 120, 130
Somalia intervention (1993–4), 154, 155
Students for a Democratic Society (SDS), 46, 50, 51–2, 61, 62
Trump administration (2017–), 223
Vietnam War (1955–75), see Vietnam War
War on Terror, 145, 156–7, 158, 186
Weather Underground Organization (WUO), 61–2, 66
Young Lords, 22, 40
Universal Citywalk, Orlando, 176
Universal Declaration of Human Rights (1948), 71, 94
University of Colorado-Boulder, 59

University of Dar es Salaam, 95, 164
Uprising (Bob Marley and the Wailers), 84–5, 90, 169, 170
Uprising Tour (1980), 85, 91
Urban Outfitters, 191
Uruguay, 46, 62, 63, 64, 65
Utas, Mats, 125

V for Vendetta, 28, 218
Vallegrande, Bolivia, 206
Van Wyk, Jermaine 'Turbo', 108
Vatican, 111
Venezuela, 59, 60, 63, 131, 190, 206
VH1, 110
Victoria, queen of the United Kingdom, 18
Vietnam War (1955–75)
    Ali and, 4
    Bin Laden and, 140
    Columbia University and, 52
    France and, 53, 54
    Guevara and, 7, 35, 36, 37, 38, 44, 45, 50, 54, 57, 61, 64
    Ho Chi Minh, 11, 21, 41, 44, 47, 54, 71
    Italy and, 53
    Mexico and, 57
    National Liberation Front (NLF), 40, 41, 53, 54, 58, 61, 62
    United Kingdom and, 44
    Uruguay and, 64
    Weather Underground Organization (WUO) and, 61–2, 66
    West Germany and, 53
Villa, Francisco 'Pancho' 20, 57
Vishnu, 162
'Viva Che!' (Fitzpatrick), 48–9, 49, 57, 61, 65, 189, 195, 198, 204, 211

Wailer, Bunny, 81, 167

# INDEX

Wailers, The, 81–5
Waitangi Day, 173
Walcott, Derek, 37
Wałęsa, Lech, 24
Walker, Alice, 87
Walmart, 178
'War' (Bob Marley and the Wailers), 74
War on Terror, 145, 156–7, 158, 186
*Washington Post*, 93
Washington, DC, United States, 35, *36*, 161–2
Washington, George, 18
'We Are the World', 154
'We Shall Overcome', 77
Weather Underground Organization (WUO), 61–2, 66
Weiss, Brad, 113–14
Weiss, Peter, 37
Wellington, New Zealand, 88
West Berlin, 22, 37, 52–4, 71, 97
West Germany (1949–90), 37, 42, 44, 46, *47*, 52–4, 58, 71, 84, 97
West Side Boys (WSB), 125–6, 128
White, Timothy, 89
Wilkerson, Cathy, 61, 62
Williams, Raymond, 39
Willoughby, Bart, 88
Wilmington, Delaware, 81
Women's rights movement, 23
Wonder Woman, 21
'Workers of the world unite!', 17
World Bank, 174

World Social Forum, 188, 189, 190
World Trade Center, *see under* September 11 attacks
World Trade Organization (WTO), 26, 188
*Wretched of the Earth* (Fanon), 50

Year of the Heroic Guerrilla (1968), 50
Yemen, 207, 208, 215
Yothu Yindi, 88
Young Lords, 22, 40
Youth International Party (Yippie), 58
Yunupingu, Mandawuy, 88

Zaffaroni, Juan, 63
Zanzibar, 147–8
Zapata, Emiliano, 12, 41, 57, 194, 195
Zapatista Army of National Liberation (EZLN), 12, 189, 193–5, 214, 223
al-Zawahiri, Ayman, 25
Zetsche, Dieter, 200–201
Zimbabwe, 70, 71, 89–90, 91, 94, 181–2
'Zimbabwe' (Bob Marley and the Wailers), 70, 89–90, 182
Zócalo, Mexico City, 57
Zuccotti Park, New York City, *204*, 223
Zurich, Switzerland, 91–2
Zvakwana-Sokwanele, 180–81